Collections For
Of Staffordsh
(Volume III)

Editor:
The William Salt Archaeological Society

Alpha Editions

This Edition Published in 2021

ISBN: 9789354412264

Design and Setting By
Alpha Editions
www.alphaedis.com
Email – info@alphaedis.com

The William Salt Archæological Society.

1900.

COUNCIL.

Nominated by the Trustees of the William Salt Library.

The Right Hon. Lord WROTTESLEY.
Captain CONGREVE.
The Ven. Archdeacon LANE.
Sir REGINALD HARDY, Bart.
Mr. W. S. BROUGH.

Elected by the Members of the Society.

Major-General The Hon. GEORGE WROTTESLEY.
The Rev. F. P. PARKER.
Sir THOMAS SALT, Bart.
The Rev. W. BERESFORD.
The Rev. E. R. O. BRIDGEMAN.

EDITORIAL COMMITTEE.

Major-General The Hon. GEORGE WROTTESLEY, 75, Cadogan Gardens.
The Rev. F. P. PARKER, The Rectory, Colton, Rugeley.
The Rev. W. BERESFORD, St. Luke's Vicarage, Leek.

TREASURER.

Mr. PERCEVAL HANBURY HARSTON.

AUDITOR.

Mr. WILLIAM MORGAN.

HONORARY SECRETARY.

Major-General The Hon. GEORGE WROTTESLEY.

HONORARY SOLICITOR.

Mr. W. H. DUIGNAN.

ASSISTANT SECRETARY.

Mr. JOHN W. BRADLEY, The William Salt Library, Stafford.

BANKERS.

LLOYD'S BANK (Limited), Stafford.

RULES OF THE SOCIETY.

I.—That the Society be called the "WILLIAM SALT ARCHÆOLOGICAL SOCIETY."

II.—The leading object of the Society shall be the editing and printing of original documents relating to the County of Stafford, to which, however, may be added papers selected by an Editorial Committee, illustrative of the same, or coming under any of the eight following heads:—

(*a*) Abstracts of the Monastic Chartularies, and of Ancient Family Deeds, with the names of witnesses and fac-similes of seals; Genealogies of Nobility and Gentry (accompanied by proofs), Heraldic Visitations, and other papers touching the general history and descent of properties and families.

(*b*) Printing and editing of the Public Records relating to the County, including the Exchequer or Pipe Rolls, the Assize Rolls, Fine Rolls, Inquisitions, Perambulations of Forests, Subsidy Rolls, and Assessments, &c., &c.

(*c*) History of Parishes and of Manors, and of Manorial Customs and Tenures, illustrated by Copies of, or reference to, original grants.

(*d*) Church Notes hitherto unpublished, such as Ecclesiastical Surveys, Extracts from Episcopal and Parish Registers, Copies of Epitaphs, and Description of Monuments and Ecclesiastical Buildings, Abstracts or Copies of Wills, &c.

(*e*) Notices of British and Roman Remains, and Roads and Buildings, and the Antiquities generally of the District.

(*f*) Autograph Letters and other Documents relating to the Civil War.

(*g*) Notices of distinguished Worthies, Broadsides, Election Squibs, &c.

(*h*) Correspondence, in which enquiries may be made and answered, on any of the above subjects, and miscellaneous information, including corrections of errors.

III.—The general affairs of the Society shall be managed by a Council of ten, of whom five shall be trustees of the William Salt Library, and nominated by them, from time to time, and five shall be elected at an Annual Meeting of the Subscribers. The Council shall be empowered to delegate, if they see fit, the selection of the papers to be printed, to an Editorial Committee. Of the Council, three shall be a quorum, and in case of equality of votes, their Chairman shall have a casting vote.

IV.—The Officers of the Society shall be a Treasurer, a Secretary, and an Auditor, to be appointed by the Council. These Offices shall be honorary, but the Council shall have power to appoint an Assistant Secretary to be paid at the discretion of the Council, as the nature of his duties may warrant.

V.—The Subscription shall be One Guinea annually, to be paid in advance, upon the first of January in each year, and such annual payment shall entitle each Subscriber to the volume issued for the year of such subscription. Any Subscriber shall be permitted to withdraw from the Society by giving notice of his intention three months before the termination of any year of Subscription.

N.B.—To save trouble, it is recommended that the Members of the Society pay their subscriptions to the Society's bankers by revocable order upon their own bankers, a printed form for which may be obtained from the Assistant Secretary.

LIST OF SUBSCRIBERS.

Allsopp, The Hon. Alfred Percy, Battenhall Mount, near Worcester.
Amphlett, John, Clent, Stourbridge.
Anson, Captain The Hon. G. A., Brocton Lodge, Stafford.
Asher & Co., Foreign Booksellers, 13, Bedford Street, Covent Garden.

Bagot, The Rt. Hon. Lord, Blithfield, Rugeley.
Bagot, Captain Josceline, Levens Hall, Milnthorpe, Westmoreland.
Bayley, B. M. Pershouse, Stonham Lodge, Tettenhall, Wolverhampton.
Bayliss, William, Ivy House, Walsall.
Beech, Rowland J., The Shaw, Cheadle, co. Stafford.
Beresford, The Rev. William, Vicar of St. Luke's, Leek.
Bill, Charles, M.P., The Woodhouse, Cheadle, Stoke-on-Trent.
Birch, Miss L. J., Parkstone House, Poole, Dorset.
Birks, Arthur, Woodfield, Rudyard, Stoke-on-Trent.
Birmingham Free Library (A. Capel Shaw, Librarian), Birmingham.
Blakiston, Matthew Folliott, Rowley Park, Stafford.
Boston (Massachusetts, U.S.A.) Public Library (Herbert Putnam, Librarian).
(*Parcels through Messrs. Kegan Paul and Co., Charing Cross Road, London.*)
Bourne, J., Hilderstone Hall, Stone, Stafford.
Bradford, The Right Hon. the Earl of, Weston Park, Shifnal, Salop.
Bree, The Venerable Archdeacon, Allesley Rectory, Coventry.
Bridgeman, C. G. O., 11, Stone Buildings, Lincoln's Inn.
Bridgeman, The Rev. Ernest R. O., Blymhill Rectory, Shifnal.
Brough, William Spooner, Leek.
Broun, Mich. A. W. Swinfen, Swinfen Hall, Lichfield.
Browne, The Rev. J. G. Cotton, Walkern Hall, Stevenage, Herts.
Bucknall, W. St. V., Lisbon (*care of Bucknall, Nephews, 22, Crutched Friars, E.C.*
Burne, Miss, Chichester Lodge, Long Ditton, Surrey.
Burton, The Right Hon. Lord, Rangemore, Burton-on-Trent.

Caddick, Edward, Wellington Road, Edgbaston, Birmingham.
Cambridge University Library, Cambridge.
Carter, W. Fowler, 33, Waterloo Street, Birmingham.
Chetham's Library, Manchester (Walter T. Brown, Librarian).
Clark, Geo. J., Dowlais House, Dowlais.
Collett, The Rev. E., Hughley Rectory, Shrewsbury.
Congreve, Capt. William, Burton Hall, Neston, Chester.
Crewe, The Rt. Hon. the Earl of, Crewe Hall, Cheshire.

Daltry, The Rev. Thos. W., F.L.S., Madeley Vicarage, Newcastle-under-Lyme.
Dartmouth, The Right Hon. Earl of, Patshull, Wolverhampton.
Davenport, Rev. G. Horatio, Foxley, Hereford.

DERRY, G., 79, Raglan Street, Fenton, Stoke-on-Trent.
DOWNING, W. H., Aldine Cottage, Kineton, Olton (*Parcels to Olton Station*).
DUIGNAN, W. H., Gorway House, Walsall.

EAGLETON, S. P., LL.D., Woodville, Compton Road, Wolverhampton.

FARNWORTH, E., Rosslyn, Coldthorn Hill, Wolverhampton.
FARRER, W., Marton House, Skipton.
FENTON, ROBERT, Newcastle-under-Lyme.
FITZHERBERT, BASIL THOMAS, Swynnerton, Stone, co. Stafford.
FLETCHER, The Rev. WILLIAM GEO. DIMOCK, M.A., F.S.A., St. Michael's Vicarage, Shrewsbury.
FOLEY, PAUL HENRY, Prestwood, Stourbridge.
FORD, JOHN WALKER, Enfield Old Park, Winchmore Hill, N.
FREER, J. H., Rugeley.

GARDNER, JOHN P., Cannock, Stafford.
GATTY, ALFRED SCOTT, York Herald, F.S.A., College of Arms, Queen Victoria Street, London, E.C.
GIBBONS, JOHN L., Ellowes Hall, Sedgeley, Staffs.
GIBBONS, W. P., Ruiton House, Dudley.
GILL, GEORGE, Highgate House, Walsall.
GOSS, W. H., Bank House, Stoke-on-Trent.
GRAZEBROOK, GEORGE, F.S.A., Sudbury, Harrow.
GRIFFIN, HARCOURT, Pell Wall, Market Drayton.
GRIFFITH, JOSEPH, Friar's Wood, Newcastle-under-Lyme.

HARDY, Sir REGINALD, Bart., Dunstall Hall, Burton-on-Trent.
HARROWBY, The Right Hon. Earl of, Sandon Hall, Stone, Stafford.
HARTLEY, GEORGE T., Wheaton Aston Hall, Stafford.
HARVARD COLLEGE, CAMBRIDGE (Massachusetts, U.S.A.) (*Parcels per Messrs. Kegan Paul and Co., Charing Cross Road, London.*)
HATHERTON, The Right Hon. Lord, Teddesley, Penkridge.
HAWKESBURY, The Right Hon. Lord, Kirkham Abbey, Yorks.
HELLIER, Col. T. B. SHAW, Woodhouse, Womborne, Wolverhampton.
HEWITT, EDWIN, 16, King Street, Hanley.
HODGSON, The Rev. J., F.S.A., Kinver Vicarage, Stourbridge.
HOLDEN, EDWARD THOMAS, Glenelg, Great Barr, Walsall.
HOLLAND, W. RICHARD, Ashbourne, Derby.
HOVENDEN, ROBERT, Heathcote Park, Hill Road, Croydon, Surrey.
HUGHES, T., Wychdon Lodge, Hixon, Stafford.
HUGHES, W. ESSINGTON, 140, Wardour Street, London, W.
HUNTER-WESTON, Lieut.-Col. GOULD, F.S.A., Hunterston, Kilbride, Ayrshire.
HUTCHINSON, Rev. SANDFORD WILLIAM, Blurton Vicarage, Stoke-on-Trent.

INGE, Rev. F. G., Baswich Vicarage, Stafford.

JACKSON, W. F. MARSH, Bearwood Hill, Smethwick.
JOBERNS, J., Aldridge Tile Works, Walsall.
JONES, W. HALL, Ablow Street, Wolverhampton.

JOYCE, M. INGLE, 16, Great Cumberland Place, London.
JOYCE, NICHOLAS, The Small Thorns, Stafford.

LANE, The Venerable Archdeacon ERNALD, Leigh Rectory, Stoke-on-Trent
LICHFIELD, The Right Hon. the Earl of, Shugborough Park, Stafford.
LICHFIELD, The Right Rev. Bishop of, Bishopstowe, Lichfield.
LICHFIELD, The Librarian of the Dean and Chapter, Cathedral Library, Lichfield.
LINCOLN'S INN, THE HON. SOCIETY OF (A. F. ETHERIDGE, Chief Librarian), Chancery Lane, W.C.
LIVERPOOL, THE FREE PUBLIC LIBRARY (PETER COWELL, Chief Librarian), William Brown Street, Liverpool.
LONDON LIBRARY (C. HAGBERG WRIGHT, Head Librarian), 12, St. James's Square, London.
LOVATT, JAMES, Brampton Hill, Newcastle-under-Lyme.

MACGREGOR, The Rev. W., The Vicarage, Tamworth.
MADAN, Mrs. F., Walford, Eccleshall.
MANCHESTER FREE PUBLIC LIBRARY (C. W. SUTTON, Chief Librarian), Manchester.
MANLEY, AUGUSTUS EAST, Manley Hall, Lichfield.
MILLS, F. W., 22A, Dorset Street, London, W.
MORETON, LOFTUS B., Pendeford Hall, Wolverhampton.
MORGAN, WILLIAM, Walton Lodge, Walton Hill, Stafford.
MORT, Lieut.-Col. FREDERICK D., Stafford.
MURRAY, Rev. D. S., Blithfield Rectory, Rugeley.

NEWCASTLE, THE FREE LIBRARY, Newcastle-under-Lyme.
NEW YORK PUBLIC LIBRARY, U.S.A. (*Parcels to care of B. F. Stevens and Brown, 4, Trafalgar Square, London.*)

OKEOVER, HAUGHTON CHARLES, Okeover, Ashbourne, Derby.

PARKER, The Rev. F. P., Colton Rectory, Rugeley.
PEARSON, J. H., Farcroft, Handsworth, Birmingham.
PERRY, FREDERICK CHARLES, Dunston Hall, Penkridge (Executors of).
PHILIPS, J. W., Heybridge, Tean, Stoke-on-Trent.
PLANT, The Rev. Prebendary S., Weston Vicarage, Stafford.

RATCLIFF, RICHARD, Stanford Hall, Loughborough.
ROBINSON, BROOKE, Barford House, Warwick.
ROBINSON, JOHN, Westwood Hall, Leek.
ROBINSON, W. P. (*care of B. F. Stevens and Brown, 4, Trafalgar Square, London.*)
ROLLASON, ARTHUR, 5, Union Street, Birmingham.
ROTTON, Sir J. F., 3, The Boltons, West Brompton, London, S.W.
ROYDS, The Rev. C. TWEMLOW, Heysham Rectory, Lancaster.

SALT, JOHN CHARLES, 61, Ennismore Gardens, London, S.W.
SALT, The Rev. EDWARD, B.A., The Rectory, Standon, Eccleshall, co. Stafford. (*Parcels to Standon Bridge Station, L. and N. W. Railway.*)
SALT, Sir THOMAS, Bart., Weeping Cross, Stafford.
SALT, THE WILLIAM (SALT) LIBRARY, Stafford.

Salt, The William (Salt) Library, Stafford (2nd copy).
Scrivener, A., Hanley.
Seckham, Samuel Lipscomb, Whittington Old Hall, Lichfield.
Slater, James, Bescot Hall, Walsall.
Smith, William, 2, Stanley Place, Leek.
Sneyd, Dryden Henry, Ashcombe Park, Leek.
Sneyd, John William, Basford Hall, Leek.
Sparrow, C. B., Corvylc, Butleigh, Glastonbury, Somerset.
Stanton, Mrs., 58, Elm Park Gardens, London, S.W.
Stoke-upon-Trent Free Library, Stoke-on-Trent.
Stone, J. H., Cavendish House, Grosvenor Road, Handsworth.
Swynnerton, The Rev. Charles (*Parcels to care of Messrs. Grindley and Co., India Agents, Parliament Street, London*).

Talbot, Rev. Arthur, Church Eaton Rectory, Stafford (*Parcels to Gnosall*).
Tildesley, James Carpenter, The Firs, Penkridge.
Twentyman, Alfred Charles, Castlecroft, Wolverhampton.

Wagner, Henry, F.S.A., 13, Half Moon Street, London, W.
Walker, Captain Robert P., 4, Rectory Place, Wolverhampton.
Walsall Free Public Library (A. Morgan, Librarian), Walsall.
Ward, Henry, Rodbaston, Penkridge.
Wedgwood Institute (T. Hulme, Curator), Burslem.
Wednesbury Free Public Library (Mr. Stanley, Librarian), Wednesbury.
West Bromwich Free Library (D. Dickenson, Librarian), West Bromwich.
Whitehead, T. N., Town Clerk, Burton-on-Trent.
Whitehouse, Benjamin, Turls Hill, Sedgeley, near Dudley.
Wiggin, Sir Henry, Bart., Metchley Grange, Harborne, Birmingham.
Windsor, The Right Hon. Lord, Hewell Grange, Bromsgrove.
Wise, Major L. L., Watts House, Bishops Lydiard, Taunton.
Wolseley, Sir Charles Michael, Bart., Wolseley Park, Rugeley.
Wolverhampton Free Library (John Elliot, Librarian), Wolverhampton.
Woods, Sir A. W., Garter King-of-Arms, College of Arms, Queen Victoria Street, London, E.C.
Wrottesley, The Right Hon. Lord, 8, Herbert Crescent, Hans Place, London, S.W.
Wrottesley, The Hon. Charles, Oaken House, Wolverhampton (*Parcels to Codsall Station, G. W. Railway*).
Wrottesley, Major-General The Hon. George, 75, Cadogan Gardens, London S.W.

The William Salt Archæological Society.

GENERAL MEETING, NOVEMBER 7TH, 1899.

THE Twenty-first Annual Meeting of the Society took place at the William Salt Library, Stafford, on the 7th November, 1899. Present: The Right Hon. the Lord Wrottesley in the Chair, the Rev. W. Beresford, the Rev. Ernest Bridgeman, the Rev. E. Collett, the Rev. F. Parker, the Rev. E. Salt, and Messrs. W. S. Brough, W. F. Carter, W. H. Duignan, N. Joyce, J. W. Philips, and Major-General the Hon. George Wrottesley, the Honorary Secretary.

The minutes of the previous meeting having been read, the Chairman called upon the Honorary Secretary to read the Report of the Editorial Committee, which was read as follows:—

REPORT OF THE EDITORIAL COMMITTEE.

The Committee have to report that in pursuance of the resolution passed at the last General Meeting, a circular was drawn up and sent to the principal residents of the County, including all Magistrates, Deputy Lieutenants, and Incumbents of Parishes, to the following effect:—

"SPECIAL APPEAL.

"At a Meeting of the William Salt Archæological Society held at Stafford on the 1st November, 1898, a resolution was unanimously passed that the present Members of the Society be asked to increase their Annual Subscription by half-a-guinea for the next two years, or until such time as the number of Subscribers reaches again a total of 200. The Society started eighteen years ago with more than 200 Members, but death vacancies and withdrawals have reduced the number at the present time to 140, whilst an estimate laid before the Meeting by the Honorary Secretary shows that a volume of average size, say of 300 to 350 pages, cannot be issued, with other incidental expenses, for a less sum than £200.

"Nearly all the important public Records relating to Staffordshire down to the reign of Henry VI. have been already printed by the efforts of the Society, and it is considered essential to continue the series to the close of the reign of Henry VII., or at least so long as the Honorary Secretary, General Wrottesley, is able to carry on his invaluable researches at the Record Office, and in connection with this subject, the Council thinks it necessary to explain that it is only through the voluntary efforts of General Wrottesley that they have been enabled to produce the number of volumes which have been issued up to this time with so small a Subscription, and that if it had been necessary to provide funds for the payment of the Abstracts from the Records now supplied gratuitously by the Honorary Secretary, the Society must have been wound up long ago.

"The Council of the Society therefore makes this appeal in the hope that the gentlemen of the County, recognising how much has been already done for Staffordshire history, will assist them to continue the work and become Subscribers to a new Series of Staffordshire Collections, of which three volumes are already in hand. The Subscription to the new Series will be one guinea annually.

"On behalf of the Council,
"J. W. BRADLEY,
"Assistant Secretary.

"The William Salt Library,
"Stafford,
"10th Nov., 1898."

The response to this circular has not been encouraging so far as new Subscribers are concerned, eight only having joined the Society, but upwards of 80 Members have consented to increase their subscriptions for two years.

The total number of Subscribers at the present date is 150, but this number will be subject to a gradual diminution by deaths and withdrawals. It becomes therefore a question for consideration whether it would be justifiable to carry on the Society after the volumes now in preparation have been issued to the Subscribers. These consist of five volumes, as under:—

1. The History of the Gresley Family.
2. The History of Weston-under-Lyzard.
3. A Volume of Records, now in print.
4. A Volume of Records, partly collected.
5. Chetwynd's History of the Pirehill Hundred, with notes by the Rev. F. Parker.

The first three volumes when issued will complete the programme proposed for the years 1898 and 1899.*

As regards the progress made in them, the Gresley History will be in the hands of Subscribers before the date of the present Meeting—the History of Weston is complete and printed all except the Index, and the latter is now in the hands of the printer. The volume of Records is complete with the exception of the last sheet, which is now in the hands of the printer, and the Index. Both these volumes will be issued early in 1900.

A difficulty, however, presents itself in the fact that the Honorary Secretary reports he is unable to collect material enough for more than 100 pages of print in the course of a year. And, therefore, even if the bulk of the volume is reduced to 250 pages, in order to meet the limited circumstances of the Society, unless new contributions are forthcoming, it will be necessary to fill 150 pages of print with other abstracts from the Records. These must be paid for, and it is doubtful whether with the present number of Subscribers there will be funds enough for this purpose. To meet this difficulty the Committee propose to prepare for press the Abstracts of Ancient Deeds in the William Salt Library, which have been made by the Assistant Secretary, and to add to them the abstracts of other deeds which were made by Mr. Hamper for the late Mr. William Salt. This will tend to fill up an important void in the Collections, for up to the present time the ancient deeds of the County have not received the attention which they deserve. It is proposed to print these abstracts in English.

The accounts of the sale of the large edition of Crecy and Calais show that a sum of £36 4*s*. was received up to the end of the year 1898, and Messrs. Harrison report that about £30 more has been received during the current year. These are the net amounts after deducting the booksellers' commission.

The Chairman proposed the adoption of the Report, which was carried.

The Chairman then called on the Assistant Secretary to read his report on the financial condition of the Society, and it was read as follows:—

* Since this Report was read it has been found impracticable to carry out this programme owing to want of funds, and it is proposed to make Volume 3 the issue for 1900.

REPORT OF THE ASSISTANT SECRETARY, DATED 7TH NOVEMBER, 1899.

The working of the Society during the past year presents some gratifying features, the first of which is that no death or withdrawal of any member has been reported.

It may be remembered that four of the vacancies reported last year were filled by the sons and a daughter of the deceased members; and a hope was expressed in the Meeting that Mr. John Bourne's son might be induced to succeed his father. As no definite refusal has been received this hope remains. It may also be well to supply an omission inadvertently made last year on this point of succession, by calling attention to the fact that after the death of the late Rev. and Hon. J. R. O. Bridgeman, *two* of his sons became Members.

Another encouraging item is the accession of EIGHT NEW MEMBERS in response to the invitation issued by the Council in 1898.

The new Members are: Captain the Hon. G. A. Anson, Messrs. J. L. Gibbons and W. H. Goss, Col. T. B. Shaw-Hellier, Mr. John Robinson, the Rev. D. S. Murray, the Rev. F. G. Inge, and Mr. W. P. Robinson.

The Membership is thus again raised to 150, if we include Mr. Bourne, whose son we hope to secure.

With this proof of extended interest in the Society, a further increase may be reasonably anticipated.

There is the case of one Member of the Society which demands the consideration and decision of the Meeting. Some now present may recall the fact that at the Annual Meeting of 1895, a gentleman introduced *three* new Subscribers; one of which was the Newcastle Free Library, which also bought a set of the Society's publications Vol. I to XV.

That gentleman had been informed by circular and letter in the ordinary course that his own subscription was in arrear, of which he complained asserting that he had paid up to date. As the records gave no evidence of such payment, a tabulated statement was prepared showing when all former sums had been entered and to which Vols. they had been credited.

In consideration of the valued service he had rendered to the Society, instructions were given that if he could not find the receipts for the payments alleged to have been made, his own memorandum of dates from the counterfoils of his cheque book would be accepted as evidence, and the claim for arrears cancelled. He agreed to this arrangement and promised to send the memo. as a voucher.

The yearly vols. have been forwarded as usual, but neither voucher for previous payments, or subsequent subscriptions have since been forthcoming.

Vol. XIV is the last for which onr accounts credit payment. For some time past no answer to either printed circular or letters has been received. Including this year's subscription, *seven guineas* are due to the Society, and it remains for the Members to take such action as they may think best.

In former years several Vols. have been returned owing to "change of address." This year *to date*, only one has thus been returned, and as the value of the previous Vol. XVIII was covered by the last Subscription paid by the missing Subscriber, the loss is not serious.

The next point claiming consideration is that of Extra Subscriptions. 140 circulars were sent to old Subscribers. Eighty signed and returned the printed promises endorsed to them. Thus about two-fifths of those who were invited to assist the Council in their financial emergency promptly responded. Two others paid the extra 10*s*. 6*d*. (since October 15th) who had not promised to do so. Thus the Extra Voluntary Subscriptions may be expected to bring in at least eighty-two guineas.

Seven of the Members—viz., Mr. Beech, Miss Burne, Lord Harrowby, Mr. Brooke Robinson, Mr. Twentyman, Mr. Ward and General Wrottesley—paid their Subscriptions for both years together.

Fifty-five paid their promised half-guineas before October 15th, and four since that date. One sent 10*s*., probably owing to a slip of the pen in filling the cheque. Fifteen omitted to transmit.

The Extra Subscriptions included in the present Balance Sheet, amount to £36 14*s*. 6*d*. The promises for 1900 may be relied upon to produce as follows :—

	£	*s*.	*d*.
15 at 21*s*. each	15	15	0
60 at 10*s*. 6*d*. each	31	10	0
The omitted	0	0	6
Four half-guineas in hand ..	2	2	0
Total	49	7	6

Or eighty-two guineas for the two years.

The analysis of the Balance Sheet may hopefully conclude by noting the sum of £36 4*s*. 1*d*., already received from sales of the special Crecy-Calais Vol., and the fears of bankruptcy which were aroused last year may be dismissed for the present by the William Salt Archæological Society.

J. W. BRADLEY, *Assistant Secretary*.

The William Salt Archæological Society.

STATEMENT OF RECEIPTS AND PAYMENTS FOR THE YEAR ENDING OCTOBER 15TH, 1899.

1898.	*Receipts.*	£ *s.* *d.*	£ *s.* *d.*
Oct. 1.	To Balance in Bank		89 7 2
Dec. 3.	„ Donation from Bernard Gilpin, Esq.		2 2 0
1899.			
Jan. 28.	„ Cheque from Norton, Rose & Co. (in error).		
Oct. 15.	„ Subscriptions and Arrears from 141 Old Subscribers:—		
	3 Vols. XVII.	3 3 0	
	3 Vols. XVIII.	3 3 0	
	(Vol. 1. New Series) 10 Vols. XIX.	10 10 0	
	(Vol. 2. „) 82 Vols. XX.	86 2 0	
	(Vol. 3. „) 2 Vols. XXI.	2 2 0	
	100		105 0 0
Oct. 15.	To Subscriptions from 8 New Subscribers. 8 Vols. XIX. = Vol. I. New Series	8 8 0	
			8 8 0
	„ Sales Vol. V, Pt. 1. and Postage	0 10 10	
	„ „ „ XVII	1 1 0	

1898.	*Payments.*	£ *s.* *d.*
Oct. 6.	By Purchase of 2 Vols. Staffordshire Collections from Mrs. Caldwell	2 2 0
Nov. 1.	„ „ 1 Vol. Staffordshire Collections, Mr. W. Morgan	1 1 0
„ 2.	„ Honorarium, Mr. J. W. Bradley, for the year 1898–1899	15 0 0
„ 2.	„ Purchase of Vols. I–III and Part 1, Vol. V, from Dr. Tylecote ..	3 0 6
„ 26.	„ Mr. W. Boyd, for Abstracts of Fines, 5–7 James I	5 0 0
1899.		
Jan. 19.	„ Mr. W. Boyd, for Abstracts of Fines, 7 to Trinity of 9 James I ..	5 0 0
Mar. 4.	„ Messrs. Harrison & Sons for issuing large paper copy of Crecy and Calais	34 18 0
„ 18.	„ Mr. J. W. Bradley to repay subscription sent by mistake (from Norton, Rose & Co.)	2 2 0
May 31.	„ Mr. W. Boyd, Abstracts of Fines, Mich. and Hillary, 9 James I ..	1 5 0

	£	s.	d.	£	s.	d.
To Sales Vol. XVIII (Crecy and Calais)	1	10	6			
„ Sales. Messrs. Harrison & Sons Special Vol. XVIII. Crecy and Calais	33	1	9			
				36	4	1
„ Extra Subscriptions (asked for 2 years) :—						
7 Members paid 21*s.* for 1899 and 1900	7	7	0			
55 „ „ 10*s.* 6*d.* for 1899 ..	28	17	6			
1 „ „ 10*s.* „ „ ..	0	10	0			
Total ..				279	17	9

Date		£	s.	d.
Sep. 29. „	The Rev. N. W. Gresley for 160 copies of "The Gresley History" at 10*s.* 6*d.*	84	0	0
Oct. 15. „	Balance in Bank	126	9	3
	Total ..	£279	17	9

Examined and found correct,

(Signed) WILLIAM MORGAN,
Hon. Auditor.
3*rd November*, 1899.

(Signed) GEORGE WROTTESLEY, MAJOR-GENERAL,
Hon. Secretary.

Mr. Parker then brought forward the question of including among their collections a history of the Wrottesley family, which was now appearing in parts in the pages of the *Genealogist*, the owners of that magazine having offered to allow the history to be reprinted by the William Salt Society on very advantageous terms, on condition, however, that it should not be issued before the final number had appeared in the *Genealogist.* Messrs. Parker and Beresford spoke very highly of the ability of the author and the excellence of that portion of the work which had been published, and the Meeting decided that the offer of the *Genealogist* should be accepted.

Mr. E. Bridgeman brought before the Meeting the question of printing the early Parish Registers of the County, as was now in progress in Shropshire, and where the attempt had proved very successful. After some debate it was considered best to postpone the question until the position of the Society was more assured.

After the usual votes of thanks, the Meeting separated.

At several of the past General Meetings of the Society, a wish has been expressed by the members present, that a portrait of the Honorary Secretary might be added to one of the volumes issued by the Society.

A photograph by Messrs. Elliott & Fry, printed by a permanent process, has accordingly been added to this volume.

CONTENTS.

VOLUME III. New Series.

Page

1. **Final Concords,** or **Pedes Finium, Staffordshire.** 5 James I. to 9 James I., inclusive. Abstracted from the originals in the Public Record Office, *by Mr. W. Boyd, and revised by the Honorary Secretary* 1–70

2. Some notes on the earlier Swynnertons of **Eccleshall** and **Chell**, and on the cross-legged effigy in Swynnerton Church, *by the Rev. Charles Swynnerton* . . 71–120

3. Extracts from the **Plea Rolls** of the reign of Henry VI., translated from the original Rolls in the Public Record Office, *by Maj.-General the Hon. George Wrottesley* 121–229

CONTENTS OF PREVIOUS VOLUMES.

VOLUME I.

The Staffordshire Pipe Rolls of 31 Henry I. (A.D. 1130) and of 1 to 35 Henry II. (A.D. 1155 to 1189); the Latin Texts extended and Notes added. *By the Rev. R. W. Eyton* .. .. pp. 1–143

The Liber Niger Scaccarii, Staffordscira, or Feodary of A.D. 1166, with Notes added. *By Colonel the Hon. G. Wrottesley* .. .. .. pp. 145–213

Notes on the Fitz Alan Fees, and those of Feudatories holding land in Staffordshire, A.D. 1166, who made no return. *By the Rev. R. W. Eyton* pp. 213–240

The Register of Roger de Norbury, Bishop of Lichfield and Coventry, from A.D. 1322 to A.D. 1358. An abstract of Contents and Remarks. *By the Right Rev. Bishop Hobhouse* .. .. pp. 241–288

The History of the Parish of Blymhill, Part I. *By the Hon. and Rev. George Bridgeman* .. .. pp. 289–384

VOLUME II.

PART I.

The Staffordshire Pipe Rolls, of the Reigns of King Richard I. and King John, A.D. 1189 to A.D. 1216. The Latin Text extended, and notes added. *By the Rev. R. W. Eyton* .. .. pp. 1 to 177

The Staffordshire Chartulary, Series I and II of Ancient Deeds. *Annotated by the Rev. R. W. Eyton* .. .. pp. 178–276

PART II.

Obligatory Knighthood, temp. Charles I., with the names of those Staffordshire gentlemen who compounded with the Commissioners, for not taking upon themselves the order of Knighthood at the coronation of that King. Extracted from the originals in the Public Record Office, *by Henry Sydney Grazebrook, Esq.* .. .. pp. 3–22

A Copy of the Arms taken in the Visitation of the co. of Stafford, in the years 1663 and 1664. By William Dugdale, Esq., Norroy King of Arms; also the names of those who disclaimed at the same date. Transcribed from the Lansdowne MS., 857, and annotated *by Henry Sydney Grazebrook, Esq.* pp. 23–65

The History of the Parish of Blymhill (continued from Vol. I and completed). *By the Hon. and Rev. George Bridgeman* .. .. .. pp. 69–147

VOLUME III.

PART I.

Staffordshire Suits, extracted from the Plea Rolls temp. Richard I. and King John, with an introduction and notes, *by Major-General the Hon. G. Wrottesley* .. .. pp. 1–163

Final Concords, or Pedes Finium, Staffordshire, temp. Richard I. and King John. Abstracted from the William Salt Transcripts, and compared with the Originals in the Public Record Office, *by Major-General the Hon. G. Wrottesley* .. .. pp. 165–177

The Staffordshire Chartulary, Series III of Ancient Deeds. Transcribed and annotated *by Major-General the Hon. G. Wrottesley* .. pp. 178–231

PART II.

The Visitation of Staffordshire, made by Robert Glover, Somerset Herald, A.D. 1583; illustrated by lithographs of Coats of Arms. Edited, with an introduction and notes, *by Henry Sydney Grazebrook, Esq.* .. pp. 1–155

A Note on the Pedigrees of the De Wasteneys Family. *By the Rev. F. P. Parker, Rector of Colton* .. .. pp. 156–162

VOLUME IV.

PART I.

Plea Rolls, temp. Henry III. Suits affecting Staffordshire tenants, taken from the Plea Rolls of the reign of Henry III., and abstracted into English. *By Major-General the Hon. G. Wrottesley* .. .. .. pp. 1–215

Final Concords, or Pedes Finium, Staffordshire, temp. Henry III. Abstracted from the William Salt Transcripts, and compared with the originals in the Public Record Office; to which have been added those of Warwickshire, and of mixed counties to which Staffordshire tenants are parties. *By Major-General the Hon. G. Wrottesley* .. .. pp. 218–263

The Chartulary of Ronton Priory, abstracted from the original MS. in the British Museum. *By Major-General the Hon. G. Wrottesley* pp. 264–295

PART II.

The History of the Parish of Church Eaton and its members, Wood Eaton, Orslow, High Onn, Little Onn, Shushions, and Marston. *By the Hon. and Rev. Canon G. T. O. Bridgeman* .. .. pp. 1–124

VOLUME V.

PART I.

An Abstract of the Contents of the Burton Chartulary, in possession of the Marquis of Anglesey at Beaudesert. *By Major-General the Hon. G. Wrottesley* .. .. pp. 1–101

The Staffordshire Hundred Rolls, temp. Henry III. and Edward I. From the originals in the Public Record Office. *By Major-General the Hon. G. Wrottesley* .. .. pp. 105–121

The Pleas of the Forest, Staffordshire, temp. Henry III. and Edward I. Translated from the originals in the Public Record Office, with an introduction and notes. *By Major-General the Hon. G. Wrottesley* pp. 123–180

PART II.

The Heraldic Visitations of Staffordshire made by Sir Henry St. George, Norroy, in 1614, and by Sir William Dugdale in the years 1663 and 1664. Edited and annotated *by H. Sydney Grazebrook, Esq.* .. .. .. pp. 1–349

VOLUME VI.

PART I.

The Stone Chartulary. An abstract of its contents from the original MS. in the British Museum. *By Major-General the Hon. G. Wrottesley* pp. 1–28

Staffordshire Pleas, taken from the Additional MS., No. 12,269, British Museum, *by the same* .. .. pp. 29–36

Extracts from the Plea Rolls, A.D. 1272 to A.D. 1294, taken from the original Rolls in the Public Record Office, with an introduction, *by the same* pp. 37–300

PART II.

A List of the Capitular Muniments at Lichfield, compiled for the Dean and Chapter. *By the Rev. Dr. C. J. Cox* .. .. pp. 1–230

VOLUME VII.

Part I.

Extracts from the Plea Rolls, A.D. 1294 to A.D. 1307. Translated from the original Rolls in the Public Record Office. *By Major-General the Hon. George Wrottesley.* With an introduction and notes .. pp. 1-191

The Exchequer Subsidy Roll of A.D. 1327. Edited, with an introduction and notes *by Major-General the Hon. G. Wrottesley* .. .. pp. 193-255

Part II.

A History of the Family of Swynnerton of Swynnerton, and of the younger branches of the same family settled at Eccleshall, Hilton, and Butterton. *By the Hon. and Rev. Canon Bridgeman* .. .. .. pp. 1-189

VOLUME VIII.

Part I.

An Account of the Military Service Performed by Staffordshire Tenants in the Thirteenth and Fourteenth Centuries. From documents in the Public Record Office. *By Major-General the Hon. G. Wrottesley* pp. 1-122

A Chartulary of the Priory of St. Thomas, the Martyr, near Stafford. Collected and edited *by the Rev. F. Parker* .. .. pp. 125-201

Part II.

History of the Manor and Parish of Castre or Castle Church. *By Mr. T. J. de Mazzinghi, M.A.*.. .. .. pp. 1-152

VOLUME IX.

Part I.

Extracts from the Assize Rolls and De Banco Rolls of the Reign of Edward II., A.D. 1307 to A.D. 1327. Translated from the original Rolls in the Public Record Office. *By Major-General the Hon. G. Wrottesley* pp. 1-118

Extracts from the Fine Rolls of the Reign of Edward II., A.D. 1307 to A.D.1327, taken from the original Rolls in the Public Record Office. *By Major-General the Hon. G. Wrottesley* .. .. pp. 120-132

Part II.

An Account of the Barons of Dudley. *By Henry Sydney Grazebrook, Esq.* pp. 1-152

VOLUME X.

Part I.

Extracts from the Coram Rege Rolls and Pleas of the Crown, Staffordshire, of the Reign of Edward II., A.D. 1307 to A.D. 1327. Translated from the original Rolls in the Public Record Office. *By Major-General the Hon G. Wrottesley* .. .. pp. 1-75

The Subsidy Roll of 6 Edward III., A.D. 1332-33. From the original Exchequer Roll in the Public Record Office, and edited, with an introduction and notes. *By Major-General the Hon. G. Wrottesley* .. .. .. pp. 79-132

Part II.

An Account of the Younger Branches of the Family of Sutton alias Dudley (in continuation of Volume IX., Part II.) *By Henry Sydney Grazebrook, Esq.* .. .. pp. 1-178

VOLUME XI.

Extracts from the Plea Rolls, 1 to 15 Edward III., translated from the original Rolls in the Public Record Office, *by Major-General the Hon. G. Wrottesley* pp. 1–123

The Final Concords, or Feet of Fines, Staffordshire, A.D. 1327 to A.D. 1547, to which have been added those of mixed counties to which Staffordshire tenants were parties, *edited by Major-General the Hon. G. Wrottesley* pp. 127-292

A Chartulary of the Augustine Priory of Trentham, *collected and edited by the Rev. F. Parker* .. .. pp. 295–336

VOLUME XII.

PART I.

Extracts from the Plea Rolls, 16 to 33 Edward III., translated from the original Rolls in the Public Record Office, *by Major-General the Hon. G. Wrottesley* .. .. pp. 1-173

Pedes Finium, or Fines of Mixed Counties, which include manors and tenements in Staffordshire, temp. Henry VII., Henry VIII., Edward VI., and Philip and Mary. Abstracted from the originals in the Public Record Office, *by Major-General the Hon. G. Wrottesley* .. .. .. pp. 177–235

Final Concords, or Pedes Finium of Staffordshire, for the 1st year of Queen Elizabeth. Abstracted from the originals in the Public Record Office, *by Mr. W. Boyd, and revised by the Honorary Secretary* .. .. pp. 235–239

The Chetwynd Chartulary, printed from the original MS. at Ingestre, with an introduction and notes, *by Major-General the Hon. G. Wrottesley* pp. 242–336

PART II.

Supplement to the History of the Manor and Parish of Blymhill, *by the Hon. and Rev. Canon Bridgeman* .. .. pp. 1–29

VOLUME XIII.

Extracts from the Plea Rolls of Edward III., and Richard II., A.D. 1360 to A.D. 1387, translated from the original Rolls in the Public Record Office, *by Major-General the Hon. G. Wrottesley* .. .. pp. 1–204

Final Concords, or Pedes Finium of Staffordshire of the reign of Elizabeth, continued from Vol. XII, 2 to 15 Elizabeth, abstracted from the original Feet of Fines in the Public Record Office, *by Mr. W. Boyd, and revised by the Honorary Secretary* .. .. pp. 207–300

VOLUME XIV.

PART I.

Extracts from the Coram Rege Rolls of Edward III., and Richard II., A.D. 1327 to A.D. 1383, translated from the original Rolls in the Public Record Office, *by Major-General the Hon. G. Wrottesley* .. .. .. pp. 1–162

The Final Concords, or Pedes Finium of Staffordshire, of the reign of Elizabeth, A.D. 1573 to A.D. 1580, abstracted from the original Documents in the Public Record Office, *by Mr. W. Boyd, and revised by the Honorary Secretary* .. .. pp. 165–217

Military Service performed by Staffordshire tenants during the reign of Richard II., from the original Rolls in the Public Record Office, *by Major-General the Hon. G. Wrottesley* .. .. pp. 221–264

PART II.

The History of the Manor and Parish of Weston-under-Lizard in the co. of Stafford, *by the Hon. and Rev. George Bridgeman* .. .. .. pp. 1–38

VOLUME XV.

Extracts from the Plea Rolls of the reigns of Richard II. and Henry IV., A.D. 1387 to A.D. 1405, translated from the original Rolls in the Public Record Office, *by Major-General the Hon. G. Wrottesley* .. .. .. pp. 1–126

The Final Concords, or Pedes Finium of Staffordshire, of the reign of Elizabeth, A.D. 1580 to A.D. 1589, abstracted from the original documents in the Public Record Office, *by Mr. W. Boyd, and revised by the Honorary Secretary* .. .. pp. 129–198

The Staffordshire Muster of A.D. 1640, from the original Muster Roll at Wrottesley, with an introduction *by Major-General the Hon. G. Wrottesley* pp. 201–231

VOLUME XVI.

Extracts from the Cheshire Plea Rolls of the reigns of Edward III., Richard II., and Henry IV., and from the De Banco and Coram Rege Rolls of Richard II and Henry IV., translated from the original Rolls in the Public Record Office, *by Major-General the Hon. G. Wrottesley* .. .. .. pp. 1–94

The Final Concords, or Pedes Finium of Staffordshire, 32 Elizabeth to the end of the reign of Elizabeth, A.D. 1589 to 1603, abstracted from the originals in the Public Record Office, *by Mr. W. Boyd, and revised by the Honorary Secretary* .. .. pp. 95–226

The Rydeware Chartulary, from the original in the possession of Sir Robert Gresley, Bart., of Drakelowe, by Isaac Herbert Jeayes, Esq., of the MS. Department, British Museum, with an Introduction *by Major-General the Hon. G. Wrottesley* .. .. pp. 227–302

VOLUME XVII.

Extracts from the Plea Rolls of the reigns of Henry V. and Henry VI., translated from the original Rolls in the Public Record Office, *by Major-General the Hon. G. Wrottesley* .. .. pp. 1–153

The Poll Tax of A.D. 1379-81 for the Hundreds of Offlow and Cuttlestone, copied from the original Roll in the Public Record Office, *by Mr. W. Boyd*; the abbreviations extended and an Introduction added *by the Honorary Secretary* pp. 157-205

Final Concords, or Pedes Finium of Mixed Counties, which include Staffordshire, abstracted from the original Fines in the Public Record Office, *by Mr. W. Boyd, and revised by the Honorary Secretary* .. .. .. pp. 208-236

The Shenstone Charters, copied from the Chartulary or Great Coucher Book of the Duchy of Lancaster in the Public Record Office, *by Mr. George Grazebrook, with notes by the late Mr. H. S. Grazebrook* .. .. pp. 239–298

VOLUME XVIII.

Part I.

The Final Concords, or Pedes Finium of Mixed Counties, which include Staffordshire *temp.* Elizabeth, abstracted from the original Fines in the Public Record Office, *by Mr. W. Boyd, and revised by the Honorary Secretary* pp. 1–21

The Final Concords, or Pedes Finium of Cities in Staffordshire *temp.* Elizabeth, *by the same* .. .. pp. 22–27

The Final Concords, or Pedes Finium of Staffordshire, 1 to 4 James I. (inclusive), *by the same* .. .. pp. 28-70

PART II.

Crecy and Calais, A.D. 1346–47, from the Rolls in the Public Record Office and a MS. in the College of Arms, as below:—

French Roll, 19 E. III., Part 2 .. .. pp. 58–65
French Roll, 20 E. III., Parts 1 and 2 .. .. .. pp. 65–115
French Roll, 21 E. III., Parts 1 and 2 .. .. .. pp. 115–136
Memoranda Rolls, Queen's Remembrancer .. .. .. pp. 136–190
The accounts for the war, by Walter de Wetewang, the Treasurer of the Household .. .. pp. 191–219
The Norman Roll of 20 E. III. .. .. pp. 219–259
The Calais Roll of 21 E. III. .. .. pp. 260–279

By Major-General the Hon. G. Wrottesley.

VOLUME I. NEW SERIES.

The Gresleys of Drakelowe. An account of the Family, and Notes of its connexions by Marriage and Descent from the Norman Conquest to the Present Day, *by Falconer Madan, M.A., Fellow of Brasenose College, Oxford.*

VOLUME II. NEW SERIES.

History of the Manor and Parish of Weston-under-Lizard. Compiled from the MSS. of the late Rev. the Hon. George T. O. Bridgeman, Rector of Wigan. *By the Rev. Ernest R. O. Bridgeman, Rector of Blymhill, and Charles G. O. Bridgeman, Esq., of 11, Stone Buildings, Lincoln's Inn, Barrister-at-Law.*

FINAL CONCORDS OR PEDES FINIUM.

STAFFORDSHIRE,

TEMP. JAMES I.

(*Continued from p.* 70, *Vol. XVIII.*)

FINAL CONCORDS. TEMP. JAMES I.

FEET OF FINES, STAFFORD. EASTER, 5 JAMES I.

(*Continued from p.* 70, *Vol. XVIII.*)

At fifteen days from Easter Day. 5 James I.

Between Alexander Jervys, complainant, and John Persehowse, gentleman, Humphrey Tudman and Eleanor, his wife, and William Siddowne and Alice, his wife, deforciants of a cottage, a garden, 20 acres of land, 2 acres of meadow, and 20 acres of pasture in **Westbromwiche** and **Brierley**.

The deforciants remitted all right to Alexander and his heirs, for which Alexander gave them £40.

At fifteen days from Easter Day. 5 James I.

Between John Wollaston, gentleman, and John Aldersey, gentleman, complainants, and Richard Wilbram, knight, and Grace, his wife, Walter Leveson, knight, Thomas Leveson, gentleman, and Richard Harrison and Ellen, his wife, deforciants of 10 acres of pasture, 20 acres of heath, and 20 acres of moor in **Pelsall, Walsall,** and **Little Wyrley**, and of a yearly rent of £10 issuing from the manor of **Little Wyrley**, with the appurtenances.

The deforciants remitted all right to the complainants and to the heirs of John Wollaston, for which the complainants gave them £240.

At fifteen days from Easter Day. 5 James I.

Between Robert Bryndley, complainant, and Philip Grove, deforciant of an acre of meadow and 2 acres of pasture in **Rowley Somerey.**

Philip remitted all right to Robert and his heirs, for which Robert gave him £40.

At fifteen days from Easter Day. 5 James I.

Between John Russell, complainant, and Thomas Bloomer and Isabella, his wife, deforciants of a messuage, a cottage, a garden, an orchard, 2 acres of land, 2 acres of meadow, and 14 acres of pasture in **Rowley.**

Thomas and Isabella remitted all right to John and his heirs, for which John gave them £40.

At fifteen days from Easter Day. 5 James I.

Between William Orme, gentleman, complainant, and John Wall and Bridget, his wife, deforciants of a messuage, a cottage, a barn, a garden, an orchard, 6 acres of land, 3 acres of meadow, 6 acres of pasture, and an acre of wood in **Rowley.**

John and Bridget remitted all right to William and his heirs, for which William gave them £40.

At fifteen days from Easter Day. 5 James I.

Between William Orme, gentleman, complainant, and Henry Wall and Jane, his wife, deforciants of 4 acres of land, 3 acres of meadow, 8 acres of pasture, and 2 acres of wood in **Rowley.**

Henry and Jane remitted all right to William and his heirs, for which William gave them £40.

At fifteen days from Easter Day. 5 James I.

Between James Turner, complainant, and John Mountforde and Elizabeth, his wife, and Thomas Mountforde, son and heir apparent of the said John, deforciants of a messuage, a cottage, 20 acres of land, 10 acres of meadow, 20 acres of pasture, common of pasture for all cattle, and common of turbary in **Baddeley** otherwise **Baddiley.**

The deforciants remitted all right to James and his heirs, for which James gave them £60.

At fifteen days from Easter Day. 5 James I.

Between Thomas Bagnalde, complainant, and Andrew Vyse, gentleman, and Elizabeth, his wife, deforciants of a messuage, a garden, an orchard, 140 acres of land, 30 acres of meadow, 100 acres of pasture, and 50 acres of wood in **Fenton Vivian** and **Botteslowe.**

Andrew and Elizabeth remitted all right to Thomas and his heirs, for which Thomas gave them £120.

At fifteen days from Easter Day. 5 James I.

Between Richard Brundley, complainant, and John Berdmore, gentleman, deforciant of 12 acres of land, 4 acres of meadow, 4 acres of pasture, an acre of wood, and 2 acres of furze and heath in **Cotton** and **Alveton.**

John remitted all right to Richard and his heirs, for which Richard gave him £41.

At fifteen days from Easter Day. 5 James I.

Between Richard Hussey, knight, complainant, and Walter Rowley, gentleman, deforciant of 3 messuages, 3 gardens, 3 orchards, 60 acres of land, 30 acres of meadow, and 50 acres of pasture in **Norton in le Moores** and **Woodhowses.**

Walter remitted all right to Richard and his heirs, for which Richard gave him £100.

At fifteen days from Easter Day. 5 James I.

Between William Fysher and Henry Grove, complainants, and Edward Grove and Anne, his wife, and Thomas Dudley, deforciants of a cottage, a barn, a garden, 14 acres of land, 10 acres of meadow, and 14 acres of pasture in **Westbromwiche.**

The deforciants remitted all right to William and Henry and the heirs of William, for which William and Henry gave them £40.

At fifteen days from Easter Day. 5 James I.

Between John Richardes, gentleman, complainant, and John Astyn, gentleman, deforciant of 6 acres of pasture in **Wolverhampton.**

John Astyn remitted all right to John Richardes and his heirs, for which John Richardes gave him £40.

At fifteen days from Easter Day. 5 James I.

Between William Orme, gentleman, complainant, and Thomas White and Margaret, his wife, deforciants of 2 cottages and 8 acres of pasture in **Rowley.**

Thomas and Margaret remitted all right to William and his heirs for which William gave them £40.

At fifteen days from Easter Day. James I.

Between Thomas Sheldon, the younger, complainant, and Thomas Dolphyn and Alice, his wife, deforciants of a cottage, a barn, a garden, an orchard, and 12 acres of pasture in **West Bromwiche.**

Thomas Dolphyn and Alice remitted all right to Thomas Sheldon and his heirs, for which Thomas Sheldon gave them £60.

At three weeks from Easter Day. 5 James I.

Between Francis Harrold, gentleman, complainant, and Richard Turner, deforciant of the advowson of the prebend of **Cloughton** otherwise **Ufton**, in the cathedral church of **Lichfield.**

Richard remitted all right to Francis and his heirs, for which Francis gave him £40.

At fifteen days from Easter Day. 5 James I.

Between Christopher Bradshawe, gentleman, complainant, and Richard Bradshawe, gentleman, and Elizabeth, his wife, deforciants of 3 messuages, 3 gardens, 160 acres of land, 30 acres of meadow, 40 acres of pasture, 100 acres of wood, 200 acres of furze and heath, and common of pasture for all kinds of cattle in **Bagnall** and **Leeke.**

Richard and Elizabeth remitted all right to Christopher and his heirs, for which Christopher gave them £120.

At fifteen days from Easter Day. 5 James I.

Between William Orme, gentleman, complainant, and William Darbye and Margery, his wife, deforciants of a messuage, a garden, an orchard, 14 acres of land, 20 acres of meadow, 24 acres of pasture, and 2 acres of wood in **Rowley.**

William Darbye and Margery remitted all right to William Orme and his heirs, for which William Orme gave them £100.

At fifteen days from Easter Day. 5 James I.

Between Walter Cradocke, gentleman, complainant, and John Cooper, gentleman, deforciant of the manor of **Dunston**, with the appurtenances, and of 3 messuages, 3 barns, 3 gardens, 3 orchards, 300 acres of land, 50 acres of meadow, 50 acres of pasture, 20 acres of furze and heath, and 16*s.* of rent in **Dunston.**

John remitted all right to Walter and his heirs, for which Walter gave him £160.

At fifteen days from Easter Day. 5 James I.

Between Thomas Tomkys, complainant, and Richard Grove, deforciant of 5 acres of pasture in **Wolverhampton.**

Richard remitted all right to Thomas and his heirs, for which Thomas gave him £40.

At fifteen days from Easter Day. 5 James I.

Between Richard Hill, clerk, complainant, and John Boylston and Elizabeth, his wife, and Ellen Belcher, widow, deforciants of 2 messuages, 2 cottages, 4 gardens, 4 orchards, 60 acres of land, 30 acres of meadow, 60 acres of pasture, 5 acres of wood, and 30 acres of furze and heath in **Dunstall** otherwise **Tunstall, Tatenell,** and **Barton under Needwood**, and of common of pasture for all cattle in the forest of **Needwood.**

The deforciants remitted all right to Richard and his heirs, for which Richard gave them £100.

At fifteen days from Easter Day. 5 James I.

Between Edward Littleton, the elder, knight, complainant, and Zacharias Babington, Doctor of Laws, and Thomasina, his wife, and William Babington, gentleman, deforciants of 2 messuages, 2 cottages, a toft, a dovecote, 2 gardens, 4 orchards, 40 acres of land, 16 acres of meadow, 30 acres of pasture, 20 acres of wood, 20 acres of furze and heath, 20 acres of marsh, 10 acres of land covered with water, 15*s.* of rent, and common of pasture for all beasts in **Curburrowe.**

The deforciants remitted all right to Edward and his heirs, for which Edward gave them £100.

At fifteen days from Easter Day. 5 James I.

Between Robert Foster and Thomas Clerke, complainants, and Thomas Wolrich, gentleman, deforciant of a messuage, 50 acres of land, 16 acres of meadow, 40 acres of pasture, and 40 acres of furze and heath in **Seighford, Cokeslane,** and **Little Bridgford.**

Thomas Wolrich remitted all right to the complainants and to the heirs of Robert, for which the complainants gave him £80.

At fifteen days from Easter Day. 5 James I.

Between Richard Chetwood, knight, and Francis Dorington, gentleman, son of Richard Dorington, deceased, complainants, and Francis Dorington, son of Francis Dorington, deceased, Matthew Dorington, and Francis Rocke and Ellen, his wife, deforciants of a messuage and a curtilage in **Stafford.**

The deforciants remitted all right to the complainants and to the heirs of Richard Chetwood, for which the complainants gave them £60.

At fifteen days from Easter Day. 5 James I.

Between Thomas Hyntes and William James otherwise Strynger, complainants, and Robert Brockhurst and Alice, his wife, and Thomas James otherwise Strynger, deforciants of a cottage, a garden, and 10 acres of land in **Westbromwich** and **Allerwich** otherwise **Aldriche.**

The deforciants remitted all right to the complainants and to the heirs of Thomas Hyntes, for which the complainants gave them £40.

At fifteen days from Easter Day. 5 James I.

Between Edward Fitzherbert, armiger, complainant, and Elizabeth Gatacre, widow, deforciant of the manor of **Swynerton,** with the appurtenances, and of 60 messuages, a mill, a dovecote, 40 gardens, 40 orchards, 600 acres of land, 160 acres of meadow, 200 acres of pasture, 2,000 acres of wood, 2,000 acres of furze and heath, 100*s.* of rent, and rents of 15 quarters of grain, 92 capons, and 176 hens, and common of pasture for all kinds of cattle, view of frankpledge, waifs, estrays, goods and chattels of felons and of fugitives, tolls, liberties, franchises, privileges, profits, and commodities whatsoever in **Swynerton, Stone, Yernefield, Beeche, Hatton, Shelton, Acton, Milne, Meese, Walford,** and **Bowers.**

Elizabeth remitted all right to Edward and his heirs, for which Edward gave her £800.

At fifteen days from Easter Day. 5 James I.

Between John Ethell, complainant, and John Egerton, knight, deforciant of the manor of **Loynton** otherwise **Lovington,** with the appurtenances, and of 4 messuages, 2 cottages, 4 tofts, 5 gardens, 5 orchards, 400 acres of land, 100 acres of meadow, 300 acres of pasture, 100 acres of wood, 400 acres of furze and heath, 100 acres of moor, 100 acres of turbary, 200 acres of land covered with water, and 8*s.* 10*d.* of rent in **Loynton** otherwise **Lovington.**

John Egerton remitted all right to John Ethell and his heirs, for which John Ethell gave him £400.

Trinity. 5 James I.

On the Morrow of Holy Trinity. 5 James I.

Between John Horsley, complainant, and John Orchard, the younger, deforciant of 2 messuages, 2 gardens, 2 orchards, 60 acres of land, 50 acres of meadow, 110 acres of pasture, 11 acres of wood, 100 acres of furze and heath, 100 acres of moor, common of pasture for all kinds of cattle, and common of turbary in **Bradnappe** and **Leeke.**

John Orchard remitted all right to John Horsley and his heirs, for which John Horsley gave him £100.

At fifteen days from the day of Holy Trinity. 5 James I.

Between Humphrey Jeffreye, complainant, and William Wightwicke and Matthew Wightwicke, deforciants of a messuage, a garden, an orchard, 100 acres of land, 20 acres of meadow, 150 acres of pasture, 20 acres of wood, 40 acres of furze and heath, and 20 acres of moor in **Woodford, Utoxater,** and **Marchington.**

William and Matthew remitted all right to Humphrey and his heirs, for which Humphrey gave them £240.

On the Morrow of Holy Trinity. 5 James I.

Between William Oliver, complainant, and Henry Jackson and Anne, his wife, deforciants of 6 acres of land, 5 acres of meadow, 4 acres of pasture, and common of pasture in **Austonefeild.**

Henry and Anne remitted all right to William and his heirs, for which William gave them £41.

* * * * * *

Between Richard Browne, complainant, and Ralph Flyer, gentleman, and Margery, his wife, deforciants of a messuage, a cottage, a toft, a garden, 3 acres of land, 2 acres of meadow, and 2 acres of pasture in **Utoxater.**

Ralph and Margery remitted all right to Richard and his heirs, for which Richard gave them £41.

On the Morrow of Holy Trinity. 5 James I.

Between John Knight, complainant, and Thomas Pope Blount, knight, deforciant of a barn, 5 acres of pasture, and common of pasture for all kinds of cattle in **Burton on Trent.**

Thomas Pope remitted all right to John and his heirs, for which John gave him £41.

At fifteen days from the day of Holy Trinity. 5 James I.

Between William Norman and Edward Mastergent, complainants, and Thomas Tixall, deforciant of a messuage, a garden, an orchard, 30 acres of land, 30 acres of meadow, and 80 acres of pasture in **Lees Hill, Utoxater, Kynston, Gratwich,** and **Loxley.**

Thomas remitted all right to William and Edward and the heirs of William, for which William and Edward gave him £100.

On the Octaves of Holy Trinity. 5 James I.

Between Thomas Smalbroke and Ambrose Rotten, complainants, and John Foxall, deforciant of 20 acres of land and 40 acres of pasture in **Bussheburye.**

John remitted all right to Thomas and Ambrose and the heirs of Thomas, for which Thomas and Ambrose gave him £41.

On the Morrow of Holy Trinity. 5 James I.

Between Walter Cotton, gentleman, complainant, and Francis Trentham, armiger, and Katherine, his wife, deforciants of 20 acres of land, 20 acres of meadow, and 40 acres of pasture in **Crakmersh** and **Strongshall** otherwise **Stromshall.**

Francis and Katherine remitted all right to Walter and his heirs, for which Walter gave them £80.

At fifteen days from the day of Holy Trinity. 5 James I.

Between Richard Stele and Thomas Rane, complainants, and John Holte, deforciant of a messuage, a garden, an orchard, 40 acres of land, 10 acres of meadow, 30 acres of pasture, and 10 acres of wood in **Madeley.**

John remitted all right to Richard and Thomas and the heirs of Richard, for which Richard and Thomas gave him £80.

On the Morrow of Holy Trinity. 5 James I.

Between William Sneyde, armiger, complainant, and Stephen Slanye, knight, and Margaret, his wife, deforciants of the manor of **Colde Norton** otherwise **Cole Norton**, with the appurtenances, and of 2 messuages, 2 cottages, 10 tofts, a dovecote, 2 gardens, 800 acres of land, 20 acres of meadow, 400 acres of pasture, 20 acres of wood, 100 acres of furze and heath, and 30*s.* of rent in **Colde Norton** otherwise **Cole Norton**, **Chebsey**, and **Somerton.**

Stephen and Margaret remitted all right to William and his heirs, for which William gave them £400.

On the Morrow of Holy Trinity. 5 James I.

Between Thomas Gilbert, complainant, and Robert Meverell, armiger, and Elizabeth, his wife, and Thomas Nabbes and Jane, his wife, deforciants of a messuage, a garden, an orchard, 10 acres of land, 10 acres of meadow, 10 acres of pasture, 60 acres of furze and heath, and common of pasture for all kinds of cattle in **Caldon.**

The deforciants remitted all right to Thomas and his heirs, for which Thomas gave them £60.

MICHAELMAS. 5 JAMES I.

On the Octaves of St. Michael. 5 James I.

Between Walter Leveson, knight, complainant, and John Leveson, gentleman, deforciant of a messuage, a cottage, 2 gardens, 15 acres of land, 4 acres of meadow, 12 acres of pasture, and 12*s.* 8*d.* of rent in **Wolverhampton.**

John remitted all right to Walter and his heirs, for which Walter gave him £60.

On the Octaves of St. Michael. 5 James I.

Between John Rothwell and William Draycott, complainants, and Richard Mountford and Agnes, his wife, deforciants of a messuage, 30 acres of land, 16 acres of meadow, 30 acres of pasture, common of pasture for all cattle, and common of turbary in **Leeke** and **Frithe** otherwise **Leekefrithe**, and of all manner of tithes whatsoever in the said tenements.

Richard and Agnes remitted all right to John and William and the heirs of John, for which John and William gave them £80.

On the Octaves of St. Michael. 5 James I.

Between Hugh Wrottesley, armiger, complainant, and William Barnesley and Isabella, his wife, deforciants of the moiety of a water-mill, 4 acres of land covered with water, and a water-course in **Womborne** and **Orton** otherwise **Overton.**

William and Isabella remitted all right to Hugh and his heirs, for which Hugh gave them £60.

On the Octaves of St. Michael. 5 James I.

Between Edmund Wyndesor, gentleman, complainant, and John Ethell, gentleman, and Katherine, his wife, deforciants of 6 acres of land, 3 acres of meadow, 10 acres of pasture, and 2 acres of wood in **Hill** and **Heighoffley.**

John and Katherine remitted all right to Edmund and his heirs, for which Edmund gave them £40.

On the Octaves of St. Michael. 5 James I.

Between Thomas Sprott, gentleman, Roger Sprott, gentleman, and Richard Henley, complainants, and Arthur Bagshawe, gentleman, and Cecilia, his wife, deforciants of a messuage, a garden, an orchard, 4 acres of land, 16 acres of meadow, 50 acres of pasture, and 16 acres of wood in **Farwell, Chorley**, and **Brendwoode.**

Arthur and Cecilia remitted all right to the complainants and to the heirs of Roger, and covenanted that they would warrant the said tenements against the heirs of Nicholas Bagshawe, deceased, father of the said Arthur, for which the complainants gave them £60.

On the Octaves of St. Michael. 5 James I.

Between Edward Craddocke, complainant, and George Crich and Jane, his wife deforciants of 2 messuages, a toft, 2 gardens, 2 orchards, 40 acres of land, 12 acres of meadow, and 40 acres of pasture in **Ashley.**

George and Jane remitted all right to Edward and his heirs, for which Edward gave them £100.

On the Morrow of All Souls. 5 James I.

Between Robert Browne and Thomas Shorte, complainants, and William Browne, deforciant of a messuage, a garden, an orchard, 20 acres of land, 10 acres of meadow, 20 acres of pasture, and 10 acres of wood in **Thornall and Madeley.**

William remitted all right to Robert and Thomas and the heirs of Robert, for which Robert and Thomas gave him £60.

On the Octaves of St. Michael. 5 James I.

Between William Winckley, complainant, and John Knight and Agnes, his wife, deforciants of 2 messuages, 2 gardens, and common of pasture for all cattle in **Burton on Trent.**

John and Agnes remitted all right to William and his heirs, for which William gave them £40.

On the Octaves of St. Michael. 5 James I.

Between John Bolton, complainant, and Thomas Coyney, the elder, gentleman, and Thomas Coyney, the younger, gentleman, deforciants of a messuage, a water-mill, a garden, an orchard, 8 acres of land, 8 acres of meadow, 10 acres of pasture, 2 acres of wood, and 20 acres of furze and heath in **Bucknall-Eves** and **Hanley.**

The deforciants remitted all right to John and his heirs, for which John gave them £60.

On the Octaves of St. Michael. 5 James I.

Between Brian Broughton and John Baduley, complainants, and Thomas Roos, gentleman, and Peter Roos, son of the said Thomas, deforciants of the manor of **Weston,** with the appurtenances, and of 4 messuages, 4 tofts, a dovecote, 4 gardens, 80 acres of land, 50 acres of meadow, 80 acres of pasture, and 20 acres of wood in **Standon, Weston,** and **Chorleton.**

Thomas and Peter remitted all right to Brian and John and the heirs of Brian, for which Brian and John gave them £240.

On the Morrow of All Souls. 5 James I.

Between John Davenport, armiger, Edward Cotton, armiger, Edmund Sutton, gentleman, and William Sutton, complainants, and Edward Sutton, gentleman, and Anne, his wife, and John Eardley, gentleman, and Alice, his wife, deforciants of a messuage, a garden, 100 acres of land, 30 acres of meadow, 100 acres of pasture, and 20 acres of wood in **Rushton Spencer, Ravenscloughe,** and **Clowdewood.**

The deforciants remitted all right to the complainants and to the heirs of John Davenport, for which the complainants gave them £120.

On the Octaves of St. Michael. 5 James I.

Between John Harpur, knight, complainant, and George Whithall, gentleman, and Mary, his wife, deforciants of a third part of the manor of **Butterton** otherwise **Butterdon,** with the appurtenances, and of 6 messuages, 2 cottages, a toft, 8 gardens, 8 orchards, 80 acres of land, 20 acres of meadow,

80 acres of pasture, 100 acres of furze and heath, 3*s.* 8*d.* of rent, and common of pasture for 24 cows in **Butter** otherwise **Butterton** otherwise **Butterdon** and **Gryn.**

George and Mary remitted all right to John and his heirs, for which John gave them £80.

On the Octaves of St. Michael. 5 James I.

Between Thomas Witherence otherwise Witheringes, complainant, and Rowland Lacon, armiger, and Ellen, his wife, and Francis Lacon, knight, deforciants of a messuage, a garden, an orchard, 60 acres of land, 30 acres of meadow, 80 acres of pasture, and 4 acres of wood in **Teene** otherwise **Teane** otherwise **Over Teane** and **Checkley.**

The deforciants remitted all right to Thomas and his heirs, for which Thomas gave them £100.

On the Octaves of St. Michael. 5 James I.

Between Christopher Thacker, gentleman, complainant, and Rowland Lacon, armiger, and Ellen, his wife, and Francis Lacon, knight, deforciants of a toft, 2 barns, 150 acres of land, 30 acres of meadow, 200 acres of pasture, and 10 acres of wood in **Teyne** otherwise **Over Teyne, Checkley,** and **Leighe** otherwise **Lee.**

The deforciants remitted all right to Christopher and his heirs, for which Christopher gave them £100.

On the Octaves of St. Michael. 5 James I.

Between Thomas Beeche, gentleman, and Thomas Strongarme, complainants, and Rowland Lacon, armiger, and Ellen, his wife, and Francis Lacon, knight, deforciants of 8 messuages, 8 gardens, 8 orchards, 400 acres of land, 50 acres of meadow, 300 acres of pasture, and 10 acres of wood in **Teyne** otherwise **Overteyne, Checkley,** and **Leighe** otherwise **Lee.**

The deforciants remitted all right to the complainants and to the heirs of Thomas Beeche, for which the complainants gave them £400.

On the Octaves of St. Michael. 5 James I.

Between Thomas Cooke, complainant, and William Cotton, gentleman, John Noble, gentleman, Edward Noble, gentleman, and Richard Kent and Emotta, his wife, deforciants of a cottage, a garden, an orchard, and 6 acres of pasture in **Brendwood.**

The deforciants remitted all right to Thomas and his heirs, for which Thomas gave them £40.

On the Octaves of St. Michael. 5 James I.

Between Robert Wood, gentleman, complainant, and Philip Wolriche and Anne, his wife, deforciants of a cottage, a garden, an acre of land, 3 acres of meadow, and 16 acres of pasture in **Shalford** and **Chebsey.**

Philip and Anne acknowledged the said tenements to be the right of Robert, and granted, for themselves and the heirs of Philip, that the cottage and an acre of land of the said tenements in **Shalford** and **Chebsey**, which Robert Wyatt and Anne, his wife, held for their lives and the life of the longest liver of them on the day this agreement was made, after the decease of the said Robert and Anne, should remain to the said Robert Wood and his heirs for ever, for which Robert Wood gave them £40.

HILLARY. 5 JAMES I.

On the Octaves of St. Hillary. 5 James I.

Between Edward Foxe, complainant, and Walter Bassett, gentleman, deforciant of 4 acres of land, 6 acres of meadow, and 20 acres of pasture in **Hynts.**

Walter remitted all right to Edward and his heirs, for which Edward gave him £60.

On the Octaves of St. Hillary. 5 James I.

Between Christopher Endesor, complainant, and Edward Bassett, armiger, and Jane, his wife, and Walter Bassett, gentleman, and Sconsolata, his wife, deforciants of a messuage, a garden, 2 acres of meadow, 80 acres of pasture, and 12 acres of wood in **Hinces** otherwise **Hintes** and **Wigginton.**

The deforciants remitted all right to Christopher and his heirs, for which Christopher gave them £80.

On the Octaves of St. Hillary. 5 James I.

Between Christopher Smyth and William Sheamondes, complainants, and Humphrey Dorlaston and Christiana, his wife, deforciants of 2 messuages, 6 cottages, 150 acres of land, 20 acres of meadow, 20 acres of pasture, 2 acres of wood, 2 acres of furze and heath, 2 acres of land covered with water, and common of pasture for all cattle in **Wigginton.**

Humphrey and Christiana remitted all right to Christopher and William and the heirs of Christopher, for which Christopher and William gave them £120.

On the Octaves of St. Hillary. 5 James I.

Between Richard Hopkys, complainant, and Alexander Jarvis and Elizabeth, his wife, deforciants of a messuage, a barn, a garden, an orchard, 6 acres of meadow, and 6 acres of pasture in **Westbromwich** and **Wednesburye.**

Alexander and Elizabeth remitted all right to Richard and his heirs, and covenanted that they would warrant the said tenements against George Boughey and Alice, his wife, and the heirs of the said George, and against Hillary Hawkes and his heirs for ever, for which Richard gave them £41.

On the Octaves of St. Hillary. 5 James I.

Between John Harpur, knight, complainant, and William Yates and Dorothy, his wife, and Nicholas Yates, son and heir apparent of the said William, deforciants of a messuage, 20 acres of land, 4 acres of meadow, 12 acres of pasture, and 10 acres of furze and heath in **Longnor** and **Alstonfield.**

The deforciants remitted all right to John and his heirs, for which John gave them £41.

On the Octaves of St. Hillary. 5 James I.

Between William Walhowse, complainant, and Francis Cartwright and Anne, his wife, deforciants of a messuage, a barn, a garden, an orchard, 60 acres of land, 10 acres of meadow, 40 acres of pasture, and 40 acres of furze and heath in **Watereyton** otherwise **Watterayeton, Kymerston** otherwise **Kynwaston,** and **Galey.**

Francis and Anne remitted all right to William and his heirs, for which William gave them £40.

EASTER. 6 JAMES I.

At fifteen days from Easter Day. 6 James I.

Between William Burbury, complainant, and Richard Almount otherwise Almond, and Alice, his wife, deforciants of 2 burgages and 2 gardens in **Burton on Trent.**

Richard and Alice remitted all right to William and his heirs, for which William gave them £60.

At fifteen days from Easter Day. 6 James I.

Between Richard Drakeford, gentleman, complainant, and Thomas Feyre and Alice, his wife, deforciants of a messuage, a barn, a garden, an orchard, 6 acres of land, 4 acres of meadow, 17 acres of pasture, 2 acres of wood, and common of pasture for all kinds of cattle in **Stretton.**

Thomas and Alice remitted all right to Richard and his heirs, for which Richard gave them £41.

At fifteen days from Easter Day. 6 James I.

Between Nicholas Allyn and William Tomkys, complainants, and John Woods and Mary, his wife, deforciants of 2 acres of land, 2 acres of meadow, and 5 acres of pasture in **Bushburye.**

John and Mary remitted all right to Nicholas and William and the heirs of Nicholas, for which Nicholas and William gave them £41.

At fifteen days from Easter Day. 6 James I.

Between Thomas Bucknall and John Beeche, the younger, complainants, and Robert Crosse and Elizabeth, his wife, deforciants of a messuage, a garden, an orchard, 20 acres of land, 10 acres of meadow, 20 acres of pasture, 6 acres of wood, common of pasture for all cattle, and common of turbary in **Harley Eves, Weston Coyney,** and **Bucknall** otherwise **Buckenhall** otherwise **Bokenhall.**

Robert and Elizabeth remitted all right to Thomas and John and the heirs of Thomas, for which Thomas and John gave them £60.

At fifteen days from Easter Day. 6 James I.

Between Thomas Morton, complainant, and Walter Chetwind, gentleman, and Eleanor, his wife, deforciants of a messuage, a garden, an orchard, 40 acres of land, 12 acres of meadow, and 40 acres of pasture in **Morton, Draycott, Howndhill, Marchington,** and **Hanbury.**

Walter and Eleanor remitted all right to Thomas and his heirs, for which Thomas gave them £100.

At one month from Easter Day. 6 James I.

Between Robert Forster, gentleman, complainant, and Thomas Wolrich, gentleman, and Frances, his wife, deforciants of a messuage, 80 acres of land, 18 acres of meadow, 40 acres of pasture, and 40 acres of furze and heath in **Cokeslane** and **Seighford.**

Thomas and Frances remitted all right to Robert and his heirs, for which Robert gave them £100.

At fifteen days from Easter Day. 6 James I.

Between Anthony Bagott, gentleman, and Hillary Hawkes, gentleman, complainants, and John Beardmore, gentleman, deforciant of a messuage, 50 acres of land, 10 acres of meadow, 40 acres of pasture, and 6 acres of wood in **Kingsley** and **Whiston.**

John remitted all right to Anthony and Hillary and the heirs of Anthony, for which Anthony and Hillary gave him £100.

At fifteen days from Easter Day. 6 James I.

Between Ralph Shyrley, gentleman, complainant, and Thomas Feyre and Alice, his wife, deforciants of 4 acres of land, 4 acres of meadow, and 34 acres of pasture in **Stretton.**

Thomas and Alice remitted all right to Ralph and his heirs, for which Ralph gave them £100.

At fifteen days from Easter Day. 6 James I.

Between John Byrche and Thomas Ball, complainants, and Thomas Jackson and Frances, his wife, and William Sheppard and Joan, his wife, deforciants of a messuage, a garden, an acre of land, and 8 acres of meadow in **Walsall** and **Little Aston.**

The deforciants remitted all right to John and Thomas and the heirs of John, for which John and Thomas gave them £40.

At fifteen days from Easter Day. 6 James I.

Between Christopher Dicken, complainant, and Thomas Badham and Frances, his wife, deforciants of a messuage, a cottage, a burgage, 2 barns, 3 gardens, 3 orchards, 20 acres of land, 10 acres of meadow, 8 acres of pasture, and 30*s.* of rent in **Stone.**

Thomas and Frances remitted all right to Christopher and his heirs, for which Christopher gave them £50.

At fifteen days from Easter Day. 6 James I.

Between Humphrey Gybons, complainant, and William Hodgettes and Joan, his wife, and Nicholas Hodgettes, deforciants of 14 acres of land, 3 acres of meadow, and 3 acres of pasture in **Hondesworthe.**

The deforciants remitted all right to Humphrey and his heirs, for which Humphrey gave them £41.

At fifteen days from Easter Day. 6 James I.

Between Francis Tonkes and Francis Woody, complainants, and John Woods, the elder, Mary, his wife, and Walter Woods, son and heir apparent of the said John, deforciants of 6 acres of meadow, 10 acres of pasture, and 6 acres of moor in **Bushebury.**

The deforciants remitted all right to the complainants and to the heirs of Francis Tonkes, for which the complainants gave them £80.

At fifteen days from Easter Day. 6 James I.

Between Richard Drakeford, gentleman, complainant, and Anne White, widow, and Thomas White, gentleman, and Elizabeth, his wife, deforciants of a messuage, a barn, 2 gardens, and an orchard in **Stafford.**

The deforciants remitted all right to Richard and his heirs, for which Richard gave them £60.

At fifteen days from Easter Day. 6 James I.

Between Thomas Thicknes, gentleman, and William Corbett, complainants, and John Everard, gentleman, and Bridget, his wife, deforciants of a messuage, a garden, an orchard, 20 acres of land, 2 acres of meadow, 24 acres of pasture, an acre of wood, and 5 acres of furze and heath in **Packington, Whittington, Tymmore, Tamhorne,** and **Horton**; and o common of pasture for all cattle in **Packington.**

John and Bridget remitted all right to Thomas and William and the heirs of Thomas, for which Thomas and William gave them £80.

At fifteen days from Easter Day. 6 James I.

Between George Hancocke, complainant, and William Wollaston otherwise Bucknall, and Margaret, his wife, Richard Walker and Joan, his wife, Anthony Phillips and Alice, his wife, and John Hall and Joan, his wife, deforciants of a messuage, a cottage, a barn, 4 acres of meadow, 80 acres of pasture, and common of pasture for all kinds of cattle in **Over Tayne.**

The deforciants remitted all right to George and his heirs, for which George gave them £80.

At fifteen days from Easter Day. 6 James I.

Between John Chapman, master of arts, and Richard Chapman, complainants, and Thomas Burton, armiger, and Katherine, his wife, and Edward Burton, armiger, and Elizabeth, his wife, deforciants of a messuage, 2 cottages, 3 gardens, 3 orchards, 40 acres of land, 30 acres of meadow, 60 acres of pasture, and 20 acres of wood in **Codsall** otherwise **Codsald** otherwise **Codsole.**

The deforciants remitted all right to John and Richard and the heirs of John, for which John and Richard gave them £120.

Trinity. 6 James I.

On the Morrow of Holy Trinity. 6 James I.

Between Edward Vaughton, complainant, and Gabriel Holland, deforciant of a messuage, a barn, a garden, and an orchard in **Tamworthe.**

Gabriel remitted all right to Edward and his heirs, for which Edward gave him £40.

On the Octaves of Holy Trinity. 6 James I.

Between John Allen, complainant, and Ralph Fitzherbert and Grisel, his wife, deforciants of 6 acres of meadow in **Wiggenton.**

Ralph and Grisel remitted all right to John and his heirs, for which John gave them £41.

At three weeks from the day of Holy Trinity. 6 James I.

Between John Peshall, armiger, complainant, and Hugh Swynerton, gentleman, John Swynerton, gentleman, and Thomas Swynerton, gentleman, deforciants of a messuage, 5 cottages, 6 gardens, 4 orchards, 140 acres of land, 20 acres of meadow, and 50 acres of pasture in **Eccleshall.**

The deforciants remitted all right to John Peshall and his heirs, for which John Peshall gave them £80.

On the Morrow of Holy Trinity. 6 James I.

Between John Ashley, complainant, and Thomas Squyer, gentleman, deforciant of a messuage, a garden, 40 acres of land, 10 acres of meadow, 40 acres of pasture, 10 acres of wood, and 10 acres of furze and heath in **Little Rydware** otherwise **Pype Rydware, Handesacre,** and **Kinges Bromley.**

Thomas remitted all right to John and his heirs, and granted that he would warrant the said tenements against William Squyer, father of the aid Thomas, and his heirs, for which John gave him £80.

On the Morrow of Holy Trinity. 6 James I.

Between Thomas Thornbury, gentleman, complainant, and William Piott otherwise Greene, gentleman, deforciant of 2 messuages, 40 acres of land, 10 acres of meadow, 10 acres of pasture, 4 acres of wood, 20 acres of furze and heath, and common of pasture for all kinds of cattle in **Chedull, Milnehowses,** and **Eves.**

William remitted all right to Thomas and his heirs, for which Thomas gave him £80.

On the Morrow of Holy Trinity. 6 James I.

Between Walter Rastell and Richard Rastell, complainants, and Henry Pynson and Alice, his wife, deforciants of a messuage, a cottage, 2 barns, 2 gardens, 10 acres of land, 7 acres of meadow, and 8 acres of pasture in **Dorlaston.**

Henry and Alice remitted all right to Walter and Richard and the heirs of Walter, for which Walter and Richard gave them £41.

At three weeks from the day of Holy Trinity. 6 James I.

Between Edmund Whyttell, complainant, and Roger Wilbraham, knight, and Mary, his wife, deforciants of a messuage, 2 cottages, 3 gardens, 3 orchards, 80 acres of land, 20 acres of meadow, 100 acres of pasture, and common of pasture for all cattle in **Overteyne, Netherteyne,** and **Checkley.**

Roger and Mary remitted all right to Edmund and his heirs, for which Edmund gave them £120.

On the Morrow of Holy Trinity. 6 James I.

Between Francis Harvey, armiger, and John Kynnersley, gentleman, complainants, and William Dawes, gentleman, deforciant of a messuage,

5 cottages, a dovecote, 6 gardens, 6 orchards, 100 acres of land, 60 acres of meadow, 100 acres of pasture, and 12 acres of wood in **Haselour** otherwise **Hasselloure**, and **Whittingeton**; and of a moiety of the manor of **Haselour** otherwise **Hasselloure**, with the appurtenances, and of 8 cartloads of furze to be taken yearly in the manor of **Haselour** otherwise **Hasselloure**.

William remitted all right to Francis and John and the heirs of Francis, for which Francis and John gave him £40.

On the Morrow of Holy Trinity. 6 James I.

Between John Birche, the younger, complainant, and John Hawkes and Anne, his wife, deforciants of a messuage, a cottage, 2 barns, 2 gardens, 2 orchards, 6 acres of land, 16 acres of meadow, and 50 acres of pasture in **Shelfeilde**, **Walsall**, and **Rushall**.

John Hawkes and Anne remitted all right to John Birche and his heirs, for which John Birche gave them £60.

On the Morrow of Holy Trinity. 6 James I.

Between Edward Mynshull, gentleman, complainant, and William Bulkley, armiger, deforciant of a messuage, 2 cottages, 10 acres of land, 4 acres of meadow, and 10 acres of pasture in **Kneyghton** otherwise **Neyghton**.

William remitted all right to Edward and his heirs, for which Edward gave him £60.

At three weeks from the day of Holy Trinity. 6 James I.

Between John Burnes and Henry Greene, complainants, and John Bolton and Alice, his wife, deforciants of a barn, 10 acres of land, and 24 acres of pasture in **Walsall**.

John Bolton and Alice remitted all right to the complainants and to the heirs of John Burnes, for which the complainants gave them £80.

At three weeks from the day of Holy Trinity. 6 James I.

Between Richard Elde, gentleman, complainant, and John Shelberie, gentleman, and Philip Chewte, gentleman, deforciants of a messuage, a garden, and 2 acres of pasture in **Ronton**; and of the rectory of **Sedgford** otherwise **Seighford**; and of the chapel of **Ronton**; and of all tithes, oblations, obventions, profits, and emoluments whatsoever yearly issuing in **Sedgford** otherwise **Seighford**, **Dodington** otherwise **Derington**, **Aston**, **Doxeye**, **Great Bridgford**, **Little Bridgford**, **Cotton**, **Clanford Grange**, **Heathcote Grange**, **Cookes Lande**, **Ronton**, **Ronton Hall**, **Hextall**, and **Broughall**.

John and Philip remitted all right to Richard and his heirs, for which Richard gave them £200.

On the Morrow of Holy Trinity. 6 James I.

Between Thomas Rudierd, armiger, John Weston, gentleman, Simon Smythe, gentleman, and John Benteley, gentleman, complainants, and William Fernyhaughe, the younger, gentleman, and Joice, his wife, deforciants of 4 messuages, 4 gardens, 40 acres of land, 20 acres of meadow, 40 acres of pasture, common of pasture for all kinds of cattle, and common of turbary in **Waterfall** and **Calton** otherwise **Caulton** otherwise **Caldon**; and of all tithes in **Fernyhaughe** and **Endon** otherwise **Yendon**.

William and Joice remitted all right to the complainants and the heirs of Thomas, for which the complainants gave them £100.

On the Octaves of Holy Trinity. 6 James I.

Between Thomas Ashley, complainant, and Ralph Fitzherbert, gentleman, and Grisel, his wife, and Thomas Thicknes and Mary, his wife, deforciants of 12 acres of meadow in **Wiggenton**.

The deforciants remitted all right to Thomas and his heirs, for which Thomas gave them £60.

At three weeks from the day of Holy Trinity. 6 James I.

Between Thomas Witherens otherwise Witheringes, gentleman, and Thomas Browne, gentleman, complainants, and Roger Wilbraham, knight, and Mary, his wife, deforciants of 2 messuages, 3 cottages, 5 gardens, 5 orchards, 300 acres of land, 30 acres of meadow, 250 acres of pasture, and common of pasture for all cattle in **Overteyne, Netherteyne,** and **Checkley.**

Roger and Mary remitted all right to the complainants, and to the heirs of Thomas Witherens, for which the complainants gave them £160.

At three weeks from the day of Holy Trinity. 6 James I.

Between Anthony Foster, gentleman, and Richard Phillippes, complainants, and Roger Wilbraham, knight, and Mary, his wife, deforciants of 21 messuages, 5 cottages, a mill, 24 gardens, 24 orchards, 2,500 acres of land, 400 acres of meadow, 1,000 acres of pasture, and common of pasture for all cattle in **Overteyne, Netherteyne,** and **Checkley.**

Roger and Mary remitted all right to Anthony and Richard and the heirs of Anthony, for which Anthony and Richard gave them £600.

On the Morrow of Holy Trinity. 6 James I.

Between Leonard Spencer, gentleman, and George Metcalfe, complainants, and Ralph Egerton, armiger, and Elizabeth, his wife, and Ralph Amerye, deforciants of a messuage, a garden, an orchard, 80 acres of land, 20 acres of meadow, 100 acres of pasture, 10 acres of wood, and 40 acres of furze and heath in **Fossebrooke** and **Dilron** otherwise **Dulverne.**

The deforciants acknowledged the said tenements to be the right of Leonard, for which Leonard and George granted them to Ralph Amerye for his life and the lives of Jane Copwood and Ralph Gallymore, and the survivor of them; rendering 52*s.* 6*d.* yearly to the said Leonard and George and to the heirs of Leonard. Leonard and George also granted the reversion of the said tenements and the said rent to Ralph Egerton and Elizabeth and to the heirs of the said Ralph Egerton for ever.

At three weeks from the day of Holy Trinity. 6 James I.

Between William Allyn, armiger, and Edmund Hamond, gentleman, complainants, and Gilbert, Earl of Shrewsbury, K.G., and Mary, his wife, Thomas, Earl of Arundel, and Alathea, his wife, William, Earl of Pembroke, K.G., and Mary his wife, Henry Grey, knight, and Elizabeth, his wife, William Hamond, gentleman, and Edward Lindsell, deforciants of the manor of **Alveton** otherwise **Awton,** with the appurtenances, and of 40 messuages, 20 tofts, a water-mill, 3 dovecotes, 40 gardens, 300 acres of land, 200 acres of meadow, 500 acres of pasture, 300 acres of wood, 1,000 acres of furze and heath, and 100*s.* of rent in **Alveton** otherwise **Awton.**

The deforciants remitted all right to the complainants and to the heirs of William Allyn, for which the complainants gave them £800.

MICHAELMAS. 6 JAMES I.

Between Roger Aldriche, complainant, and George Aldriche, gentleman, and Thomasine, his wife, deforciants of a messuage, a barn, 8 acres of meadow, and 12 acres of pasture in **Handsacre.**

George and Thomasine remitted all right to Roger and his heirs, for which Roger gave them £60.

On the Octaves of St. Michael. 6 James I.

Between Thomas Smythe, complainant, and John Hayes and Margaret, his wife, deforciants of 4 acres of meadow in **Little Bloxwiche.**

John and Margaret remitted all right to Thomas and his heirs, for which Thomas gave them £40.

On the Octaves of St. Michael. 6 James I.

Between Thomas Baylie, complainant, and Richard Baylie otherwise Baylison, and Margaret, his wife, deforciants of 2 cottages, a garden, and an acre of land in **Little Bloxwich.**

Richard and Margaret remitted all right to Thomas and his heirs, for which Thomas gave them £40.

On the Morrow of All Souls. 6 James I.

Between William Cotton and Margaret, his wife, complainants, and Robert Bett, deforciant of 2 messuages, 2 barns, 2 gardens, 2 orchards, 50 acres of land, 10 acres of meadow, 6 acres of pasture, and common of pasture for all kinds of cattle in **Ansley** and **Rolston.**

Robert remitted all right to William and Margaret and the heirs of Margaret, for which William and Margaret gave him £60.

On the Octaves of St. Michael. 6 James I.

Between Hugh Wrottesley, armiger, complainant, and Thomas Burnett, deforciant of the manor of **Womborne** and **Overton** otherwise **Orton**, with the appurtenances, and of 300 acres of furze and heath and 20*s.* of rent in **Womborne** and **Overton** otherwise **Orton.**

Thomas remitted all right to Hugh and his heirs, for which Hugh gave him £60.[1]

On the Morrow of St. Martin. 6 James I.

Between William Corbett, complainant, and Walter Aston, knight, deforciant of a messuage, a garden, an orchard, 2 acres of meadow, 20 acres of pasture, 40 acres of furze and heath, and common of pasture for all cattle in **Packington** and **Swynfen.**

Walter remitted all right to William and his heirs, for which William gave him £41.

[1] Amongst the Wrottesley muniments destroyed by the disastrous fire of December, 1898, there was an Indenture dated 20 April, 6 James I, by which Thomas Burnett agreed to convey the manors of Womborne and Orton to Hugh Wrottesley, Esquire, and attached to these papers there was a memorandum dated 1584, stating that "William Buffray, lord of Womborne, Netherpenne, and Orton had issue John Buffray, who had issue Jane, which Jane married with John Burnett, which John had issue Thomas Burnett, which Thomas Burnett had issue Robert Burnett, which Robert had issue Thomas Burnett, now lord of Womborne and Orton." There was also amongst the same muniments an original deed dated 6 Hen. VIII, by which Thomas Burnett, of Netherpenne, granted to Robert Burnett, his son, and to the heirs of his body, all his lands and tenements, with homages, wards, marriages, eschaets, &c., in Womborne and Orton, and failing such heirs, to his daughters Margaret, Maud, and Agnes successively in tail. Notwithstanding the above Fine, which does not appear to have been contested at the time, Sir Gilbert Wakering, of Rickmansworth, co. Herts, claimed to hold the manor; and the Inquisition on his death, dated 3 April, 21 James I, stated he had held the manors of Womborne, Seisdon, and Tresell, co. Stafford. Amongst the Wrottesley muniments there was also an abstract of documents, with this title: "A breviate of such Court Rolls, and other evidences which concerne the pretended manor late Sir Gilbert Wakering's some time the Lord Sheffield's, formerly Balsters and Babingtons, heretofore Sir Roger Hillary's and lastly William Woodhouse's, from whom it was purchased by Walter Wrottesley Esqr. now owner thereof." It will be seen by this that Shaw's account of the descent of the manor is very inaccurate. The Walter Wrottesley, Esq., who made this last purchase was the first Baronet, who died in 1659.

On the Octaves of St. Michael. 6 James I.

Between John Swayne, gentleman, complainant, and William Kyng, the elder, deforciant of a messuage, a garden, an orchard, 100 acres of land, 40 acres of meadow, 100 acres of pasture, and 10 acres of wood in **Honesworthe** otherwise **Hondesworthe**.

William remitted all right to John and his heirs, for which John gave him £160.

On the Octaves of St. Michael. 6 James I.

Between James Bennett, complainant, and Hugh Baylye and Margaret, his wife, deforciants of a messuage, a garden, an orchard, 20 acres of land, 2 acres of meadow, and 10 acres of pasture in **Fulforde** and **Hilderston** otherwise **Hilderson**.

Hugh and Margaret remitted all right to James and his heirs, for which James gave them £60.

On the Morrow of All Souls. 6 James I.

Between Andrew Vyse and Peter Rose, gentleman, complainants, and William Maclesfeilde, armiger, and Ursula, his wife, and Peter Maclesfeilde, gentleman, son and heir apparent of the said William, and Joan, his wife, deforciants of a messuage, a garden, an orchard, 36 acres of land, 8 acres of meadow, and 16 acres of pasture in **Meare** and **Aston**.

The deforciants remitted all right to the complainants and to the heirs of Andrew, for which the complainants gave them £80.

On the Octaves of St. Michael. 6 James I.

Between John Parker, complainant, and Humphry Berdmore, gentleman, and George Berdmore, gentleman, and Barbara, his wife, deforciants of a messuage, a garden, an orchard, 72 acres of land, 6 acres of meadow, 20 acres of pasture, 40 acres of furze and heath, and 1*s.* 6*d.* of rent in **Hatton** and **Swynnerton**.

The deforciants remitted all right to John and his heirs, for which John gave them £80.

On the Octaves of St. Michael. 6 James I.

Between Thomas Walsted, complainant, and Edward Stanford, armiger, and Mary, his wife, deforciants of 20 acres of meadow in **Great Barre**.

Edward and Mary remitted all right to Thomas and his heirs, and covenanted that they would warrant the said tenements against the heirs of Robert Stanford, knight, for which Thomas gave them £80.

On the Morrow of All Souls. 6 James I.

Between Roger Aldriche, complainant, and Thomas Salte, gentleman, deforciant of 12 acres of pasture in **Yoxall**.

Thomas remitted all right to Roger and his heirs, for which Roger gave him £41.

At one month from the day of St. Michael. 6 James I.

Between John Wood, complainant, and Mary Parker, widow, and John Parker, deforciants of a messuage, a garden, an orchard, 30 acres of land, 10 acres of meadow, 20 acres of pasture, and common of pasture for all kinds of cattle in **Chesterfeild** and **Shenston**.

The deforciants remitted all right to John Wood and his heirs, for which John Wood gave them £60.

At fifteen days from the day of St. Martin. 6 James I.

Between Walter Leveson, knight, complainant, and John Leveson, knight, deforciant of 5 messuages, 2 cottages, 5 barns, a water-mill, 5 gardens, 5 orchards, 100 acres of land, 40 acres of meadow, 220 acres of pasture, 150 acres of wood, 60 acres of furze and heath, 40 acres of moor, and 20 acres of land covered with water in **Wyllenhall** otherwise **Wylnall**, **Bentley**, **Wednesfeild**, **Prestwood**, and **Poolehayes**.

John remitted all right to Walter and his heirs, for which Walter gave him £300.

On the Octaves of St. Michael. 6 James I.

Between William Beeche, complainant, and Henry Stephenson, clerk, and Elizabeth, his wife, deforciants of the sixth part of 8 acres of land, 8 acres of meadow, 8 acres of pasture, and 4 acres of wood in **Olcott** and **Tunstall**.

Henry and Elizabeth remitted all right to William and his heirs, for which William gave them £40.

On the Octaves of St. Michael. 6 James I.

Between John Weston, gentleman, complainant, and Richard Mintridge, gentleman, and Anne, his wife, deforciants of a messuage, 40 acres of land, 4 acres of meadow, 40 acres of pasture, and 12 acres of wood in **Madeley** and **Whitmore**.

Richard and Anne remitted all right to John and his heirs, for which John gave them £60.

On the Octaves of St. Michael. 6 James I.

Between William Sneyde, armiger, complainant, and Matthias Bacon, gentleman, and Elizabeth, his wife, deforciants of a messuage, a garden, an orchard, 70 acres of land, 12 acres of meadow, 70 acres of pasture, and 20 acres of wood in **Swynnorton**, **Newcastle under Lyme**, **Benteley**, and **Whytmore**.

Matthias and Elizabeth remitted all right to William and his heirs, for which William gave them £121.

On the Octaves of St. Michael. 6 James I.

Between William Whorwood, gentleman, and Gerard Whorwood, complainants, and Richard Gibbyns and Ellen, his wife, deforciants of 6 acres of pasture in **Bryerley**.

Richard and Ellen remitted all right to William and Gerard and to the heirs of William, for which William and Gerard gave them £40.

On the Octaves of St. Michael. 6 James I.

Between George Illesley otherwise Ilseley, complainant, and Robert Towers and Katherine, his wife, deforciants of 2 messuages, 30 acres of land, 10 acres of meadow, 30 acres of pasture, and common of pasture for all cattle in **Bonehill**, **Drayton-Bassett**, **Hopwas**, **Phaseley**, and **Hyntes**.

Robert and Katherine remitted all right to George and his heirs, for which George gave them £60.

On the Octaves of St. Michael. 6 James I.

Between Thomas Selvester, complainant, and William Selvester, deforciant of a messuage, 30 acres of land, 12 acres of meadow, 50 acres of pasture, and 5 acres of wood in **Fotherley** and **Shenston**.

William remitted all right to Thomas and his heirs, for which Thomas gave him £60.

On the Octaves of St. Michael. 6 James I.

Between William Fernihaulgh, complainant, and William Thorley and Anne, his wife, deforciants of 2 messuages, a toft, 16 acres of land, 15 acres of meadow, 20 acres of pasture, 6 acres of wood, common of pasture for all cattle, and common of turbary in **Heyton**, and of all tithes of hemp and flax in **Heyton**.

William Thorley and Anne remitted all right to William Fernihaulgh and his heirs, for which William Fernihaulgh gave them £200.

On the Octaves of St. Michael. 6 James I.

Between William Brooke and Robert Pickin, complainants, and John Greene, deforciant of 2 messuages, 30 acres of land, 10 acres of meadow, 40 acres of pasture, and 4 acres of wood in **Aston in Hales.**

John remitted all right to William and Robert and to the heirs of William, for which William and Robert gave him £60.

On the Octaves of St. Michael. 6 James I.

Between William Orme, gentleman, complainant, and Philip Grove and Anne Grove, daughter and heir apparent of the said Philip, deforciants of 2 acres of land, 6 acres of meadow, and 6 acres of pasture in **Rowley.**

Philip and Anne remitted all right to William and his heirs, for which William gave them £41.

On the Octaves of St. Michael. 6 James I.

Between Leonard Sheldon, complainant, and John Boylston and Elizabeth, his wife, deforciants of a messuage, 15 acres of land, 10 acres of meadow, 20 acres of pasture, and common of pasture for all kinds of cattle, and common of turbary in **Caldon**, **Calton**, and **Waterfall.**

John and Elizabeth remitted all right to Leonard and his heirs, for which Leonard gave them £41.

On the Octaves of St. Michael. 6 James I.

Between Simon Greysley, armiger, and Edward Broughton, gentleman, complainants, and Thomas Wolseley, armiger, deforciant of 5 messuages, 4 cottages, 9 gardens, 400 acres of land, 80 acres of meadow, 200 acres of pasture, and 10 acres of wood in **Hyckston** otherwise **Huckston** otherwise **Hyckson**, **Uttoxator**, **Little Bromshulfe** otherwise **Bromshill**, and **Loxley.**

Thomas remitted all right to Simon and Edward and to the heirs of Simon, for which Simon and Edward gave him £400.

On the Octaves of St. Michael. 6 James I.

Between Ralph Amerye and Richard Henshawe, complainants, and William Amerye, deforciant of a messuage, a garden, an orchard, 20 acres of land, 8 acres of meadow, 60 acres of pasture, and common of pasture for all kinds of cattle in **Forsebroke** and **Dulherne** otherwise **Dilhorne.**

William remitted all right to Ralph and Richard and to the heirs of Ralph, for which Ralph and Richard gave him £100.

On the Octaves of St. Michael. 6 James I.

Between George Barboure, gentleman, and Pacquett Pulton, complainants, and Sampson Pulton and Elizabeth, his wife, deforciants of 3 messuages, 3 barns, 100 acres of land, 60 acres of meadow, 40 acres of pasture, 20 acres of furze and heath, 10 acres of moor, and 20 acres of marsh in **Hilderston.**

Sampson and Elizabeth remitted all right to the complainants and to the heirs of George, for which the complainants gave them £120.

On the Octaves of St. Michael. 6 James I.

Between Richard Browne, clerk, complainant, and William Langton, gentleman, and John Langton, clerk, deforciants of 5 acres of meadow and 20 acres of pasture in **Kyngsbromley**, **Curborowe**, **Somerfield**, and **Damefield.**

William and John remitted all right to Richard and his heirs, for which Richard gave them £60.

On the Octaves of St. Michael. 6 James I.

Between Ralph Flyer, armiger, complainant, and Walter Bassette, of Hyntes, gentleman, and Sconsolata, his wife, deforciants of 2 messuages, 2 gardens, 100 acres of land, 20 acres of meadow, 100 acres of pasture, 80 acres of wood, and 100 acres of furze and heath in **Hyntes**,

Walter and Sconsolata remitted all right to Ralph and his heirs, for which Ralph gave them £240.

On the Octaves of St. Michael. 6 James I.

Between Andrew Michell and William Perry, complainants, and John Fulwood and Richard Fulwood and Anne, his wife, deforciants of 4 acres of meadow in **Sedgley** and **Etingsall.**

The deforciants remitted all right to Andrew and William and to the heirs of Andrew, for which Andrew and William gave them £40.

On the Octaves of St. Michael. 6 James I.

Between Francis Backhouse otherwise Chamberlyn and Robert Backhouse otherwise Chamberlyn, complainants, and Robert Grosvenor, gentleman, and William Grosvenor, gentleman, deforciants of a messuage, a garden, an orchard, 6 acres of land, 28 acres of meadow, 110 acres of pasture, and 6 acres of wood in **Cotton, Clanford, Dodington** otherwise **Derrington, Haughton,** and **Rowton.**

Robert Grosvenor and William remitted all right to the complainants and to the heirs of Francis, and covenanted that they would warrant the said tenements against Thomas Grosvenor, father of the said Robert, and his heirs, for which the complainants gave them £120.

On the Octaves of St. Hillary. 5 James I.

And afterwards recorded on the Octaves of St. Michael. 6 James I.

Between Lawrence Monckes, complainant, and Lawrence Rope, gentleman, deforciant of a messuage, a garden, an orchard, 60 acres of land, 20 acres of meadow, 60 acres of pasture, 10 acres of wood, and 100 acres of furze and heath in **Radwoode** and **Meyre.**

Lawrence Rope remitted all right to Lawrence Monckes and his heirs, for which Lawrence Monckes gave him 130 marks.

On the Octaves of St. Michael. 6 James I.

Between Robert Meverell, armiger, and Elizabeth, his wife, complainants, and Elizabeth Leighton, widow, deforciant of 150 acres of land, 30 acres of meadow, and 220 acres of pasture in **Throwley.**

Elizabeth Leighton acknowledged the said tenements to be the right of Robert, for which Robert and Elizabeth, his wife, granted them to Elizabeth Leighton, to have and to hold to the said Elizabeth for 13 years; rendering one grain of pepper yearly to the said Robert and Elizabeth and to the heirs of Robert.

At fifteen days from the day of St. Martin. 6 James I.

Between William Aston, gentleman, complainant, and Walter Aston, knight, and Gertrude, his wife, Edward Aston, gentleman, and Thomas Aston, gentleman, deforciants of a messuage, 2 barns, a water-mill, a garden, an orchard, 320 acres of land, 40 acres of meadow, 160 acres of pasture, 500 acres of wood, 20 acres of furze and heath, 6 acres of land covered with water, and a water-course in **Wolseley, Hulton, Mylton, Sneyde, Greene,** and **Bucknall.**

The deforciants remitted all right to William and his heirs, for which William gave them £200.

On the Morrow of St. Martin. 6 James I.

Between Thomas Chetwyne, gentleman, and Thomas Comberford, gentleman, complainants, and John Stubbs and Priscilla, his wife, and Thomas . . . and Cecilia, his wife, deforciants of a messuage, a garden, an orchard, 20 acres of land, and 10 acres of pasture in **Gorseforthe Greene** and **Longdon.**

The deforciants remitted all right to the complainants and to the heirs of Thomas Chetwyne, for which the complainants gave them £60.

On the Morrow of All Souls. 6 James I.

Between James Whitehall, gentleman, complainant, and Edmund Sutton, gentleman, and Alice, his wife, Francis Pott, gentleman, Stephen Sutton, and John Whitehurst, deforciants of all tithes, oblations, obventions, mortuaries, and emoluments issuing from 8 messuages, 2 cottages, 200 acres of land, 60 acres of meadow, 250 acres of pasture, 20 acres of wood, and 100 acres of furze and heath in **Barsforde** otherwise **Berisforde** and **Chedulton.**

The deforciants remitted all right to James and his heirs, for which James gave them £100.

Hillary. 6 James I.

On the Octaves of St. Hillary. 6 James I.

Between Henry Atwood, gentleman, complainant, and Richard Luccocke and Margery, his wife, deforciants of 9 acres of meadow, 14 acres of pasture, and an acre of land covered with water in **Horborne.**

Richard and Margery remitted all right to Henry and his heirs, for which Henry gave them £40.

On the Octaves of St. Hillary. 6 James I.

Between John Curtler, complainant, and Henry Walle and Jane, his wife, deforciants of 2 cottages, 2 gardens, and 18 acres of pasture in **Rowley.**

Henry and Jane remitted all right to John and his heirs, for which John gave them £40.

On the Octaves of the Purification. 6 James I.

Between Robert Wolferston, armiger, and Edmund Wolferston, gentleman, complainants, and Hersey Wulverston otherwise Wolfreston otherwise Wolferston, armiger, deforciant of the manor of **Stotfold** otherwise **Stotfolde** otherwise **Statfold**, with the appurtenances, and of 7 messuages, 2 cottages, 6 tofts, a dovecote, 7 gardens, 7 orchards, 500 acres of land, 50 acres of meadow, 200 acres of pasture, 20 acres of wood, 100 acres of furze and heath, and 5*s.* of rent in **Stotfold** and **Hawnton.**

Hersey remitted all right to Robert and Edmund and to the heirs of Robert, for which Robert and Edmund gave him £240.

On the Octaves of the Purification. 6 James I.

Between Thomas Browne and James Austen, complainants, and Henry, Earl of Huntingdon, and Elizabeth, his wife, Walter Hastinges, armiger, Thomas Spencer, armiger, and Thomas Harvey, gentleman, deforciants of 20 messuages, 6 cottages, 4 tofts, 30 gardens, 30 orchards, 400 acres of land, 30 acres of meadow, 700 acres of pasture, 100 acres of wood, 500 acres of furze and heath, 100 acres of moor, 100 acres of marsh, common of pasture for all cattle, common of turbary, and 8*s.* of rent in **Caverswall** otherwise **Careswall, Dilron** otherwise **Dillorne, Stanton More** otherwise **Stante More Stone, Fosbroke, Fulford, Kingesley, Chedull, Draycott,** and **Brodoke.**

The deforciants remitted all right to the complainants and to the heirs of Thomas Browne, for which the complainants gave them £400.

On the Octaves of St. Hillary. 6 James I.

Between George Craddocke, complainant, and Anne Woodhouse otherwise Seckerson, Mary Woodhouse otherwise Seckerson, and Margery Woodhouse otherwise Seckerson, deforciants of a messuage, a barn, a stable, a garden, and of the moiety of a barn in **Stafford.**

The deforciants remitted all right to George and his heirs, for which George gave them £60.

EASTER. 7 JAMES I.

At fifteen days from Easter Day. 7 James I.

Between Richard Adderley, armiger, and Ralph Fenton, complainants, and John Hollins, gentleman, deforciant of 3 messuages, 6 barns, 3 gardens, 3 orchards, 300 acres of land, 50 acres of meadow, 700 acres of pasture, 60 acres of wood, and 600 acres of furze and heath in **Chedulton** and **Chedle** otherwise **Chedull.**

John remitted all right to Richard and Ralph and to the heirs of Richard, for which Richard and Ralph gave him £300.

At fifteen days from Easter Day. 7 James I.

Between Francis Kynder, complainant, and Thomas Norris and Jane, his wife, Walter Jones and Anne Jones otherwise Colborne, deforciants of 2 messuages, a barn, 2 gardens, an orchard, and 4 acres of land in **Tibington** otherwise **Tipton.**

The deforciants remitted all right to Francis and his heirs, for which Francis gave them £40.

At fifteen days from Easter Day. 7 James I.

Between Richard Smythe, complainant, and William Walhowse, gentleman, and Elizabeth, his wife, deforciants of 24 acres of land in **Breewood** and **Hatton.**

William and Elizabeth remitted all right to Richard and his heirs, for which Richard gave them £41.

At one month from Easter Day. 7 James I.

Between Charles Waringe, gentleman, and Richard Foxe, complainants, and Richard Coxe, deforciant of a moiety of 2 messuages, a cottage, 50 acres of land, 10 acres of meadow, 80 acres of pasture, 4 acres of wood, and 6 acres of moor in **Aldriche** otherwise **Aldridge, Walsall,** and **Great Barr.**

Richard Coxe remitted all right to the complainants and to the heirs of Charles, for which the complainants gave him £60.

At three weeks from Easter Day. 7 James I.

Between Sylvester Hayes, complainant, and Margaret Nechilles, widow, and Thomas Nechilles and Mary, his wife, deforciants of 30 acres of land in **Wednesfeild** and **Nechilles.**

The deforciants remitted all right to Sylvester and his heirs, for which Sylvester gave them £60.

At fifteen days from Easter Day. 7 James I.

Between Francis Middelton and William Sherratt, complainants, and Thomas Lathropp, gentleman, and Mary, his wife, deforciants of a messuage, a toft, 2 barns, a garden, an orchard, 17 acres of land, 10 acres of meadow, 64 acres of pasture, 6*d.* of rent, and pasture for 1 beast in **Daddesley Leas,** with the appurtenances, in **Leigh** otherwise **Lee, Withington, Daddesley,** and **Feild.**

Thomas and Mary remitted all right to Francis and William and to the heirs of Francis, for which Francis and William gave them £60.

At fifteen days from Easter Day. 7 James I.

Between Henry Goughe and John Goughe, complainants, and Walter Leveson, knight, and Anne, his wife, deforciants of a messuage, 2 cottages, 3 gardens, 3 orchards, 70 acres of land, 10 acres of meadow, 40 acres of pasture, and 4 acres of wood in **Oldfallinge** and **Bushburye.**

Walter and Anne remitted all right to Henry and John and to the heirs of Henry, for which Henry and John gave them £80.

At fifteen days from Easter Day. 7 James I.

Between John Barnett, the elder, complainant, and William Merryman and Joan, his wife, deforciants of a messuage, 20 acres of land, 2 acres of meadow, 6 acres of pasture, and 60 acres of furze and heath in **Cotton** and **Alveton**.

William and Joan remitted all right to John and his heirs, for which John gave them £60.

At fifteen days from Easter Day. 7 James I.

Between Stephen Pratt, complainant, and Thomas Wolseley, armiger, deforciant of 2 acres of meadow in **Gospell end** and **Sedgeley**.

Thomas remitted all right to Stephen and his heirs, for which Stephen gave him £40.

At fifteen days from Easter Day. 7 James I.

Between Agnes Sneyde, complainant, and Margaret Midleton, widow, and John Midleton, deforciants of a messuage, a garden, and an orchard in **Newcastle under Lyme**.

Margaret and John remitted all right to Agnes and her heirs, for which Agnes gave them £40.

At fifteen days from Easter Day. 7 James I.

Between Henry Butler, complainant, and John Beardmore, gentleman, and Margaret, his wife, deforciants of a messuage, a garden, and an orchard in **Whiston-Eaves** and **Whiston-Lees**; and of a moiety of 5 messuages, 5 gardens, 50 acres of land, 31 acres of meadow, 60 acres of pasture, 60 acres of wood, 100 acres of moor, 100 acres of turbary, and of common of pasture for all cattle in **Whiston-Eaves, Whiston-Lees,** and **Kyngeley.**

John and Margaret remitted all right to Henry and his heirs, for which Henry gave them £80.

At fifteen days from Easter Day. 7 James I.

Between William Bowyer, gentleman, and Robert Forster, gentleman, complainants, and Thomas Wolrich, gentleman, deforciant of 5 messuages, 5 gardens, 5 orchards, 70 acres of land, 20 acres of meadow, 30 acres of pasture, and common of pasture for all kinds of cattle in **Aston near Doxey, Ernefeild** otherwise **Ernfen, Little Brichford,** and **Seighford** otherwise **Segford.**

Thomas remitted all right to William and Robert and to the heirs of William, for which William and Robert gave him £160.

At fifteen days from Easter Day. 7 James I.

Between Humphrey Bate, the elder, Humphrey Jurden, gentleman, and Robert Hunt, complainants, and John Clerke, gentleman, and Jane, his wife, deforciants of a moiety of a messuage, a cottage, 16 acres of land, 4 acres of meadow, 2 acres of pasture, and an acre of wood in **Dunseley, Whittington, Kynver** otherwise **Kynfarre,** and **Kynges Swynforde.**

John and Jane remitted all right to the complainants and to the heirs of Humphrey Bate, for which the complainants gave them £40.

At fifteen days from Easter Day. 7 James I.

Between John Chippingdale, Doctor of Laws, complainant, and Richard Holland, clerk, and Alice, his wife, deforciants of 3 messuages, 3 gardens, 3 orchards, 60 acres of land, 12 acres of meadow, 24 acres of pasture, an acre of wood, and common of pasture for all cattle in **Barton under Needewood.**

Richard and Alice remitted all right to John and his heirs, for which John gave them £100.

At five weeks from Easter Day. 7 James I.

Between John Longmer, gentleman, and George Miller, gentleman, complainants, and Thomas Leighe, gentleman, and John Leighe, gentleman, deforciants of a messuage, a dovecote, a garden, an orchard, 100 acres of land, 30 acres of meadow, 100 acres of pasture, 20 acres of wood, and 20 acres of furze and heath in **Enfeild Morffe** and **Swinford Regis.**

The deforciants remitted all right to John and George and to the heirs of John Longmer, for which John and George gave them £160.

At five weeks from Easter Day. 7 James I.

Between Thomas Birche, the elder, and Thomas Addyes, complainants, and Humphrey Wirley, armiger, and Knightley, his wife, deforciants of 12 acres of land, 12 acres of meadow, 80 acres of pasture, 4 acres of wood, an acre of land covered with water, and common of pasture for all kinds of cattle in **Great Barre, Aldridge,** and **Wednesbury.**

Humphrey and Knightley remitted all right to the complainants and to the heirs of Thomas Birche, for which the complainants gave them £80.

At five weeks from Easter Day. 7 James I.

Between Matthew Bale, gentleman, complainant, and William Bradborne, armiger, deforciant of a yearly rent of £11 *6s.* *5d.* issuing from 8 messuages, 10 gardens, 10 orchards, 120 acres of land, 100 acres of meadow, 140 acres of pasture, 60 acres of wood, and *15s.* *5d.* of rent in **Hampstall Ridware** and **Nethertowne.**

William remitted all right to Matthew and his heirs, for which Matthew gave him £220.

At fifteen days from Easter Day. 7 James I.

Between David Fawkener otherwise Sawyer, complainant, and John Weston, gentleman, and Alice, his wife, deforciants of a messuage, 2 gardens, and 10 acres of pasture in **Eccleshall.**

John and Alice remitted all right to David and his heirs, for which David gave them £41.

At fifteen days from Easter Day. 7 James I.

Between George Abney, gentleman, and Clement Rossington, complainants, and John Boyllston, deforciant of a messuage, a cottage, 2 gardens, an orchard, 60 acres of land, 30 acres of meadow, 80 acres of pasture, 6 acres of wood, and common of pasture for all kinds of cattle in **Hanburye, Faude,** and **Cotton.**

John remitted all right to George and Clement and to the heirs of George, for which George and Clement gave him £160.

At fifteen days from Easter Day. 7 James I.

Between Walter Richardes, complainant, and Rowland Cartwright and Alice, his wife, deforciants of 2 cottages and 4 acres of pasture in **Wolverhampton.**

Rowland and Alice remitted all right to Walter and his heirs, for which Walter gave them £40.

At fifteen days from Easter Day. 7 James I.

Between William Pierson and Roger Harvie, complainants, and John Everard, gentleman, deforciant of 8 messuages, 2 water-mills, 8 gardens, 8 orchards, 200 acres of land, 50 acres of meadow, 60 acres of pasture, 10 acres of wood, 40 acres of furze and heath, and common of pasture for all cattle in **Whittington** and **Lichfeild.**

John remitted all right to William and Roger and to the heirs of William, for which William and Roger gave him £160.

At fifteen days from Easter Day. 7 James I.

Between George Copwood, the younger, gentleman, son and heir apparent of William Copwood, gentleman, and Bassett Copwood, gentleman, complainants, and the said William Copwood, gentleman, deforciant of 4 messuages, 4 cottages, 6 gardens, 4 orchards, 40 acres of land, 10 acres of meadow, 100 acres of pasture, 10 acres of wood, 100 acres of furze and heath, and common of pasture for all kinds of cattle in **Dulverne** otherwise **Dylron, Fosbrooke, Careswall, Chedulton,** and **Consall.**

William Copwood remitted all right to the complainants and to the heirs of George, for which the complainants gave him £100.

At one month from Easter Day. 7 James I.

Between Humphrey Welles, armiger, complainant, and Anne Coxon, widow, deforciant of 8 acres of pasture in **Horecrosse, Agarsley,** and **Yoxall.**

Anne remitted all right to Humphrey and his heirs, for which Humphrey gave her £41.

At fifteen days from Easter Day. 7 James I.

Between Richard Dayken and John Walton, complainants, and Roger Sprott, gentleman, and Margaret, his wife, Thomas Sprott, gentleman, son and heir apparent of the said Roger, and Mary, his wife, and Edward Sprott, gentleman, deforciants of a messuage, a cottage, 2 gardens, 2 orchards, 10 acres of land, 16 acres of meadow, 16 acres of pasture, and 10 acres of wood in **Brendwood** and **Chorley.**

The deforciants remitted all right to Richard and John and to the heirs of Richard, for which Richard and John gave them £41.

At fifteen days from Easter Day. 7 James I.

Between Richard Wright, complainant, and Elias Dudson, gentleman, and Frances, his wife, and John Smyth and Anne, his wife, deforciants of 8 acres of meadow and 10 acres of pasture in **Bromley Pagetts** otherwise **Abbottes Bromley.**

The deforciants remitted all right to Richard and his heirs, for which Richard gave them £60.

At fifteen days from Easter Day. 7 James I.

Between Hillary Hawkes, gentleman, and Humphrey Batkyn, complainants, and William Tomkynson and Agnes, his wife, and Humphrey Tomkynson, deforciants of 2 messuages, 2 gardens, 2 orchards, 24 acres of land, 12 acres of meadow, 20 acres of pasture, 2 acres of wood, and 10 acres of furze and heath in **Bryneton, Coldwyche, Stowe, Charteley, Grynley,** and **Kingeston.**

The deforciants remitted all right to the complainants and to the heirs of Hillary, for which the complainants gave them £60.

At fifteen days from Easter Day. 7 James I.

Between William Agard, armiger, and John Chadwick, gentleman, complainants, and Thomas Sprott, the elder, gentleman, Roger Sprott, gentleman, and Thomas Sprott, the younger, gentleman, deforciants of 8 messuages, 10 tofts, 3 mills, 2 dovecotes, 20 barns, 10 gardens, 10 orchards, 200 acres of land, 100 acres of meadow, 400 acres of pasture, 20 acres of wood, 40 acres of furze and heath, 40 acres of fresh marsh, and 20*s.* of rent in **Ashmerbroke, Great Abnoll, Little Abnoll, Pype, Chorley, Elmehurst, Farwall, Brendwood, Chelderhey end, Leycroft,** and **Norton under Cannock** otherwise **Canck.**

The deforciants remitted all right to William and John and to the heirs of William, for which William and John gave them £500.

At fifteen days from Easter Day. 7 James I.

Between Humphrey Tew and William Tew, complainants, and William Kniveton, armiger, deforciant of 34 acres of land, an acre of meadow, 22 acres of pasture, an acre of wood, an acre of moor, an acre of marsh, and common of pasture for all cattle in **Freford** otherwise **Frayforde**, **Streethay**, **Curbourough**, **Elmehurst**, **Fisherwick**, **Whittington**, **Morfall** otherwise **Morghall**, **Fulfen**, and **Longdon**.

William Kniveton remitted all right to Humphrey and William and to the heirs of Humphrey, and covenanted that he would warrant the said tenements against the heirs of Jane Kniveton, deceased, mother of the said William, and against the heirs of Elizabeth Pollard, deceased, aunt of the said William, for which Humphrey and William Tew gave him £60.

At fifteen days from Easter Day. 7 James I.

Between John Rigges, the younger, complainant, and Margaret Midleton, widow, and John Midleton, deforciants of a cottage, a curtilage, a barn, and a garden in **Newcastle under Lyme**.

Margaret and John Midleton remitted all right to John Rigges and his heirs, for which John Rigges gave them £40.

At fifteen days from Easter Day. 7 James I.

Between Ambrose Arden, armiger, and Ralph Wedgwood, gentleman, complainants, and John Wedgwood, armiger, and Margaret, his wife, deforciants of 2 messuages, a cottage, 3 gardens, 30 acres of land, 30 acres of meadow, 20 acres of pasture, 40 acres of wood, common of pasture for all kinds of cattle, and common of turbary in **Bagnald** otherwise **Bagenholte** otherwise **Bagenold**, **Blackwood**, **Gretton**, and **Horton**; and of all manner of tithes issuing or growing in a messuage called *le Mosse*, with the appurtenances, and in 40 acres of land in **Parke Hayes**, **Langett**, **Englondfeild**, and **Pottocke**.

John and Margaret remitted all right to Ambrose and Ralph and to the heirs of Ambrose, for which Ambrose and Ralph gave them £100.

At fifteen days from Easter Day. 7 James I.

Between John Rooper, knight, and Edward Savage, armiger, complainants, and Ralph Breerton, knight, deforciant of the manors of **Ipstones**, **Cresswalle**, and **Blymhill** otherwise **Blymhull**, with the appurtenances, and of 100 messuages, 40 cottages, 40 tofts, 4 mills, 3 dovecotes, 200 gardens, 200 orchards, 4,000 acres of land, 500 acres of meadow, 4,000 acres of pasture, 1,000 acres of wood, 3,000 acres of furze and heath, 1,000 acres of moor, 1,000 acres of marsh, 200 acres of land covered with water, and £10 of rent in **Ipstones**, **Cresswalle**, **Blymhill** otherwise **Blymhull**, **Brinton**, **Orpley** otherwise **Arpley**, **Chedleton**, **Alton** otherwise **Alveton**, **Leeke**, **Rushton**, **Sharpcliffe**, **Castorne**, **Kingley** otherwise **Kingsley**, and **Foxeweist** otherwise **Foxewist**; and also of the advowsons of the churches of **Blymhill** otherwise **Blymhull** and **Cresswalle**.

Ralph remitted all right to John and Edward and to the heirs of John, for which John and Edward gave him £1,000.

At fifteen days from Easter Day. 7 James I.

Between Thomas Carter, complainant, and Humphrey Wyrley, armiger, and Knightley, his wife, deforciants of a messuage, a garden, an orchard, 40 acres of land, 12 acres of meadow, 20 acres of pasture, 12 acres of wood, 80 acres of furze and heath, and 60 acres of moor in **Honnesworthe** otherwise **Handesworthe** and **Purye Barrye**.

Humphrey and Knightley granted the said tenements to Thomas, to be held by him for 99 years if the said Thomas Charles Stanley, son of Roger Stanley, gentleman, and Edward Wyllys, son of Henry Wyllys, or any of them should so long live; rendering yearly to the said Humphrey and Knightley and to the heirs of Humphrey £21, for which Thomas gave them £80.

At fifteen days from Easter Day. 7 James I.

Between John Whitehall, complainant, and Henry, Earl of Huntingdon, and Elizabeth, his wife, Walter Hastings, armiger, Thomas Spencer, armiger, and Thomas Harvie, gentleman, deforciants of a messuage, a . . . . . orchard, 30 acres of land, 16 acres of meadow, 40 acres of pasture, an acre of wood, common of pasture for all cattle, and common of turbary in **Careswall** otherwise **Caverswall** otherwise **Careswell**, and **Dillorne** otherwise **Dillerne**.

The deforciants remitted all right to John and his heirs, for which John gave them £60.

At fifteen days from Easter Day. 7 James I.

Between George Craddock, gentleman, complainant, and Henry, Earl of Huntingdon, and Elizabeth, his wife, Walter Hastinges, armiger, Thomas Spencer, armiger, and Thomas Harvey, gentleman, deforciants of 2 messuages, 2 cottages, 2 tofts, a water-mill, a dovecote, 2 gardens, 2 orchards, 80 acres of land, 50 acres of meadow, 300 acres of pasture, 100 acres of wood, 100 acres of furze and heath, 100 acres of moor, 100 acres of marsh, common of pasture for all kinds of cattle, and common of turbary in **Caverswall** otherwise **Careswall**, **Dylhorne** otherwise **Dylron** otherwise **Dyllerne**, **Stanton More** otherwise **Stante Mere, Stone, Fysbroke, Fulford, Kingesley, Chedull, Draycott**, and **Brodoke**.

The deforciants remitted all right to George and his heirs, for which George gave them £200.

At fifteen days from Easter Day. 7 James I.

Between Edward Shadwell, gentleman, and John Shadwell, gentleman, complainants, and John Dickens, gentleman, and Jane, his wife, Humphrey Dashfen and Joice, his wife, Rose Dashfen, widow, and Humphrey Grove and Elizabeth, his wife, deforciants of 2 messuages, a cottage, 2 gardens, 2 orchards, 40 acres of land, 20 acres of meadow, 20 acres of pasture, 2 acres of wood, 10 acres of furze and heath, 10 acres of moor, 3 acres of marsh, and common of pasture for all cattle in **Kynfare, Morffe**, and **Enfeild**; and of a free fishery in the water of **Spittell Brooke**.

The deforciants remitted all right to the complainants and to the heirs of Edward Shadwell, for which the complainants gave them £800.

At fifteen days from Easter Day. 7 James I.

Between Thomas Tyldesley, armiger, John Peshall, armiger, Edward Windsore, armiger, and Edmund Breres, gentleman, complainants, and Richard Fletewood, armiger, deforciant of the manors of **Caldwich, Wootton under Weever, Quicksill, Prestwood**, and *le Verd* of **Elaston**, with the appurtenances; and of 100 messuages, 100 cottages, 200 barns, 500 tofts, 3 water-mills, 2 dovecotes, 200 gardens, 1,000 acres of land, 500 acres of meadow, 1,000 acres of pasture, 1,000 acres of wood, 1,000 acres of furze and heath, 1,000 acres of moor, and 40*s*. of rent in **Caldwich, Wootton under Weever, Elaston, Quicksill, Prestwood, Stanton, Northwood, Ramsore, Calton, Alton, Farley**, and **Wast**; and of the rectory of **Elaston**; and of the advowson of the vicarage of the church of **Elaston**; and also of the view of frankpledge in **Caldwich, Wootton**, and *le Verd* of **Elaston**.

Richard remitted all right to the complainants and to the heirs of Thomas Tyldesley, for which the complainants gave him £800.

[1] On the Quindene of Easter. 7 James I.

Between Thomas Henshawe, gentleman, and Richard Forde, complainants,

[1] From "Notes of Fines."

and William Smythe and Joan, his wife, and Anne Beardmore, deforciants of a messuage, a garden, an orchard, 50 acres of land, 20 acres of meadow, 60 acres of pasture, 10 acres of wood, common of pasture for all cattle, and common of turbary in **Whiston-Eves, Chedull** otherwise **Chedle**, and **Kingeley.**

The deforciants remitted all right to Thomas and Richard and to the heirs of Thomas, for which Thomas and Richard gave them £80.

TRINITY. 7 JAMES I.

On the Morrow of Holy Trinity. 7 James I.

Between Matthew Smyth, complainant, and Robert Orgill and Anne, his wife, deforciants of a messuage, a garden, an orchard, and 2 acres of pasture in **Branston** and **Burton.**

Robert and Anne remitted all right to Matthew and his heirs, for which Matthew gave them £40.

On the Morrow of Holy Trinity. 7 James I.

Between Walton Aston, knight, complainant, and William, Lord Paget and Leticia, his wife, deforciants of 52 acres of meadow in **Great Heywood** and **Shutborowe.**

William and Leticia remitted all right to Walter and his heirs, for which Walter gave them £100.

On the Morrow of Holy Trinity. 7 James I.

Between Roger Ryley, Nicholas Chadwick, and Roger Janance, complainants, and Robert Riley, deforciant of a messuage, a garden, an orchard, 10 acres of land, 4 acres of meadow, and 6 acres of pasture in **Tunstidd** and **Alstonfeild.**

Robert remitted all right to the complainants and to the heirs of Roger Riley, for which the complainants gave him £41.

On the Morrow of Holy Trinity. 7 James I.

Between Edward Bosson and William Hulme, complainants, and John Looker, gentleman, and Robert Whithead, gentleman, and Katherine, his wife, deforciants of 2 messuages, 2 gardens, 20 acres of ground, 5 acres of meadow, 20 acres of pasture, and 2 acres of wood in **Betteley.**

The deforciants remitted all right to Edward and William and to the heirs of Edward, for which Edward and William gave them £41.

On the Morrow of Holy Trinity. 7 James I.

Between Thomas Glover, complainant, and John Harrison and Joan, his wife, deforciants of a messuage, a toft, 2 gardens, 2 orchards, 35 acres of land, 8 acres of meadow, 27 acres of pasture, 12 acres of turbary, and common of pasture for all cattle in **Chedle** and **Eves.**

John and Joan remitted all right to Thomas and his heirs, for which Thomas gave them £60.

On the Morrow of Holy Trinity. 7 James I.

Between Simon Jasson, complainant, and Thomas Gresley, knight, and George Gresley, armiger, son and heir apparent of the said Thomas, deforciants of a messuage, a toft, a garden, an orchard, 40 acres of land, 16 acres of meadow, and 60 acres of pasture in **Colton, Admaston,** and **Colwych.**

Thomas and George remitted all right to Simon and his heirs, for which Simon gave them £100.

On the Morrow of Holy Trinity. 7 James I.

Between George Craddocke, gentleman, complainant, and John Baker and Cecilia, his wife, deforciants of 2 messuages, 2 gardens, 2 orchards, 26 acres of land, 5 acres of meadow, 10 acres of pasture, and common of pasture for all cattle in **Brockton, Barkeswich** otherwise **Baswiche,** and in the **Forest of Cannock.**

John and Cecilia remitted all right to George and his heirs, for which George gave them £80.

At fifteen days from the day of Holy Trinity. 7 James I.

Between John Gregg, gentleman, complainant, and Thomas Pope Blount, knight, deforciant of 2 cottages, 2 gardens, 2 orchards, 40 acres of land, 20 acres of meadow, 100 acres of pasture, 80 acres of wood, 20 acres of furze and heath, and 2*s.* 6*d.* of rent in **Kyngston** otherwise **Kynston** and **Uttoxater,** and of the rectory of **Kyngston** otherwise **Kynston**; also of all tithes in **Kyngston** and the advowson of the vicarage of the church of **Kyngston** otherwise **Kynston.**

Thomas remitted all right to John and his heirs, for which John gave him £80.

On the Morrow of Holy Trinity. 7 James I.

Between Thomas Stoke, gentleman, and Richard Drakeford, gentleman, complainants, and Edward Littleton, the elder, knight, and Margaret, his wife, and Edward Littleton, the younger, knight, deforciants of the manor of **Pilletonhall,** with the appurtenances, and of 14 messuages, 4 tofts, 2 dovecotes, 14 gardens, 14 orchards, 300 acres of land, 90 acres of meadow, 350 acres of pasture, 100 acres of wood, 300 acres of furze and heath, 20 acres of land covered with water, and common of pasture in **Pilletonhall, Huntington, Cannock, Acton-Trussell,** and **Bednall.**

The deforciants remitted all right to Thomas and Richard and to the heirs of Thomas, for which Thomas and Richard gave them £400.

On the Morrow of Holy Trinity. 7 James I.

Between Walter Aston, knight, complainant, and Thomas Greysley, knight, and Mary, his wife, and George Greysley, armiger, and Susan, his wife, deforciants of the manor of **Colton,** with the appurtenances, and of 22 messuages, 4 cottages, 20 tofts, 2 water-mills, 22 gardens, 22 orchards, 1,200 acres of land, 400 acres of meadow, 1,300 acres of pasture, 500 acres of wood, 100 acres of furze and heath, common of pasture for all cattle, and 26*s.* 8*d.* of rent in **Colton, Newland, Blythford, Blythbury, Admaston, Hill-Ridware, Mavison-Ridware, Byshton,** and **Colwiche**; and also of a free fishery in the water of **Trent**; and also of the advowson of the church of **Colton**; and of a moiety of all tithes in **Colton.**

The deforciants remitted all right to Walter and his heirs, for which Walter gave them £1,000.

MICHAELMAS. 7 JAMES I.

At one month from the day of St. Michael. 7 James I.

Between Thomas Thorneburye, complainant, and John Knight and Joan, his wife, deforciants of a messuage, 20 acres of land, 6 acres of meadow, 16 acres of pasture, and common of pasture and common of turbary in **Chedull.**

John and Joan remitted all right to Thomas and his heirs, for which Thomas gave them £60.

At one month from the day of St. Michael. 7 James I.

Between John Widdowes, complainant, and Thomas Jukes and Elizabeth, his wife, deforciants of a messuage, 3 gardens, 20 acres of land, 5 acres of meadow, 20 acres of pasture, and 5 acres of wood in **Madeley** and **Bowerende.**

Thomas and Elizabeth remitted all right to John and his heirs, for which John gave them £60.

At one month from the day of St. Michael. 7 James I.

Between William Fynney, complainant, and John Beardmore, gentleman, deforciant of a messuage, 40 acres of land, 16 acres of meadow, 40 acres of pasture, 6 acres of wood, 10 acres of furze and heath, common of pasture for all cattle, and common of turbary in **Lees** and **Kingsley.**

John remitted all right to William and his heirs, for which William gave him £40.

At one month from the day of St. Michael. 7 James I.

Between William Kelsall, clerk, complainant, and John Ethell, gentleman, and Katherine, his wife, deforciants of 2 messuages, a garden, an orchard, 15 acres of land, 4 acres of meadow, and 15 acres of pasture in **Audeley.**

John and Katherine remitted all right to William and his heirs, for which William gave them £80.

At one month from the day of St. Michael. 7 James I.

Between Richard Gest and John Gest, complainants, and John Swayne and Elizabeth, his wife, deforciants of a messuage, 2 gardens, 2 orchards, 40 acres of land, 16 acres of meadow, 20 acres of pasture, 10 acres of moor, and an acre of land covered with water in **Honnesworth.**

John Swayne and Elizabeth remitted all right to the complainants and to the heirs of Richard Gest, for which the complainants gave them £80.

At one month from the day of St. Michael. 7 James I.

Between John Jodrell, gentleman, and William Fernihoughe, complainants, and George Holden, deforciant of 6 messuages, 12 acres of land, 3 acres of meadow, 16 acres of pasture, and common of pasture for all cattle in **Abbottes Bromley** and **Bagottes Bromley.**

George remitted all right to John and William and to the heirs of John, for which John and William gave him £100.

[1] At one month from the day of St. Michael. 7 James I.

Between Roger Harvie, complainant, and Robert Stounford, gentleman, and Magdalen, his wife, George Midlemore, the elder, gentleman, and George Midlemore, the younger, gentleman, deforciants of 5 messuages, 3 cottages, 7 gardens, 7 orchards, 120 acres of land, 16 acres of meadow, 16 acres of pasture, 6 acres of wood, 20 acres of furze and heath, and common of pasture for all cattle in **Whittington, Fisherwicke, Timore, Tamhorne, Lichfeild, Chedull,** and **Dylron.**

The deforciants remitted all right to Roger and his heirs, and covenanted that they would warrant the said tenements against Jane Midlemore, deceased, mother of the said George Midlemore, the younger, for which Roger gave them £100.

At one month from the day of St. Michael. 7 James I.

Between Thomas Gamull, gentleman, and Thomas Hatfeilde, gentleman, complainants, and William Bartram, and Thomas Bissell and Margaret, his wife, deforciants of a messuage, a garden, an orchard, 100 acres of land, 30

[1] The rest of the Fines of this term are taken from the "Notes of Fines."

acres of meadow, 100 acres of pasture, 20 acres of wood, 100 acres of furze and heath, and common of pasture for all cattle in **Barlaston**.

The deforciants remitted all right to the complainants and to the heirs o Thomas Gamull, for which the complainants gave them £120.

At one month from the day of St. Michael. 7 James I.

Between Richard Foxe, gentleman, and Elizabeth, his wife, complainants, and Edmund Whittell and Elizabeth, his wife, deforciants of a messuage, 2 cottages, 3 gardens, 3 orchards, 80 acres of land, 20 acres of meadow, 100 acres of pasture, and common of pasture for all cattle in **Over Teyne, Netherteyne**, and **Checkley**.

The deforciants remitted all right to Richard and Elizabeth and to the heirs of Richard, for which Richard and Elizabeth gave them £100.

At one month from the day of St. Michael. 7 James I.

Between Thomas Chetwind, gentleman, and Francis Chamberlen, gentleman, complainants, and Thomas Wolrich, gentleman, deforciants of a messuage, a dovecote, a garden, an orchard, 60 acres of land, 20 acres of meadow, 80 acres of pasture, 10 acres of wood, 20 acres of furze and heath, and common of pasture for all cattle in **Ancott** otherwise **Oncott, Seighford, Walton**, and **Little Brichforde**.

Thomas Wolrich remitted all right to Thomas Chetwind and his heirs, for which Thomas Chetwind gave him £120.

At one month from the day of Holy Trinity. 7 James I.

And afterwards at one month from the day of St. Michael. 7 James I.

Between George Craddock, gentleman, and Matthew Craddock, gentleman, complainants, and Edward, Lord Stafford, deforciant of a messuage, a garden, an orchard, 80 acres of land, 12 acres of meadow, 12 acres of pasture, 20 acres of furze and heath, and common of pasture in **Cokeslane** otherwise **Cookeslow** and **Seighford**.

Edward remitted all right to the complainants and to the heirs of Matthew, for which the complainants gave him £60.

At one month from the day of St. Michael. 7 James I.

Between Francis Woodhowse, complainant, and Thomas Burnett and Alice, his wife, deforciants of 4 acres of land, 6 acres of meadow, and 6 acres of pasture in **Over Penne** and **Nether Penne**.

Thomas remitted all right to Francis and his heirs, for which Francis gave him £40.

At one month from the day of St. Michael. 7 James I.

Between William Smyth, complainant, and George Holden and Katherine, his wife, deforciants of 4 acres of pasture in **Abbottes Bromley** otherwise **Pagettes Bromley**.

George and Katherine remitted all right to William and his heirs, for which William gave them £40.

At one month from the day of St. Michael. 7 James I.

Between Alexander Goodwyn, complainant, and John Clarke and Elizabeth, his wife, and Richard Clarke, deforciants of a messuage, a barn, a garden, and an orchard in **Bromley Pagettes** otherwise **Abbottes Bromley**.

The deforciants remitted all right to Alexander and his heirs, for which Alexander gave them £40.

At one month from the day of St. Martin. 7 James I.

Between Thomas Mylls, James Compson, and Humphrey Bradeley, complainants, and Denis Bradeley, gentleman, and Judith, his wife, deforciants of 6 acres of land, 5 acres of meadow, and 42 acres of pasture in **Kingeswinforde**.

Denis and Judith remitted all right to the complainants and to the heirs of Thomas, for which the complainants gave them £41.

At one month from the Feast of St. Michael. 7 James I.

Between John Tymyns and Beatrice, his wife, complainants, and Richard Bradeley, deforciant of a cottage, a smithy, a garden, an orchard, 2 acres of meadow, and 5 acres of pasture in **Sedgeley.**

Richard acknowledged the said tenements to be the right of Beatrice, for which John and Beatrice granted them to Richard; to be held by the said Richard for one week; after that term to remain to Thomas Bayles and Richard Hanmett, the younger, and to the heirs of the said Thomas for ever.

At one month from the Feast of St. Michael. 7 James I.

Between Baptist Hicks, knight, complainant, and Edward Stanley, knight, and Sebastian Harvie, citizen and alderman of London, and Mary, his wife, deforciants of the manor of **Kibbulston** otherwise **Kebbleston** otherwise **Kebulston** otherwise **Cubleston,** with the appurtenances, and of 60 messuages, 20 tofts, 4 mills, 10 dovecotes, 80 gardens, 20 acres of land, 400 acres of meadow, 1,000 acres of pasture, 300 acres of wood, 3,000 acres of furze and heath, and £4 of rent in **Kibbulston, Mayforth, Oelton** otherwise **Olton, Beryhill, Kevenall, Spotts, Mothershall, Cotwalton,** and **Woodhowses.**

The deforciants remitted all right to Baptist and his heirs, for which Baptist gave them £600.

At one month from the Feast of St. Michael. 7 James I.

Between Lewis Packer, complainant, and John Goodwyn and Anne, his wife, deforciants of 2 messuages, 2 gardens, 2 orchards, 50 acres of land, 12 acres of meadow, 40 acres of pasture, and common of pasture for all kinds of cattle in **Gayton, Weston on Trent, Fosbrooke, Dilron** otherwise **Dilhorne,** and **Careswall**; and of the fourth part of 2 cottages and 6 acres of land in **Gayton.**

John and Anne remitted all right to Lewis and his heirs, for which Lewis gave them £100.

At one month from the Feast of St. Michael. 7 James I.

Between Robert Toone, gentleman, and Callingewood Saunders, gentleman, complainants, and William Caldwall, gentleman, and Elizabeth, his wife, deforciants of a moiety of the manor of **Ansley** otherwise **Anseley,** with the appurtenances, and of 6 messuages, 3 tofts, a barn, 6 gardens, 2 orchards, 20 acres of land, 6 acres of meadow, 23 acres of pasture, an acre of wood, 100 acres of furze and heath, and 2*s.* 4*d.* of rent in **Ansley** otherwise **Anseley, Burton upon Trent,** and **Burton extra.**

William and Elizabeth remitted all right to the complainants and to the heirs of Robert, for which the complainants gave them £80.

At one month from the Feast of St. Michael. 7 James I.

Between Thomas Crompton, armiger, complainant, and William Sparry, gentleman, deforciant of a third part of a messuage, a garden, 10 acres of land, 35 acres of meadow, 86 acres of pasture, and 16*s.* 6*d.* of rent in **Stafford, Forbrige, Burton, Ricarscote, Hopton, Whitgreave, Tillington, Creswall, Tixsall, Ingestre,** and **Castle Parysshe**; and of all tithes of grain, sheaves, corn, hay, fruit, wool, lambs, &c., in **Stafforde, Forbrige, Burton, Ricarscote, Hopton, Whitgreave, Tillington, Creswall, Tixsall, Ingestre,** and **Castle Parysshe**; and also of 26*s.* 8*d.* of rent for a portion of tithes issuing from the rectory of **Castle Parysshe,** and 16*s.* for a portion of tithes issuing from the rectory and church of the Blessed Mary in the town of **Stafford,** and 26*s.* 8*d.* for a portion of tithes issuing from the rectory and church of **Hopton,** and of the third part of a pension of 16*s.* 8*d.* issuing from the rectory and church of **Creswall,** and of a pension of 3*s.* 4*d.* issuing from the rectory and church of **Ingestre**, and of a pension of 6*s*. 8*d*. issuing from the rectory and church of **Tixsall**, and of 3*s*. 4*d*. every third year for procurations issuing from the rectory and church of **Ingestre**, and of 3*s*. 4*d*. every third year for procurations issuing from the rectory and church of **Creswall**.

William remitted all right to Thomas and his heirs, for which Thomas gave him £300.

At one month from the Feast of St. Michael. 7 James I.

Between Thomas Docksie, complainant, and Thomas Clowes and Elizabeth, his wife, and Lawrence Clowes and Margaret, his wife, deforciants of 6 acres of meadow and 20 acres of pasture in **Leeke** and **Leekefrithe**.

The deforciants remitted all right to Thomas Docksie and his heirs, for which Thomas Docksie gave them £80.

At one month from the Feast of St. Michael. 7 James I.

Between John Weston and Edward Shorte, complainants, and John Brunner, deforciant of 5 messuages, 3 cottages, 8 gardens, 8 orchards, 100 acres of land, 40 acres of meadow, 60 acres of pasture, 20 acres of furze and heath, and common of pasture for all cattle in **Whitmore, Hallywell, Aston, Kneighton**, and **Merewelane**.

John Brunner remitted all right to the complainants and to the heirs of John Weston, for which the complainants gave him £120.

At one month from the Feast of St. Michael. 7 James I.

Between John Rothwell and John Carlett, complainants, and John Fynnye, the younger, deforciant of a messuage, a garden, 20 acres of land, 15 acres of meadow, 10 acres of pasture, 4 acres of wood, and common of pasture for all kinds of cattle, and common of turbary in **Leeke, Lowe Horton**, and **Longsdon**.

John Fynnye remitted all right to the complainants and to the heirs of John Rothwell, for which the complainants gave him £60.

At one month from the Feast of St. Michael. 7 James I.

Between Urian Leigh, knight, Richard Wilbraham, knight, Thomas Ravenscrofte, armiger, and John Doune, armiger, complainants, and Ralph Egerton, armiger, and Richard Egerton, knight, son and heir apparent of the said Ralph, deforciants of the manors of **Dulverne** otherwise **Dilron** and **Beffcotte**, with the appurtenances, and of 16 messuages, 8 cottages, 8 tofts, a mill, 20 gardens, 20 orchards, 800 acres of land, 200 acres of meadow, 600 acres of pasture, 200 acres of wood, 400 acres of furze and heath, 300 acres of moor, 200 acres of turbary, and 30*s*. of rent in **Dulverne** otherwise **Dilron, Beffcotte, Fossebrooke, Awdeley, Biggenhall, Hill, Talke, Cowley, Fulforde**, and **Chedull**.

The deforciants remitted all right to the complainants and to the heirs of Urian, for which the complainants gave them £600.

At one month from the Feast of St. Michael. 7 James I.

Between Edward Manwaringe, armiger, and Thomas Brett, complainants, and Thomas Baddeley and John Baddeley, deforciants of a messuage, a water-mill, a garden, an orchard, 300 acres of land, 40 acres of meadow, 200 acres of pasture, 20 acres of wood, and 30 acres of furze and heath in **Knotton, Bradwall**, and **Woolstington** otherwise **Owsington**.

Thomas Baddeley and John remitted all right to the complainants and to the heirs of Edward, for which the complainants gave them £340.

At one month from the Feast of St. Michael. 7 James I.

Between Humphrey White and Richard Hadley, complainants, and William Lowe, and William Bissell and Eleanor, his wife, deforciants of a message, a cottage, 2 barns, a garden, an orchard, 5 acres of land, 4 acres of meadow, and 8 acres of pasture in **Westbromwiche**.

The deforciants remitted all right to Humphrey and Richard and to the heirs of Humphrey, for which Humphrey and Richard gave them £40.

At one month from the Feast of St. Michael. 7 James I.

Between John Garbett and John Tonge, complainants, and William Garbett and Elizabeth, his wife, and Thomas Burnett and Katherine, his wife, deforciants of a messuage, 50 acres of land, 3 acres of meadow, and 7 acres of pasture in **Netherpen**.

The deforciants remitted all right to the complainants and to the heirs of John Garbett, for which the complainants gave them £80.

On the Morrow of All Souls. 7 James I.

Between William Stodderd, complainant, and Anthony Brocke, gentleman, and Henry Brocke, gentleman, deforciants of 2 messuages, a cottage, 3 gardens, 140 acres of land, 12 acres of meadow, 100 acres of pasture, 10 acres of wood, and 20 acres of furze and heath in **Shelton**, **Hanley**, **Fenton Vyvian**, and **Loueton**.

Anthony and Henry remitted all right to William and his heirs, for which William gave them £120.

On the Morrow of All Souls. 7 James I.

Between Thomas Jourdan, complainant, and Edward Leghe, knight, and Anne, his wife, and Henry Leghe, armiger, deforciants of 12 acres of meadow in **Allerwiche** otherwise **Aldriche**.

The deforciants remitted all right to Thomas and his heirs, for which Thomas gave them £41.

On the Morrow of All Souls. 7 James I.

Between Henry Cookes, gentleman, complainant, and Walter Littleton, gentleman, and Alice, his wife, and Alice Littleton, daughter of the said Walter and Alice, deforciants of a messuage, a garden, an orchard, 40 acres of land, 30 acres of meadow, 60 acres of pastnre, 20 acres of wood, 20 acres of furze and heath, 10 acres of moor, and common of pasture in **West Bromwiche**.

The deforciants remitted all right to Henry and his heirs, for which Henry gave them £80.

On the Morrow of All Souls. 7 James I.

Between Ambrose Arden, gentleman, complainant, and Richard Barboure, gentleman, deforciant of a messuage, 22 acres of land, 5 acres of meadow, 25 acres of pasture, and 5 acres of wood in **Yoxall**.

Richard remitted all right to Ambrose and his heirs, and covenanted that he would warrant the said tenements against the heirs of Nicholas Barboure, deceased, father of the said Richard, for which Ambrose gave him £80.

On the Morrow of All Souls. 7 James I.

Between William Scott, the younger, complainant, and Edward Newman, gentleman, and Joan, his wife, and William Crosse and Agnes, his wife, deforciants of 10 acres of land, 20 acres of meadow, 60 acres of pasture, and 30 acres of wood in **Great Barr**, **Walsall**, and **Wednesburye**.

The deforciants remitted all right to William Scott and his heirs, for which William Scott gave them £80.

HILLARY. 7 JAMES I.

On the Octaves of St. Hillary. 7 James I.

Between Walter Walhouse, gentleman, complainant, and William Walhouse, gentleman, William Henney, John Henney, John Swancote, Elizabeth Norton, Anne Ensore, widow, Roger Goughe and Mary, his wife, Edward Webbe, Thomas Burne and Margaret, his wife, William Lynhill, John Madeley, and John Perkyn, deforciants of $\frac{11}{25}$ths of 50 acres of wood and 200 acres of furze and heath in **le Haye of Galighe** otherwise **Galey Haye**, within the forest of **Cannock**; and also of $\frac{11}{25}$ths of the view of frankpledge, free warrens, chases, knights' fees, wards, marriages, escheats, heriots, reliefs, fines, amercements, mines, quarries, courts, goods and chattels of felons and of fugitives, felons of themselves, deodands, alienations, tolls, customs, ways, herbage, poundage, liberties and franchises in **le Haye of Galighe** otherwise **Galey Haye**, in the forest of **Cannock.**

The deforciants remitted all right to Walter and his heirs, for which Walter gave them £60.

On the Octaves of St. Hillary. 7 James I.

Between Bartholomew Colcloughe, gentleman, complainant, and Henry Goodwyn, gentleman, deforciants of a messuage, 20 acres of land, 10 acres of meadow, 10 acres of pasture, and an acre of wood in **Fosbrooke.**

Henry remitted all right to Bartholomew and his heirs, for which Bartholomew gave him £41.

On the Octaves of St. Hillary. 7 James I.

Between Thomas Fodon, gentleman, and Edward Everdon, complainants, and Edward James, the elder, gentleman, and Isabella, his wife, deforciants of a cottage, a toft, 100 acres of land, 30 acres of meadow, 100 acres of pasture, 10 acres of wood, 100 acres of furze and heath, and 20 acres of moor in **Penckrych, Water Eyton, Somerford, Brerewcod, Engleton, Robaston,** and **Ealey.**

The deforciants remitted all right to the complainants and to the heirs of Thomas, for which the complainants gave them £80.

On the Octaves of the Purification. 7 James I.

Between Richard Weston, gentleman, complainant, and Walter Aston, knight, and Gertrude, his wife, deforciants of a messuage, a garden, 40 acres of land, 30 acres of meadow, 200 acres of pasture, 30 acres of furze and heath, and 10 acres of moor in **Ridgley, Armitage, Wolsley,** and **Brereton.**

Walter and Gertrude remitted all right to Richard and his heirs, and covenanted that they would warrant the said tenements against the heirs of Edward Aston, knight, deceased, father of the said Walter, and against the heirs of Walter Aston, knight, deceased, grandfather of the said Walter, for which Richard gave them £100.

On the Octaves of St. Hillary. 7 James I.

Between John Nicken, complainant, and Richard Chatterley and Dorothy, his wife, deforciants of a cottage, a garden, and 38 acres of pasture in **Hatherton** otherwise **Hatherdon.**

Richard and Dorothy remitted all right to John and his heirs, for which John gave them £41.

On the Octaves of St. Hillary. 7 James I.

Between Henry Boylson and John Cowper, complainants, and John Awcocke, deforciant of a messuage, 5 acres of land, and 2 acres of meadow in **Coton, Draycott,** and **Hanbury.**

John Awcocke remitted all right to the complainants and to the heirs of Henry, for which the complainants gave him £41.

On the Octaves of St. Hillary. 7 James I.

Between Edmund Waringe, gentleman, complainant, and Roger Sprott, gentleman, and Thomas Sprott, gentleman, and Mary, his wife, deforciants of 2 messuages, a toft, 2 water-mills, a windmill, 40 acres of land, 10 acres of meadow, 20 acres of pasture, 100 acres of wood, 10 acres of marsh, 8 acres of land covered with water, and a water-course in **Cannocke, Leacrofte, Norton-Kaynes**, and **Brendwood.**

The deforciants remitted all right to Edmund and his heirs, for which Edmund gave them £100.

On the Octaves of St. Hillary. 7 James I.

Between Thomas Crompton, armiger, complainant, and William Bartram and Elizabeth, his wife, and Thomas Bissell and Margaret, his wife, deforciants of 3 messuages, a toft, 3 gardens, 24 acres of land, 20 acres of meadow, 60 acres of pasture, 6 acres of wood, 6 acres of furze and heath, and common of pasture for all cattle in **Cocknage** and **Trentham.**

The deforciants remitted all right to Thomas Crompton and his heirs, for which Thomas Crompton gave them £80.

On the Octaves of St. Hillary. 7 James I.

Between Richard Wright, complainant, and John Clarke and Elizabeth, his wife, and Richard Clarke, deforciants of a messuage and 2 acres of pasture in **Bromley Pagettes** otherwise **Abbottes Bromley.**

The deforciants remitted all right to Richard Wright and his heirs, for which Richard Wright gave them £40.

On the Octaves of St. Hillary. 7 James I.

Between Henry Butler, complainant, and Lawrence Whithall and Jane, his wife, deforciants of the manor of **Whiston**, with the appurtenances, and of 20 acres of land, 10 acres of meadow, 20 acres of pasture, 40 acres of wood, 500 acres of moor, 100 acres of turbary, and common of pasture for all kinds of cattle in **Whiston.**

Lawrence and Jane remitted all right to Henry and his heirs, for which Henry gave them £120.

On the Octaves of St. Hillary. 7 James I.

Between Richard Barnefilde, armiger, and John Coyney, gentleman, complainants, and James Skrimshaw, armiger, and Eleanor, his wife, deforciants of a messuage, a garden, 20 acres of land, 20 acres of meadow, and 60 acres of pasture in **Hales.**

James and Eleanor remitted all right to Richard and John and to the heirs of Richard, for which Richard and John gave them £100.

On the Octaves of St. Hillary. 7 James I.

Between John Millington, complainant, and William Seabrooke and Emma, his wife, deforciants of a moiety of 3 burgages and 9 acres of land in **Newburgh** otherwise **Newborow**, and of common of pasture for all cattle in **Newburgh** otherwise **Newborow.**

William and Emma remitted all right to John and his heirs, for which John gave them £40.

On the Octaves of St. Hillary. 7 James I.

Between Daniel Danvers, gentleman, and George Pudsey, gentleman, complainants, and William Cotton, gentleman, and Thomas Cotton, gentleman, deforciants of 3 messuages, 8 cottages, 4 gardens, 6 orchards, 30 acres of land, 20 acres of meadow, 200 acres of pasture, 6 acres of wood, and common of pasture for all kinds of cattle in **Hombridge** otherwise **Hamerwiche, Cracmarshe, Brendwodd** otherwise **Brundwood, Elmerst, Stowe,** and **Longdowne.**

William and Thomas remitted all right to Daniel and George and to the heirs of Daniel, for which Daniel and George gave them £160.

On the Octaves of St. Hillary. 7 James I.

Between Thomas Moreton, gentleman, and William Wollaston, complainants, and Benedict Bradley and Jane, his wife, and William Garbett and Elizabeth, his wife, deforciants of a messuage, a cottage, 80 acres of land, 10 acres of meadow, 40 acres of pasture, and 4 acres of wood in **Orton** otherwise **Overton** and **Womborne.**

The deforciants remitted all right to Thomas and William Wollaston and to the heirs of Thomas, for which Thomas and William Wollaston gave them £120.

At fifteen days from the day of St. Hillary. 7 James I.

Between Thomas Jordan, William Jordan, William Scott, John Scott, and Edmund Harrison, complainants, and Edward Leighe, knight, and Anne, his wife, and Henry Leighe, esquire, deforciants of 2 cottages, 20 acres of land, 16 acres of meadow, 30 acres of pasture, 20 acres of wood, 10 acres of furze and heath, and common of pasture for all cattle in **Great Barre** and **Aldrich.**

The deforciants remitted all right to the complainants and to the heirs of Thomas Jordan, for which the complainants gave them £80.

On the Octaves of St. Hillary. 7 James I.

Between John Chadwicke, gentleman, and Gerard Stanley, gentleman, complainants, and Henry Sewall and Mary, his wife, deforciants of a fourth part of the manor of **Mavesyn** otherwise **Maveson Ridware,** with the appurtenances, and of 4 messuages, 2 cottages, a water-mill, 100 acres of land, 20 acres of meadow, 120 acres of pasture, 20 acres of wood, and 60*s*. of rent, and of common of pasture for all cattle in **Mavesyn** otherwise **Maveson Ridware** and **Rugeley,** and of a free fishery in the water of **Trent;** and also of a fourth part of the advowson of the church of **Ridware.**

Henry and Mary remitted all right to John and Gerard and to the heirs of John, for which John and Gerard gave them £80.

On the Octaves of the Purification. 7 James I.

Between William Bowyer, armiger, complainant, and Walter Aston, knight, and Gertrude, his wife, deforciants of 3 messuages, 100 acres of land, 6 acres of meadow, 500 acres of pasture, and 500 acres of furze and heath in **Leeke, Bradnapp,** and **Mixton Hay;** and also of all manner of tithes in **Mixton Hay.**

Walter and Gertrude remitted all right to William Bowyer and his heirs, for which William Bowyer gave them £200.

On the Octaves of St. Hillary. 7 James I.

Between John Astyn, gentleman, complainant, and Edward Cricheley, gentleman, Walter Petitt, gentleman, and Dorothy, his wife, and Thomas Cricheley, gentleman, deforciants of 3 messuages, 2 cottages, 5 gardens, 5 orchards, 100 acres of land, 40 acres of meadow, 160 acres of pasture, 14 acres of wood, 40 acres of furze and heath, 4 acres of land covered with water, and common of pasture for all cattle in **Norton subtus Cannocke, Great Worley,** and **Little Worley.**

The deforciants remitted all right to John and his heirs, for which John gave them £300.

On the Octaves of St. Hillary. 7 James I.

Between Thomas Foxe and Henry Foxe, complainants, and Hugh Gresbroke and Margaret, his wife, Edward Foxe and Elizabeth, his wife, and Walter Bassett, gentleman, deforciants of a messuage, 2 gardens, 120 acres of land, 13 acres of meadow, 120 acres of pasture, 2 acres of wood, 3 acres of moor, 1 acre of land covered with water, and common of pasture for all kinds of cattle in **Hynts.**

The deforciants remitted all right to Thomas and Henry and to the heirs of Thomas, for which Thomas and Henry gave them £200.

EASTER. 8 JAMES I.

At one month from Easter Day. 8 James I.

Between Richard Squyre, complainant, and Henry Squyre, deforciant of a cottage, a garden, an orchard, 2 acres of land, an acre of meadow, and 5 acres of pasture in **Honsworth** and **Smethwicke.**

Henry remitted all right to Richard and his heirs, for which Richard gave him £41.

At fifteen days from Easter Day. 8 James I.

Between William Shelley, the younger, complainant, and William Shelley, the elder, deforciant of a messuage, a cottage, 60 acres of land, 6 acres of meadow, and 50 acres of pasture in **Aston**, **Stone**, and **Walton.**

William Shelley, the elder, remitted all right to William Shelley, the younger, for which William Shelley, the younger, gave him £80.

At fifteen days from Easter Day. 8 James I.

Between Thomas Pratt, complainant, and Thomas Pyrry, deforciant of 2 acres of land in **Tresle.**

Thomas Pyrry remitted all right to Thomas Pratt and his heirs, for which Thomas Pratt gave him £40.

At fifteen days from Easter Day. 8 James I.

Between John Gilbert, Thomas Robotham, and Robert Morton, complainants, and William Amery and Mary, his wife, deforciants of 10 acres of land, 2 acres of meadow, and 15 acres of pasture in **Marchington.**

William and Mary remitted all right to the complainants and to the heirs of John, for which the complainants gave them £60.

At fifteen days from Easter Day. 8 James I.

Between Thomas Harrison, complainant, and James Warner and Mary, his wife, deforciants of a moiety of a messuage, 20 acres of land, 7 acres of meadow, 30 acres of pasture, and 6 acres of wood in **Chedull** and **Hatchley.**

James and Mary remitted all right to Thomas and his heirs, and covenanted that they would warrant the said moiety against the heirs of George Warner, gentleman, deceased, against John Whitehurste and his heirs, and against William Wood and his heirs, for which Thomas gave them £60.

At fifteen days from Easter Day. 8 James I.

Between William Garbett and Thomas Perrye, complainants, and Thomas Burnett, deforciant of 6 acres of land, 8 acres of meadow, and an acre of wood in **Overpenne** and **Netherpenne.**

Thomas Burnett remitted all right to the complainants and to the heirs of William, for which the complainants gave him £40.

At fifteen days from Easter Day. 8 James I.

Between James Skrymshere, armiger, complainant, and James Greene, deforciant of a messuage, a garden, an orchard, 80 acres of land, 20 acres of meadow, 60 acres of pasture, 4 acres of wood, and common of pasture for all cattle in **Gebertsley** otherwise **Jeberdsley, Tunstall, Heigh Offley,** and **Eccleshall.**

James Greene remitted all right to James Skrymshere and his heirs, for which James Skrymshere gave him £80.

At fifteen days from Easter Day. 8 James I.

Between William Pillesburye, complainant, and Richard Turnocke and Alice, his wife, deforciants of a messuage, a garden, an acre of land, an acre of meadow, and common of pasture for all kinds of cattle, and common of turbary in **Heaton**, and of all kinds of tithes of flax and hemp in **Heaton**, and of a moiety of a barn and an oven in **Heaton.**

Richard and Alice remitted all right to William and his heirs, for which William gave them £40.

On the Morrow of the Ascension. 8 James I.

Between Thomas Thicknes, gentleman, complainant, and William Knyveton, armiger, deforciant of 6 acres of meadow, 6 acres of pasture, and 6 acres of moor in **Tammenhorne** otherwise **Tamhorne** and **Horton.**

William remitted all right to Thomas and his heirs, and covenanted that he would warrant the said tenements against the heirs of Jane Knyveton, deceased, mother of the said William, and against the heirs of Elizabeth Pollard, deceased, aunt of the said William, for which Thomas gave him £60.

At fifteen days from Easter Day. 8 James I.

Between Thomas Russell, complainant, and John Lawrance, deforciant of a messuage, a cottage, a shop, 2 barns, a garden, and 12 acres of meadow in **Rowley Regis.**

John remitted all right to Thomas and his heirs, for which Thomas gave him £41.

At fifteen days from Easter Day. 8 James I.

Between Edward Howe and Christopher Mawe, complainants, and James Phillipes and Anne, his wife, deforciants of 4 acres of land in **Nether Tayne,** and of common of pasture for six cattle in **Teaneleas**, in **Nether Teane.**

James and Anne remitted all right to Edward and Christopher and to the heirs of Edward, for which Edward and Christopher gave them £41.

At fifteen days from Easter Day. 8 James I.

Between Thomas Berdemore, gentleman, and Walter Povy, complainants, and George Houlden, deforciant of a messuage, 6 cottages, 7 gardens, 7 orchards, 33 acres of land, 6 acres of meadow, and 33 acres of pasture in **Bromley Pagettes** and **Bromley Bagottes.**

George remitted all right to Thomas and Walter and to the heirs of Thomas, for which Thomas and Walter gave him £60.

At fifteen days from Easter Day. 8 James I.

Between Humphrey Tayler, complainant, and John Stockley and Agnes, his wife, deforciants of a messuage, a garden, an orchard, 2 acres of land, an acre of pasture, and common of pasture for all cattle in **Yoxall.**

John and Agnes remitted all right to Humphrey and his heirs, for which Humphrey gave them £40.

At fifteen days from Easter Day. 8 James I.

Between John Persehowse, gentleman, complainant, and William Sheppardе and Joan, his wife, deforciants of 2 messuages and 2 gardens in **Walsall.**

William and Joan remitted all right to John and his heirs, for which John gave them £40.

At fifteen days from Easter Day. 8 James I.

Between Thomas Johns, complainant, and William Cowan and Margaret, his wife, deforciants of a cottage, a garden, an orchard, 7 acres of land, an acre of meadow, and an acre of pasture in **Overpen.**

William and Margaret remitted all right to Thomas and his heirs, for which Thomas gave them £40.

At fifteen days from Easter Day. 8 James I.

Between Thomas Smythe, complainant, and Walter Aston, knight, deforciant of 5 messuages, 5 gardens, 5 orchards, 16 acres of meadow, and 80 acres of pasture in **Utoxator** and **Utcetter Woodland**.

Walter remitted all right to Thomas and his heirs, for which Thomas gave him £80.

At five weeks from Easter Day. 8 James I.

Between Walter Aston, gentleman, complainant, and Walter Aston, knight, and Gertrude, his wife, deforciants of 4 messuages, 4 barns, a watermill, a dovecote, 4 gardens, 4 orchards, 60 acres of land, 60 acres of meadow, 200 acres of pasture, 100 acres of wood, 4 acres of furze and heath, 6 acres of moor, and 6 acres of land covered with water in **Longdon**, **Curborowe**, **Elmehurst**, **Kynges Bromley**, and **Handsacre**.

The deforciants remitted all right to Walter Aston, gentleman, and his heirs, for which Walter gave them £100.

At fifteen days from Easter Day. 8 James I.

Between Richard Bowyer, gentleman, complainant, and Walter Aston, knight, deforciant of a messuage, a garden, an orchard, 14 acres of land, 6 acres of meadow, 14 acres of pasture, 10 acres of furze and heath, common of pasture and common of turbary in **Milwich**, **Sandon**, and **Leighe**.

Walter remitted all right to Richard and his heirs, for which Richard gave him £41.

At one month from Easter Day. 8 James I.

Between William Fleeminge otherwise Greene, complainant, and John Fulwood and Matilda, his wife, Richard Fulwood and Anne, his wife, and George Jesson and Eleanor, his wife, deforciants of a messuage, a cottage, a barn, a garden, an orchard, 2 acres o meadow, and 20 acres of pasture in **Colseley** and **Sedgeley**.

The deforciants remitted all right to William and his heirs, for which William gave them £60.

At fifteen days from Easter Day. 8 James I.

Between William Lacon, armiger, complainant, and Francis Lacon, knight, deforciant of the manor of **Overtene** otherwise **Overteane**, with the appurtenances, and of 2 cottages, 2 gardens, 2 orchards, 2 acres of land, 400 acres of furze and heath, 10*s*. of rent, and rent of a pound of pepper in **Overtene** otherwise **Overteane**; and also of the advowson of the church of **Checkley**.

Francis remitted all right to William and his heirs, for which William gave him £80.

At fifteen days from Easter Day. 8 James I.

Between Roger Stanley and Thomas Lane, complainants, and John Squyre, gentleman, deforciant of 6 cottages, 6 gardens, 8 acres of land, 2 acres of meadow, 8 acres of pasture, 4 acres of furze and heath, and 32*s*. of rent in **Honsworth**, **Smethwicke**, **Purry Barre**, and **Westbromwiche**.

John remitted all right to Roger and Thomas and to the heirs of Thomas, for which Roger and Thomas gave him £60.

At fifteen days from Easter Day. 8 James I.

Between William Cooke and William Hulme, complainants, and Francis Aspinall, gentleman, and Katherine, his wife, deforciants of 13 messuages 4 cottages, 14 gardens, 14 orchards, 300 acres of land, 100 acres of meadow, 120 acres of pasture, and 20 acres of wood in **Amerton**, **Hickson**, **Newton Kinson**, **Calohill**, and **Bromley Regis**.

Francis and Katherine remitted all right to the complainants and to the heirs of William Cooke, for which the complainants gave them £300.

At fifteen days from Easter Day. 8 James I.

Between John Harryson, Henry Stone, and Thomas Gorwey, complainants, and William Hollys and Mary, his wife, Hugh Hollys, John Hollys, and George Hollys, deforciants of a cottage, 9 acres of meadow, and 6 acres of pasture in **Aldrich**.

The deforciants remitted all right to the complainants and to the heirs of John Harryson, for which the complainants gave them £60.

At fifteen days from Easter Day. 8 James I.

Between George Stoneor, the elder, complainant, and Thomas Harrison and Anne, his wife, deforciants of $\frac{2}{3}$rds of a messuage, a garden, an orchard, 30 acres of land, 10 acres of meadow, 10 acres of pasture, and 4 acres of wood in **Gretton** and **Horton**, and of common of pasture for all manner of cattle, and common of turbary in **Gretton** and **Horton**.

Thomas and Anne remitted all right to the complainants and to the heirs of George, for which the complainants gave them £41.

At fifteen days from Easter Day. 8 James I.

Between Ralph Mountford and John Horsley, complainants, and William Smythe, deforciant of all manner of tithes, oblations, and emoluments issuing from 4 messuages, 70 acres of land, 36 acres of meadow, 70 acres of pasture, and 12 acres of wood in **Leeke**, **Lowe**, **Padwicke**, and **Ypstones**.

William remitted all right to Ralph and John and to the heirs of Ralph, and covenanted that he would warrant the said tithes, etc., against Thomas Smythe, father of the said William, and his heirs for ever, for which Ralph and John gave him £60.

At fifteen days from Easter Day. 8 James I.

Between John Beresford and George Crichlowe, the younger, complainants, and George Tittringeton and Joan, his wife, and Henry Tittringeton and Dorothy, his wife, deforciants of 2 messuages, 80 acres of land, 20 acres of meadow, 20 acres of pasture, 100 acres of furze and heath, and 4*d.* of rent in **Alstonfeild** and **Narrowdall**.

The deforciants remitted all right to the complainants and to the heirs of John, for which the complainants gave them £100.

At one month from Easter Day. 8 James I.

Between William Draffgate and William Woode, complainants, and Anne Barboure, widow, deforciant of 3 messuages, 3 gardens, 3 orchards, 10 acres of land, 6 acres of meadow, 16 acres of pasture, and common of pasture for all kinds of cattle in **Agarsley** and **Neweboroughe**.

Anne remitted all right to the complainants and to the heirs of William Draffgate, for which the complainants gave her £60.

At fifteen days from Easter Day. 8 James I.

Between Richard Callengewood, complainant, and Nicholas Breton, armiger, and Edward Breton, gentleman, deforciants of 54 acres of land, 2 acres of meadow, 12 acres of pasture, an acre of wood, 20 acres of furze and heath, 6 acres of moor, 4 acres of marsh, and common of pasture for all kinds of cattle in **Tamworth**, **Wiggenton**, **Comberford**, **Coton**, and **Hoppwas**.

Nicholas and Edward remitted all right to Richard and his heirs, and covenanted that they would warrant the said tenements against the heirs of John Breton, father of the said Nicholas, and against the heirs of Nicholas Breton, father of the said John, for which Richard gave them £80.

At fifteeen days from Easter Day. 8 James I.

Between Walter Giffard, armiger, and Reginald Brome, armiger, complainants, and Roger Fowke, armiger, and Katherine, his wife, deforciants of the manors of **Ingleton, Little Worley,** and **Norton under Cannocke,** with the appurtenances, and of 10 messuages, 30 cottages, a water-mill, a dovecote, 40 gardens, 40 orchards, 300 acres of land, 160 acres of meadow, 300 acres of pasture, 40 acres of wood, 600 acres of furze and heath, 100 acres of moor, 20 acres of land covered with water, 65*s.* of rent, and common of pasture for all kinds of beasts in **Ingleton, Brewood, Chillington, Little Worley, Norton under Cannocke,** and **Pelsall.**

Roger and Katherine remitted all right to Walter and Reginald and to the heirs of Walter, for which Walter and Reginald gave them £800.

At fifteen days from Easter Day. 8 James I.

Between William Clowes, James Hooley, William Holme, and Richard Holme, complainants, and William Downes and Joan, his wife, deforciants of a messuage, 7 acres of land, 5 acres of meadow, 7 acres of pasture, and 2 acres of wood in **Heyton,** and of all tithes issuing from the said tenements, and of the moiety of a water-mill in **Heyton.**

William Downes and Joan remitted all right to the complainants and to the heirs of William Clowes, for which the complainants gave them £41.

At fifteen days from Easter Day. 8 James I.

Between Richard Parkes, complainant, and Thomas Colmore, gentleman, and Elizabeth, his wife, deforciants of 2 messuages, a cottage, a toft, 4 gardens, 60 acres of land, 20 acres of meadow, 100 acres of pasture, 10 acres of wood, 6 acres of moor, and 4 acres of furze and heath in **Cannocke** otherwise **Canke** and **Penkcrich;** and of the ninth part of 30 acres of meadow in **Cannocke** otherwise **Canke;** and also of the third part of the office of Forester or Keeper of the Hay of **Chistlyn Hay** within the forest or chase of **Cannocke** otherwise **Canke;** and of the herbage and after-pannage of the same hay, and of all profits, commodities, and advantages to the same office or Hay belonging or pertaining.

Thomas and Elizabeth remitted all right to Richard and his heirs, for which Richard gave them £100.

At fifteen days from Easter Day. 8 James I.

Between George Craddocke, gentleman, complainant, and James Nowell, gentleman, and Mary, his wife, Edward Nowell, gentleman, and Elizabeth, his wife, and Henry Nowell, gentleman, deforciants of a messuage, 4 cottages, 2 tofts, 6 gardens, 6 orchards, 40 acres of land, 30 acres of meadow, 250 acres of pasture, 20 acres of wood, 120 acres of furze and heath, and common of pasture for all cattle in **Pelsall, Wolverhampton, Little Wirley, Esington, Bloxwich, Russhall, Homeriche, Walsall,** and **Goscott.**

The deforciants remitted all right to George and his heirs, for which George gave them £200.

At fifteen days from Easter Day. 8 James I.

Between Thomas Voughton, complainant, and Nicholas Breton, armiger, and Edward Breton, gentleman, deforciants of 60 acres of land, 2 acres of meadow, an acre of wood, 20 acres of furze and heath, 6 acres of moor, 4 acres of marsh, and common of pasture for all kinds of cattle in **Tamworth, Wiggenton, Comberford, Coton,** and **Hoppwas.**

Nicholas and Edward remitted all right to Thomas and his heirs, and covenanted that they would warrant the said tenements against the heirs of John Breton, father of the said Nicholas, and against the heirs of Nicholas Breton, father of the said John, for which Thomas gave them £80.

At fifteen days from Easter Day. 8 James I.

Between Thomas Saunders, gentleman, and Simon Jasson, gentleman, complainants, and John Bradshawe, gentleman, and Ellen, his wife, and Gervase Piggott, gentleman, and Jane, his wife, Walter Grosvenor, gentleman, and Ellen, his wife, and Isabella Bradshawe, deforciants of a messuage, a dovecote, a garden, an orchard, 5 acres of land, 5 acres of meadow, 15 acres of pasture, and common of pasture for all kinds of cattle in **Burton on Trent**, and of a free fishery in the water of **Trent**.

The deforciants remitted all right to Thomas and Simon and to the heirs of Thomas, for which Thomas and Simon gave them £60.

At fifteen days from Easter Day. 8 James I.

Between Anthony Kynnersley, armiger, complainant, and Henry, Earl of Huntingdon, deforciant of the manors of **Caverswall** otherwise **Careswall** otherwise **Cariswall**, and **Dilrone** otherwise **Dulverne**, with the appurtenances, and of 4 cottages, 30 acres of land, an acre of meadow, 2 acres of pasture, 200 acres of furze and heath, common of pasture, and free warren in **Caverswall** otherwise **Careswall** otherwise **Cariswall**, **Dilrone** otherwise **Dulverne**, **Stone**, **Fosbrooke**, **Whitehurst**, **Holme**, **Braddock** otherwise **Brodoke**, **Fulford**, **Kingsley**, and **Stallington**, and of the fairs and markets of **Caverswall** otherwise **Careswall** otherwise **Cariswall**; and also of two-thirds of a cottage, a shop, a water-mill, and a garden in **Blithbridge** and **Fosbrooke**.

The Earl remitted all right to Anthony and his heirs, for which Anthony gave him £160.

At fifteen days from Easter Day. 8 James I.

Between Richard Berington, armiger, complainant, and Edward Stanford, armiger, and Mary, his wife, deforciants of the manor of **Rowley**, with the appurtenances, and of a messuage, 68 acres of land, 43 acres of meadow, 64 acres of pasture, 10 acres of wood, and 60*s*. of rent in **Rowley**, **Castle**, and **Stafford**; and of the site of the late monastery of the "Austen Friers" near the town of **Stafford**, with the appurtenances, in **Stafford**; and also of all tithes of sheaves of corn, grain, hay, calves, lambs, sucking pigs, and wool, and all other tithes in **Castle**, **Rowley**, and **Billington**.

Edward and Mary remitted all right to Richard and his heirs, for which Richard gave them £100.

At fifteen days from Easter Day. 8 James I.

Between Edward Littleton, the younger, knight, complainant, and Thomas Burie and Elizabeth, his wife, deforciants of 14 acres of land, 6 acres of meadow, 4 acres of pasture, and common of pasture in **Penkriche**.

Thomas and Elizabeth remitted all right to Edward and his heirs, for which Edward gave them £41.

At fifteen days from Easter Day. 8 James I.

Between Robert Hussey, armiger, complainant, and Richard Hussey, knight, and others, deforciants of tenements in **Bardeley**.[1]

TRINITY. 8 JAMES I.

On the Morrow of Holy Trinity. 8 James I.

Between William Collinson, complainant, and Henry Squyer, deforciant of a messuage, 40 acres of land, 20 acres of meadow, and 20 acres of pasture in **Howndsworth**.

[1] Fine missing. Taken from the Index.

Henry granted the said tenements to William; to be held by him and his heirs for 21 years next after the decease of John Squyer, father of the said Henry, rendering 12*d.* yearly to the said Henry and his heirs, for which William gave him £80.

On the Morrow of Holy Trinity. 8 James I.

Between Edward Cartwright, complainant, and Walter Chetwynd, knight, deforciant of a messuage, a toft, 2 barns, a garden, an orchard, 40 acres of land, 2 acres of meadow, 40 acres of pasture, 3 acres of wood, 4 acres of heath, and common of pasture for all kinds of cattle in **Heckeley** otherwise **Hecley**, **Bagottes Bromley**, and **Pagettes Bromley**.

Walter remitted all right to Edward and his heirs, for which Edward gave him £60.

On the Morrow of Holy Trinity. 8 James I.

Between Hugh Wrottesley, armiger, complainant, and Thomas Burnett, deforciant of a cottage, a garden, an orchard, 5 acres of meadow, and 15 acres of pasture in **Overton** otherwise **Orton**.

Thomas remitted all right to Hugh and his heirs, for which Hugh gave him £60.

On the Morrow of Holy Trinity. 8 James I.

Between William Lowton, complainant, and Thomas Lowton, deforciant of 2 messuages, 2 cottages, a water grain-mill, 2 gardens, 2 orchards, 500 acres of land, 12 acres of meadow, and 120 acres of pasture in **Huntley** and **Chedull**.

Thomas remitted all right to William and his heirs, for which William gave him £100.

On the Morrow of Holy Trinity. 8 James I.

Between Richard Stretton, complainant, and Nicholas Breton, armiger, and Edward Breton, gentleman, deforciants of an orchard and an acre of pasture in **Tamworth**.

Nicholas and Edward remitted all right to Richard and his heirs, for which Richard gave them £41.

On the Morrow of Holy Trinity. 8 James I.

Between William Endsore, gentleman, complainant, and Walter Bassett, gentleman, deforciant of 12 acres of meadow in **Hyntes**.

Walter remitted all right to William and his heirs, for which William gave him £80.

At fifteen days from the day of Holy Trinity. 8 James I.

Between William Bache and Thomas Bache, complainants, and John Button and Walter Button, son and heir apparent of the said John, deforciants of 40 acres of land, 3 acres of meadow, and 20 acres of pasture in **Overpen** and **Netherpen**.

John and Walter remitted all right to William and Thomas and to the heirs of Thomas, for which William and Thomas gave them £80.

On the Morrow of Holy Trinity. 8 James I.

Between Humphrey Wildey, complainant, and Nicholas Breton, armiger, and Edward Breton, gentleman, deforciants of a messuage, 3 cottages, 4 gardens, 4 orchards, 18 acres of land, 3 acres of meadow, 3 acres of pasture, 10 acres of furze and heath, 6 acres of moor, 4 acres of marsh, and common of pasture for all kinds of cattle in **Wiggenton**, **Comberford**, **Coton**, and **Hoppwas**.

Nicholas and Edward remitted all right to Humphrey and his heirs, for which Humphrey gave them £80.

On the Morrow of Holy Trinity. 8 James I.

Between John Gravener, gentleman, and Francis Wightwicke, gentleman, complainants, and Humphrey Wightwicke, deforciant of 10 messuages, 10 gardens, 10 acres of land, 2 acres of meadow, 40 acres of pasture, and 10 acres of furze and heath in **Wolverhampton** and **Overpen.**

Humphrey remitted all right to John and Francis and to the heirs of John, for which John and Francis gave him £100.

At three weeks from the day of Holy Trinity. 8 James I.

Between Matthew Craddocke, gentleman, and William Bowyer, gentleman, complainants, and Thomas Wolrich, gentleman, deforciant of 2 messuages, a cottage, 3 gardens, 3 orchards, 80 acres of land, 26 acres of meadow, 35 acres of pasture, and common of pasture in **Cokeslane** otherwise **Cookesland, Little Brichford,** and **Seighford.**

Thomas remitted all right to Matthew and William and to the heirs of Matthew, for which Matthew and William gave him £80.

On the Morrow of Holy Trinity. 8 James I.

Between Walter Leveson, knight, and Robert Chapman, gentleman, complainants, and Peter Maclesfeild, armiger, deforciant of the manor of **Meyre,** with the appurtenances, and of 8 messuages, 8 cottages, a dovecote, 16 gardens, 10 orchards, 600 acres of land, 50 acres of meadow, 300 acres of pasture, 20 acres of wood, and 1,000 acres of furze and heath in **Meyre, Aston, Meyreway, Sidway, Radwood, Audeley, Chesterton,** and **Garsall** otherwise **Garingshall.**

Peter remitted all right to Walter and Robert and to the heirs of Walter, for which Walter and Robert gave him £400.

On the Morrow of Holy Trinity. 8 James I.

Between William Scott, John Scott, and William Jorden, complainants, and Edward Leigh, knight, and Anne, his wife, and Henry Leigh, armiger, deforciants of 30 acres of pasture, 60 acres of wood, and common of pasture for all cattle in **Great Barre, Aldrich,** and **Rushall.**

The deforciants remitted all right to the complainants and to the heirs of William Scott, for which the complainants gave them £80.

On the Morrow of Holy Trinity. 8 James I.

Between John Sallam and Mary Paynton, complainants, and Anthony Sallam and Joan, his wife, deforciants of the moiety of a messuage, 40 acres of land, 10 acres of meadow, 30 acres of pasture, and 20 acres of wood in **Copenhall.**

Anthony and Joan granted the said moiety, and whatsoever they had therein for the term of their lives and the life of the longest liver of them, to John and Mary; to be held by the said John and Mary for the lives of the said Anthony and Joan and the life of the longest liver of them; for which John and Mary gave them £60.

On the Morrow of Holy Trinity. 8 James I.

Between Edward Coke, knight, Chief Justice of the King's Bench, Robert Bulleyn, gentleman, and John Pepys, gentleman, complainants, and Francis Lacon, knight, and Margaret, his wife, and Alfred Kellett, deforciants of the manor of **Knyghtley** otherwise **Knightley,** with the appurtenances, and of 20 messuages, 10 cottages, 6 tofts, 2 water-mills, a dovecote, 20 gardens, 500 acres of land, 300 acres of meadow, 1,000 acres of pasture, 400 acres of wood, 200 acres of furze and heath, 10 acres of moor, and 70*s.* of rent in **Knyghtley, Gnosall** otherwise **Gnos Hall** otherwise **Gnowsall, Chatwall, Wynnington, Maccleston, Knighton** near **Adbaston,** and **Hill** otherwise **Hill House.**

The deforciants remitted all right to the complainants and to the heirs of Edward Coke, for which the complainants gave them £200.

At three weeks from the day of Holy Trinity. 8 James I.

Between John Coker, gentleman, complainant, and Walter Harecourt, knight, and Dorothy, his wife, and Robert Harecourt, armiger, deforciants of the manor of **Chebsey** and **Shalford**, with the appurtenances, and of 24 messuages, 6 cottages, a water-mill, a dovecote, 30 gardens, 30 orchards, 400 acres of land, 200 acres of meadow, 1,400 acres of pasture, 12 acres of wood, and 20*s.* 6*d.* of rent in **Chebsey** and **Shalford**, and of the view of frankpledge in **Chebsey** and **Shalford**.

The deforciants remitted all right to John and his heirs, and covenanted that they would warrant the said tenements against the heirs of Robert Harecourt, armiger, deceased, for which John gave them £800.

Michaelmas. 8 James I.

On the Octaves of St. Martin. 8 James I.

Between Robert Walker, complainant, and Walter Hill and Ellen, his wife, deforciants of a garden, an orchard, 6 acres of meadow, 40 acres of pasture, an acre of wood, and common of pasture for all cattle, and of the moiety of a messuage and 100 acres of land in **Stawne**.

Walter and Ellen remitted all right to Robert and his heirs, for which Robert gave them £80.

On the Octaves of St. Michael. 8 James I.

Between Ralph Mountford and Thomas Cliffe, complainants, and Lawrence Cliffe, gentleman, deforciant of 2 messuages, a cottage, 100 acres of land, 60 acres of meadow, 120 acres of pasture, 10 acres of wood, and common of pasture for all kinds of cattle, and common of turbary in **Bradnoppe** and **Leeke.**

Lawrence remitted all right to Ralph and Thomas and to the heirs of Ralph, for which Ralph and Thomas gave him £120.

On the Octaves of St. Michael. 8 James I.

Between Edward Poyser, complainant, and John Harrison, deforciant of 2 acres of meadow in **Ansley**.

John remitted all right to Edward and his heirs, and covenanted that he would warrant the said tenement against Edward Blunt and his heirs, and against Edward Manuringe and his heirs, for which Edward gave him £40.

On the Octaves of St. Michael. 8 James I.

Between William Bowyer, gentleman, and Thomas Tomkes, gentleman, complainants, and George Johnson and Ellen, his wife, deforciants of 10 acres of land in **Stafford** and **Foryate Stafford** otherwise **Stafford Foryate.**

George and Ellen remitted all right to William and Thomas and to the heirs of William, for which William and Thomas gave them £40.

On the Octaves of St. Michael. 8 James I.

Between Edward Bott, complainant, and Robert Bott, deforciant of 2½ burgages and 2 acres of land in **Uttoxator**.

Robert remitted all right to Edward and his heirs, for which Edward gave him £60.

On the Octaves of St. Michael. 8 James I.

Between Henry Stone, gentleman, complainant, and Walter Fowlar, armiger, and Edward Fowlar, gentleman, son and heir apparent of the said Walter, deforciants of 3 messuages, 3 gardens, 40 acres of land, 2 acres of meadow, and 40 acres of pasture in **Wallsall**, **Rushall**, **Goscott**, and **Caldmore.**

Walter and Edward remitted all right to Henry and his heirs, for which Henry gave them £100.

At fifteen days from the Day of St. Martin. 8 James I.

Between Humphrey Jem, Richard Jem, and John Cocker, complainants, and John Everard, gentleman, and Bridget, his wife, deforciants of a cottage, a garden, an orchard, an acre of land, 2 acres of meadow, and 10 acres of pasture in **Whyttyngton.**

John Everard and Bridget remitted all right to the complainants and to the heirs of Humphrey, for which the complainants gave them £60.

On the Octaves of St. Michael. 8 James I.

Between Richard Parkes, complainant, and John Astyn, gentleman, and Katherine, his wife, deforciants of 40 acres of land, 50 acres of pasture, and 10 acres of wood in **Norton under Cannock.**

John and Katherine remitted all right to Richard and his heirs, for which Richard gave them £80.

On the Octaves of St. Michael. 8 James I.

Between Walter Stanley, armiger, complainant, and John Bate and Samuel Arden and Mary, his wife, deforciants of a messuage, a barn, a garden, an orchard, an acre of land, an acre of meadow, and 2 acres of pasture in **Westbromwiche.**

The deforciants remitted all right to Walter and his heirs, for which Walter gave them £40.

On the Octaves of St. Michael. 8 James I.

Between Erasmus Mowsley, complainant, and Edward Ethershawe and Martha, his wife, deforciants of a messuage, a garden, and an orchard in **Tamworth.**

Edward and Martha remitted all right to Erasmus and his heirs, for which Erasmus gave them £40.

On the Octaves of St. Michael. 8 James I.

Between Lawrence Whitwall, complainant, and William Clarke, deforciant of a messuage, a garden, an orchard, 50 acres of land, 15 acres of meadow, 50 acres of pasture, 10 acres of wood, 100 acres of moor, common of pasture for all kinds of cattle, and common of turbary in **Weston** and **Wetley Moore.**

William remitted all right to Lawrence and his heirs, for which Lawrence gave him £80.

On the Octaves of St. Michael. 8 James I.

Between Edward Littleton, the younger, knight, complainant, and Arthur Lowe, gentleman, and Susan, his wife, and Anthony Lowe, gentleman, deforciants of a messuage, a garden, an orchard, 10 acres of land, 10 acres of meadow, 70 acres of pasture, 6 acres of wood, and common of pasture in **Longdon.**

The deforciants remitted all right to Edward and his heirs, for which Edward gave them £100.

On the Morrow of St. Martin. 8 James I.

Between John Heaton and Ralph Heaton, the younger, complainants, and Walter Aston, knight, deforciant of a messuage, a garden, 40 acres of land, 15 acres of meadow, 20 acres of pasture, 5 acres of furze and heath, common of pasture for all kinds of cattle, and common of turbary in **Bradnapp** and **Moreage.**

Walter remitted all right to John and Ralph and to the heirs of John, for which John and Ralph gave him £41.

On the Octaves of St. Michael. 8 James I.

Between William Lownes, complainant, and Thomas Wordesley and Margaret, his wife, deforciants of a cottage, a garden, an orchard, 10 acres of land, an acre of meadow, 6 acres of pasture, and common of pasture for all cattle in **Brewoode** and **Somerford**.

Thomas and Margaret remitted all right to William and his heirs, for which William gave them £40.

On the Octaves of St. Michael. 8 James I.

Between Edmund Darbye, complainant, and William James and Mary, his wife, deforciants of a cottage, a barn, a garden, and 5 acres of pasture in **Westbromwich**.

William and Mary remitted all right to Edmund and his heirs, for which Edmund gave them £41.

On the Octaves of St. Michael. 8 James I.

Between George Cotton, gentleman, complainant, and Lewis Packer and Anne, his wife, deforciants of 2 messuages, 2 gardens, 2 orchards, 50 acres of land, 12 acres of meadow, 40 acres of pasture, and common of pasture for all kinds of cattle in **Gayton, Weston on Trent, Fosbrooke, Dilron** otherwise **Dilhorne**, and **Careswall**, and of the fourth part of 2 cottages and 6 acres of land in **Gayton**.

Lewis and Anne remitted all right to George and his heirs, for which George gave them £100.

At fifteen days from the day of St. Martin. 8 James I.

Between Richard Baxter and Robert Sarrels, complainants, and Robert Orme, gentleman, and Alice, his wife, deforciants of 2 messuages, 2 gardens, 2 orchards, 16 acres of land, 4 acres of meadow, 16 acres of pasture, and 2 acres of wood in **Whyttington** and **Fyssherwicke**.

Robert Orme and Alice remitted all right to Richard and Robert Baxter and to the heirs of Richard, for which Richard and Robert Baxter gave them £41.

On the Octaves of St. Michael. 8 James I.

Between Edward Cole, Henry Cole, and John Cole, complainants, and William Cole, deforciant of a messuage, a cottage, 2 gardens, 2 orchards, 20 acres of land, 6 acres of meadow, and 64 acres of pasture in **Westbromwich**.

William remitted all right to the complainants and to the heirs of Edward, for which the complainants gave him £80.

On the Octaves of St. Michael. 8 James I.

Between John Greene, complainant, and John Hollins, gentleman, and Robert Whitehall, gentleman, deforciants of a cottage, a toft, a garden, 12 acres of pasture, and 2 acres of wood in **Chedull**.

The deforciants remitted all right to John Greene and his heirs, for which John Greene gave them £60.

On the Octaves of St. Michael. 8 James I.

Between Thomas Crompton, complainant, and John Allen and Agnes, his wife, deforciants of a cottage, a toft, 16 acres of land, 14 acres of meadow, 14 acres of pasture, 3 acres of wood, 4 acres of furze and heath, and common of pasture for all kinds of cattle in **Chedull**.

John and Agnes remitted all right to Thomas and his heirs, for which Thomas gave them £60.

At one month from the day of St. Michael. 8 James I.

Between Richard Pott, gentleman, complainant, and Thomas Wolrich, gentleman, and Robert Forster and Margaret, his wife, deforciants of a messuage, a garden, an orchard, 20 acres of land, 8 acres of meadow, 10 acres of pasture, 3 acres of wood, 10 acres of furze and heath, and common of pasture for all cattle in **Seighford** otherwise **Sedgeford**.

The deforciants remitted all right to Richard and his heirs, for which Richard gave them £60.

On the Octaves of St. Michael. 8 James I.

Between George Cowper and Robert Cowper, gentleman, complainants, and Henry Wood, gentleman, and Anne, his wife, deforciants of 4 messuages, 4 burgages, a toft, 9 gardens, 60 acres of land, 20 acres of meadow, 60 acres of pasture, 10 acres of wood, 100 acres of heath, and 100 acres of moor in **Balterley** and **Newcastle.**

Henry and Anne remitted all right to George and Robert and to the heirs of George, for which George and Robert gave them £100.

At fifteen days from the day of St. Martin. 8 James I.

Between Robert Sharpe, Humphrey Hatchett, and John Ansted, complainants, and John Everard, gentleman, and Bridget, his wife, deforciants of a messuage, a garden, an orchard, 17 acres of land, 2 acres of meadow, and 20 acres of pasture in **Whyttyngton.**

John Everard and Bridget remitted all right to the complainants and to the heirs of Robert, for which the complainants gave them £41.

On the Octaves of St. Michael. 8 James I.

Between Samuel Pype, gentleman, complainant, and John Brooke, gentleman, deforciant of 50 acres of pasture and 10 acres of wood in **Bobington** otherwise **Bovington.**

John remitted all right to Samuel and his heirs, for which Samuel gave him £60.

On the Octaves of St. Michael. 8 James I.

Between Richard Higgens, complainant, and Thomas Asheforde and Joan, his wife, deforciants of 20 acres of pasture, 4 acres of wood, and common of pasture in **Smethwicke.**

Thomas and Joan remitted all right to Richard and his heirs, for which Richard gave them £40.

On the Octaves of St. Michael. 8 James I.

Between John Dutton, complainant, and Thomas Hasterley, deforciant of a messuage, a garden, an orchard, 11 acres of land, 2 acres of meadow, and 3 acres of pasture in **Purrye Barre.**

Thomas remitted all right to John and his heirs, for which John gave him £41.

On the Octaves of St. Michael. 8 James I.

Between Henry Towneshend, knight, and Dorothy, his wife, complainants, and Francis Bucke, gentleman, deforciant of the manors of **Hilton** and **Estington** otherwise **Esington**, with the appurtenances, and of 10 messuages, 10 gardens, 10 orchards, 200 acres of land, 200 acres of meadow, 300 acres of pasture, 200 acres of wood, 200 acres of furze and heath and £3 of rent in **Hilton, Essington, Wolverhampton, Penkridge, Shareshill, Great Sarden, Little Sarden, Walsall,** and **Blockwich.**

Francis remitted all right to Henry and Dorothy and to the heirs of Dorothy, for which Henry and Dorothy gave him £240.

At one month from the day of St. Michael. 8 James I.

Between William Stoddard, complainant, and Anthony Brocke, gentleman, and Anne, his wife, and Henry Brocke, gentleman, and Joan, his wife, deforciants of 2 messuages, a cottage, 3 gardens, 140 acres of land, 12 acres of meadow, 100 acres of pasture, 10 acres of wood, and 20 acres of furze and heath in **Shelton, Hanley, Fenton Vivian,** and **Loncton.**

The deforciants remitted all right to William and his heirs, for which William gave them £100.

At one month from the day of St. Michael. 8 James I.

Between Walter Mynors, armiger, complainant, and William Milward, armiger, deforciant of a messuage, 2 cottages, 3 tofts, 3 gardens, 3 orchards, 80 acres of land, 40 acres of meadow, 80 acres of pasture, and common of pasture for all kinds of cattle in **Draycott**, **Sudbury**, **Brcadheade**, **Overton**, **Madeley Holme** otherwise **Madeley Home**, and **Morton**.

William remitted all right to Walter and his heirs, for which Walter gave him £120.

On the Octaves of St. Martin. 8 James I.

Between Richard Weston, gentleman, and William Browne, gentleman, complainants, and Walter Mynors, armiger, and Mary, his wife, deforciants of a messuage, 2 cottages, 3 tofts, 3 gardens, 3 orchards, 80 acres of land, 40 acres of meadow, and 80 acres of pasture in **Draycott**, **Sudbury**, **Broadheade**, **Overton**, **Madeley Holme** otherwise **Madeley Home**, and **Morton**.

Walter and Mary remitted all right to Richard and William and to the heirs of Richard, for which Richard and William gave them £120.

On the Octaves of St. Michael. 8 James I.

Between Robert Clowes, complainant, and William Thorley, gentleman, and Anne, his wife, and George Thorley, son and heir apparent of the said William, deforciants of a messuage, a cottage, 2 gardens, 30 acres of land, 10 acres of meadow, 30 acres of pasture, 10 acres of wood, and common of pasture for all kinds of cattle, and common of turbary in **Heyton** otherwise **Heaton** otherwise **Hayton**.

The deforciants remitted all right to Robert and his heirs, for which Robert gave them £41.

On the Octaves of St. Michael. 8 James I.

Between Richard Drakeford, gentleman, complainant, and Thomas Hall and Ellen, his wife, and Thomas White, deforciants of 2 messuages, 4 cottages, a mill, 4 gardens, 2 orchards, an acre of land, an acre of meadow, an acre of pasture, and common of pasture in **Stafford** and **Foryate Stafford** otherwise **Stafford Foryate**.

The deforciants remitted all right to Richard and his heirs; and Thomas White covenanted that he would warrant the said tenements against the heirs of Francis White, deceased, father of the said Thomas, for which Richard gave them £41.

At fifteen days from the day of St. Martin. 8 James I.

Between Richard Harryes, gentleman, and Thomas Mempas, complainants, and Ambrose Graye, armiger, and George Graye, armiger, deforciants of a messuage, 20 acres of land, 10 acres of meadow, and 70 acres of pasture in **Bobbington**.

Ambrose and George remitted all right to Richard and Thomas and to the heirs of Richard; and Ambrose covenanted that he would warrant the said tenements against Margaret Graye, wife of the said Ambrose, for which Richard and Thomas gave them £60.

On the Octaves of St. Michael. 8 James I.

Between Judith Corbett, widow, complainant, and John Duncalffe and Joice, his wife, and William Duncalffe, deforciants of a messuage, a garden, an orchard, 6 acres of land, 6 acres of meadow, 6 acres of pasture, 20 acres of urze and heath, and common of pasture for all cattle in **Chedull**.

The deforciants remitted all right to Judith and her heirs, and John and William covenanted that they would warrant the said tenements against James Cowper and his heirs, for which Judith gave them £41.

On the Octaves of St. Michael. 8 James I.

Between George Vernon, armiger, Thomas Rudiarde, armiger, Thomas Kynaston, armiger, and John Weston, gentleman, complainants, and John Fernihaugh, gentleman, and William Fernihaugh, gentleman, deforciants of 4 messuages, 4 gardens, 4 orchards, 50 acres of land, 20 acres of meadow, 50 acres of pasture, common of pasture for all kinds of cattle, and common of turbary in **Waterfall** and **Calton** otherwise **Caulton** otherwise **Caldon**, and of all tithes in **Endon** otherwise **Yendon**.

The deforciants remitted all right to the complainants and to the heirs of George Vernon, for which the complainants gave them £100.

On the Octaves of St. Martin. 8 James I.

Between John Egerton, knight, and Francis Leigh, knight, complainants, and Thomas Leigh, knight, and Katherine, his wife, deforciants of the manor of **Hampstall Ridware** otherwise **Hamstall Ridware** otherwise **Ridware Hampstall** otherwise **Ridware Hamstall**, with the appurtenances, and of 20 messuages, 10 cottages, 2 water-mills, 20 gardens, 20 orchards, 500 acres of land, 200 acres of meadow, 100 acres of pasture, 200 aeres of wood, 200 acres of furze and heath, 20 acres of land covered with water, and free warren in **Hampstall Ridware**, **Rowley**, and **Agarsley** otherwise **Agardsley**, and of the two parks called **Rowley Parke** and **Ridware Parke**; and also of the advowson of the church of **Hampstall Ridware**.

Thomas and Katherine remitted all right to John and Francis and to the heirs of John, for which John and Francis gave them £200.

On the Octaves of St. Michael. 8 James I.

Between Judith Corbett, widow, complainant, and John Draycote and Anne, his wife, deforciants of 6 messuages, 4 cottages, 10 gardens, 10 orchards, 140 acres of land, 80 acres of meadow, 100 acres of pasture, 100 acres of furze and heath, and 40*s*. of rent in **Chedull**, and of a moiety of the manor of **Chedull**, with the appurtenances, and of 3 messuages, a water-mill, 3 gardens, 3 orchards, 40 acres of land, 40 acres of meadow, 100 acres of pasture, 200 acres of wood, 300 acres of furze and heath, £18 of rent, view of frankpledge, wards, marriages, reliefs, heriots, escheats, fines, amercements, fairs, markets, and tolls in **Chedull**, **Parkhall**, **Blackehaughe**, **Delfehowses**, **Milnehowses**, **Huntley**, **Brockhowses**, **Littley**, **Comslowe**, **Woodhead**, **Thornebury Hall**, **Shawe**, **Bothehall**, **Chedull**, **Bouthes Birchenfeld**, and **Abone Parke**; and also of a moiety of the advowson of the church of **Chedull**.

John and Anne remitted all right to Judith and her heirs, for which Judith gave them £700.

On the Octaves of St. Michael. 8 James I.

Between Sampson Parkes, John Tetlowe, and Lawrence Bevell, complainants, and Robert Meverell, armiger, and Elizabeth, his wife, and Thomas Nabbes and Jane, his wife, deforciants of 3 messuages, 3 gardens, 3 orchards, 30 acres of land, 30 acres of meadow, 30 acres of pasture, 100 acres of furze and heath, and common of pasture for all kinds of cattle in **Waterfall**.

The deforciants remitted all right to the complainants and to the heirs of Sampson, for which the complainants gave them £100.

On the Octaves of St. Michael. 8 James I.

Between William Pye and Humphrey Pye, complainants, and John Chapman and Thomasina, his wife, Richard Chapman and Mary, his wife, William Southwell and Joan, his wife, and Thomas Cartwright and Anne, his wife, deforciants of 6 acres of land, 8 acres of meadow, 10 acres of pasture, and 2 acres of wood in **Haughton**.

The deforciants remitted all right to the complainants and to the heirs of Humphrey; and John and Thomasina covenanted that they would warrant the said tenements against the heirs of John Chapman, father of the said John; and Richard and Mary covenanted that they would warrant the said tenements against the heirs of John Chapman, father of the said Richard, for which the complainants gave them £41.

HILLARY. 8 JAMES I.

On the Octaves of St. Hillary. 8 James I.

Between William Hunte and John Turton, complainants, and George Hawe, deforciant of 2 messuages, 4 cottages, 6 gardens, 40 acres of land, 20 acres of meadow, 60 acres of pasture, 20 acres of wood, and 40 acres of furze and heath in **Walsall** and **Shelfeilde**.

George remitted all right to William and John and to the heirs of William, for which William and John gave him £100.

On the Octaves of St. Hillary. 8 James I.

Between Gervase Hall, gentleman, complainant, and Walter Bickford and Joan Bickford, widow, and Elizabeth Bickford, deforciants of a messuage, a stable, and a garden in **Wolverhampton**.

The deforciants remitted all right to Gervase and his heirs, for which Gervase gave them £40.

On the Octaves of the Purification of the Blessed Mary. 8 James I.

Between John Mytton, armiger, complainant, and Humphrey Whitmore and Sarah, his wife, deforciants of a toft, 16 acres of land, 3 acres of meadow, and 3 acres of pasture in **Horsebrooke**.

Humphrey and Sarah remitted all right to John and his heirs, for which John gave them £60.

On the Octaves of St. Hillary. 8 James I.

Between William Hunte and John Turton, complainants, and John Haule, deforciant of 2 messuages, 6 cottages, 8 gardens, 40 acres of land, 20 acres of meadow, 60 acres of pasture, 10 acres of wood, and 40 acres of furze and heath in **Walsall, Westbromwich, Great Bloxsiche**, and **Rushall**.

John Haule remitted all right to the complainants and to the heirs of William, for which the complainants gave him £100.

On the Octaves of St. Hillary. 8 James I.

Between John Brinley, complainant, and Walter Aston, knight, deforciant of a messuage, a toft, a water-mill, a garden, 26 acres of land, 12 acres of meadow, 26 acres of pasture, 3 acres of wood, and common of pasture for all kinds of cattle, and common of turbary in **Bradnap** and **Morage**.

Walter remitted all right to John and his heirs, and covenanted that he would warrant the said tenements against the heirs of Edward Aston, knight, deceased, father of the said Walter, and against the heirs of Walter Aston, knight, deceased, grandfather of the said Walter, for which John gave him £41.

On the Octaves of St. Hillary. 8 James I.

Between John Hall, complainant, and John Ferrers, knight, deforciant of a message, a garden, and an orchard in **Tamworth**.

John Ferrers remitted all right to John Hall and his heirs, for which John Hall gave him £41.

On the Octaves of St. Hillary. 8 James I.

Between Philip Jackson, complainant, and Edward Leigh, knight, and Anne, his wife, and Henry Leigh, armiger, deforciants of a cottage, 4 acres of land, 2 acres of meadow, and 18 acres of pasture in **Rushall, Hawrden,** and **Gorsticott.**

The deforciants remitted all right to Philip and his heirs, for which Philip gave them £41.

At fifteen days from the day of St. Hillary. 8 James I.

Between George Banester, complainant, and Robert Bullock and Joan, his wife, deforciants of a messuage, a garden, an orchard, 3 acres cf land, 2 acres of pasture, and 10 acres of furze and heath in **Longdon,** and of common of pasture for all kinds of cattle in the **Forest of Cannock.**

Robert and Joan remitted all right to George and his heirs, for which George gave them £41.

On the Octaves of St. Hillary. 8 James I.

Between Nicholas Moseley and John Cupper, complainants, and Roger Fowke, gentleman, and Mary, his wife, deforciants of 2 messuages, 2 gardens, 2 orchards, 170 acres of land, 38 acres of meadow, 100 acres of pasture, and 4 acres of wood in **Wolverhampton** and **Darlaston.**

Roger and Mary remitted all right to Nicholas and John and to the heirs of John, for which Nicholas and John gave them £200.

On the Octaves of St. Hillary. 8 James I.

Between William Aston, gentleman, complainant, and Walter Aston, knight, deforciant of 2 messuages, a cottage, a toft, 2 barns, 2 gardens, 2 orchards, 85 acres of land, 18 acres of meadow, 80 acres of pasture, 12 acres of wood, 5 acres of furze and heath, common of turbary, and common of pasture for all kinds of cattle in **Milwich, Garsall** otherwise **Garingsall, Marchington,** and **Hanburie.**

Walter remitted all right to William and his heirs, for which William gave him £100.

On the Octaves of the Purification. 8 James I.

Between Thomas Clowes, complainant, and Walter Aston, knight, deforciant of a messuage, a garden, 4 acres of land, common of pasture for all cattle, and common of turbary in **Bradnap** and **Moredge.**

Walter remitted all right to Thomas and his heirs, for which Thomas gave him £60.

On the Octaves of St. Hillary. 8 James I.

Between James Lawnder and Thomas Pycken, complainants, and Ralph Bold and Parnell, his wife, deforciants of 6 acres of land and 10 acres of pasture in **Sondon.**

Ralph and Parnell remitted all right to James and Thomas and to the heirs of James, for which James and Thomas gave them £41.

On the Octaves of the Purification. 8 James I.

Between Edward Waldron and Thomas Wootton, complainants, and Alfred Kellett, gentleman, and Francis Kellett, gentleman, deforciants of a messuage, a garden, an orchard, 12 acres of land, 10 acres of meadow, and 20 acres of pasture in **Wootton** and **Eccleshall.**

Alfred and Francis remitted all right to Edward and Thomas and to the heirs of Edward, for which Edward and Thomas gave them £60.

At fifteen days from the day of St. Hillary. 8 James I.

Between Robert Fewkes, complainant, and Edward Harvey, William Harvey, John Huntbach otherwise Walton, and Mary Huntbach otherwise

Walton otherwise Harvie, deforciants of 2 messuages, 2 gardens, 2 orchards, 4 acres of land, and 14 acres of pasture in **Hetly** and **Bagettes Bromley**.

The deforciants remitted all right to Robert and his heirs, for which Robert gave them £41.

On the Octaves of St. Hillary. 8 James I.

Between Thomas Bradeley, complainant, and Richard Grove, deforciant of a messuage, a tan-house, and an acre of pasture in **Wolverhampton**.

Richard remitted all right to Thomas and his heirs, for which Thomas gave him £40.

On the Octaves of St. Hillary. 8 James I.

Between Richard Ockoulde and Edward Phillippes, complainants, and Thomas Gervies, armiger, and Dorothy, his wife, deforciants of the manor of **Chackill** otherwise **Chackull**, with the appurtenances, and of 200 acres of land, 40 acres of meadow, and 200 acres of pasture in **Chackill** otherwise **Chackull**, **Aspley**, **Charnes**, and **Eccleshall**.

Thomas and Dorothy remitted all right to Richard and Edward and to the heirs of Richard, for which Richard and Edward gave them £300.

On the Octaves of St. Hillary. 8 James I.

Between John Egerton, knight, and Francis Leigh, knight, complainants, and Anthony Fitzherbert, armiger, deforciant of the manor of **Hampstall Ridware** otherwise **Hamstall Ridware** otherwise **Ridware Hampstall** otherwise **Ridware Hamstall**, with the appurtenances, and of 20 messuages, 10 cottages, 2 water-mills, 20 gardens, 20 orchards, 500 acres of land, 200 acres of meadow, 1,000 acres of pasture, 200 acres of wood, 200 acres of furze and heath, 20 acres of land covered with water, and free warren in **Hampstall Ridware**, **Rowley**, and **Agarsley** otherwise **Agardsley**, and of the two parks called **Rowley Parke** and **Ridware Parke**; and also of the advowson of the church of **Hampstall Ridware**.

Anthony remitted all right to John and Francis and to the heirs of John for which John and Francis gave him £400.

Easter. 9 James I.

At fifteen days from Easter Day. 9 James I.

Between Hugh Sheldon, complainant, and Thomas Whiston and Katherine, his wife, deforciants of a messuage, a garden, 15 acres of land, 6 acres of meadow, 12 acres of pasture, common of pasture for all kinds of cattle, and common of turbary in **Cauldon**.

Thomas and Katherine remitted all right to Hugh and his heirs, for which Hugh gave them £41.

At fifteen days from Easter Day. 9 James I.

Between Stephen Baylye and John Parker, complainants, and Thomas Thicknes, gentleman, and Mary, his wife, deforciants of a messuage, a garden, an orchard, and 16 acres of pasture in **Whittyngton** and **Tamhorne**.

Thomas and Mary remitted all right to Stephen and John and to the heirs of Stephen, for which Stephen and John gave them £41.

At fifteen days from Easter Day. 9 James I.

Between George Licett, complainant, and John Ampe, gentleman, and Sarah, his wife, deforciants of a messuage, a barn, a garden an orchard, 4 acres of land, 3 acres of meadow, and 10 acres of pasture in **Curboroughe** and **Elmehurst**.

John and Sarah remitted all right to George and his heirs, for which George gave them £41.

At fifteen days from Easter Day. 9 James I.

Between Thomas, Lord Gerard, complainant, and Walter Chetwynd, knight, deforciant of a messuage, a garden, an orchard, 80 acres of land, 10 acres of meadow, 80 acres of pasture, 20 acres of wood, 20 acres of furze and heath, and common of pasture for all kinds of cattle in **Rudge**, **Asheley**, and **Stawne** otherwise **Standon**.

Walter remitted all right to Thomas and his heirs, and covenanted that he would warrant the said tenements against William Chetwynd, knight, brother of the said Walter, and against the heirs of John Chetwynd, armiger, deceased, father of the said Walter, for which Thomas gave him £120.

At fifteen days from Easter Day. 9 James I.

Between Humphrey Vaughton and Thomas Pemberton, complainants, and Richard White, the younger, and Joan, his wife, deforciants of 2 acres of land, 8 acres of meadow, and 10 acres of pasture in **Handesworthe**.

Richard and John remitted all right to Humphrey and Thomas and to the heirs of Humphrey, for which Humphrey and Thomas gave them £60.

At fifteen days from Easter Day. 9 James I.

Between Robert Homersley and Humphrey Warner, gentlemen, complainants, and Thomas Homersley, the elder, deforciant of a messuage, a garden, 40 acres of land, 10 acres of meadow, 30 acres of pasture, 30 acres of wood, common of pasture for all kinds of cattle, and common of turbary in **Chedleton**, and of all tithes and emoluments in the said tenements.

Thomas remitted all right to Robert and Humphrey and to the heirs of Robert, for which Robert and Humphrey gave him £100.

At fifteen days from Easter Day. 9 James I.

Between Francis Dorington, complainant, and Godfrey Grene and Nicholas Grene, deforciants of a messuage, 5 cottages, and 3 gardens in **Stafford**.

Godfrey and Nicholas remitted all right to Francis and his heirs, for which Francis gave them £60.

At fifteen days from Easter Day. 9 James I.

Between Judith Corbet, widow, complainant, and John Allen and Anne, his wife, deforciants of a messuage, a garden, an orchard, 20 acres of land, 6 acres of meadow, 40 acres of pasture, 3 acres of wood, 40 acres of furze and heath, and common of pasture for all kinds of cattle in **Kingesley**, **Broadoke**, **Chedull**, and **Parkhall**.

John and Anne remitted all right to Judith and her heirs, for which Judith gave them £60.

At fifteen days from Easter Day. 9 James I.

Between Roger Pott and Thomas Pott, gentlemen, complainants, and Francis Pott, gentleman, and Anne, his wife, deforciants of 2 messuages, a toft, 2 gardens, 2 orchards, 68 acres of land, 30 acres of meadow, 20 acres of pasture, 20 acres of wood, 10 acres of furze and heath, and 10 acres of marsh in **Roughee**, **Roughey**, and **Chedulton**.

Francis and Anne remitted all right to Roger and Thomas and to the heirs of Roger, for which Roger and Thomas gave them £100.

At fifteen days from Easter Day. 9 James I.

Between Richard Jevon, the elder, gentleman, complainant, and John Marshe, gentleman, deforciant of an acre of land, 3 acres of meadow, 13 acres of pasture, and 2 acres of wood in **Sedgeley**.

John remitted all right to Richard and his heirs, for which Richard gave him £41.

At fifteen days from Easter Day. 9 James I.

Between Thomas Sprott, gentleman, complainant, and Walter Aston, gentleman, and Joice, his wife, deforciants of a messuage, a barn, a water-mill, a garden, an orchard, 20 acres of land, 40 acres of meadow, 80 acres of pasture, 20 acres of wood, 20 acres of moor, and 2 acres of land covered with water in **Longdon**, **Curborough**, and **Elmehurst**.

Walter and Joice remitted all right to Thomas and his heirs, for which Thomas gave them £120.

At fifteen days from Easter Day. 9 James I.

Between Henry Langeley and Isabella, his wife, complainants, and Thomas Bonus and Joan, his wife, deforciants of a cottage, a garden, an orchard, 14 acres of land, 2 acres of meadow, and an acre of pasture in **Whittyngton**, **Horton**, **Fissherwicke**, **Tymmore**, and **Tamhorne**.

Thomas and Joan remitted all right to Henry and Isabella and to the heirs of Henry, for which Henry and Isabella gave them £41.

At fifteen days from Easter Day. 9 James I.

Between Richard Adderley, armiger, and Ellen, his wife, complainants, and Humphrey Agard, gentleman, deforciant of a messuage, a barn, 2 gardens, 2 acres of meadow, 8 acres of pasture, and common of pasture for all cattle in **Newborrowghe** and **Needwood**.

Humphrey remitted all right to Richard and Ellen and to the heirs of Richard, for which Richard and Ellen gave him £41.

At fifteen days from Easter Day. 9 James I.

Between John Chadwicke, gentleman, and Thomas Smyth, gentleman, complainants, and John Langton, clerk, and Matilda, his wife, deforciants of 2 messuages, 2 gardens, 2 orchards, 40 acres of land, 20 acres of meadow, and 50 acres of pasture in **Curborow-Darvell**, **Elmehurste**, **Curborow-Somerfeild**, **Morfall**, and **Strethay**.

John Langton and Matilda remitted all right to the complainants and to the heirs of John Chadwicke, for which the complainants gave them £100.

At fifteen days from Easter Day. 9 James I.

Between Leonard Pownder, complainant, and Edward Littleton, the younger, knight, and Mary, his wife, deforciants of 3 acres of meadow in **Kinges Bromley**.

Edward and Mary remitted all right to Leonard and his heirs, for which Leonard gave them £41.

At fifteen days from Easter Day. 9 James I.

Between Thomas Thicknes, William Dawes, and Richard Tew, gentleman, complainants, and John Everard, gentleman, and Bridget, his wife, deforciants of 2 messuages, 3 cottages, 4 gardens, 4 orchards, 120 acres of land, 10 acres of meadow, 20 acres of pasture, 40 acres of furze and heath, and common of pasture for all kinds of cattle in **Whyttyngton**, **Fyssherwicke**, and **Horton**.

John and Bridget remitted all right to the complainants and to the heirs of Thomas, for which the complainants gave them £120.

At fifteen days from Easter Day. 9 James I.

Between Thomas Mason, complainant, and Hugh Tomkis and Mary, his wife, and Thomas Lacon and Thomasine, his wife, deforciants of a messuage and a garden in **Wolverhampton**.

The deforciants remitted all right to Thomas Mason and his heirs, for which Thomas Mason gave them £60.

At fifteen days from Easter Day. 9 James I.

Between Richard Almond, gentleman, complainant, and German Poole, knight, deforciant of 100 acres of pasture and an acre of wood in **Hanburye** and **Marchington**.

German remitted all right to Richard and his heirs, for which Richard gave him £100.

At one month from Easter Day. 9 James I.

Between William Garbett, complainant, and Thomas Burnett, deforciant of 4 messuages, a mill, a dovecote, 150 acres of land, 10 acres of meadow, 60 acres of pasture, and 4 acres of wood in **Overpenne**, **Netherpenne**, and **Orton** otherwise **Overton**.

Thomas remitted all right to William and his heirs for which William gave him £120.

At fifteen days from Easter Day. 9 James I.

Between Thomas Browne and John Woode, complainants, and John Austen, gentleman, and Susan, his wife, deforciants of 40 acres of land, 6 acres of meadow, and 20 acres of furze and heath in **Stone**, **Normicote**, **Meyre**, and **Meyrelane end**.

John Austin and Susan remitted all right to the complainants and to the heirs of Thomas, for which the complainants gave them £60.

At fifteen days from Easter Day. 9 James I.

Between Thomas Smythe, complainant, and Richard Ford and Anne, his wife, and Ellen Bradshawe, deforciants of 20 acres of pasture, 4 acres of wood, 20 acres of furze and heath, and common of pasture for all cattle in **Chedull** otherwise **Chedle**, **Parkhall**, and **Dilverne**.

The deforciants remitted all right to Thomas and his heirs, for which Thomas gave them £41.

At fifteen days from Easter Day. 9 James I.

Between Robert Bateman, Ralph Baylie, Thomas Alcock, and Hugh Bateman, complainants, and William Royle, gentleman, and Margaret, his wife, deforciants of a messuage, a garden, an orchard, 60 acres of land, 20 acres of meadow, 30 acres of pasture, and common of pasture for all kinds of cattle in **Tutburie**, **Woodhowsen**, and **Fawde**.

William and Margaret remitted all right to the complainants and to the heirs of Robert, for which the complainants gave them £100.

At fifteen days from Easter Day. 9 James I.

Between George Boulton, complainant, and Richard Henshawe and Elizabeth, his wife, deforciants of a messuage, a garden, an orchard, 20 acres of land, 4 acres of meadow, 4 acres of pasture, 4 acres of wood, and 20 acres of furze and heath in **Dillarne** otherwise **Dulverne**, **Forsbrooke**, **Draycote**, **Karswall**, and **Stone**.

Richard and Elizabeth remitted all right to George and his heirs, for which George gave them £60.

At one month from Easter Day. 9 James I.

Between John Starkey, complainant, and John Austyn, gentleman, deforciant of 4 messuages, 4 gardens, 10 acres of land, 10 acres of meadow, and 20 acres of pasture in **Norton** and **Little Wyrley**.

John Austyn remitted all right to John Starkey and his heirs, for which John Starkey gave him £60.

At fifteen days from Easter Day. 9 James I.

Between John Hurdman and Robert Launder, complainants, and John Allen and Margaret, his wife, deforciants of 30 acres of land, 18 acres of pasture, and 8 acres of wood in **Hilderson** and **Garsall**.

John Allen and Margaret remitted all right to John Hurdman and Robert and the heirs of John Hurdman, for which John Hurdman and Robert gave them £41.

At fifteen days from Easter Day. 9 James I.
Between Walter Cotton, gentleman, Thomas Sprott, gentleman, and William Sherratt, complainants, and Thomas Cotton, gentleman, and Frances, his wife, deforciants of 2 messuages, 2 cottages, 10 acres of land, 15 acres of meadow, 20 acres of pasture, 5 acres of wood, and common of pasture for all cattle in **Crakemarshe, Strongshall, Creighton, Elmehurst**, and **Brendwoode.**
Thomas Cotton and Frances remitted all right to the complainants and to the heirs of Walter, and covenanted that they would warrant the said tenements against William Cotton, gentleman, father of the said Thomas, and his heirs, for which the complainants gave them £41.

At fifteen days from Easter Day. 9 James I.
Between John Rawlyn, complainant, and John Elkyn and Margaret, his wife, deforciants of a messuage, a garden, an orchard, 10 acres of land, 10 acres of meadow, 10 acres of pasture, an acre of wood, and 20 acres of furze and heath in **Dillorne** otherwise **Dilvorne.**
John Elkyn and Margaret remitted all right to John Rawlyn and his heirs, for which John Rawlyn gave them £41.

At fifteen days from Easter Day. 9 James I.
Between Robert Pershall, gentleman, complainant, and Francis Lacon, knight, deforciant, of a messuage, a garden, an orchard, 50 acres of land, 10 acres of meadow, 40 acres of pasture, and 100 acres of furze and heath in **Bushops Offley** otherwise **Byshops Offleye, Eccleshall, Tunstall**, and **Adbaston.**
Francis remitted all right to Robert and his heirs, for which Robert gave him £100.

At fifteen days from Easter Day. 9 James I.
Between James Bennett and John Shalcrosse, complainants, and Roger Allen and Margaret, his wife, and James Aldrich and Margery, his wife, deforciants of a messuage, a garden, 20 acres of land, 6 acres of meadow, and 40 acres of pasture in **Fulford and Stone.**
The deforciants remitted all right to the complainants and to the heirs of James Bennett, for which the complainants gave them £60.

At fifteen days from Easter Day. 9 James I.
Between John Clarke and Humphrey Vawle, complainants, and Thomas White, gentleman, and Elizabeth, his wife, and Anne White, widow, deforciants of 30 acres of land, 10 acres of meadow, and 20 acres of pasture in **Ronton** and **Haughton.**
The deforciants remitted all right to John and Humphrey and the heirs of John, for which John and Humphrey gave them £100.

At fifteen days from Easter Day. 9 James I.
Between Thomas Wright, John Thickens, and Edward Thickens, complainants, and Thomas Hurt, gentleman, and Eleanor Hurt, widow, deforciants of 3 messuages, 2 cottages, 30 acres of land, 30 acres of meadow, 60 acres of pasture, and 2 acres of wood in **Marchington, Marchington Woodland,** and **Tutbury,** and of common of pasture for all cattle in the forest of **Needwood.**
Thomas Hurt and Eleanor remitted all right to the complainants and to the heirs of Thomas Wright, for which the complainants gave them £100.

At fifteen days from Easter Day. 9 James I.

Between William Cluloe and William Adderley, complainants, and Timothy Meller, deforciant of a messuage, a garden, 30 acres of land, 6 acres of meadow, 30 acres of pasture, 10 acres of furze and heath, common of pasture for all kinds of cattle, and common of turbary in **Leeke Fryth**, **Leeke**, and **Hasselwood**, and of all kinds of tithes and emoluments in the said tenements.

Timothy remitted all right to the complainants and to the heirs of William Cluloe, for which the complainants gave him £60.

At fifteen days from Easter Day. 9 James I.

Between William Brooke, gentleman, and Thomas Smythe, gentleman, complainants, and John Chadwick, gentleman, and Joice, his wife, and Gerard Stanley, gentleman, and Elizabeth, his wife, deforciants of the manor of **Maveson** otherwise **Mavesyn Ridware**, with the appurtenances, and of 10 messuages, 3 cottages, 10 barns, a mill, 10 gardens, 10 orchards, 300 acres of land, 60 acres of meadow, 300 acres of pasture, 120 acres of wood, 60 acres of furze and heath, £6 of rent, and common of pasture for all cattle in **Maveson** otherwise **Mavesyn Ridware** and **Rugeley**, and of a free fishery in the water of **Trent**; and also of the advowson of a moiety of the church of **Maveson** otherwise **Mavesyn Ridware**.

The deforciants remitted all right to William and Thomas and to the heirs of William, for which William and Thomas gave them £500.

At five weeks from Easter Day. 9 James I.

Between Peter Leighe, knight, George Booth, knight, Ralph Ashton, armiger, and James Anderton, armiger, complainants, and Thomas, Lord Gerard, deforciant of the castles of **Healey** and **Tyrley**, with the appurtenances; and of the manors of **Gerardes Bromley**, **Audeley**, **Tillington**, **Asheley**, and **Tyrley** otherwise **Tyrlighe**, with the appurtenances; and of 200 messuages, 2 water-mills, a windmill, 2 dovecotes, 7 tofts, 200 gardens, 6,000 acres of land, 1,800 acres of meadow, 6,000 acres of pasture, 1,800 acres of wood, 2,000 acres of furze and heath, 100 acres of moor, 40 acres of land covered with water, and £10 of rent in **Gerardes Bromley**, **Asheley**, **Wynnyngton**, **Podmore**, **Owre** otherwise **Ore**, **Rydge**, **Willughbridge**, **Chackyll**, **Audeley**, **Heyley**, **Betley**, **Boterley** otherwise **Balterley**, **Talke on the Hill**, **Knowle ende**, **Yardeley ende**, **Bignoll ende**, **Halmore ende**, **Meydeley** otherwise **Madeley ende**, **Parke ende**, **Tillington**, **Tyrley** otherwise **Tyrlighe**, **Drayton**, **Blore**, **Bloreheathe**, **Almyngton**, **Hales**, **Ockley**, **Great Dreyton**, **Little Dreyton**, and **Knowle**; and of the mines of ironstone and water-courses in **Tunstall**; and also of the advowson of the church of **Asheley**.

Thomas remitted all right to the complainants and to the heirs of Peter Leighe, for which the complainants gave him £2,600.

Of the Quindene of Easter. 9 James I.[1]

Between Francis Trentham, armiger, complainant, and Leonard Hatfielde, the elder, and Katherine, his wife, Leonard Hatfield, the younger, and Jane, his wife, and Thomas Hatfield, deforciants of 2 messuages, 8 cottages, 10 barns, 10 gardens, 10 orchards, 100 acres of land, 30 acres of meadow, 100 acres of pasture, 10 acres of wood, 100 acres of furze and heath, and 40 acres of moor in **Hilderston**.

The deforciants remitted all right to Francis and his heirs, for which Francis gave them £240.

[1] From Notes of Fines.

TRINITY. 9 JAMES I.

At fifteen days from the day of Holy Trinity. 9 James I.

Between Edmund Harington, gentleman, Simon Presse, clerk, Richard Webster, and John Couper, complainants, and John Everard, gentleman, and Bridget, his wife, deforciants of 2 water-mills, a garden, an orchard, 20 acres of land, 30 acres of meadow, and 10 acres of wood in **Whittington.**

John Everard and Bridget remitted all right to the complainants and to the heirs of Edmund, for which the complainants gave them £60.

At three weeks from the day of Holy Trinity. 9 James I.

Between John Digby, gentleman, and John Ridgeley, gentleman, complainants, and Humphrey Thickbrome, gentleman, and Barbara, his wife, deforciants of the manor of **Thickbrome**, and of 8 messuages, a water-mill, 600 acres of land, 50 acres of meadow, 400 acres of pasture, 30 acres of wood, and 200 acres of furze and heath in **Thickbrome** and **Wyford.**

Humphrey and Barbara remitted all right to the complainants and to the heirs of John Digby, for which the complainants gave them £300.

On the Morrow of Holy Trinity. 9 James I.

Between Edmund Noell, gentleman, complainant, and Philip Noell, gentleman, deforciant of 4 messuages, 2 cottages, 2 tofts, a dovecote, 6 gardens, 6 orchards, 20 acres of land, 70 acres of meadow, 600 acres of pasture, 100 acres of wood, 100 acres of furze and heath, 100 acres of marsh, 16*s.* of rent, and common of pasture in **Hilcott** otherwise **Newbolt, Chebsey, Ecclesall, Badnall**, and **Halfeheade.**

Philip remitted all right to Edmund and his heirs, for which Edmund gave him £600.

On the Morrow of Holy Trinity. 9 James I.

Between Sampson Stubbes and Thomas Whiston, complainants, and William Pyott otherwise Greene, deforciant of 2 messuages, a cottage, 3 gardens, 3 orchards, 100 acres of land, 20 acres of meadow, 80 acres of pasture, 5 acres of wood, 100 acres of furze and heath, and common of pasture for all cattle in **Chadull** otherwise **Chadle** and **Parkhall.**

William remitted all right to Sampson and Thomas and to the heirs of Sampson, for which Sampson and Thomas gave him £200.

On the Octaves of Holy Trinity. 9 James I.

Between Joseph Mayne, gentleman, and Edward Penne, gentleman, complainants, and Matthew Bata and Elizabeth, his wife, and William Bradbourn, esquire, deforciants of £11 6*s.* 5*d.* of rent issuing from 20 messuages, 30 tofts, 30 gardens, 30 orchards, 200 acres of land, 40 acres of meadow, 100 acres of pasture, 100 acres of wood, 20 acres of furze and heath, and 20 acres of moor in **Ridware, Hampstall Ridware, Pipe Ridware, Maveson Ridware,** and **Nethertowne.**

The deforciants remitted all right to Joseph and Edward and to the heirs of Joseph, for which Joseph and Edward gave them £226.

On the Morrow of Holy Trinity. 9 James I.

Between Robert Jackson and William Brackley, complainants, and Walter Royle, clerk, and Susan, his wife, and William Royle, son of the said Walter, deforciants of 10 acres of meadow in **Burton on Trent.**

Walter and Susan remitted all right to Robert and William and to the heirs of Robert, for which Robert and William gave them £41.

On the Morrow of Holy Trinity. 9 James I.
Between Thomas Wolseley, armiger, complainant, and Walter Aston, knight, and Gertrude, his wife, deforciants of 2 messuages, a cottage, 3 gardens, 3 orchards, 70 acres of land, 20 acres of meadow, 80 acres of pasture, and 20 acres of wood in **Hickson** otherwise **Hixston, Draynton** otherwise **Dreygnton, Stowe, Colwiche**, and **Lea.**
Walter and Gertrude remitted all right to Thomas and his heirs, for which Thomas gave them £120.

On the Morrow of Holy Trinity. 9 James I.
Between William Hawkes, complainant, and Anthony Bagott, gentleman, and Thomas Arblaster, gentleman, deforciant of 10 acres of meadow, 10 acres of pasture, and 4 acres of wood in **Longdon** and **Bromley Regis.**
Anthony and Thomas remitted all right to William and his heirs, for which William gave them £60.

On the Morrow of Holy Trinity. 9 James I.
Between Thomas Wolseley, armiger, complainant, and Francis Aspinall, gentleman, and Katherine, his wife, and Thomas Aspinall, deforciant of 3 messuages, 3 gardens, 3 orchards, 40 acres of land, 12 acres of meadow, 24 acres of pasture, and common of pasture for all kinds of cattle in **Hickeson** otherwise **Hixston.**
The deforciants remitted all right to Thomas Wolseley and his heirs, for which Thomas Wolseley gave them £41.

On the Morrow of Holy Trinity. 9 James I.
Between Thomas Bowyer, gentleman, and John Bentley, gentleman, complainants, and Walter Rowley, gentleman, John Murrhall, and Thomas Greaves, deforciants of a messuage, 3 cottages, 3 gardens, 25 acres of land, 20 acres of meadow, 30 acres of pasture, 5 acres of wood, and common of turbary in **Heytley, Overheytley**, and **Norton in les Moores** otherwise **Norton on les Moores.**
The deforciants remitted all right to the complainants and to the heirs of Thomas Bowyer, for which the complainants gave them £41.

MICH. 9 JAMES I.

On the Octaves of St. Michael. 9 James I.
Between Thomas Cookes and George Nutshawe, complainants, and John Cookes and Ellen, his wife, Sampson Cookes, and William Cookes, deforciants of a messuage, a garden, an orchard, 12 acres of land, an acre of meadow, 12 acres of pasture, 2 acres of wood, and 20 acres of furze and heath in **Hilderston.**
The deforciants remitted all right to Thomas and George and to the heirs of Thomas, for which Thomas and George gave them £41.

On the Octaves of St. Michael. 9 James I.
Between Henry Agard, gentleman, complainant, and William Belcher, deforciant of a messuage, a cottage, 2 gardens, an orchard, 12 acres of land, 5 acres of meadow, and 7 acres of pasture in **Dunstall** otherwise **Tunstall.**
William remitted all right to Henry and his heirs, for which Henry gave him £41.

On the Octaves of St. Michael. 9 James I.
Between Sylvester Hayes, gentleman, complainant, and John Pyrry,

deforciant of 2 acres of meadow and 12 acres of pasture in **Wolverhampton, Wednesfeild, Willnall,** and **Nechills.**

John remitted all right to Sylvester and his heirs, for which Sylvester gave him £60.

On the Octaves of St. Michael. 9 James I.

Between Hugh Wrottesley, armiger, complainant, and Thomas Burnett, deforciant of a messuage, a cottage, 2 gardens, 2 orchards, 16 acres of land, and an acre of pasture in **Womborne.**

Thomas remitted all right to Hugh and his heirs, for which Hugh gave him £41.

On the Octaves of St. Michael. 9 James I.

Between Thomas Cowper, the younger, complainant, and Henry Flackett, deforciant of a messuage, a garden, an orchard, 28 acres of land, 26 acres of meadow, 38 acres of pasture, 2 acres of wood, 100 acres of furze and heath, and common of pasture for all cattle in **Combridge, Crakemarshe, Rocestor, Checkley,** and **Uttoxeter.**

Henry remitted all right to Thomas and his heirs, for which Thomas gave him £80.

On the Octaves of St. Michael. 9 James I.

Between Gilbert Wakering, knight, and Henry Stone, complainants, and John Hockin and Dorothy, his wife, deforciants of a toft, a garden, 40 acres of land, 20 acres of meadow, and 100 acres of pasture in **Wallsall, Esington,** and **Bushburie.**

John and Dorothy remitted all right to Gilbert and Henry and to the heirs of Henry, for which Gilbert and Henry gave them £100.

At one month from the day of St. Michael. 9 James I.

Between Samuel Westwood, complainant, and Nicholas Paston and Joice, his wife, deforciants of 2 acres of land, 2 acres of meadow, and 7 acres of pasture in **Rowley.**

Nicholas and Joice remitted all right to Samuel and his heirs, for which Samuel gave them £40.

On the Octaves of St. Michael. 9 James I.

Between John Gallymore, complainant, and Francis Stoddart and Alice, his wife, deforciants of a messuage, a garden, an orchard, 6 acres of land, 3 acres of meadow, 20 acres of pasture, and common of pasture in **Draycott.**

Francis and Alice remitted all right to John and his heirs, for which John gave them £41.

On the Octaves of St. Michael. 9 James I.

Between John Garbett, gentleman, complainant, and John Perrye, deforciant of 14 acres of land and 4 acres of meadow in **Wolverhampton, Wednesfeild,** and **Nechills.**

John Perrye remitted all right to John Garbett and his heirs, for which John Garbett gave him £41.

On the Octaves of St. Michael. 9 James I.

Between Edward Hill, Francis Adye, and Richard Archbolde, complainants, and Walter Aston, gentleman, and Joice, his wife, deforciants of a cottage, 10 acres of land, 14 acres of meadow, and 30 acres of pasture in **Longdon.**

Walter and Joice remitted all right to the complainants and to the heirs of Edward for ever, for which the complainants gave them £41.

At one month from the day of St. Michael. 9 James I.

Between Godfrey Needham and Robert Bill, complainants, and Richard Bill and Elizabeth, his wife, deforciants of a messuage, 3 cottages, 4 gardens, 4 orchards, 22 acres of land, 10 acres of meadow, 20 acres of pasture, 20 acres of furze and heath, and common of pasture for all kinds of cattle in **Farley**.

Richard and Elizabeth remitted all right to Godfrey and Robert and to the heirs of Godfrey for ever, for which Godfrey and Robert gave them £60.

On the Octaves of St. Michael. 9 James I.

Between John Hood, complainant, and Thomas Vall and Anne, his wife, deforciants of a messuage, a garden, an orchard, 60 acres of land, 8 acres of meadow, 20 acres of pasture, and common of pasture for all cattle in **Ricardescote, Burton**, and **Forbridge.**

Thomas and Anne remitted all right to John and his heirs, and covenanted that they would warrant the said tenements against the heirs of Robert Vall, deceased, father of the said Thomas, and against the heirs of Thomas Vall, deceased, grandfather of the said Thomas, for which John gave them £80.

On the Octaves of St. Michael. 9 James I.

Between Michael Heynes, complainant, and Walter Leveson, knight, deforciant of 3 acres of land and 2 acres of meadow in **Wolverhampton.**

Walter remitted all right to Michael and his heirs, for which Michael gave him £41.

On the Octaves of St. Michael. 9 James I.

Between Walter Aston, gentleman, and William Orme, complainants, and Edward Hill and Margery, his wife, deforciants of 4 acres of meadow in **Longdon.**

Edward and Margery remitted all right to Walter and William and to the heirs of William, for which Walter and William gave them £41.

On the Octaves of St. Michael. 9 James I.

Between Simon Gresley, armiger, and Edward Broughton, armiger, complainants, and Thomas Wolseley, armiger, and Ellen, his wife, deforciants of 5 messuages, 4 cottages, 9 gardens, 400 acres of land, 80 acres of meadow, 200 acres of pasture, and 10 acres of wood in **Hickston** otherwise **Huckston** otherwise **Hyckson, Uttoxator, Little Bromshulfe** otherwise **Bromshill,** and **Loxley.**

Thomas and Ellen remitted all right to Simon and Edward and to the heirs of Simon for ever, for which Simon and Edward gave them £300.

On the Octaves of St. Michael. 9 James I.

Between John Garbett, gentleman, complainant, and John Pyrry, deforciant of a messuage, a barn, a stable, a garden, an orchard, 6 acres of land, an acre of meadow, 10 acres of pasture, and common of pasture for all cattle in **Wolverhampton, Wednesfeild,** and **Nechills.**

John Pyrry remitted all right to John Garbett and his heirs, for which John Garbett gave him £41.

On the Octaves of St. Michael. 9 James I.

Between William Orme, complainant, and Walter Aston, gentleman, and Joice, his wife, deforciants of a messuage, 2 barns, a garden, an orchard, 20 acres of land, 20 acres of meadow, 40 acres of pasture, 20 acres of furze and heath, an acre of land covered with water, and common of pasture for all kinds of cattle in **Longdon.**

Walter and Joice remitted all right to William and his heirs, and covenanted that they would warrant the said tenements against the heirs of Walter Aston, knight, for which William gave them £60.

On the Octaves of St. Michael. 9 James I.

Between Zacharias Taylor, complainant, and Edward Underhill and Mary, his wife, deforciants of a moiety of 2 acres of land and 12 acres of pasture in **Shenston** and **Foderley**.

Edward and Mary remitted all right to Zacharias and his heirs, for which Zacharias gave them £40.

On the Octaves of St. Michael. 9 James I.

Between Thomas Browne and William Knight, complainants, and Thomas Wright and Katherine, his wife, deforciants of a messuage, a garden, an orchard, 20 acres of land, 5 acres of meadow, 13 acres of pasture, 2 acres of wood, and 20 acres of furze and heath in **Longton, Fenton, Culvert** otherwise **Culwart, Meyre,** and **Meyr Lane Ende**.

Thomas Wright and Katherine remitted all right to Thomas Browne and William and to the heirs of Thomas Browne for ever, for which Thomas Browne and William gave them £60.

On the Octaves of St. Michael. 9 James I.

Between John Colclughe, complainant, and William Pyott otherwise Greene and Henry Pyott otherwise Greene, deforciants of 4 acres of meadow in **Chedle**, and of a moiety of 4 acres of pasture in **Chedle**.

William and Henry remitted all right to John and his heirs, for which John gave them £40.

On the Octaves of St. Michael. 9 James I.

Between Thomas Bagnald, complainant, and Thomas Cowper, the younger, and Thomas Cowper, the elder, and Margaret, his wife, deforciants of a messuage, a garden, an orchard, 20 acres of land, 10 acres of meadow, 20 acres of pasture, 2 acres of wood, 40 acres of furze and heath, and common of pasture for all kinds of cattle in **Butterton**.

The deforciants remitted all right to Thomas Bagnald and his heirs, for which Thomas Bagnald gave them £41.

At one month from the day of St. Michael. 9 James I.

Between Thomas Sprott, complainant, and Thomas Arblaster, armiger, deforciant of 10 acres of land, 30 acres of meadow, 30 acres of pasture, 2 acres of wood, and 10 acres of moor in **Longdon** and **Elmehurst**.

Thomas Arblaster remitted all right to Thomas Sprott and his heirs, for which Thomas Sprott gave him £60.

On the Octaves of St. Michael. 9 James I.

Between William Hodgetts and Richard Jevon, the younger, complainants, and John Marshe, gentleman, deforciant of 22 acres of land and 2 acres of meadow in **Sedgeley**.

John remitted all right to William and Richard and to the heirs of Richard for ever, for which William and Richard gave him £40.

On the Octaves of St. Michael. 9 James I.

Between John Birche, the younger, complainant, and John Hawkes and Anne, his wife, deforciants of 2 acres of meadow and 50 acres of pasture in **Shelfielde** and **Walsall**.

John Hawkes and Anne remitted all right to John Birche and his heirs, for which John Birche gave them £60.

On the Octaves of St. Michael. 9 James I.

Between Jerome Bowes, knight, and John Bowes, gentleman, complainants, and Walter Heveningham, armiger, deforciant of the manors of **Aston near Stone, Pype, Haunton,** and **Clifton**, with the appurtenances, and of 20 messuages, 20 cottages, 40 gardens, 40 orchards, 100 acres of land,

60 acres of meadow, 100 acres of pasture, 100 acres of furze and heath, 20 acres of wood, 10 acres of moor, and common of pasture for all kinds of cattle in **Aston near Stone, Walton, Burston** otherwise **Burweston, Stoke Stone, Fulford, Sandon, Hardwicke, Pype, Haunton,** and **Clifton**; and of free warren in **Clifton**, and also of the advowson of the church of **Clifton.**

Walter remitted all right to Jerome and John and to the heirs of Jerome for ever, for which Jerome and John gave him £320.

On the Octaves of St. Michael. 9 James I.

Between Anthony Tunsteed, gentleman, and John Chetwind, gentleman, complainants, and Thomas Wolseley, armiger, and Ellen, his wife, deforciants of 16 messuages, 10 cottages, 200 acres of land, 20 acres of meadow, 100 acres of pasture, 4 acres of wood, 10 acres of furze and heath, 10 acres of moor, and of the third part of a messuage, 10 acres of land, 3 acres of meadow, and 10 acres of pasture in **Ridgley, Brereton, Armitage, Hansacre, Longdon,** and **Little Heywood.**

Thomas and Ellen remitted all right to Anthony and John and to the heirs of Anthony for ever, for which Anthony and John gave them £200.

On the Octaves of St. Michael. 9 James I.

Between Edward Stanford, armiger, complainant, and William Rowley and Alice, his wife, deforciants of a cottage, a garden, 30 acres of land, and 6 acres of moor in **Purye Barre** otherwise **Perrie Barre.**

William and Alice remitted all right to Edward and his heirs, for which Edward gave them £41.

On the Octaves of St. Michael. 9 James I.

Between William Turner, the younger, complainant, and John Gill and Elizabeth, his wife, and Ralph Gill and Grace, his wife, deforciants of 27 acres of land, 26 acres of pasture, and 60 acres of furze and heath in **Fosbrooke** otherwise **Forsbrooke** and **Dillerne.**

The deforciants remitted all right to William and his heirs, for which William gave them £41.

On the Octaves of St. Michael. 9 James I.

Between Robert Whitgreve, armiger, and Humphrey Whitgreve, gentleman, complainants, and Philip Wolrich and Anne, his wife, deforciants of 16 acres of meadow and 26 acres of pasture in **Chebsey.**

Philip and Anne remitted all right to Robert and Humphrey and to the heirs of Robert for ever, for which Robert and Humphrey gave them £41.

On the Octaves of St. Michael. 9 James I.

Between George Kempe, complainant, and Edmund Godwyn and Joan, his wife, and John Godwyn, deforciants of 2 cottages, 2 gardens, 2 orchards, 3 acres of land, 6 acres of pasture, 10 acres of furze and heath, and common of pasture for all kinds of cattle in **Bromley Pagettes** and **Bromley Hurst.**

The deforciants remitted all right to George and his heirs, for which George gave them £41.

On the Octaves of St. Michael. 9 James I.

Between John Boylston and Elizabeth, his wife, complainants, and John Alcocke, deforciant of 10 acres of land, 16 acres of meadow, 32 acres of pasture, and common of pasture for all kinds of cattle in **Faulde** and **Cotton.**

John Alcocke acknowledged the said tenements to be the right of John Boylston, for which John Boylston and Elizabeth granted them to John Alcocke; to be held by him from the Feast of St. Michael the Archangel last past for 80 years, rendering yearly to the said John Boylston and Elizabeth and to the heirs of John one grain of pepper if it be demanded.

On the Morrow of St. Martin. 9 James I.

Between John Chetwind, armiger, and John Smythe, gentleman, complainants, and Walter Aston, knight and baronet, and Gertrude, his wife, deforciants of the manor of **Hulton**, with the appurtenances, and of 18 messuages, a water-mill, a dovecote, 18 gardens, 500 acres of land, 200 acres of meadow, 400 acres of pasture, 400 acres of wood, 500 acres of furze and heath, 100 acres of moor, 10 acres of land covered with water, 8*s.* of rent, and common of pasture for all kinds of cattle, and of the view of frankpledge in **Hulton, Sneyde, Mylton, Bucknall, Baddiley, Burdeslam** otherwise **Burslam, Uveley, Stoke,** and **Newcastle under Lyme.**

Walter and Gertrude remitted all right to the complainants and to the heirs of John Chetwind, for which the complainants gave them £500.

On the Octaves of St. Michael. 9 James I.

Between Robert Roper and Anthony Clarke, complainants, and Elizabeth Moleford, widow, and Richard Brodrepp, armiger, and Mary, his wife, deforciants of 16 messuages, 16 barns, 5 tofts, 16 gardens, 16 orchards, 260 acres of land, 76 acres of meadow, 690 acres of pasture, 20 acres of wood, 20 acres of furze and heath, and common of pasture for all kinds of cattle in **Lee** otherwise **Ley, Dodsley, Withington, Nobold, Foale, Checkeley banke, Middleton greene,** and **Field.**

The deforciants remitted all right to Robert and Anthony and to the heirs of Robert, for which Robert and Anthony gave them £500.

On the Octaves of St. Michael. 9 James I.

Between William Willaston, armiger, complainant, and Robert Harecourte, armiger, deforciant of the manors of **Ellenhall** otherwise **Elnhale** otherwise **Elnall,** and **Ronton,** with the appurtenances, and of the site of the late monastery of **Ronton**; and also of 30 messuages, 10 tofts, 30 gardens, 20 orchards, 1,600 acres of land, 300 acres of meadow, 1,000 acres of pasture, 200 acres of wood, 700 acres of furze and heath, 50 acres of moor, 100 acres of fresh marsh, 20*s.* of rent, common of pasture, and view of frankpledge in **Ellenhall** otherwise **Elnhale, Ronton, Seithteford, Hethehowse grange, Gnosshall, Great Britchford, Little Britchford** otherwise **Brunchford, Wootton, Walton, Lotford,** and **Knightley**; and of the rectory of **Ellenhall** otherwise **Elnhale.**

Robert remitted all right to William and his heirs, for which William gave him £1,600.

On the Octaves of St. Michael. 9 James I.

Between Thomas Cowper, the younger, complainant, and Thomas Flackett and Elizabeth, his wife, deforciants of a messuage, 3 cottages, 3 gardens, 3 orchards, 24 acres of land, 27 acres of meadow, 36 acres of pasture, 3 acres of wood, 100 acres of furze and heath, and common of pasture for all kinds of cattle in **Combridge, Crakemarshe, Rocester, Checkley,** and **Uttoxeter.**

Thomas Flackett and Elizabeth granted the said tenements to Thomas Cowper; to be held by him for the lives of the said Thomas Flackett and Elizabeth and the life of the longest liver of them, for which Thomas Cowper gave them £80.

On the Morrow of St. Martin. 9 James I.

Between Edward Stanford, armiger, and William Stanley, armiger, complainants, and Walter Leveson, knight, and Anne, his wife, and Thomas Leveson, armiger, deforciants of the manors of **Ashemores, Heathe, Shareshull, Great Saredon, Little Saredon, Coven, Brinsford, Seawall, Wobaston** otherwise **Wybaston, Willenhall, Hilton, Hatherton, Moumore,** and **Fether-**

ston, with the appurtenances, and of 100 messuages, 7 water-mills, a windmill, 2 dovecotes, 2,000 acres of land, 500 acres of meadow, 2,000 acres of pasture, 1,000 acres of wood, 2,000 acres of furze and heath, 500 acres of moor, and £10 of rent in **Wolverhampton, Ashemores, Heathe, Wednesfeild, Shareshull, Great Saredon, Little Saredon, Coven, Brinsford, Seawall, Wobaston** otherwise **Wybaston, Willenhall, Hilton, Hatherton, Monmore, Fetherston, Bradley, Cannocke, Overpenne, Netherpenne, Michall, Coton, Gouldthorne, Bushburye, Prestwood,** and **Poolehayles** ; and of the **Hay** of **Chistlyn**, within the forest of **Cannock**, and of free warren in the same **Hay** ; and of the rectory of **Overpenne** ; and also of all kinds of tithes, oblations, and obventions whatsoever in **Wolverhampton, Ashemores, Heathe, Wednesfeild, Wobaston** otherwise **Wybaston, Willen Hall, Hilton, Hatherton, Moumore, Fetherston, Pelshall, Bradley, Bilston, Tunstall,** and **Coton** ; and of the advowson of the vicarage of the church of **Overpenne**.

The deforciants remitted all right to Edward and William and to the heirs of Edward for ever, for which Edward and William gave them £1,600.

Hillary. 9 James I.

On the Octaves of St. Hillary. 9 James I.

Between Walter Leveson, knight, complainant, and Edward, Lord Duddeley, deforciant of a messuage, a garden, 100 acres of land, 100 acres of meadow, 200 acres of pasture, 100 acres of furze and heath, and 40 acres of moor in **Sedgeley** ; and also of all tithes of sheaves of grain and hay in **Sedgeley**.

Edward, Lord Duddeley, remitted all right to Walter and his heirs, and covenanted that he would warrant the said tenements against the heirs of Edward, Lord Duddeley, deceased, father of the said Edward, for which Walter gave him £240.

On the Octaves of St. Hillary. 9 James I.

Between John Bowman, plaintiff, and John Olliver and Ellen, his wife, William Olliver, and Lawrence Jackson, deforciants of 6 acres of land, 5 acres of meadow, 4 acres of pasture, and common of pasture for all kinds of cattle in **Austonefeilde**.

The deforciants remitted all right to John Bowman and his heirs, for which John Bowman gave them £41.

On the Octaves of St. Hillary. 9 James I.

Between Thomas Allatt, complainant, and Humphrey Harecourt, armiger, and Bridget, his wife, deforciants of 3 messuages, 3 gardens, 3 orchards, 200 acres of land, 24 acres of meadow, and 20 acres of pasture in **Mylnemeese**.

Humphrey and Bridget remitted all right to Thomas and his heirs, for which Thomas gave them £120.

On the Octaves of St. Hillary. 9 James I.

Between Thomas Clemson, complainant, and John Crosswey and Richard Crosswey, son of the said John, and Anne, his wife, deforciants of 5 acres of pasture in **Enfeld**.

The deforciants remitted all right to Thomas and his heirs, for which Thomas gave them £40.

On the Octaves of St. Hillary. 9 James I.

Between John Wilson, the younger, complainant, and John Wilson, the elder, and Joan, his wife, deforciants of a messuage, 2 gardens, 2 orchards, and 2 acres of land in **Stafford**.

John Wilson, the elder, and Joan remitted all right to John Wilson, the younger, and his heirs, for which John Wilson, the younger, gave them £41.

On the Octaves of St. Hillary. 9 James I.

Between William Horton, complainant, and Robert Kilvart and Elizabeth, his wife, deforciants of a messuage, a garden, an orchard, 200 acres of land, 40 acres of meadow, 4 acres of pasture, 10 acres of wood, and 100 acres of furze and heath in **Shredicott** and **Bradley**.

Robert and Elizabeth granted the said tenements to William, and whatsoever they had therein for the term of the said Elizabeth's life; to be held by the said William for the said Elizabeth's life, for which William gave them £160.

On the Octaves of the Purification of the Blessed Mary. 9 James I.

Between Robert Barkeley, armiger, complainant, and Francis Lacon knight, deforciant of the manor of **Hopton**, with the appurtenances, and of 18 messuages 5 cottages, 600 acres of land, 200 acres of meadow, 800 acres of pasture, 200 acres of wood, 500 acres of furze and heath, and 20*s.* of rent in **Hopton**.

Francis remitted all right to Robert and his heirs, for which Robert gave him £500.

On the Morrow of the Purification of the Blessed Mary. 9 James I.

Between John Persehowse, gentleman, and Humphrey Tudman, complainants, and Rowland Tudman and Alice, his wife, deforciants of a messuage, a barn, a garden, 5 acres of land, and 50 acres of pasture in **Sedgeley** and **Colseley**.

Rowland and Alice remitted all right to John and Humphrey and to the heirs of Humphrey, for which John and Humphrey gave them £41.

On the Octaves of St. Hillary. 9 James I.

Between William, Lord Pagett, complainant, and Edward Littleton, knight, deforciant of a messuage, 20 acres of land, 4 acres of meadow, and 10 acres of pasture in **Cannock** and **Longdon**.

Edward remitted all right to William, Lord Pagett, and his heirs, for which William gave him £41.

On the Octaves of St. Hillary. 9 James I.

Between Edward Sherwood, the elder, and Edward Sherwood, the younger, complainants, and Griffin Baker and Edward Baker, deforciants of a messuage, 2 cottages, 2 barns, and 2 gardens in **Dorlaston**.

The deforciants remitted all right to the complainants and to the heirs of Edward Sherwood, the elder, for which the complainants gave them £40.

On the Octaves of St. Hillary. 9 James I.

Between Richard Newton, complainant, and Francis Motteram and Margery, his wife, deforciants of 10 acres of land, 4 acres of meadow, and 6 acres of pasture in **Willeslock** and **Utoxetur**.

Francis and Margery remitted all right to Richard and his heirs, for which Richard gave them £60.

On the Octaves of St. Hillary. 9 James I.

Between Anthony Kynnersley, armiger, complainant, and Thomas Cowop and Richard Cowop, deforciants of 2 messuages, 2 gardens, 2 orchards, 40 acres of land, 40 acres of meadow, 40 acres of pasture, and common of pasture for all kinds of cattle in **Leigh**, and of a free fishery in the water of **Blithe**.

Thomas and Richard remitted all right to Anthony and his heirs, for which Anthony gave them £120.

On the Octaves of St. Hillary. 9 James I.

Between Francis Trentham, armiger, complainant, and Anthony Kynnersley, armiger, and Francis Kynnersley, gentleman, son and heir apparent of the said Anthony, deforciants of 2 messuages, a toft, 2 gardens, 2 orchards,

30 acres of land, 20 acres of meadow, 130 acres of pasture, 20 acres of wood, and common of pasture for all kinds of cattle in **Hanbury, Marchington** and **Marchington Woodland**.

Anthony and Francis Kynnersley remitted all right to Francis Trentham and his heirs, for which Francis Trentham gave them £100.

On the Octaves of St. Hillary. 9 James I.

Between Michael Moseley, gentleman, complainant, and Francis Whorwood, gentleman, and Jane, his wife, deforciants of a messuage, a cottage, a water-mill, 2 barns, 2 gardens, 2 orchards, 10 acres of land, 8 acres of meadow, 14 acres of pasture, 2 acres of wood, and 2 acres of land covered with water in **Luttley**.

Francis and Jane remitted all right to Michael and his heirs, for which Michael gave them £41.

On the Octaves of St. Hillary. 9 James I.

Between John Persehowse, gentleman, and Mary, his wife, complainants, and Robert Willymott, Richard Alporte and Elizabeth, his wife, Thomas Poyser and Katherine, his wife, and William Alporte, deforciants of 24 acres of pasture in **Walsall**.

The deforciants remitted all right to John and Mary and to the heirs of John, for which John and Mary gave them £41.

ADDITIONS

TO

THE HISTORY OF THE SWYNNERTONS,

PRINTED IN VOL. VII,

"STAFFORDSHIRE COLLECTIONS,"

BY

THE REV. CHARLES SWYNNERTON, F.S.A.

THE EARLIER SWYNNERTONS OF ECCLESHALL.

ARMS.—*Argent*, a cross formee flory *sable*, over all a bend *gules*.
(College of Arms.)

THE common ancestor of the Swynnertons of Eccleshall, of both the earlier and the later houses, and in short of all the Swynnertons of succeeding ages, was JOHN DE PARVA SUGENILLA (Little Sugnall), living in the reigns of Richard I and King John.

His real patronymic was "Swynnerton." A generation before it would have been "Fitz-Aelen" (Alan).

His wife was Petronilla de Derueslawe (Dorslow), co-heiress of Dorslow hard by Little Sugnall, and she was the mother of John, his heir.

Reasons for these statements will be given early in the following pages, from which it will be seen that the estate of Little Sugnall, however acquired, and that that of Dorslow, remained with his direct descendants during the whole of the thirteenth century and beyond.

In the Chartulary of Stone Priory near Eccleshall are preserved numerous charters of Robert de Magna Sugnall, and Petronilla his wife, who was one of the three daughters of Engenulf de Gresley and Alina his wife, the lady of Darlaston.[1] No fewer than ten of these charters of King John's time are witnessed by a tenant in Eccleshall named "John de Suinnerton," while twelve of them bear the witness of "Robert de Suinnerton," who was at that period the lord of Swynnerton. The name of the latter, however, stands frequently first on the list, while John's comes near the end, showing that he was only a cadet. That he was of the whole blood and nearly related to Robert cannot be doubted, because it was only in that very generation that the Swynnertons had begun to discard the patronymic "fitz-Alan" in its various forms, and to adopt the manorial cognomen "de Swynnerton."[2]

[1] See Chartulary in "Staff. Coll.," VI, I, 1-28.
[2] So Eyton. See "Staff. Coll.," II, 251.

Nothwithstanding the relative positions of their names, however, on the attestation clauses of the Priory deeds, the probability is that they were brothers. Their surnames are identical, though their holdings are different, and that circumstance, at that early date, constitutes strong evidence in itself. Nor was it necessary, or even usual, that the name of a younger brother should follow immediately after the name of his eldest brother in an attesting clause, of which fact we have another example in this very Chartulary, where in a deed of A. de Bellocampo, once wife of William Malbanc, the names of William Panton and Norman Panton, the two younger sons of Ivo Panton, Baron of Wem (*ob.* 1175–6), by his second wife Alice, daughter of Norman de Verdon, are separated by the intervening names of Robert fitz Pagan and Ivo de Walton.[1] It is true John de Swynnerton's son John will have married his cousin-germain Margery (v. *postea*), but such breach of canonical rule (if it was a breach, the law of God not forbidding it) was common enough in those times, when Dispensations were often issued by the Ordinaries, as representing the Pope, on the usual conditions. That Robert and John were also related closely either to the Gresleys or the Sugnalls their frequent attestation of these deeds sufficiently declares.[2]

But it is a singular fact that, when we leave the charters of the monks of Stone, and turn to the *Curia Regis* Rolls of King John, we do not discover in them the name of John de *Suinnerton* linked with that of Robert de Sugnall, as in the charters. What we do find, however, associated with Robert de Sugnall's name is that of John de *Sugnall.* Instead of Robert de Sugnall and John de *Suinnerton*, we have Robert de Sugnall and John de *Sugnall.* The truth is, the two Sugnalls lay side by side, their boundaries were co-terminous, and litigation between the two tenants was to be expected. It is in John de Sugnall, then, of the Rolls that I detect John de Suinnerton of the Stone Chartulary.

The Pleas of the Crown for the first year of the reign of King John, heard at Lichfield on the 29th September (1199), shew that an Assize assembled to enquire if Wimer the father of Reginald had been seised in his demesne, as of fee, of half a virgate of land with appurtenances in Derueslawe (Dorslow) on the day of his

[1] "Staff. Coll.," VI, Part I, p. 19.

[2] Robert and John de Swynnerton attest deeds of both Petronilla and her sister Dionisia. I am of opinion that Petronilla's first husband, of kin to herself, and father of her son *Johannes Bastardus*, was probably one connecting link.

death, which land is held by John de Suggenilla and Petronilla his wife, who say that the said Petronilla has a certain elder sister who holds a moiety of the said half-virgate of land, and that they themselves hold the other moiety. And Reginald says that on the day of view they themselves held the whole of the aforesaid half-virgate, and that afterwards they demised the said moiety to the sister of the said Petronilla.

The suit was finally concorded on the 4th October in the same year, when John, Petronilla, and *Margaret* acknowledged the land to be the right of Reginald, to be held by him and his heirs of them and their heirs by the service of 16*d.* yearly.[1]

The suit proves that John de Sugnall had entry into this Dorslow land only in right of his wife Petronilla, and it shows too that Reginald was arrière tenant under Petronilla and Margaret.

(Petronilla de Derneslawe (Dorslow) may have been a daughter of Gamel de Deureslawe who in 35 Hen. II (1188–1189) was fined half a mark for default of appearance of one Suanilda, for whom he had gone bail;[2] and the grand-daughter of Gamel who witnessed a deed of Ernald fitz-Odo to the monks of Stone in 1136;[3] and the great-grand-daughter of Gamel who was slain by Liulf de Audley before 31 Hen. I (1129–1130), for which the said Liulf incurred the enormous fine of 200 marks, 10 deer-hounds, and 10 hawks.[4] In 31 Hen. I (1129–30) a tenant of Gamel fitz-Griffin owes 40*s.*, a fine incurred in a suit of treasure-trove.[5] It is more likely, however, that Gamel de Dorslow was arrière tenant.)

Here is another suit. On the Assize Roll of 5 John (1203) four knights, Walter de Witefield, John Sautcheverell, Ralf de Blore, and Ralf de Knutton, are summoned to make recognition between Robert de Suggenhull and John de Suggenhull concerning three virgates of land with appurtenances in Suggenhull, whereupon the said John de Suggenhull puts himself on the Great Assize of the Lord the King for an inquest as to which of the two has the greater right in that land. The Final Concord is not extant, a separate entry merely showing that John de Suggenhille, in order to have it, fined half a mark by the pledge of Osbert de Witindon, the Bishop's seneschal.[6] Here the case closes. The piece of land

[1] *Curia Regis* Rolls, 1 John, Record Office.
[2] "Staff. Coll.," Vol. I, pp. 136, 138.
[3] *Ibid.*, Vol. VI, Part I, p. 23.
[4] *Ibid.*, Vol. I, p. 3.
[5] *Ibid.*, Vol. I, pp. 3–10.
[6] Assize Roll, 5 John, *ibid.*

in dispute was claimed probably by Robert de Sugnall as a portion of Magna Sugnall, as on the occasion of a similar dispute, perhaps over the same land, in the reign of Edward I. (See *postea.*)

John de Sugnall of the Rolls, if thus identical with "John de Suinnerton" of the Stone charters[1] (as we shall show also from other evidence presently), must have lived through the reign of King John, as he continues to be a witness in the priory Chartulary up to about the year 1216, if not beyond. I suppose him to have died about 1220, and to have been succeeded by a son "JOHN DE PARVA SUGGINHILLE" (II), who in 12 Hen. III (1227) was the defendant in a suit about a tenement in Parva Sugnall.[2] He it was who must have married Margery, the lady of Swynnerton, sister and heir of Sir Robert de Swynnerton, who died about 1245. She was his cousin, and he obtained with her the manor of Swynnerton, which he transmitted.

That John de Swynnerton, the husband of Margery, came from Eccleshall is proved by the fact that he was a tenant there, for he was the lord of Peshal. And that he was a Swynnerton by blood may be proved, at this stage, in two ways:—

(1.) By the fact that his grandson Roger succeeded to Swynnerton in 1284 as one of the heirs male to the exclusion of nearer heirs in the female line. Roger de Swynnerton did not descend from Margery at all, but from a former match of John, Margery's husband.[3]

(2.) By the testimony of arms. This is a class of evidence which is too much neglected, yet it is safe to say that in tracing the history of families in the thirteenth and fourteenth centuries, it is of the highest importance. John, the husband of Margery de Swynnerton, could never have passed on the Swynnerton arms to a son by a former wife unless he had been himself a Swynnerton. Yet this is precisely what he did. His son Richard de Peshal, and his descendants, bore the Swynnerton arms pure and simple, differenced merely by an escutcheon or canton.[4] And that Richard was by a former wife and

[1] *John de Suinerton* occurs as chief witness after Hugh Waite in a deed of Cecilia de Freford (? Bereford), daughter of Roger Waite of Rickerscote (*viv.* 1166), which could not have passed later than 1190, and which may have passed earlier. ("Staff. Coll.," Vol. VII, Part I, p. 7.)

[2] "Staff. Coll.," Vol. IV, p. 37.

[3] *Ibid.*, Vol. VII, Part I, pp. 12, 13.

[4] Heralds' Visitations.

not by Margery, the last representative of the right line of the Norman lords of Swynnerton, is proved by the fact that neither he nor his son succeeded to Swynnerton on the death of Sir John de Swynnerton, Margery's only surviving son, without issue, in 1284.[1]

John de Swynnerton of Parva Sugnall, of Dorslow, of Peshal, and lastly (on his marriage with Margery), of Swynnerton, had been married, as we have stated, to a former wife. Who was she? A pedigree of the Peshals, in Burke's "Royal Descents," gives her name as Eleanor, and says that she was the sister and heir of Robert the son of Stephen de Peshal in Eccleshall, and with this the evidence available certainly agrees, for John named one of his sons Stephen and another Robert. The history of Peshal, then a divided manor, is also in accord. Thus Chetwynd, the Staffordshire historian, says: "that the whole of Peshall not pertaining to Thomas de Peshall and his sister Dorea,[2] together with the *royalty*, was purchased by Sir John de Swynnerton, knight, of Robert son of Stephen de Peshall, who sold him all his own lands there, and all too that he had purchased of Thomas son of Thomas de Peshall aforesaid, together with all rents, homages, &c., &c., all which were by Sir John given to a younger son, Richard, who seating himself here assumed the name (of Peshall), and was progenitor of that family, which in succeeding ages rose to very great eminence and esteem in this and neighbouring counties."[3]

Erdeswick, writing in 1600, gives the actual deed, thus:—

"*Ego Robertus filius Stephani de Peshale dedi &c. domino Johanni de Swinerton totam terram meam in Peshale cum domibus redditibus servitiis homagiis wardis releviis et escaetis et totam terram quam emi de Thome filio Thome de Peshale*"—(and then the

[1] Staff. Coll.," Vol. VII, part I, p. 12.

[2] Observe—

8 Ed. I.—*Thomas de Peshale* sued William de *Sogenhulle* and Dora his wife for a debt of £100.

9 Ed. I.—*Thomas de Goldene* sued William de *Sogenhulle* and Doreya his wife for a debt of £100.

("Staff. Coll.," Vol. VI, p. 105, and Vol. VI, p. 120.)

This Thomas was Thomas son of Thomas de Peshale. (*Ibid.*, p. 132.)

11 Ed. I, Mich., *Staff.*, Roger bishop of C. and L. has licence of concord with William de *Peshale* and Doreia his wife in a plea of warranty of charter. (Vol. VI, p. 131.)

Here Thomas de Peshale and Thomas de Goldene are identical, and so are William de Sogenhulle and William de Peshale.

[3] From the Chetwynd MSS. *penes* the Earl of Shrewsbury.

testes to the deed)—"*Sir Robert de Knightley, Sir Rob. de Bromley, Sir Philip de Mutton, Reg. de Charnes, Thos de Titnesoure, Ivo de eadem, Robto de Joneston et aliis.*"[1]

Lastly, Sir John de Swynnerton's arms, as given in the College of Arms, was the Swynnerton cross flory, surmounted by a shield of pretence for Peshal.

John de Swynnerton had other sons by his first wife besides Richard de Peshal, namely:—

1. "John de Suggenhull" (III). It was in accordance with a fixed rule in the family, as in many other feudal families, that in all senior branches the eldest son should be named after his father. It was so among the Norman lords of Swynnerton, among the Swynnerton lords of the later line, among the Swynnertons of Isewall, and those of Hilton, just as in the junior branches, the Swynnertons of Whitmore and of Butterton, the heir was invariably named after the grandfather. John de Suggenhull then was the eldest, and his father must have given him Parva Sugnall during his lifetime, probably after marrying his second wife. John married Alditha, daughter and co-heiress of Adam de Bures, but he must have died comparatively early without issue, as Parva Sugnall seems to have gone to a younger brother, Robert.—

   On the 27th January, 1248, there was a final concord at Lichfield between Felicia, daughter of Adam de Bures, Thomas de Chatkulum and Sarra his wife, Richard de Boys and Basilia his wife, Nicholas de Chatkulum and Avice his wife, *John de Suggenhull* and *Alditha* his wife, on the one side, and Vivian de Standon on the other, concerning twelve acres of land in Standon. Vivian acknowledged the land to be the right of Felicia, Sarra, Basilia, Avice, and Alditha, forever. ("Staff. Coll.")

[1] Erdeswick's MSS., British Museum, p. 26. The whole of the persons who figure in this deed can be shown from the Plea Rolls to have been living early in Henry III, and the authenticity of the deed cannot be questioned. It is also worthy of note that Thomas de Peshall is sometimes named in the Plea Rolls "Thomas de Golden." Compare "Ormus de Gulden" of Erdeswick, the grandfather of Alina, who in a deed quoted in Ward's "Stoke-upon-Trent" styles herself "Lady of Darlaston."

2. "Robert de Swynnerton." A comparison of the following extracts forms my reasons for thinking that he succeeded John de Parva Sugnall III, and, at the same time, completes the foregoing argument of origin and descent:—

(*a*.) In 1266 Robert de *Suggenhull* and Thomas de Pessale were admitted to the King's peace by the Sheriff through the Bishop of Coventry and Leichfield, as having made their submission after the rebellion of Simon de Montfort.[1]

(*b*.) About 1270 "Robto de *Sugenhull*" is a name attached to an original deed at Charnes, together with "Thom̄. de Derneslowe" and "Stepho de Slyndon." [By Suggenhull we must understand Parva Sugnall, as Magna Sugnall was then held by Stephen de Swynnerton in right of his wife Joan, daughter and heir of Roger de Waure, who had acquired it from Robert de Magna Sugnall of King John's time.]

(*c*.) In 1272, 56 Hen. III, Robert de *Swynnerton* had a dispute with Richard de Whytefeld (of Eccleshall) in the manor-court of Swynnerton, and received from him a wound from a knife, whereupon he killed his assailant, and fleeing for sanctuary to Swynnerton Church he acknowledged the deed before the coroner, and abjured the kingdom. It was subsequently shown, however, that he had died from his wound.[2] This was in 1272. His estate must have passed into the hands of the Sheriff for a year and a day, and in 1274, 3 Ed. I, "John de *Parva Sogenhulle*" (IV) witnesses a deed now in original at Charnes, as well as other deeds ranging from 1272 to 1309, in some of which he appears as "John de Sugenhull" simply.[3]

(*d*.) In 8 Ed. I (1279), August 24th, an assize was held to decide if John de *Parva Sugenhull*, Cecilia his mother,[4] and others named, had unjustly disseised

[1] "Staff. Coll.," Vol. VIII, p. 118.

[2] *Ibid.*, Vol. IV, p. 212.

[3] Deeds at Charnes *penes* the Rev. G. Vernon Yonge.

[4] This Cecilia was a daughter of John lord of Charnes, and sister of Reginald his son and successor. She was sister also to Juliana (occurring 1271), who married Roger de Broughton *alias* de Napton, also an Eccleshall tenant. (From an

Nicholas son of Simon de Aspelegh and Avice his wife of an acre of land in Great Sugnall. John answered for all the defendants, and stated that the land in question was in *Little Sugnall* and not in Great Sugnall, and if it was decided that the land was in Great Sugnall, he added that ROBERT *his father* had died seised of it.[1]

(*e.*) In 1292, 21 Ed. I, some unknown malefactors broke open the mill of Staundon, and killed Roger de Dereslowe (Dorslow), and fled. Hue and cry of the men of Eccleshall being raised, one of the malefactors, Robert le Porcher, fleeing the King's peace, was beheaded. Philip, son of Hamon, the finder, is not suspected, but, not appearing, is attached by two Eccleshall tenants, JOHN SON OF ROBERT DE SWYNNERTON and Robert Overy of Walford.[2]

There was no John son of Robert de *Swynnerton*, then a tenant in Eccleshall, or anywhere else, unless he was John son of Robert de *Parva Sugnall*. That the father's name is mentioned so long after his death was in accordance with a prevailing custom, serving in this case to distinguish John son of Robert de Swynnerton of Parva Sugnall from John son of Stephen de Swynnerton of Magna Sugnall. It was fitting too that the finder should be attached by John de Swynnerton, for Roger de *Dorslow* must have been one of his tenants, if not his own brother.

The extract just quoted is the key to the whole position, proving as it does that the manor of Parva Sugnall had descended in ordinary course to the direct posterity of John de Suggenhull of 1199, and completing the chain of evidence by which I have shown that the ancestor of all the Swynnertons of the thirteenth and succeeding centuries was the aforesaid "John de Suggenhille" of the *Curia Regis* Rolls of 1 John, *alias dictus*, "John de Suinnerton" of the Chartulary of the monks of Stone.

(*f.*) A quotation from Erdeswick will crown the general

inspection of the original deeds at Charnes.) Among those deeds there is one beginning—"*Sciant omnes &c. quod ego Cecilia relicta Roberti de Parva Sugenhull.*" (No date.)

[1] "Staff. Coll.," Vol. VI, Part I, p. 146.

[2] Assize Roll, 21 Ed. I, *m.* 24.

argument :—"Little Sugnal and DORSLOW hard by were holden by John de Parva Sugenhull of the bishop by *octavam partem feodi.* 24 E. I."[1]

Here we have Little Sugnall and Dorslow rated together as one-eighth of a knight's fee. They are one inheritance. The heir of the one is also the heir of the other. Petronilla and Margaret in the time of Richard I, and K. John, were evidently then the co-heirs of both places. Margaret, having no children, grants her rights in both to her sister Petronilla and her husband John. John, Petronilla's husband, in pleas of land, is naturally and properly described by his territorial designation—"John de Parva Suggenhille." In his purely personal character, as a witness to deeds in the Stone Chartulary, he describes himself just as naturally and properly by his true patronymic—"John de Suinnerton."

Of John's other sons by his first wife there were—

3. Stephen concerning whom and whose descendants we will treat presently.
4. Nicholas. That there was such a son I have no doubt whatever. He was known as "Nicholas de Aspley," as Stephen de Swynnerton was sometimes known as "Stephen de Aspley." He became a monk, and rose to the position of prior of St. Thomas of Canterbury near Stafford. He was one of the three executors of the will of (his step-mother) Margery, lady of Swynnerton, the relict of (his father) John, of Eccleshall and Swynnerton.[2]
5. (Simon de Aspley may also have been a son. The Swynnertons were probably not all supporters of de Montford, though the memory of that hero was long cherished in many a household in the baptismal name Simon. The name Simon was also largely in vogue in the twelfth century, and one Simon fitz-Alwin, who was amerced 2 marks for a *novel disseisin* in 33 Hen. II (1186), was doubtless a Swynnerton. Simon de Aspley had a son Nicholas, nicknamed "the Fisher," who had been enfeoffed in part of the Sugnall lands. His son William married Dorea, daughter and heir of Thomas de

[1] Erdeswick, Add. MSS., Brit. Mus., p. 61.
[2] The *Liber Albus*, Lichfield.

Peshall, so that he is sometimes known as William de Sugnall, and sometimes as William de Peshall—another example of the confusion in personal names prevailing at the period. William had another son William, who was slain.)[1]

But we must follow the fortunes of the second son of Sir John de Swynnerton:—

STEPHEN DE SWYNNERTON is known also as Stephen de Uselwall (Isewall), Stephen de Aspley, and perhaps also as Stephen de Slyndon. He was the ancestor of the earlier Swynnertons of Isewall, and owed his advancement in life to his marriage with Joan, daughter and heir of Roger de Waure of Eccleshall, who brought him Great Sugnall, Isewall, and possessions at Aspley and Slyndon, all in the Bishops' Liberty of Eccleshall.

Uselwall, Isewall, Isewell, or Eyeswell[2] as it is now called, was an estate, now reduced to a field of four acres, by the town of Eccleshall, at present in the possession of the writer, a direct descendant of Stephen de Swynnerton and Joan de Waure. The name appears to have arisen from a little perennial spring traditionally said to be good for sore eyes. This spring still exists. It fed the now drained moat of the old house of Isewall, in which the Eccleshall Swynnertons lived for centuries, but which stands no longer. This mansion was one of the three burgages in Eccleshall belonging to Roger de Waure in 1225, to which right of housebote, haybote, and firebote in the Bishops' forests pertained, as fully appears in Bishop Alexander's charter of that date, which is quoted, *in extenso*, in a suit of 45 Ed. III (1376), by which Humphrey de Swynnerton of Isewall sought to recover his forest-rights against Robert, Bishop of Coventry and Lichfield.[3] Roger de Waure was in high favour with Bishop Alexander and his predecessors in the reigns of Richard I and John, holding some important office under them, probably that of Seneschal, as the charter plainly sets forth, and acquiring large estates duly enumerated therein.

Stephen de Swynnerton appears to have been a great friend and companion-in-arms of his half-brother John de Swynnerton,

[1] "Staff. Coll.," VII, 166.

[2] *Wall*, a spring of water, from base *wal-a* (A.S. *weall-an*, to spring up); Teutonic base, *wall* to well up (Skeat). To the well of Isewall came people with sore eyes from time immemorial.

[3] Plea Rolls, Staff., 50 Ed. III, Easter, *m*. 124.

Margery's last surviving son, and lord of Swynnerton from 1267-8 to 1284.

In October, 1265, Stephen de *Uireswell* (*Isewall*), John de Swynereston (Swynnerton), and Henry de Swynereston, together with William de Trumwyne and many others, chiefly of Eccleshall, were impleaded by Odo de Hodenet for having entered the manor of the said Odo, during the disturbances in the kingdom, and taken away his goods and chattels. The defendants did not appear, and the Sheriff was ordered to distrain them, etc., and produce them at Hillary.[1]

The John de Swynnerton mentioned in the foregoing was the lord of Swynnerton, and his interest in the manor of Hodnet is an item in the history of the times too interesting to be passed over:

In the time of Richard I, Odo de Hodynot enfeoffed Robert de Swynnerton, lord of Swynnerton, in three carucates of land at Peplow, a member of Hodnet, of which Robert was in seisin in 1203.[2] Robert de Swynnerton dying in 1224 the right descended to his son Robert, and by a fine dated 25th November, 1231, Ralph fitz Odo (de Hodnet) as tenant surrenders three virgates of land and a mill in Peplow to Robert de Swynnerton for an annuity of 40*s*., receivable half-yearly at Swynnerton. This Robert de Swynnerton was the last of his house in the right line male, and these rights therefore went to his sister's husband Sir John de Swynnerton, who transmitted them to their son Roger, who dying without issue left them to his brother John above-mentioned. This John de Swynnerton, who had raided the manor of Odo de Hodnet during Simon de Montford's rebellion as above noted, made a fine with Richard de Hodnet in 1284 by which his paternal interest in Peplow as aforesaid passed on his death without issue to the said Richard de Hodnet.[3]

To return to Stephen Swynnerton of Isewall, Aspley, and Sugnall:

In 53 Hen. III (1269), on the 20th May, before the King, Richard Brun appeared against Robert Cotes, Simon Burgilon, Adam le Fevre of Swynnerton, and six others, for having come to his house at Eston, and taken from him *vi et armis* 13 marks

[1] "Staff. Coll.," Vol. VII, Part I, p. 9. Staffordshire generally was with King John; but Erdington, the Sheriff, names Baldwin de Hodnet as one of the most disaffected. (Vol. II, 170.)

[2] Eyton's "Shropshire." Also suit Ludlow *v*. Hodnet, 42 Ed. III, Plea Rolls, *De Banco*, *m*. 385.

[3] *Ibid.*

in money, and a horse of the value of 6 marks, etc. Defendants did not appear, and the Sheriff was ordered to distrain them, and returned that John, lord of *Somerton* (Swynnerton), and *Stefanus de Aspele* stood bail for Robert de Cotes.[1]

In a Standon deed, No. 8, in original, at the Stafford Library, which must have passed about 1272, John, lord of Swynnerton, and Stephen his brother ("*Hiis testibus Johanne domino de Swinnerton Stephano fratre ejus*" etc.) are the principal witnesses. This deed concerns a concession of lands in Chorlton, a member of Eccleshall, from Robert son of Simon de Chorlton to William son of Robert de Cotes.

In three deeds among the charters of Mr. Vernon Yonge at Charnes in Eccleshall, which must have passed not later than 1270, Stephen de Swynnerton appears as "Stephen de Espley" (Aspley), "Stephen de Espeleye," and "Stephen de Slyndon."

In 3 Ed. I (1275), on the Monday next before the Feast of St. Bartholomew (*i.e.* 22nd August), Stephen de Swynnerton occurs as a juror in an inquisition taken at Stafford, as well as in a suit tried at the Bishop's Court at Lichfield.[2]

In the same year Agnes, the widow of John de Wytemor, sued Stephen de Swynnerton for one-third of a messuage and two bovates of land in Cherleton (Chorlton), and Roger de Burgilon for one-third of a messuage and ten acres of land in Wytemor as her dower. The defendants claimed a view, and subsequently called to warranty the heir, namely, John son of John de Wytemor, etc.[3]

It is of importance that we should note that according to this entry, while Roger de Burgilon had become possessor of a messuage and ten acres of land in Whitmore, Stephen de Swynnerton had purchased a messuage and two bovates of land in Chorlton, for both call to warranty the heir of John de Whitmore, the former tenant. This was perhaps the estate held *temp.* Ed. III by Richard de Swynnerton the Palmer, and it was sufficiently extensive to justify a new name "de Chorlton" to Stephen or his successor. Of this manor the priors of St. Thomas of Canterbury near Stafford were the mesne lords.

On the Sunday after the Ascension, 4 Ed. I (17th May, 1276), John de Swynnerton and Stephen de *Uselewalle* are two

[1] "Staff. Coll.," Vol. IV, p. 172.

[2] *Ibid.*, Vol. VII, Part I, p. 12.

[3] *Ibid.*

of the jurors at the inquisition taken after the death of Henry de Audley. (He had been killed by a fall from his horse in Ireland.)[1]

Stephen de Swynnerton must have died within a year of this date. His eldest son Roger inherited half Great Sugnall, and probably Isewall also; but if so, he must have given Isewall to his younger brother John when he himself succeeded his uncle John in 1284 as lord of Swynnerton, concerning which and his successors Canon Bridgeman has written at length in his "History of the Swynnertons." ("Staff. Coll.," Vol. VII.)

But the two bovates of land and the messuage which his father acquired from John de Whitmore in Chorlton must, I think, have come to John too, if at least he is the John de Chorlton referred to in the following:—In Trinity Term, 18 Ed. I (1290), Roger de Swynnerton was attached to answer the plea of Robert Chell, that he, with *John de Cherleton*, James de Hayton, William son of William de Cherleton, and Gilbert de Swynnerton had ill-treated, taken, and imprisoned at Swynnerton the said Robert de Chell, etc.[2]

JOHN DE SWYNNERTON OF ISEWALL.

In a feodary called Kirby's Quest,[3] compiled in 1284 or perhaps a little earlier, we read that Great Sennhall (Sugnall) was then held by Roger and John, the sons of Stephen (de Swynnerton) de *Aspley*, who held it of John Muriel who held it of the Bishop by the service of one-fourth part of a knight's fee.

In 12 Ed. I (1283–4) John, son of Stephen de Swynnerton, gives 20*s.* for a writ of *ad terminum*. In 19 Ed. I he fines for a writ of *pone*.[4]

In 15 Ed. I (1286–7) Justices are appointed to take the assize of novel disseisin which John son of Stephen de Swynnerton

[1] *Inq.*, p.m. 4 Ed. I, No. 50. *Inq.* 4 Ed. I, 1275–6. *Henry de Audley.* Two of the jury—John de Swynnerton and Stephen de *Uselewalle*. This Henry de Audley had rents of assize *in Newcastle*, and of the mill of Chauldon.

[2] Stephen probably left other sons also, namely, Adam de Sugnall, and Richard, Hugh, and Henry de Chell. Richard was probably in orders, and the parson of Swynnerton who occurs in 6, 7, and 8 Ed. II (1312–1314).

[3] John Kirby, Bishop of Ely and treasurer to Edward I, died in 1290. It was in June, 1282, that he was sent by the King to obtain a subsidy from the shires and boroughs. (Stubbs.)

[4] "Staff. Coll.," Vol. VII, Part I, p. 13. A writ *ad terminum* was when land had been leased for a term of years, or for a life or lives, and the term had expired. A writ *pone* was one for transferring a suit to the higher court at Westminster.

arraigned against Roger (de Meuland), Bishop of Coventry and Lichfield, concerning tenements in Eccleshall.[1]

In 20 Ed. I (1292-3) John de Swynnerton appeared against Roger de Meuland, Bishop of Coventry and Lichfield, concerning tenements in Eccleshall.[2]

By deed without date, but which must have passed between 1290 and 1299, Roger, Bishop of Coventry and Lichfield, conceded to John de Swynnerton and his heirs housebote and haybote, and a reasonable supply of dead wood for his hearth, out of his forest of Blore.[3] Witnesses—Nich. de Audley, William de Mere, etc.

In 23 Ed. I (1295) John de Swynnerton, William de Mere, and others were in the retinue of Nicolas de Audley in the expedition into Wales. Letters of protection were dated 27th April.[4]

In 25 Ed. I (1297) the King sent to the Justices a writ in these words:—Here follow letters of protection for Nicolas de Alditheley (Audley), Robert de Standon, Roger de Swynnerton, John de Ebroicis (Devereux), Roger le Burgelun, John de Swynnerton, and Richard de Chetelton, who by the King's command, and in his retinue (*cum rege*), were about to set out for parts beyond sea, to last for a year. Dated at Sevenoaks, 5th August.[5]

The former of these two extracts refers to Edward's third Welsh war, which occupied him until May, 1295, when he captured Madoc and returned to London. The second refers to his expedition into Flanders against the French. He embarked on the 22nd August, 1297, and returned in March, 1298. Roger de Swynnerton, lord of Swynnerton, never lived to return, as he was dead by February. It is to be noted that both brothers were in the train of the King, and as they were also under the banner of Lord Audley, they must have been Audley tenants. Roger, in fact, was Audley's sub-tenant at Great Chelle, and John had probably a holding in the Liberty of Newcastle, of which the Audleys had purchased the rents of assize.

In 31 Ed. I (1302-3) John de Swynnerton sued Katrine, formerly wife of Nicholas de Alditheleg (Audley), and James de Stafford, for a sum of £40 which they owed him. By W. Howard.[6]

[1] Patent Rolls, 15 Ed. I, *m.* 10.
[2] *Ibid.*, 20 Ed. I.
[3] "Staff. Coll.," Vol. VII, Part I, p. 13.
[4] *Ibid.*, Vol. VIII, p. 16.
[5] *Ibid.*, Vol. VIII, p. 44.
[6] Banco Roll, Trinity, *m.* 140. This W. Howard, a Judge, is the unknown ancestor of the Dukes of Norfolk.

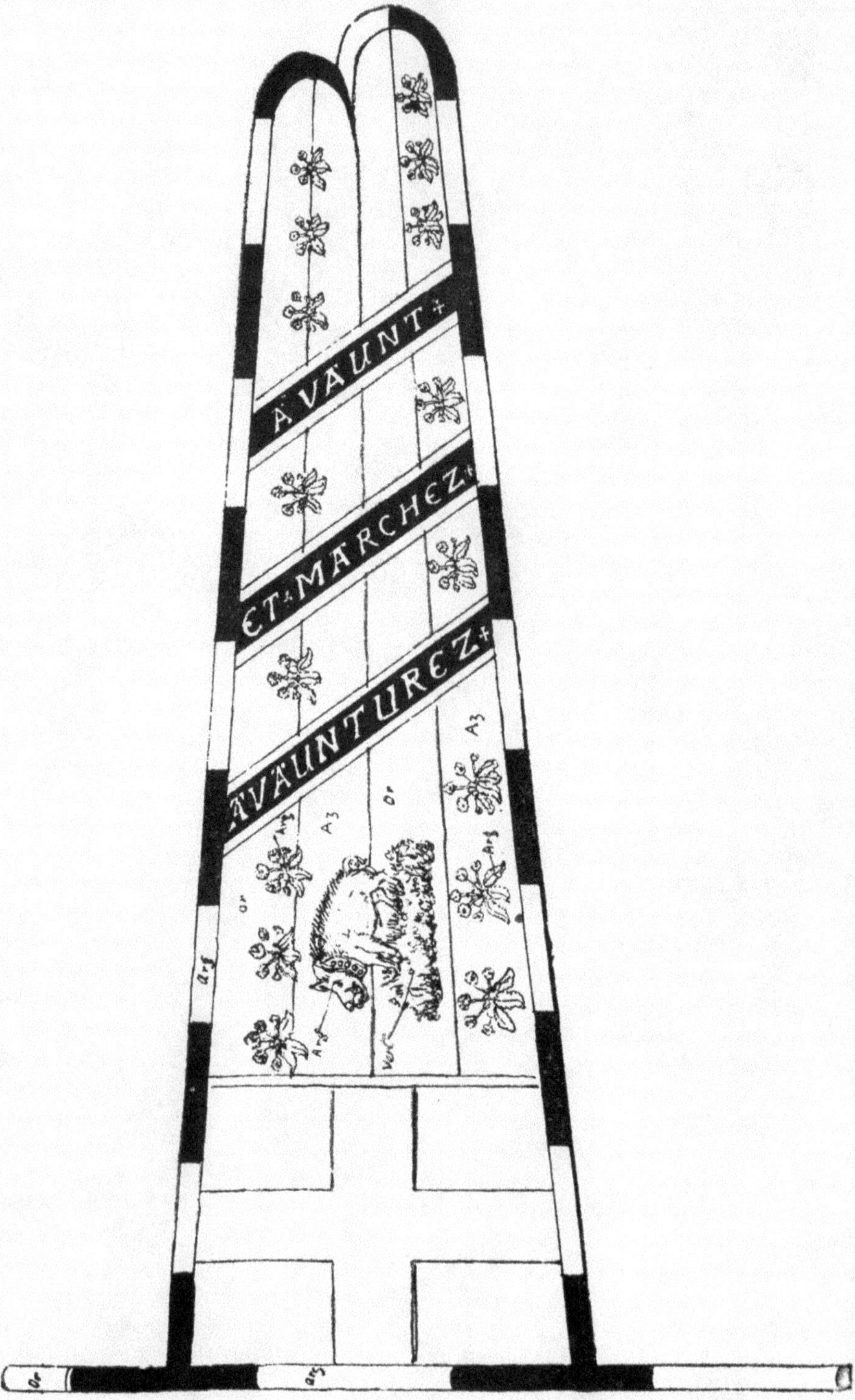
A VAUNT
ET MARCHEZ
AVAUNTUREZ

A SWYNNERTON STANDARD.—(From an emblazoned MS. at the Heralds' College.)

In 33 Ed. I (1304–5) there was a suit between Adam le Bedel and John de Swynnerton concerning tenements in *Great Sugnall*.[1]

In 34 Ed. I (1306) John de Swynnerton had letters of protection as being in the retinue of Thomas, Earl of Lancaster, in the war in Scotland. Dated Westminster, 6th June.[2]

John de Swynnerton was there as a *serviens*, *i.e.* a squire or serjeant-at-arms, mounted and equipped in all points like a knight, but without the rank. This notice proves him to have been a tenant of Thomas, Earl of Lancaster, and his holding was probably in the Earl's manor of Newcastle. He would have been differenced in the field by the Swynnerton coat—a cross flory *sable*, debruised by a bend *gules*—(which in subsequent times was assumed by the later Swynnertons of Isewall), a bend *gules* being one of the earliest differences in Heraldry, pertaining to the reigns of Hen. III and Ed. I.[3] And his motto will have been, not *Avaunturez, et marchez avaunt*, which was the knightly motto of the Head of the family at Swynnerton,[4] but *Avauncez et archez bien*, a motto which has descended to his present representatives, and which indicates a race of squires and of mounted archers, not knights. Neither John de Swynnerton of Isewall nor his son was a knight, nor were any of the subsequent Swynnertons of Isewall.

John de Swynnerton's suit against Katrine, relict of Nicholas de Audley, recurs at Michaelmas, 33 Ed. I (1305), and in the same regnal year (1306) John de Swynnerton stated that she had bound herself to him for that sum on the Saturday after the Feast of St. Matthew, 29 Ed. I (1301), to be repaid by instalments of 10 marks at Newcastle-under-Lyme, and he produced her bond. Katrine appeared by attorney and acknowledged her bond, for which John remitted his damages and £10 of the debt. John is therefore to recover £30.[5]

In 1 Ed. II (1307), according to a presentment made by a jury in 1323, John (de Swynnerton) of *Uselwall* appears to have been concerned in the death of Henry de Salt of Stafford, the names of the Swynnerton faction being given in the following order:—Roger de Swynnerton, knight, John de Swynnerton, knight (of Hilton), Richard de Swynnerton, Stephen de Swynnerton, *John de Uselwall*, Nicholas de Swynnerton, parson of the church

[1] Patent Rolls. [2] "Staff. Coll.," Vol. VIII, p. 27.

[3] See the contemporary Norman-French roll of the siege of Caerlaverock, where a bend debruising the paternal arms for younger branches of noble families is in full vogue.

[4] College of Arms. [5] Banco Roll, 33 Ed. I, *m.* 201.

of Moccleston, Richard de Whethales, John de Whetales, Richard de Chelle, Henry de Chelle, Robert de Aston near Stone, and many others.

In 2 Ed. II (1308), "John de Swynnerton of Eccleshall" has a suit against John son of Simon de Aspley and others concerning tenements in Magna Sugnall.[1]

In 4 Ed. II (1310), at the general proffer of knight-service to the King, taken at Twedemouth before Sir Bartholomew de Badlesmere, Lieutenant to the Constable of England, and Sir Nicholas de Segrave, Marshal of the King's host, Thomas, Earl of Lancaster, acknowledged the services of six knights' fees for all his lands in England, to be performed by Roger de Swenerton, John de Twyford, Peter de Lemeseye, and William Trussell,[2] knights, and John de Swenerton, John de Nortle (? Norton), Richard de Lymsey, and Roger de Kent, sergeants, with barded horses.[3]

Here again we have evidence that Roger de Swynnerton who, as lord of Swynnerton, was a vassal of Lord Stafford, and that his uncle John who, as a tenant in Eccleshall, was a vassal of the Bishops, were vassals also, by virtue of holdings elsewhere, of the Earls of Lancaster. These holdings were, in part at least, Chell, which, as a member of the seignory of Wolstanton, was held by the Earl of Lancaster, and of him by the Audleys, and of them by the Swynnertons, and part also in the Earl's manor of Newcastle-under-Lyme, especially Whitmore and Knutton, members of that manor.

We now come to a curious note by Walter Chetwynd, the Staffordshire antiquary of the seventeenth century, which is quoted by the Hon. the Rev. Canon Bridgeman in his "History of the Swynnertons." It runs thus: "Between Seabridge and Hanchurch there is a little village where there are two ancient families, the one of the Swinnertons and the other of the Buttertons." And in speaking of the former Chetwynd adds: "John de Swinnerton purchased all the lands there of William Badkin of Fulford in 7 Ed. II" (1313).

[1] "Staff. Coll.," Vol. X, p. 54.

[2] This must have been the Sir William Trussell who, as proctor of the Estates of the Realm, proclaimed to Edward II in Kenilworth Castle, in 1327, his deposition. It is noteworthy that three branches of the Trussells bore the Swynnerton coat differenced by *gules* for the cross flory instead of *sable*, and that one branch of the Swynnertons displayed the same difference. (Glover and Edmondson.)

[3] I do not understand this entry, unless it speaks only of lands *outside the Honour of Lancaster.*

The "little village" here referred to can only be Butterton itself, and must be identical with "a certain little village of Newcastle (meaning of the Liberty or Manor thereof) which is of the territory of the parish of Trentham,"[1] mentioned in a charter of Roger de Weseham, Bishop of Coventry and Lichfield, between 1245 and 1256, which gives a detailed list of all the ecclesiastical appurtenances of Trentham, of which appurtenances this "viculus" was one. From this charter it would seem that anciently (whatever it may be now) Butterton was a hamlet of the parish of Trentham, and yet lay within the bounds of the royal Liberty of Newcastle-under-Lyme, and was subject therefore to the *Magna Curia*, or general manor-court, which periodically assembled at the borough of Newcastle.[2] It was, in fact, a member of one of the lesser manors comprised in the Liberty. But of which of them? The following extract will prove that it was of the fee of Whitmore, if not wholly, at least in part:—

By deed enrolled, dated from London on Thursday the Feast of St. Catherine (25th Nov.), 13 Ed. III (1339), and witnessed by John de Delves, Ralph Burgynion and others, John son of William de Bromley releases to William de Bromley, clerk, his brother, all the rights he had to lands and tenements, etc., which the said William held of his enfeoffment in *Botterton within the demesne of Whitmore*.[3]

It is not certain who the John de Swynnerton mentioned by Chetwynd was. He may have been Sir John de Swynnerton (I) of Hilton, the Seneschal of Cannock Forest in right of his wife Anne de Montgomery, as surmised by Canon Bridgeman. In the absence of evidence, however, he may just as likely have been the latter's uncle, John de Swynnerton of Isewall, of whom we are now treating. Extracts will be given presently which would seem to support the latter theory. I strongly suspect, however, that Chetwynd is mistaken in his date, and that for "7 Edw. II," we must read "7 Ric. II." My reasons for this suspicion will be found in my account of "Some Forgotten Swynnertons of the 14th Century."

[1] The passage runs thus:—"*Trentham cum omnibus pertinenciis suis scilicet Berlaston Betteleye dimidiam Baltredeleye quidam viculus Novi Castelli qui est de territorio parochie de Trentham*," etc. ("Staff. Coll.," Vol. XI, p. 303.)

[2] By *Inq. temp.* Hen. III without date the pasture in Boterton belonging to the *King's manor of Newcastle* was valued at 2*s.* (*Inq.* at Stafford.)

[3] "Staff. Coll.," Vol. XI, p. 97.

In the Spring of 5 Ed. II (1312) occurred the first rebellion of the King's cousin-germain, Thomas, Earl of Lancaster, which resulted in the capture of Piers Gaveston at Scarborough Castle, and his summary execution on Blacklow Hill on the 19th June. Nicolas de Audley was one of the ring-leaders on that occasion, and he was attended by John de Swynnerton of Isewall, the *serviens* of Thomas, Earl of Lancaster, mentioned in a previous paragraph, who therefore is the "John" of the following pardon:—

In 7 Ed. II (1313), on Oct. 16th, John de Swynnerton and Roger de Swynnerton with many others received the King's pardon for having been present in arms, with Thomas, Earl of Lancaster, when Piers Gaveston was beheaded on Blakelow Hill. John's name precedes that of Roger, though he was only a squire, but on the other hand he was Roger's uncle and a veteran.[1]

In the same year (1313), on the 13th May, five months before the issue of the pardons, John de Swynnerton had letters of protection to go to parts beyond the sea in the retinue of John de Cherleton, a great lord who had married the heiress of the last Welsh Prince of Powis.[2] The two entries—this and the former—cannot possibly refer to the same John de Swynnerton. The rebel was in disgrace, at any rate up to the 16th October, whereas the other was in favour, for he was with Edmund de Mauley, the Steward of the King's household, being part of the suite of the King into France, whither he went that year with his Queen and a great following on May 23rd, for the coronation of the King of Navarre at Paris. John de Swynnerton of *Hilton* was then a young knight, holding of the King *in capite*, and, as we shall show, he remained firm in his allegiance throughout both rebellions, and it was he, not John de Swynnerton of Isewall, who went with King and Queen to France. The latter was then languishing in prison.

In 8 Ed. II (1314) John de Swynnerton (of Isewall) granted to Walter, Bishop of Coventry and Lichfield, a croft in Eccleshall, which Adam le Flechere formerly held, called Doggescroft, a piece of land called Grymeshalgh, and other places, the witnesses being John de Hastang, Roger de Swynnerton, Thomas de Halghton,

[1] Rymer's *Foedera*. Also "Staff. Coll.," Vol. VIII, p. 31.
[2] *Ibid.*, Vol. II, p. 12.

knights, Adam de Whetales,[1] and others. The opening words of the quit-claim run thus: "Inasmuch as for a long time a dispute and an altercation had existed between the lord Walter, bishop of Coventry and Lichfield, of the one part, and me, *John de Swynnerton, lord of Isewelle*, of the other."[2]

This Bishop was Walter de Langton, the great finance minister of Edward I and Edward II. He became the Royal Treasurer in 1295, and Bishop of Lichfield in 1296. In 1301 he was suspended on a charge of adultery, concubinage, simony, and intercourse with the devil, but the Pope acquitted him, and Edward restored him. He was Bishop until 1322. One of the most powerful and unscrupulous men of his day, all through his episcopate he amassed wealth from every conceivable source for his new shrine of St. Chad, which he built at a cost of £2,000, the new Lady Chapel, his new palace, a great precinct wall, and his other princely additions to the cathedral at Lichfield, as well as for his improvements to his castle of Eccleshall.

In the same year (1314) John Peche had a suit against Roger de Swynnerton and John de Swynnerton *senior*, each for a debt of £20.[3]

The campaign in Scotland, notorious for the rout of Bannockburn, occurred in 1314, the battle being fought on June 24th. Thomas, Earl of Lancaster, had refused the summons. All the Audleys however were there, viz. Hugh, senior; Hugh, junior; James son of James; and Nicolas de Audley. And John Swynnerton of Isewall, as usual, must have followed the Audley banner. And he probably did good service in that campaign, otherwise it is not possible to explain why he rose at once to favour, as the following testifies:—

In March, 1315, the King granted to John de Swynnerton of Eccleshall that he and his heirs forever should have right of free-warren in all his demesne lands at Sogenhall in co. Stafford. Dated at Westminster, 8th March, *by the King himself*.[4]

In the same year he was murdered, when his age could scarcely have been over fifty, as his elder brother Roger was a minor in 1278. On the 4th October, 1315, Justices were appointed by the King

[1] Adam de Whetale, *alias* de Peshale. His son Adam was indicted for the death of the granton's son John in 1337. See *infra*.

[2] *Liber Albus* de Lichfield, p. 129.

[3] "Staff. Coll.," Vol. IX, p. 51.

[4] Charter Rolls, 8 Ed. II.

to inquire who the malefactors were who had maliciously slain John de Swinnerton at Eccleshall.[1]

In the same year Gilbert Cotsmere, Robert Fisher, Thomas Porter, and Geoffrey Gilberdesman were lodged in Stafford gaol for the murder of John de Swynnerton, but Fulk le Strange, William Trussell senior, and William Stafford were appointed to set them at liberty.[2]

JOHN SON OF JOHN DE SWYNNERTON of Isewall succeeded in 1315.

The Scotch Roll of 11 Ed. II (1317–18) shows that Hugh de Audley senior was serving that year in the marches of Scotland, and that James de Audley, afterwards to be so famous, was in his retinue. The Letters of Protection mention a John de Swynerton and a John de Swinerton, one of whom should be John de Swynnerton of Isewall.

In 14 Ed. II (1320), at Michaelmas, Agnes, formerly wife of Robert de Knotton, sued Hugh Doucesone for a third of ten acres of land and four acres of meadow in *Knotton,* and William Baly for a third of three acres, and James de Audley for a third of two acres and 2*s*. rent, and William de Mere for a third of 10*s*. rent, and she sued John le Burgoynon and *John son of John de Swonnerton* for a third of an iron mine in the same vill, which she claimed as dower.[3]

At the same time Agnes, formerly wife of Robert de Knotton, sued Thomas Baban and Margaret his wife for a third of a messuage and two acres of meadow in Knotton, and she sued Richard Lagon for a third of six acres of land, and William de Snede for a third of three acres, and William son of Nicholas de Thiknes for a third of 22*d*. rent, and *John son of John de Swonnerton* for a third of two parts of a mill in the same vill, which she claimed as dower.[4]

Earlier in the volume we find John le Burgoynon sued by Margaret the relict of John de Arden for one-third the manor of Knotton, excepting a water-mill and a mine—evidently the mill and the mine mentioned in the two previous pleas as held by John le Burgoynon and John de Swynnerton.[5]

[1] Patent Rolls, *m*. 20, *in dorso,* 8 Ed. II.
[2] *Ibid.*, *m*. 8.
[3] Plea Rolls, *De Banco*, *m*. 314, *dorso*, quoted p. 82, Vol. IX "Staff. Coll."
[4] *Ibid.*, *m*. 158 *dorso* ("Staff. Coll.," Vol. IX, p. 83).
[5] *Ibid.*, Vol. IX, p. 55.

John le Burgoynon or Burgylon was thus in seisin of the manor of Knutton. He was lord also of Clayton, and had lands and tenements in Whitmore, where the Burgulons appear to have resided. All these, in the manor of Newcastle, were held under the Earl of Lancaster.

When Thomas, Earl of Lancaster, again revolted in 1321, the Audleys, including Hugh de Audley who had married the King's niece, also revolted with him. Roger de Swynnerton of Swynnerton and John de Swynnerton of Hilton remained firm in their allegiance, being governors of royal castles; in fact, it was during that crisis that Roger had the custody of the Tower, while the latter was Sheriff also of cos. Stafford and Salop. Not so John de Swynnerton of Isewall, however, who again followed the fortunes of the house of Audley. Towards the end of February, 1322, the Earl, being then in retreat towards the north, made an ineffectual stand at the bridge of Burton, and there John de Swynnerton of Isewall, with many others, was taken prisoner. The battle of Boroughbridge was fought on the 16th March, and Thomas, Earl of Lancaster, in his turn summarily beheaded just outside his own castle of Pomfret. Many others were hanged, and many merely suffered fine and imprisonment. Among the latter was John de Swynnerton of Isewall. His life was spared on the payment of a fine of £40, and he was discharged from prison, having taken oath and given security for his good behaviour, and promised that he would loyally serve the King in his wars. His bond and recognizance were dated at York, 11th July, 16 Ed. II (1323).[1]

In 17 Ed. II (1323) the Hundred of Pirehill, co. Stafford, presented that Peter de Lymesi, John de Twyford, and Thomas Wither, knights, and *John son of John de Iselewall*, and others named (in other words, the Audley faction), were with the Earl of Lancaster at the bridge of Burton, and were all taken on that occasion. Afterwards the Sheriff was ordered to produce them on the morrow of the Purification.[2]

[1] As one example, among many, to show that John de Swynnerton of Hilton was not an adherent of Thomas, Earl of Lancaster, we quote the following:—"In presentments made in the co. of Stafford on 12th December, 17 Ed. II (1323), John de Swynnerton (of Hilton) is accused of having in March, 16 Ed. II (1322), *in the exercise of his office as Sheriff*, despoiled the fugitives from the field of Boroughbridge, in that he had taken two horses worth 40 marks, which belonged to Roger Damory, the King's enemy and rebel, and which should have been forfeited to the King, etc. ("Staff. Coll.," Vol. IX, p. 99.)

[2] "Staff. Coll.," Vol. X, p. 54.

In the same year the jury of the vill of Newcastle-under-Lyme presented that Peter de Lymesey, knight, *John de Uselwall*, Henry del Peek, William his brother, Ralf del Shaw of Knotton, and six others named of Knotton, with many more of that locality, were at the bridge of Burton assisting the Earl of Lancaster against the King in 1322. The Sheriff was ordered to attach them. A postscript shows that subsequently they all appeared, and were fined sums varying from 40*d.* to 1 mark, and found sureties for good behaviour.[1]

On the same date the same jury presented that Thomas de Warwyk, formerly clerk of the Countess of Helegh, like a common malefactor, in full market at Newcastle-under-Lyme, in 13 Ed. II (1319), insulted Roger son of Roger de Swynnerton and beat and maltreated him, and that Richard de Swynnerton, William the Smith of Chelle, and others named, beat and wounded the said Thomas de Warwyk almost to death, and that Henry, the clerk of the Countess of Helegh, Henry de Peleter, and *John de Iselwalle,* at Newcastle, on a market day in 13 Ed. II, came like common malefactors, and beat and wounded Agnes wife of Robert del Bakhous, etc.[2] It will thus be seen that John de Swynnerton (II) of Isewall was now banded with a faction hostile to that of his cousins, Roger de Swynnerton of Swynnerton and John de Swynnerton of Hilton.

In 1325, 18 Ed. II, John de Swynnerton (of Isewall) received a writ of military service, being commanded to be at Portsmouth on the Sunday next after Mid-Lent, "bien et nettement mountez et armez et apparaillez," to accompany Earl Warrenne to Gascony and Guienne, and the writ which was tested at Ravensdale on the 7th January reminded him that he owed his life to a promise that he would serve the King. On the 20th February he received a writ to the same purport, and mention was made that he had been previously summoned on such service by Letters of Privy Seal.[3]

In 19 Ed. II (1325), in November, Justices were appointed to take the assize of novel disseisin which William de Joneston arraigned against *John son of John de Swynnerton* and others concerning tenements in Eccleshall and Great Sugenhall.[4]

In 20 Ed. II (1326) Henry de Burgh, carpenter, sued *John*

[1] "Staff. Coll.," Vol. X (from *Coram Rege* Rolls. *m.* 8). [2] *Ibid.*, *m.* 9.
[3] Parliamentary Writs. [4] Patent Rolls, 19 Ed. II, *m.* 20, *in dorso.*

son of John de Uselwall for two messuages and two acres of land in Eccleshall.[1]

In 6 Ed. III (1332) Roger de Swynnerton the younger (heir to Swynnerton), by his essoin, sued Nicholas son of Adam le Bedel of Madeley, and Henry servant of John Burgylon, in a plea that they, together with *John de Uselwalle*, Henry de Sugenhull, John Burguloun, Roger Burguloun, and Thomas Yokkynson of Knutton, had taken, *vi et armis*, his goods and chattels from Knutton to the value of £40. Defendants did not appear, etc.[2]

By two deeds, both dated 7 Ed. III (1333), *John son of John de Swynnerton of Uselwell* remits for himself and his heirs to Roger, Bishop of Coventry and Lichfield, all the right, etc., which he has to all manner of estovers of wood, as well in housebote, haybote, and fyrebote, as in other estovers and *necessariis*, which he was wont to take and enjoy in the same Bishop's park of Blore, and in all other woods of the said Bishop within the manor of Eccleshale.[2]

In 8 Ed. III (1334) John de Swynnerton again surrenders by charter to Bishop Roger certain rights in Eccleshall.[3]

In 9 Ed. III, Trinity Term (1335), John de *Uselwalle* sued Philip le Barker of Eccleshale, and William his son, for breaking, *vi et armis*, into his close at Eccleshale, and taking his goods and chattels to the value of £10. Defendants did not appear, etc.[4]

On the 10th February, 1336, John de Swynnerton had a writ dated Knaresborough, and another dated Westminster, May 6th, for the war in Scotland.

In 10 Ed. III (1336) John de *Uselwall*, with many others, are indicted for pillaging the house of John de Stafford, knight, at Sandon.[5]

The next year the case was resumed *coram rege*;[6] but as the name of John de Isewall no longer appears on the record, and as, in the year after, Roger lord of Swynnerton died seised of Isewall, the inference is that the interim John de Swynnerton of Isewall had died. In point of fact, he had been murdered, as his father

[1] "Staff. Coll.," Vol. IX, p. 116.

[2] John de Swynnerton of Isewall, as we have seen, was of the opposite party to Roger de Swynnerton in the rebellion of 1322. ("Staff. Coll.," Vol. X, p. 128; *Ibid.*, Vol. XIV, p. 28.)

[3] *Liber Albus*, p. 128.

[4] "Staff. Coll.," Vol. X, p. 44 (*Coram Rege*).

[5] *Ibid.*, Vol. IX, p. 71.

[6] *Ibid.*, Vol. XIV, p. 50. (*Coram Rege*, Michaelmas 11 Ed. III, *apud Cantuar.*)

THE DESCENT OF THE EARLIER SWYNNERTONS OF ECCLESHALL.

Alen, Norman lord of Swynnerton, etc., held of Robt. de Stafford, 1086. ╤

Robert fitz-Alen, lord of Swynnerton, etc., 1122–1154. ╤

Robert fitz-Alen, lord of Swynnerton, etc., 1158–1189. ╤

"Robert de Suinnerton," lord of Swynnerton, etc., *ob.* 1224.

Petronel, co-heir of Little Sugnall and Dorslow, oc. 1199. ╤ "John de Suinnerton," *jure uxoris* lord of Parva Sugnall, oc. *circa* 1190–1215.

Robert de Swynnerton, etc., *ob. s p.* 1245–6.

Margery, sister and heir, *ob.* 1255. 2nd wife. ╤ John de Swynnerton, lord of Parva Sugnall, Peshall, and Swynnerton, *ob.* 1254. ╤ (Elenor de Peshall.) 1st wife.

Aldith, dau. and co-heir of Adam de Bures, occ. 1248. = John de Parva Sugnall, oc. 1248 (*ob. s.p.*).

Steph. of Isewall, etc., *ob.* 1276. ╤ Joan, dau. and heir of Roger de Waure.

Robert of Parva Sugnall, killed in 1272. ╤ Cecily, dau. of John de Charnes, rel. 1279.

Richard de Peshall.
Nicolas de Aspley.
(? Simon de Aspley.)

Roger de Swynnerton, lord of Swynnerton, *ob.* 1298. ╤ Joan, dau. of Rob. Hastang.

John de Swynnerton of Isewall, killed 1315.

John de Swynnerton of Isewall, killed 1337, *s.p.*

Stephen, Parson of Swynnerton.

John of Parva Sugnall; held Parva Sugnall and Dorslow of the Bishop, 24 Ed. I.

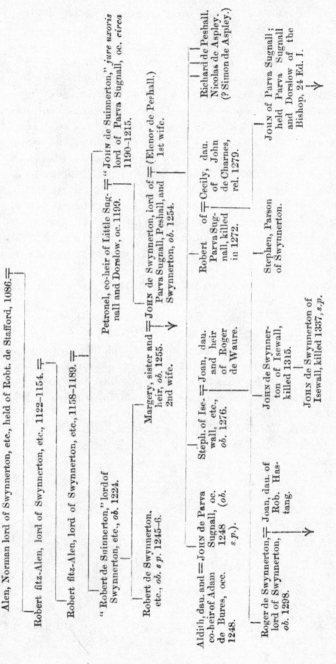

Note.—Observe the succession of *Johns* of Sugnall.

was murdered before him, on Saturday the 1st day of October, 1337, and a kinsman, Adam de Peshale, was arrested for the crime. The following entries refer to this deplorable deed:—

Gaol Delivery made at Stafford before Roger Hillary and John de Peyto, Justices, etc., on the Thursday next after the Feast of the Annunciation 12 Ed. III. No. 131—

Staff. Adam de Peshale, Roger Marion,[1] and William son of Philip le Barker of Eccleshale, indicted before John Gentille, the steward of the Bishop's Liberty of the manor of Eccleshale, for feloniously killing John de *Uselwalle* at Eccleshale on the Saturday after the Feast of St. Michael 11 Ed. III, were acquitted. *m. 2, dorso.*[2]

Staff. Adam de Peshale, indicted before John le Gentille, the Bishop's steward, for aiding and abetting Roger Marion,[1] and William son of Philip, who had feloniously killed John de *Uselwalle* at Eccleshale, was acquitted. *m. 2, dorso.*[2]

Staff. Robert, son of Stephen le Bedel of Eccleshale, who had been indicted before Ralph de Grendon, the Coroner, for feloniously killing John de *Uselwalle* at Eccleshale in 11 Ed. III, was acquitted. *m. 2, dorso.*[2]

Adam de Peshale, *alias* de Whetales, was a son of Adam de Whetales, and one of the party of Roger de Swynnerton of Swynnerton.[3] By descent he was himself a Swynnerton.[4]

Thus ended the last of the earlier Swynnertons of Isewall in Eccleshall, and, as his lands passed at once into the hands of his cousin Roger de Swynnerton of Swynnerton, it is certain that he left no issue. The later line of Swynnerton of Isewall has been treated of by Canon Bridgeman in his *History of the Family of Swynnerton* in Volume VII of the "Collections," from which most of these evidences have been taken.

[1] Roger Marion was of Swynnerton, and of the suite of Sir Roger de Swynnerton. "Staff. Coll.," Vol. VIII, p. 56.

[2] "Staff. Coll.," Vol. XVI, p. 7.

[3] *Cf.* pp. 56 and 79, "Staff. Coll.," Vol. IX.

[4] According to the *Visitations* of 1583, this Adam de Peshall was second son (by his second wife, the heiress of Weston-super-Lyzard) of Adam de Peshall (I), and grandson of Richard de Swynnerton. He was his mother's heir at Weston. (See *ante*, p. 76.)

NOTES ON THE EARLIER HISTORY OF GREAT SUGNALL IN THE LIBERTY OF ECCLESHALL, CO. STAFFORD.

I.

1. In 1166 Great Sugnall was held by Robert Joceran, *i.e.* Robert the son or descendant of Joceran, at ¼th f.m.[1]

2. His son it may have been who as Robert de Magna Sugnall, married Petronilla of Darlaston, a daughter of Engenulf de Gresley and Alina, daughter of Robert fitz Orm. For convenience we shall call him Robert de Sugnall (II).

3. Robert de Sugnall (III), who died before 1233, had sold most of his patrimony to Roger de Waure, so that his widow, pleading in 1233, stated that Robert, his son and heir, held nothing of the inheritance of his father.[2]

4. Robert de Sugnall (IV), the son referred to, was then a minor, and he may have been a minor also in 1242, because *Testa de Nevill* states that Great Sugnall was held by the *heir* of Robert de Sugnall.

5. He was still living in 1252–3, because the Inquisition of William Muriel of that year mentions the fact.[3] But he was dead by 1255–6, because Margery de Swynnerton had been guardian of his "*heirs*," but was then herself dead.[4]

6. These "heirs" must have been infant daughters, two or more. The Bishop, as chief lord of the fee, had conceded their wardship and marriage to Margery, lady of Swynnerton, and her executors on her death had surrendered those rights again to the Bishop.[5]

7. William Muriel, dying in 1252–3, left a son and heir, John Muriel, at that time 18 years old.[3]

8. Thirty years after, in 1284, Kirby's Quest says that Great Sugnall is held by ¼ f.m. by Roger and John, sons of Stephen (de Swynnerton) of Aspley, and that they hold it of John Muriel, who holds of the Bishop. In other words, we have John Muriel holding the *status* of Robert de Sugnall at Great Sugnall, from which it would appear that John Muriel had married one of the "heirs" of the last Robert de Sugnall.

[1] Pipe Roll of 1166.
[2] "Staff. Coll.," IV, p. 85.
[3] *Inq.* in copy, Wm. Salt Lib., Stafford.
[4] "Staff. Coll.," VII, Part 2, p. 8
[5] According to feudal rule the care of a minor belonged to the next kinsman who could not inherit. (Stubbs.)

II.

In the Stone Chartulary, Robert, lord of Swynnerton from *circa* 1190 to 1224, is several times the most honoured witness in the deeds concerning lands granted by Robert de Sugnall and Petronilla de Gresley his second wife, by whom he had no issue.[1]

In 12 Hen. III (1227) Robert de Swynnerton joins Robert de Sugnall as surety for William de Erdington, a bailiff of the Earl of Chester.[2]

These phenomena indicate close relationship; and the relationship is almost certainly this:—that the first wife of Robert de Sugnall (II), and the mother of his heir, was a sister of Robert de Swynnerton, his contemporary. In other words, Robert de Swynnerton and Robert de Sugnall of the Stone Chartulary were brothers-in-law. To support this theory there is the following evidence:—

In the *Liber Albus* of Lichfield is preserved a quit-claim (without date) from the executors of Margery de Swynnerton, late lady of Swynnerton, to Roger de (Wescham), Bishop of Coventry and Lichfield, of all the right which the said Lady Margery had, by concession of the Lord Bishop, to the custody of the heirs and lands of the late Robert de Sugenhull in Espel (Aspley) and Sugenhull, and also to the marriage of the heirs of the said Robert.[3]

This custody must have been conceded to Margery as a right; and her right must have been the usual feudal law and right of the nearest of kin who could not inherit; which would be precisely the position she would occupy with regard to the heirs of the last Robert de Sugnall, if the match above-noted had taken place. This fact, as I regard it, will be best understood by a reference to the following pedigree:—

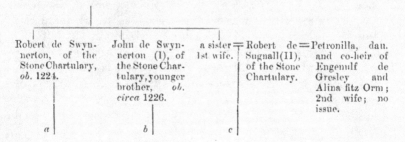

Robert de Swynnerton, of the Stone Chartulary, *ob.* 1224.	John de Swynnerton (I), of the Stone Chartulary, younger brother, *ob. circa* 1226.	a sister = 1st wife.	= Robert de Sugnall (II), of the Stone Chartulary.	= Petronilla, dau. and co-heir of Engenulf de Gresley and Alina fitz Orm; 2nd wife; no issue.
a	*b*	*c*		

[1] "Staff. Coll.," VI, Part 1, pp. 1-20.
[2] *Ibid.*, IV, 72.
[3] *Ibid.*, VII, Part 2, p. 8.

a | b | c |

Robert, *ob. s.p.* 1246.

X Margery, lady of Swynnerton, custos of the heirs of Sugnall, *ob.* 1256; *2nd wife.* = John de Swynnerton (II), *ob.* 1254. = (Eleanor, dau. and heir of Stephen de Peshall); *1st wife.*

Robert de Sugnall (II), dead in 1233.

Roger de Swynnerton, son and heir, *ob. s.p.*

John, brother and heir, *ob. s.p.*

John de Swynnerton (III), of Parva Sugnall, and other sons.

Robert de Sugnall (III), a minor in 1242; dead before 1255.

X Daughters and heirs in ward to Margery, Lady of Swynnerton.

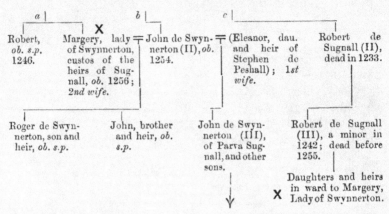

It will be thus seen that the nearest of kin who *could* inherit was the issue male of John de Swynnerton (II) *by his first wife;* and that the nearest of kin *who could not inherit* was Margery de Swynnerton, to whom, therefore, was conceded the custody of the heirs of the last Robert de Sugnall.

Canon Bridgeman does not mention the names of Margery de Swynnerton's executors. They were—

1. Roger, Prior of Trentham.
2. Nicholas de Aspley, Prior of St. Thomas, near Stafford.
3. Stephen de Hunteback, chaplain.[1]

Nicholas de Aspley must have been a brother of Stephen de Aspley, and one of Margery's step-sons. How Great Sugnall came to the Swynnertons from Roger de Waure, who acquired it from Robert de Sugnall (III), is told in my account of the earlier Swynnertons of Eccleshall.

NOTE.—Referring to the circumstance that, in the attestation-clauses of the Stone Chartulary, Sir Robert de Swynnerton often heads the list of witnesses, while his younger brother John de Swynnerton as often comes near the end (see p. 74), there is a deed of Hervey Bagot of 1194–5, edited by Eyton in "Staff. Coll.," II, 226, where, of eighteen witnesses, Adam de Audley heads the list, while his two sons, Adam and Henry, enter last but two.

These examples are instances of the well-known fact that the precedence of age and rank was very strictly observed on all such occasions. Indeed, a witness-clause will often afford a clue, not merely to status, but even to approximate age.

[1] *Liber Albus* at Lichfield.

SWYNNERTON OF CHELL, CO. STAFFORD.

NOTES ON THE EARLIER HISTORY OF THE MANOR OF GREAT CHELL, CO. STAFFORD.

The Swynnerton holding at Chell, as we learn from a suit of 14–15 Ed. I (1286) consisted of four messuages and four bovates of land with appurtenances at *Great Chelle*, which they held as arrière tenants under the Audleys, who had obtained the chief rents and the seignory of that place from Engenulf de Gresley and Alina.

Erdeswick says that Ormus de Guldene, among other manors, held the manor of Chell.

Ormus had at least two sons, Robert and Ralf. Of these Ralf fitz Orm had a daughter and heir, Emma, who married Adam de Audley, and Robert had a daughter, Alina, who married Engenulf de Gresley.

Henry III's confirmation to Henry de Audley of all his lands shows that Audley and Cheddleton—*i.e.* not the land, for that had been the Audleys long before, but the mesne-lordship of them[1] came to Adam his father of the gift of Nicholas de Verdon, to whom Erdeswick believes him to have been related, and that Adam de Audley had "of the gift of Engenulf de Gresley and of Alina his wife, Tunstall, Chaddersley, CHELLE, and Normancote."

But Chell, with Tunstall, Chadderley, Thursfield, Bradwell, and Normancote, had formed part of the Staffordshire Seigneury, believed by Eyton to have been added to the Domesday Honour of Chester, previously to 1153, probably by Henry I, in favour of Earl Raoul le Meschin, who, succeeding his father, Earl Raoul (I) in 1128, married about that time the King's granddaughter. And when it is certified by the Crown (see *Rot. Cart.*, 21 Hen. III) that Earl Ranulf (III) gave Henry de Audley the whole rent of Chell, Tunstall, Chadderley, Thursfield, Bradwell, and Normancote, the presumption is that the Earl merely released that which

[1] "Staff. Coll.," I, 234.

had been previously due to himself as Suzerain. (So Eyton. See "Staff. Coll.," I, 234.)

It would appear then that the gift of Engenulf and Alina of the manor of Chell, etc., had constituted Adam de Audley *mesne* tenant instead of themselves under the Earl of Chester; and that the gift of Earl Ranulf (III) to Henry de Audley constituted the latter, tenant *sine medio* of the same places *under the King.* But when the King (Henry III) conferred his Crown lands in those parts of Staffordshire on his younger son Edmund Crouchback, with the Earldom of Lancaster, then the Audleys would again hold Chell, etc., as *mesne* tenants, but this time of the Honour of Lancaster.

Adam de Audley had three sons, Adam who died without issue, the aforementioned Henry, the founder of the barony, and William.

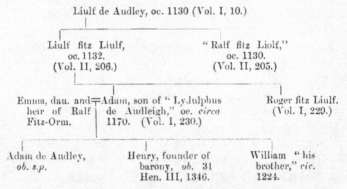

Liulf de Audley, oc. 1130 (Vol. I, 10.)

Liulf fitz Liulf, oc. 1132. (Vol. II, 206.)

"Ralf fitz Liolf," oc. 1130. (Vol. II, 205.)

Emma, dau. and heir of Ralf Fitz-Orm. = Adam, son of "Lydulphus de Audleigh," oc. *circa* 1170. (Vol. I, 230.)

Roger fitz Liulf. (Vol. I, 229.)

Adam de Audley, *ob. s.p.*

Henry, founder of barony, *ob.* 31 Hen. III, 1346.

William "his brother," *cir.* 1224.

In a deed of about 1225, by which John son of Ralf de Cnotton confirms to Ralf son of John de Wytemore all the tenements in Wytemore which John de Wytemore, father of Ralf, held of Ralf de Cnotton, father of John, among ten witnesses, the two first in order are the Lords *Henry de Haudeley* and *Robert de Swynnerton.*[1]

To a concord, dated the Feast of St. Peter ad Vincula, A.G. 1242, between the Abbot of Hilton, of the one part, and the Prior of Trentham, of the other, the witnesses in order are: "the Lords Simon then Abbot of Combermere, *Henry de Audley, James de Audley his son, Robert de Swinnerton,* William Pantulf, Geoffrey Griffin, Robert de Mere, with Robert de Badenale, Ralf de Waure, Ranulf de Bevile, and others."[2]

[1] Original deed *penes* Rev. C. Swynnerton.
[2] "Staff. Coll.," Vol. XI, pp. 314, 315.

All these witnesses were men of the first rank in the district. Thus to take the second deed, the Abbot of Combermere was probably visitor of both Hilton[1] and Trentham. Henry de Audley, the first Baron Audley, founded the Abbey of Hilton in 1223. James de Audley his son, a favourite of Henry III, was subsequently one of the King's Council of Twelve in 1259, and a lord of the Welsh marches. Swynnerton was lord of Swynnerton Pantulf, a grandson of Ivo Pantulf, Baron of Wem, by Alice daughter of Norman de Verdon, was lord of Cubblestone; Griffin, of Clayton; Robert de Badenhale was then Seneschal of Trentham; Ralf, if identical with Roger de Waure, held office under the Bishops, and was a large tenant in Eccleshall; Ralf Bevile of Longton was a great benefactor of the priory of Trentham: all had domains close to Trentham and Hilton.

It is to be noted that in the former deed Robert de Swynnerton's name stands second, coming immediately after that of Henry de Audley himself, and that in the latter deed it stands fourth, coming immediately after that of James de Audley the son and heir, and before even William Pantulf's. The inference is that he was *near of kin* to the Lord Henry de Audley. An Audley may have married a Swynnerton, but the following extracts make it quite clear that a Swynnerton had married a lady of the house of Audley :—

1. On the Octaves of Michaelmas, 6th Oct., 1251, Margaret, the wife of Robert de Mere, put in her place her husband, or Robert de Weston, *versus* Pavia, widow of RICHARD DE CHELL, in a plea of dower.[2]

2. In June, 1263, Isolda, the widow of Robert son of Robert de Mere, sued Roger de Swynnerton for one-third of two virgates of land in Acton and Shelton (in Swynnerton), and one-third of a rent of 8 marks in CHELLE, which she claimed as dower.[3]

3. At the assize at Lichfield on the morrow of Holy Trinity, 56 Hen. III (1272), John de Swyneforton (Swynnerton) appeared, and conceded to Hugh de Beumeys and Isolda his wife a third part of three virgates of land and 7*s.* 6*d.* of rent in Shelton, Acton, and CHELLE, as the dower of the same Isolda, which she had of the gift of Robert de Mere her first husband, the COUSIN of the aforesaid John, *whose heir he is.*[4]

[1] Not the Hilton of the subsequent Swynnertons of Hilton, which was in quite another part of Staffordshire.

[2] "Staff. Coll.," Vol. IV, p. 122.

[3] *Ibid.*, pp. 156, 157.

[4] *Ibid.*, p. 192.

These extracts prove that Chell had belonged to Margery, the daughter of Richard de Chell, that either her mother or her grandmother therefore must have been an Audley, and that the *alias* of her husband, Richard de Chell, must have been Richard de Swynnerton.

If we suppose that her grandmother was an Audley, her husband will have been Robert, lord of Swynnerton, who died about 1190. Her marriage portion will have been Chell, and Chell will have descended to Richard, her younger son, who dying, left a daughter and heir Margery, cousin of Margery, lady of Swynnerton, and wife of Robert de Mere. Of course it may have been Richard himself who married an Audley, but in either case the result is the same. I suppose the lady's name to have been Margery, and that the two later Margerys were named after her. Hence the following pedigree:—

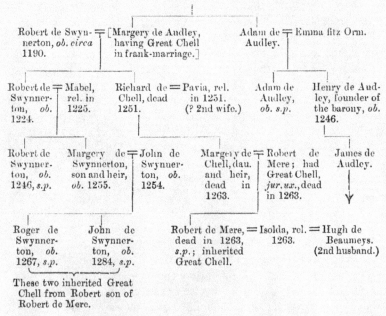

Robert de Swynnerton, *ob. circa* 1190. = [Margery de Audley, having Great Chell in frank-marriage.]

Adam de Audley. = Emma fitz Orm.

Robert de Swynnerton, *ob.* 1224. = Mabel, rel. in 1225.

Richard de Chell, dead 1251. = Pavia, rel. in 1251. (? 2nd wife.)

Adam de Audley, *ob. s.p.*

Henry de Audley, founder of the barony, *ob.* 1246.

Robert de Swynnerton, *ob.* 1246, *s.p.*

Margery de Swynnerton, son and heir, *ob.* 1255. = John de Swynnerton, *ob.* 1254.

Margery de Chell, dau. and heir, dead in 1263. = Robert de Mere; had Great Chell, *jur. ux.*, dead in 1263.

James de Audley.

Roger de Swynnerton, *ob.* 1267, *s.p.*

John de Swynnerton, *ob.* 1284, *s.p.*

These two inherited Great Chell from Robert son of Robert de Mere.

Robert de Mere, dead in 1263, *s.p.*; inherited Great Chell. = Isolda, rel. 1263. = Hugh de Beaumeys. (2nd husband.)

John de Swynnerton, who died without issue, must have left Chell as well as Swynnerton to his nephew and successor Roger, the eldest son of his half-brother, Stephen de Swynnerton of Isewall. Thus:—

At the Michaelmas Assizes of 14–15 Ed. I. (1286), the Sheriff of Staffordshire was ordered to take with him four discreet and lawful knights of his county, and *in propria persona* to proceed to the court of Edmund the King's brother, at Newcastle-under-Lyme, and in full court there to cause to be recorded the suit which was in the court by the King's writ between John de Wytemore, Adam son of William de Alsager, Roger de Pyvelesdon and Joan his wife, Robert le Mareschal, and Gilbert son of Geoffrey de Aston, plaintiffs, and Roger son of Stephen de Useleswell, tenant of four messuages and four bovates of land with the appurtenances in GREAT CHELLE, as to which the said Roger son of Stephen complained that a false judgment had been given, and to have the record in court at this term, together with four legal men of the same court who were present at the record. And John and the others now appeared, and William de Mere, Geoffrey de Cokenegge, Thomas de Baddeley, and Richard Lee, the four men of the court to whom the record had been entrusted to produce it in court, never came. The Sheriff is therefore ordered to distrain and produce them on the morrow of the Purification, and the same day is given to the other parties. At the ensuing Hillary Term, however, Roger son of Stephen de Useleswall, who brought a writ of false judgment against John de Wytemore, Adam son of William de Allesager and others did not appear to prosecute it, and the suit is dismissed.[1]

In 16 Ed. I Roger de Swynnerton gives half a mark for a writ of *ad terminum*.

At Michaelmas, 1288, Roger son of Stephen de Swynemerton (Swynnerton) gives 40s. for licence of concord with Roger de Pulesdon and Joan his wife in a plea of convention, and they have a chirograph. In this final concord Roger son of Stephen de Swynnerton appears as complainant against Roger de Pywelesdon and Juliana (Joan) his wife, deforciants in a plea concerning the ninth part of the manor of Swynnerton, of Beche, and CHELLE, which deforciants acknowledge to belong to complainant, and they remitted the same to complainant for ever. For this acknowledgment complainant gave deforciants one sore sparrow-hawk.

Again:—In Trinity Term, 18 Ed. I (1290), Roger de Swynnerton is *in misericordia* for several defaults of appearance. He is attached to answer the plea of Robert Chelle, that he, with John de Cherleton, James de Hayton, William son of William de Cherleton, and Gilbert de Swynnerton had ill-treated, taken, and imprisoned at Swynnerton the said Robert Chelle, on the Monday

[1] "Staff. Coll.," Vol. VII, Part 2, pp. 15, 16.

after the Feast of St. James, 17 Ed. I (1289), and detained him a prisoner for fifteen days, until he was delivered by the King's precept, for which he claimed 100s. damages. Roger appeared and denied the injury, and stated that after the death of Richard, the brother of Robert Chelle who had held of him a messuage and virgate of land in CHELLE in villeinage, the said Robert had fined 30s. for entry into the said tenement to be held in villeinage of him, and because he had refused to pay the fine he had taken him as his villein, and put him into gaol, as it was lawful for him to do.[1]

Roger de Swynnerton died in 1298,[2] and was succeeded by his eldest son Roger, who died both Baron and Banneret in 1338, having demised his rights in Chell before his death. Thus:—

Matilda, formerly wife of Roger de Swynnerton, sued Richard de Peshale, chivaler, for a third of a rent of 40s. in CHELLE, which she claimed as dower. Richard stated that he held the rent for his life only by a demise of the said Roger de Swynnerton, who had afterwards granted the reversion of it to Thomas de Swynnerton and his heirs, and he could not answer to the plea of Matilda without the said Thomas: as Matilda did not deny this, the Sheriff was ordered to summon the said Thomas for the Quindene of Holy Trinity.

Nevertheless, the Roger who died in 1298 may have made a grant in Chell to a younger brother, name at present unknown, and the four "de Chells," apparently brothers, who were of the faction of Roger de Swynnerton in the reign of Edward II, may have been sons of that younger brother. The principal members of that faction were these:—

Roger de Swynnerton, knight,
John de Swynnerton, knight,
Richard de Swynnerton, man-at-arms,
Stephen de Swynnerton, man-at-arms,
Nicholas de Swynnerton, clerk,
Alexander de Swynnerton,
} brothers.

John de Swynnerton of Isewall, man-at-arms, uncle of the foregoing.
Richard de Whetales.
John de Whetales.
Richard de Chelle, clerk.

[1] "Staff. Coll.," Vol. VII, Part 2, p. 17.
[2] Rot. Claus., 26 Ed. I.

William de Chelle.
Hugh de Chelle.
Henry de Chelle.

The Whetales were certainly Swynnertons, since they were identical with the Peshales, who were Swynnertons, and the Rolls are not without indications that these Chells were also Swynnertons, and if so they may have been sons of the supposed younger brother above referred to.—

[*De Banco*, 9 *E. II* (1315), *Mich.* Anna, formerly wife of Adam de Whetale by Richard de *Whetale* her attorney, sues Juliana, etc. for dower.

Ibidem. Anna, formerly wife of Adam de Whetales by Richard de *Peshale* her attorney, sues Juliana, etc. for dower. (Same suit.)[1]

Richard de Whetales *alias* de Peshale was in fact Anna's step-son.[2]

Again in a suit, *Coram Rege*, of Mich., 9 Ric. II, "John de *Whethales* of Albrighton" is also named "John de *Peshale*" in the same pleadings.][3]

[POSTSCRIPTUM.]

A "Richard fitz-Alwin," who was probably a Swynnerton, occurs in a suit of *Mort d'Ancestor* concerning land of the Templars in "Kel" in 1 John (1199).[4] In the same year, as *Ricardus filius Alani*, he fined a mark for his pledges.[5] He was deceased in 1213, when Godehouda, his widow, was suing Geoffrey Savage for her dower in "Walcot."[6]

This Richard fitz-Alan may possibly have been a younger son of "Robert fitz-Alan" of Swynnerton, deceased 1190, and father of Richard de Chell. And his wife, Godonda, may possibly have been the member of the family of Audley, whose marriage-portion was Chell. Even if that were so, the argument of this paper would be fortified rather than weakened.

ON VARIATIONS IN EARLY PERSONAL NAMES.

Consider :—

I.—Necessity of distinction.

II.—The extreme unwillingness on the part of the Normans to adopt the barbarous place-names of the subject Saxons.

a.—This seen in such surnames as *Dapifer*, *Constabularius*, *Forestarius*, etc.

b. —Many Normans had recourse to the prefix "fitz." But as in "Fitz-Alan" this also became a source of confusion. Hence possibly differences in spelling, as "Fitz-Eelen," "Fitz-Ailwin," etc.

[1] "Staff. Coll.," Vol. IX, p. 56.
[2] *Ibid.*, p. 79, and Heralds' Visitations of 1583.
[3] *Ibid.*, Vol. XVI, pp. 27–28.
[4] "Staff. Coll.," III, 57.
[5] *Ibid.*, II, 95.
[6] *Ibid.*, III, 160.

III.—The policy of Henry I, and Henry II, did much to break down the barriers between the two races, and taught Normans to be proud of being Englishmen.

IV.—By the accession of Richard I, place-cognomens were well established, and Robert de Swynnerton of Swynnerton (for example) can no longer be confused with any possible Robert fitz-Alan of Coton.

V.—Multiplied possession, however, formed a new evil, as men were named sometimes after one estate, sometimes after another, and it was not the reign of Edward II, or early Edward III, that the *caput* of family gave the fixed name to the race. Meanwhile, however, the onfusion among surnames is so great and so bewildering in those early times, that General Wrottesley suggests that the better plan would be to translate the French "de" into its English equivalent, excepting in those cases where it marks the general patronymic, or generic name, of the family. Take, as an example, John de Swynnerton of Isewall, where "de Swynnerton" has become generic. In his quit-claim to Roger, Bishop of Coventry and Lichfield, he appears as "Johannes de Swynnerton de Iselwelle." Here, naturally, we should translate the second "de," but not the first—John de Swynnerton of Isewall. But this John constantly appears under the form of "Johannes de Iselwelle," which is merely a local or residential name. Wherever there is evidence that, as in this case, a name is not generic, but merely residential, or local, or territorial, it would certainly be best to render the "de" into "of." *John of Isewelle* would suggest at once the *hiatus*, which could be supplied within brackets; thus,—*John* (*de Swynnerton*) *of Isewelle.*

NOTE TO pp. 98-100.—Incidental and undesigned testimony is afforded by this paper, corroborating the statement, that "Robert de Suinnerton" and "John de Suinnerton" of the Stone Chartulary were two brothers (See pp. 73-76.)

THE CROSSED-LEGGED FIGURE IN SWYNNERTON CHURCH.

BY THE

REV. C. SWYNNERTON.

ON THE CROSS-LEGGED EFFIGY IN SWYNNERTON CHURCH.

BEFORE coming directly to the subject of this paper, it will be necessary first of all to settle certain preliminary dates in order to show that at the time of the Crusade of 1191 there was living at Swynnerton a knight, not only sufficiently young to incur the risks of that expedition, but also of such an age as to be still comparatively young at the time of his death; the reason of which will appear presently.

Early in the reign of Henry II we have evidence of a difference of opinion between "Robert fitz-Eelen,"[1] the lord of Swynnerton, and the canons of Stone Priory regarding the right of presentation to Swynnerton Church. An inspection of a charter of Helyas, the Archdeacon of Stafford, which Eyton shows to have passed in or soon after 1155, reveals the fact that this dispute had been of a very protracted character, the wording of the deed distinctly stating that there had been a long controversy between the two parties as to their respective claims. "Robert fitz-Eelen," the lord of the vill, had evidently, some years before, presented to the living two secular priests (for there were then two incumbents) Osbert and another Osbert.[2] From the tenour of similar disputes in subsequent times, it is probable that the quarrel was brought to a crisis by a refusal on the part of the two rectors to pay as a condition of undisturbed possession an annual pension claimed originally by the Priory of Kenilworth, but then appurtenant to the daughter house of Stone. At last Bishop Walter Duredent, who died in 1159, was induced to interfere. He sent Helyas the Archdeacon to the spot, who, when

[1] He was the son of Alen the Domesday tenant of Swynnerton co. Staff. and Rauceby co. Linc., and probably brother and heir of Alan the husband of Eylina, daughter of Enisan de Walton, who gave her inheritance in Walton to the monks of Stone ("Staff. Coll.," Vol. II, 298.)

[2] It is not at all unlikely that these two Osberts were father and son.

he was come, summoned before him the two incumbents, and compelled them to surrender the church of "Swinnerton" on the altar of the blessed Mary in the church of Stone. This they accordingly did, and professedly it was done "with the assent of Robert fitz-Eelen, which Robert of the aforesaid vill of Swinnerton is lord." The rest of the charter in which Helyas records this arrangement translates thus:—"Above all, the aforesaid clergy have pledged themselves on oath in the same place, that, with the church, and for the church, of Stone, they will everywhere devote themselves, body and soul, and specially to defend and to retain the aforesaid church of Swinnerton to the canons of Stone, as that which legally and *parochially* of the said church of Stone it is well known to be, and that they will never side against it with anyone"—(*cum aliquo*, meaning, apparently, the lord of the vill).[1]

Robert fitz-Eelen was not himself present at this characteristic scene, as his name nowhere appears among the witnesses, and I am of opinion that, when old and infirm, he had been induced to waive his rights, and to assent to the arrangement of the monks, his two chaplains, Osbert and Osbert, for this concession being allowed to remain in possession.

It would appear likely, then, that "Robert fitz-Eelen," whom we know to have been in possession in 1122[2] died about the time of the date of this deed, that is to say, some time between 1155 and 1159.

From the record of a similar dispute which raged in the reign of King John,[3] we learn that "Robert fitz-Eelen" left a son and successor also named Robert, who as "Robertus filius Alani" attests a deed of Robert de Stafford, which Eyton proves to have passed between 1158 and 1165.[4] In the *Liber Niger* of 1166 we meet with him again, where "Robert fitz-Aelen" is returned as

[1] This deed *in extenso* is quoted with notes in "Staff. Hist. Coll.," Vol. III, p. 185. Domesday Book makes no mention of any Church of Swynnerton in 1086. Probably it did not form a separate parish at all, for this deed declares that even so late as 1154 it was *parochially* but a portion of the great parish of Stone. Nevertheless a church had been built there, probably before 1100, portions of which still remain, and practically it had been constituted a parish, but it remained always dependent, to the extent of two marks yearly, to the mother-parish of Stone.

[2] "Staff Hist. Coll.," Vol. II, 195–197. [3] *Ibid.*, Vol. VI, 30.

[4] *Ibid.*, Vol. II, 261.

holding a knight's fee at Swynnerton, co. Stafford, and one half a knight's fee at Rauceby, co. Lincoln, under the barons of Stafford.[1]

Towards the end of his life he, like his father, would appear to have been involved in controversy with the monks of Stone regarding the advowson of the church. There was a vacancy in the living; there was a dispute as to the patronage; the Bishop had again to interfere; Robert fitz-Aelan was induced to confirm his father's concession, and the Prior and Canons carried the day by presenting their own man, "Adam the Chaplain."[2]

The Plea Rolls of 2 Hen. III (1217) show that this Robert confirmed his father's concession in the time of Bishop Hugh, and Bishop Hugh of Lichfield was elected in 1185. "Robert fitz-Aelen" therefore was living after 1185. That he was dead before 1190 I accept as certain, and as the fact directly concerns the subject of this paper I now give my reasons for thinking so:—

In 1 John (1199) Stephen de Hatton claimed against "Robert de Swynnerton" four virgates of land which his father had leased to *Robert the father of the said Robert de Swynnerton* for a term which had then expired.[3]

This entry proves that "Robert fitz-Aelen" was dead in 1199.

In the same year Walter de Cherleton arraigned "Robert de Swynnerton" for having injured him by unjustly raising a certain stank after the second coronation of Richard I (1194). The main issue before the court was—Did Robert de Swynnerton raise the stank after the coronation or before? The defendant's plea was that he did not raise it after the coronation, and the jury found in his favour. He must have raised it *before* 1194.[4]

This entry proves that "Robert fitz-Aelen" was dead in 1194.

Once more: it is not "Robert fitz-Aelen," but "Robertus de Swinertona," who attested a deed of Hervey Bagot, which Eyton shows to have passed between 1185 and 1190.[5]

It is, then, evident that Robert fitz-Aelen died some time before the year 1190, and that before that date also—that is, by the date of the accession of Richard I—he was succeeded by a son "Robertus de Swinertona," who, as Eyton observes, was the first of the race of the Domesday "Aslen" to call himself "de Swinerton." His

[1] "Staff. Hist. Coll.," Vol. I, 174.

[2] *Ibid.*, Vol. VI, 30.

[3] *Ibid.*, Vol. III, 59, 60. The expired term was doubtless twenty-one years. See a suit of this same Stephen de Hatton *alias* Stephen de Chatkull, *Curia Regis Rolls*, 1 John; "Staff. Coll.," III, 56.

[4] *Ibid.*, Vol. III, 56 (from Assize Roll of 1 John).

[5] *Ibid.*, Vol. II, 261.

name frequently occurs in the Plea Rolls and charters of the time, and Canon the Hon. G. O. Bridgeman, in his "History of the Swynnertons," proves that he died in or just before the year 1224.[1]

Having thus settled that point, namely, that the Robert de Swynnerton who was deceased by 1224 was the lord of Swynnerton at the date of Richard's Crusade in 1192, we have next to examine the evidence as to his having accompanied that monarch to Cyprus and Palestine.

1. The Lincolnshire Hundred Roll of 3 Ed. I (1274–5) states that the Hospitallers of Maltby held half a knight's fee in Rauceby by the gift of Robert de Swynnerton 100 years before.[2] The statement, however, need not be understood literally. It speaks in round numbers, and the hundred years are a rough calculation. It may, and it probably does, refer to the time of Richard's Crusade.
2. Robert de Swynnerton's overlord, Robert de Stafford, then like himself a young man, accompanied by his younger brother Nicholas, joined that Crusade, and where the overlord went many of his knights would follow.
3. That many of them did follow is proved thus:—The amount of scutage of Wales remitted to Robert de Stafford by the King for taking the Cross was the exact amount sanctioned for a Baron and nine of his vassal knights.[3] It is most improbable that, of these nine, Robert de Swynnerton should not have been one. He was young and doubtless aglow with the prevailing enthusiasm; he was drawn by the ties of kindred,[4] and impelled by the obligations of feudalism, and he represented one of the most considerable knightly families in Staffordshire.
4. But the Rolls are not without other indications that Robert de Swynnerton was absent from England at this period. Hardly had Richard I left for the East when his brother John began to undermine his authority and to exercise tyranny. The result was seen in provincial disturbances. In Staffordshire there appears to have been an insurrection, and the Pipe Roll of Michaelmas, 1191, which deals with the events of the previous twelve months, shows

[1] "Staff. Hist. Coll.," Vol. VII, Part 1, 5. [2] *Ibid.*, Vol. I, 174.

[3] Eyton works this out in one of the early volumes of the "Staff. Hist. Coll."

[4] Both General Wrottesley and Canon Bridgeman expressed their opinion that "Aslen" de Swynnerton, the Norman grantee, was related to Robert de Stafford.

that large sums had been expended by the Sheriff in the maintenance of men-at-arms, who had been called out for the preservation of the peace.[1] At Newcastle a strong garrison of knights was maintained at great expense.[2] Offenders had been imprisoned in the King's gaol at Stafford. Among the latter apparently was Nicholas de Tittensor, a neighbour, and, I think, a kinsman, of Robert de Swynnerton.

Tittensor adjoined Swynnerton so closely that one of its members, Beech, was included within the boundaries of Swynnerton parish. Nicholas de Tittensor, apparently too advanced in years to go himself, had sent his son and heir, Richard de Stoke, on Crusade with Robert de Stafford his lord.[3] He was mesne lord of both Tittensor and Stoke (in Stone), and he appears to have put his son Richard in seisin of Stoke, as well as of Aston, a portion of Stoke, long before King Richard's accession.[4] All these places were in the great parish of Stone, adjoining the parish and manor of Swynnerton.

It was during his son's absence over sea with the King that Nicholas de Tittensor was found a prisoner in the royal castle or gaol of Stafford. He was allowed to compound his offence, whatever it was, for a round fine. To obtain the full sum necessary he was compelled to part with a portion of his son's inheritance. Half the whole vill of Stoke, with its appurtenances, namely, two virgates of land with half of the demesne, he sold to his superior, Robert fitz-Payne, for 100s. of silver, and a gold ring to Sybil, his wife.[5] A similar grant (of the other half), with the half service which Robert fitz-Payne owed him for 100 acres and a virgate in Aston (*quas tenet de dominio meo de Stoke*), he gave to the Prior and Canons of Stone. And this he did, as he says himself, as a return to the monks for the sum of xv marcs (100s.), which they gave him "*ad redemptionem meam dum captus eram apud Stafford*," for his deliverance when a captive at Stafford.[6]

The latter transaction is comprised in three deeds in

[1] Pipe Rolls, 3 Ric. I, "Staff. Coll.," II, 10, 11.
[2] *Ibid.* [3] *Ibid.*, VII, Part 2, p. 1. [4] "Staff. Coll.," III, 32.
[5] *Ibid.* [6] *Ibid.*, VI, Part 1, 18.

the Stone Chartulary, which passed after the news of Robert de Stafford's death on Crusade had arrived in England, and after Hervey Bagot, the husband of Milisent, Robert de Stafford's sister and heir, had offered 100 marcs for seisin of the Barony of Stafford in right of his wife, that is, some time in the year 1191–2.[1] And the point to note is this,—that the monks of Stone, to establish their right in the property as firmly as possible, in the absence of the heir, scoured the country round about Stone and Swynnerton for substantial witnesses, whom they brought together to the enormous number of eighteen. In this list, conspicuous by its absence, the name of Robert de Swynnerton does not appear.[2] Where was he? Evidently he was absent on Crusade in the company of his kinsman, Richard de Stoke of Tittensor, and the rest of the nine knights who had followed Robert de Stafford to the Holy Land.[3] "*Transfretavit in servitio Regis Ricardi*," to quote Richard de Stoke's own words in the suit by which, on his return home, he vainly strove to quash the alienation of so much of his inheritance, on the plea that his father, during his absence on service with the King, had held those lands of his only in trust, as his Seneschal.[4]

5. Two out of every three of those who engaged in that Crusade are estimated to have died of dysentery at Acre. Robert and Nicholas de Stafford, from whatever cause, both perished there or elsewhere.[5] The survivors were nursed back to health by the Knight Hospitallers who acted as an "Army Medical Department." They were repaid by grants of land, some of these grants being really sales effected by sick knights to raise the necessary funds for the journey home. There can be little doubt that the grant of the half knight's fee at Rauceby to the Knight-Hospitallers was one such sale effected by Robert de Swynnerton when stricken with disease or wounds, or when pressed for money, at Acre or Ascalon.[6]

1 "Staff. Hist. Coll.," II, 27. 2 *Ibid.*, VI, Part 1, 17. 3 *Ibid.*, II, 9.

4 *Ibid.*, III, 32, 33. Richard de Stoke pleaded that his father had enfeoffed him by deed twenty years before. Unfortunately the deed was not forthcoming.

5 "Staff. Hist. Coll.," II, 28.

6 So argues General Wrottesley, and the argument is sound.

o face page 117.

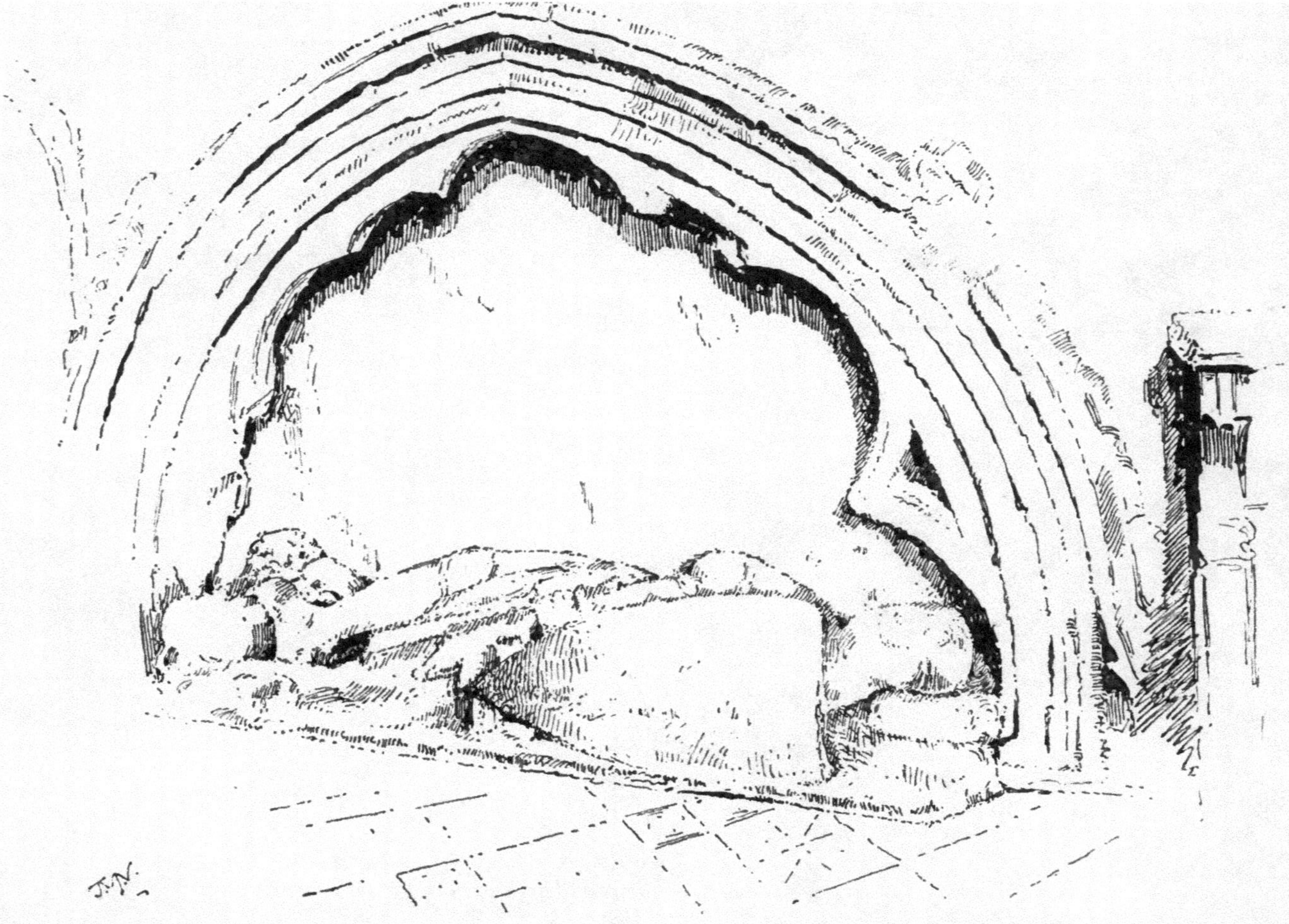

CROSS-LEGGED EFFIGY IN SWYNNERTON CHURCH.—(From a sketch by J. M. NICHOLSON, Isle of Man.)

6. The Norman-French motto, *Avaunturez et marchez avaunt*,[1] was said in a tradition preserved by the Swinnertons of Butterton to have been "conferred on an ancestor for valour in engaging and overcoming in single combat a Saracen champion in the Holy Wars."[2] Tradition is not of the nature of judicial evidence; but every tradition contains a germ of truth, and its testimony becomes important when, as in this case, it is supplemented by evidence of a more direct character.

This then is our second point, and we have now in the third place to consider the style of the effigy, traditionally known as the "Old Crusader," which lies in the chancel of Swynnerton Church.

This effigy is a recumbent figure of a cross-legged knight. Carved, as it is, in some local free-stone, it has unfortunately suffered from the wear and tear of time. It lies close to the floor in a niche on the south side of the chancel, the position (as generally understood) of the tomb of a founder. But it is curious that one of the sedilia, of which there remain only two, appears to have been encroached upon to make room for it, suggesting the bare possibility of its having been moved from some other part of the church, especially as the canopy over it is of a decidedly later date. The sculptured figure measures 6 feet 2 inches from head to foot: it lies partly on one side, and it is clothed in complete mail. The head rests on a plain square cushion. Round the head may be traced the usual slight fillet-like rim or projection, indicating possibly some fashion of skull-cap of velvet worn beneath, just as within memory the wild warriors of our Indian North-West Frontier wore a similar cap beneath their linked mail. The features, greatly worn, are exposed. The right hand is in the act of drawing or restoring the heavy cross-hilted sword which hangs by two straps secured to a broad leathern belt. The left hand grasps the scabbard. The legs are crossed at the knee, and the feet rest on a dog or on a lion couchant.[3] On the heels were plain prick-spurs. Above and below the knee may

[1] College of Arms. The differenced form of the motto, claimed by the Swinnertons of Butterton, was *Avauncez et archez bien*, indicating an offshoot from the main stem, not of knights, but of squires and mounted archers.

[2] From a pedigree of Swinnerton of Butterton dated 1713.

[3] "Thou shalt go upon the lion—the young lion shalt thou tread under thy feet." (Ps. xci, 13.)

be traced a band indicating apparently the use of a leathern knee-cap. On the left arm hangs an early Norman convex shield, which is 34 inches in length, 19 inches broad at the top, and 16 inches broad in the middle. The original model must have been even longer, probably the full yard, as it narrows rapidly from the centre down, and like the figure looks much worn, the point especially. The evidence of the shield, its dimensions and its form, led the late Mr. Planchè, Somerset Herald, to attribute the work to the first half of the twelfth century (1125). The bands above and below the knee suggest a date considerably later, though it has yet to be proved that (leathern) knee-caps were never worn before the middle of the thirteenth century. There is no inscription on the tomb, which itself is an argument of greater antiquity, and the surface of the shield is quite plain. In all respects it bears a very close resemblance to the effigy of Maurice Berkeley de Gaunt in the Mayor's chapel at Bristol, who was buried there in 1230, excepting that the latter figure does not carry a shield.

The foregoing considerations constitute a mass of accumulative evidence tending to show that a lord of Swynnerton accompanied Richard Cœur-de-Lion to the Holy Land in 1191, and those who, with Mr. Planchè, the late Somerset Herald, regard this uninscribed figure as early work, will be disposed to identify it with Sir Robert de Swynnerton, whose claims are thus set forth. In other words, its date would range from 1224 to 1230.

There is, however, another alternative with claims on our attention which cannot be ignored, and that is, that the figure marks the tomb of Sir John de Swynnerton of Sugnall, who, even before he acquired Swynnerton, and much else besides, by his marriage with his cousin Margaret, the heiress of Swynnerton, was already a man of much wealth. This John de Swynnerton died lord of Swynnerton about 1254, and the arguments in his favour are these:—

1. He was the founder of a new line of lords of Swynnerton.
2. He was almost certainly a second founder of the church, which, originally Norman throughout, must have been rebuilt by him in the Early English style of Gothic architecture, which characterizes the middle of that century, and which the fabric displays to the present day. This fact would have entitled him to interment in

that part of the new chancel reserved for a founder, the very spot, in fact, occupied by the effigy. And the same hypothesis would account for the removal of one of his own Early English *sedilia* for the purpose of affording sufficient space for the admission of body and figure in the niche designed for it in the south wall.

3. So far as the dates allow us to judge, Sir John de Swynnerton died a comparatively young man, and, as we shall see, the inmate of the tomb also died a comparatively young man.
4. His wife, Margery, lady of Swynnerton in her own right, survived him, and what so likely as that she should have placed a monument to his memory there?
5. During the whole of Henry III's time English gentlemen were constantly going to and from Jerusalem, as the Plea Rolls of that period testify. Many were the Crusades of that time, and it is far more probable than improbable that John de Swynnerton followed the fashion of his day.

If, therefore, it cannot be conceded that the effigy belongs to the earlier date, it might be safely assigned to the later one, that is, to a date not earlier than 1255. In other words, if the figure is not the portrait of Sir Robert de Swynnerton of King Richard's time, who was one of the crusaders of 1191 beyond any reasonable doubt, it is probably that of Sir John de Swynnerton of King Henry's time, from whom all succeeding lords of Swynnerton hailed their direct descent.

But whatever the history of the figure, it certainly marks the present resting-place of one of the earliest lords of Swynnerton, and not only so, but the resting-place of the very knight whose image reposes above, for beneath it there is a grave or burial chamber carefully built with ashlar work, which, on being opened by some accident during the restoration of the church in 1856 was found to contain the body lying exactly, and close under, the stone figure, and *corresponding with it in length*—6 feet 2 inches. Portions of his arms were found within, what appeared to have been a lance-head, and other fragments of iron, but greatly consumed by rust. The corpse had been wrapt in lead a quarter of an inch thick, made to fit close to the form, but it was burst open, as is usually found to be the case with leaden coffins. There appeared to have been a coffin of wood outside the lead, but it was reduced to a soft kind of powder. The skeleton was very perfect. *All the teeth were sound and firmly fixed in the jaws,* excepting two in the front, which were missing. The bones were still clothed with flesh as in life, or rather with the semblance thereof, but it fell to dust soon after exposure to the air. The beard was in perfect preservation and of a *reddish brown.* The rector, the Rev. W. Taylor, who gave me this account, inspected the tomb in company with Mr. Thomas Fitzherbert, the lord of the manor, almost immediately after it had been broken open. The masonry was at once restored, and the dead left once more to rest in peace. But the accident which had disturbed him was scarcely one to be regretted, since it revealed to us a vision of a mediaeval knight as he really was. He rises before us lofty in stature, ruddy in complexion, with auburn locks, and in the vigour of life. Two of his front teeth have been driven in by a lance-thrust. His weapons of war lie by his side, and, if he was a companion of Cœur-de-Lion, we are at liberty to imagine the resolution with which he may have used them, whether at the storming of Buffavento, or on the walls of long-beleaguered Acre.

EXTRACTS FROM THE PLEA ROLLS TEMP. HENRY VI.

BY

MAJOR-GENERAL THE HON. GEORGE WROTTESLEY.

(*Continued from p. 153, Vol. XVII.*)

EXTRACTS FROM THE PLEA ROLLS
TEMP. HENRY VI.

(*Continued from p.* 153, *Vol. XVII.*)

CORAM REGE. MICH., 2 H. VI.

Staff. The Sheriff had been ordered to arrest William Perton, parson of the church of Blumenhulle, Roger Waryng, of Trescote, gentilman, and John, son of Richard Robyns, of Briggenorth, chapman, and produce them at this term to answer for their redemption on account of a trespass and conspiracy against William Leveson, of Hampton, co. Stafford, gentilman, of which they had been convicted; and the Sheriff now returned they could not be found. He was therefore ordered to put them into *exigend;* and if they did not appear, they were to be outlawed. *m.* 13 *Rex.*

Staff. The King sued the Abbot of Bordesle for the next presentation to the church of Kynefar, and the King's attorney (Thomas Greswold) stated that one Henry de Mortimer was formerly seised of the manor and advowson of Kynefare, holding the same of King Edward III *in capite* by the service of one-fourth of a knight's fee, and had presented to the church his clerk, John Lutteley, and he had afterwards granted the advowson of the church to one Walter Attewode, and to his heirs, without the license of the King; and the said Walter had granted the same to the abbot of Bordesle, the license of the King not having been first obtained, and afterwards, when the church became vacant by the resignation of John Lutteley, King Edward III had presented his clerk, Roger Clove, who had been admitted and instituted by the Ordinary; and as the church was now vacant by the death of Roger Clove, it pertained to the King to present to it.

The abbot denied that the advowson of the church had been alienated without the King's license, but admitted that King Edward III had presented the said Roger; but he stated that long after this date King Edward III, by his Letters Patent dated 37 E. III, had granted the advowson to John Acton, then abbot of Bordesley and to the convent; and King Richard II had confirmed these Letters Patent in the third year of his reign; and the same abbot had presented to the church his clerk, Nicholas Grendon, who had been admitted and instituted. The King's attorney repeated his plea, and denied that at the date of the Letters Patent King Edward III was seised of the advowson, and appealed to a jury, which was to be summoned for the Octaves of St. Hillary. Repeated postscripts extending over many terms show no jury had been empannelled. *m.* 35 *Rex.*

CORAM REGE. MICH., 3 H. VI.

Warw. A jury had presented before William Mountfort, chivaler, and John Weston, Justices of the Peace in co. Warwick, on the Tuesday before Michaelmas, 2 H. VI, that Edmund Ferrers, of Bromwyche in co. Warwick, chivaler, John Ruggeley, the abbot of Murywall, Robert Langham, lord of Goysull, co. Warwick, armiger, William Neuport, of Lichefeld, co. Stafford, armiger, Roger Yermonger, of Lichefeld in co. Stafford, gentilman, William atte Welle, of Bromley in co. Stafford, armiger, Thomas Nefeve, of Ruggeley in co. Stafford, gentilman, Robert Overton, of Overton, co. Warwick, yoman, Thomas Percok, prior of the Hospital of St. John, Lychefeld, chaplain, John Seynt Jone, of Lychefeld, yoman, William Arderne, the younger, of Merston, co. Warwick, gentilman, John Nowell, of Lychefeld, yoman, Robert Baxter, of Lychefeld, yoman, Robert Kerkylton, of Cruddeworth, co. Warwick, fletcher, and eleven others named, on the Sunday before the Feast of the Exaltation of the Holy Cross, 2 H. VI, as rebels and disturbers of the King's peace, armed in the manner of war, with habergyns, polaxes, swords, and bows and arrows, with many others who were unknown to the number of nearly 200, had raised an insurrection at Birmyngham [*modo de Ryot et Rowte*] against the form of the Statute "*de armis non portandis*," and had broken into the manor of Birmyngham *vi et armis* and had expelled William de Birmyngham, chivaler, the Lady Joan, his wife, and his sons and daughters, with their household (*cum familia sua*), and had beaten, wounded, and ill-treated their servants, etc. And which presentment the King had commanded to be brought before him to be terminated in this Court.

And the said Edmund Ferrers, knight, and the others above-named now appeared, and denied the indictment and appealed to a jury; and as regarded the intrusion into the manor, they pleaded that the presentment was *non sufficiens in lege*, inasmuch as it never mentioned the owner of the manor. Thomas Greswold, the King's attorney, pleaded it was sufficient, and the case was adjourned to Hillary term for the judgment of the Court. A long postscript shews repeated adjournments before judgment was delivered; but it was held at length that the presentment was not sufficiently definite, and the defendants were discharged. *m.* 20 *Rex.*

Staff. Thomas Salewey, of Cank, son of John Salewey, of Cank, yoman who had been outlawed on an indictment for various misdemeanours which he had not appeared to answer, now surrendered on the 29th November, and was committed to the custody of Thomas Strangways the Marshal. He afterwards produced Letters Patent of the King pardoning him for the transgression, and prayed he might be released on the payment of a Fine. He was therefore discharged. *m.* 20 *Rex, dorso.*

Staff. John Kyngesley, armiger, who had been indicted with Hugh Erdeswyk, Thomas de Swynerton, Thomas Stanley, William Egerton, John Myners, John Delves, Hugh Damport, and others, for divers trespasses, misprisions, and felonies contained in a petition to Parliament in 11 H. IV, appeared in Court and produced the pardon of the King's grandfather dated 24 April, 12 H. IV. *m.* 23 *Rex.*

CORAM REGE. MICH., 4 H. VI.

Staff. The Sheriff had been ordered to summon Robert Erdeswyk, of Great Sandon, co. Stafford, squyer, to answer to the King for having given a certain livery of cloth (*quandam liberatam pannorum*) to William de

Knyghton, of co. Stafford, yoman, when he was neither of his household nor holding any office under him (*non est familiaris seu officiarius*) against the Statute. Robert did not appear, and the Sheriff returned he could not be found. He was therefore ordered to arrest and produce him on the Octaves of St. Hillary. *m.* 5 *Rex.*

CORAM REGE. MICH., 5 H. VI.

Staff. It had been presented before Humfrey, Earl of Stafford, and Richard Lone, and their Fellow Justices of the Peace, that Alana, late wife of William Latoner, of Lichefeld, wedowe, had feloniously stolen, on the Monday after the Feast of the Close of Easter, 3 H. VI, at Lichefyld, a *lanacrum* worth 13*s.* 4*d.* of the goods and chattels of Thomas Stanley, armiger, and which indictment the King for certain causes wished to be determined in this Court. And Alana now surrendered, and was committed to the Marshalsea; and being brought before the Court, pleaded she was not guilty, and appealed to a jury which was to be summoned for the Octaves of St. John the Baptist. And Alana was admitted to bail on the sureties of Richard Hord, of co. Salop, gentilman, William Lawley, of co. Salop, gentilman, John Greswold,[1] of co. Warwick, gentilman, and William Coton, of co. Stafford, gentilman. After several adjournments for want of a jury, the case was sent to be tried before the Justices of Assize at Stafford at Michaelmas, 6 H. VI, when a jury stated she was not guilty. *m.* 7 *Rex.*

On another membrane of this roll Alana had brought an appeal against several persons for the death of her husband.

Staff. A jury had been summoned to return a verdict whether William Birmyngeham, of Coventre, knight, Thomas Austyn, of Birmyngeham, yoman, John Blakemere, of Weston under Lesyord, yoman, and William Drover, of Birmyngeham, hostiler, were guilty of divers felonies and trespasses of which they had been indicted,[2] and the defendants had been admitted to bail on the sureties of Thomas Erdyngton, of Erdyngton, co. Warwick, gentilman, John Warveley, of Warveley, co. Stafford, gentilman, John Peshale, of On, co. Stafford, gentilman, and Ralph Frebody, of Bobyngton, co. Stafford, gentilman; and Thomas Austyn and the said John and William Drover now appeared, and William Birmyngeham being solemnly called did not appear. His manucaptors were therefore to be arrested, and the Sheriff was ordered to put him into *exigend*, and if he did not appear, to outlaw him, and if he appeared, to produce him on the Morrow of All Souls. *m.* 13 *Rex, dorso.*

CORAM REGE. MICH., 6 H. VI.

Staff. Elizabeth, late wife of Robert Colbourne, appealed John Byrde, of Lychefeld, mercer, John Ridware, of Lychefeld, husbondman, Thomas Jayler, hostiler, Richard Coucher, coucher, John Taverner, viteller, William Bedenhale, hosyer, Robert Taillour, taillour, Bernard Sporiour, sporiour, John Strangelford, mercer, William Beek, hosyer, William Neuport, armiger, John More, hostiler, William Sherman, hosyer, John Hethe, draper,

[1] Thomas Greswold at this date was the Attorney General, and it is probable that the latter had taken up the cause of the unfortunate Alana out of pity for her.

[2] The felony imputed to them was robbing Edmund Ferrers of divers goods and chattels at Sedgeley several years before this date.

Nicholas Hauley, chaplain, John Barre, barker, John Pereson, husbondman, Richard Colleman, courtholder, John atte Yate, writer, Henry Alwhite, milleward, and John Rideware, barker,[1] all of Lychefeld, to answer for the death of her husband; together with John Mayot, of Lichefeld, taillour, and Margery, his wife, Thomas Rodesford, of Lychefeld, laborer, John Couper, of Lychefeld, couper, John Fletcher, of Lychefeld, fletcher, John Bedenhale, of Kyngesbromley, yoman, Alice, wife of the said Robert Taillour, John Lyppetort, of Lychefeld, taillour, and John Leverych, of Lychefeld, souter, who had not surrendered.

Elizabeth appeared in person, and stated that at Lychefeld on the Tuesday the Vigil of St. Barnabas, 5 H. VI, about the seventh hour after noon, John Mayot, whom she appealed as principal, had struck Robert Colbourne, her late husband, with a dagger in the breast and given him a mortal blow, of which he had died. And that John Byrde, whom she accused as a principal, had struck her husband a mortal blow on the head with a staff called a keystaf; and Thomas Rodesford, whom she accused as a principal, had stabbed her husband in the back with a dagger; and that the said John Ridware, the younger, Thomas Jayler, Richard Coucher, and the others named were present aiding and abetting the said John Mayot, John Byrde, and Thomas Rodesford in committing the felony; and that John Taverner on the same day had knowingly received John Mayot after the felony, and William Neuport had likewise knowingly received the said John Mayot at Lychefeld the same night, and Nicholas Hanley had knowingly received Thomas Rodesford after the felony; and she accused Margery, the wife of John Mayot, John Couper, John Fletcher, John Bedenhale, Alice, the wife of Robert Taillour, John Lyppetort, and John Leveryche, whom she would have appealed as accessories, if they had been present, of procuring, abetting, and assisting the others in the felony; and that John Fletcher had knowingly received John Mayot on the Feast of St. Barnabas, 5 H. VI, at Lychefeld, and John Bedenhale on the Monday after the Feast of St. John the Baptist, 5 H. VI, had knowingly received John Mayot at Colton. The defendants who had appeared denied the felony, and appealed to a jury; and John Byrde in addition pleaded his name was John Bryd. Elizabeth replied that at the date the writ was issued he was known both as John Bryd and John Byrde, and repeated her plea against him; and John Byrde was committed to the Marshalsea, but afterward released on bail, William Lychefeld, knight, William Venables, armiger,[2] William Gyles, of London, grocer, and Roger Wyllenhale, of co. Stafford, gentilman, standing as sureties for him. A postscript shews that after many adjournments through defect of juries, Elizabeth eventually failed to appear to prosecute her appeal, and her suit was dismissed; but the defendants had to answer for the felony to the King, and Peter de la Pole, of Rodburne, co. Derby, gentilman, Roger Wylnale, of Lychefeld, gentilman, William Gyles, of London, grocer, and John London, of Lychefeld, yoman, became sureties for their appearance either *coram Rege* or at the assizes at Stafford on the Monday after the Feast of St. Peter *in Cathedra* 7 H. VI. *m.* 15.

Staff. John Kyngesley, armiger, sued William Venables, late of Edlaston, co. Cheshire, the younger, gentilman, Richard de Bryndelegh, late of Wystanton, co. Chester, yoman, John de Bryndelegh, of Wystanton, yoman, Robert de Cholmondelegh, late of Edlaston, yoman, Henry Chaloner, of Dulverne, co. Stafford, yoman, Ralph Vicares, of Careswalle, co. Stafford, yoman, John Smyth, of Careswalle, yoman, Robert Perkyn, of Flosbroke, co. Stafford, grome, and twelve others named, for a robbery and breach of the peace. None of the defendants appeared, and the Sheriff was

[1] Elsewhere called John Ridware, the elder.
[2] In other parts of the proceeding William is stated to be of Caverswall.

ordered to arrest and produce them on the Quindene of St. Hillary. *m. 20 dorso.*

Staff. A jury had presented before John Bagot, knight, and Richard Lone, Justices of the Peace at Stafford, on the Monday after the Feast of the Conception of the Blessed Mary, that when John Goldesmith, of Tamworth, goldesmyth, had been indicted in the 1st year of the King's reign at Lychefeld for fabricating at Tamworth 40 nobles of base money, one Roger Wilnehale, of Lichefeld, gentilman, the clerk of the said Justices, had abstracted and embezzled the indictment with a view of favouring the said John Goldesmyth, and had handed it to the said John, to the King's great damage and subversion of his laws. And the King for certain reasons had caused the said indictment to be brought into his Court, to be heard and terminated there.

Roger now surrendered, and was given into the custody of the Marshal and being brought before the Court he pleaded not guilty, and appealed to a jury, and was admitted to bail.

After several adjournments, the case was finally tried by the Justices of Assize at Stafford, when a jury found that Roger was not guilty. *m. 7 Rex, dorso.*

CORAM REGE. MICH., 7 H. VI.

Warw. Thomas Fitzherberd, of Norbury, co. Derby, gentilman, who had been outlawed in co. Warwick at the suit of Matilda, late wife of John Balterley, for the death of her husband, surrendered, and was committed to the Marshalsea; and being brought before the Court, he pleaded that there was a manifest error in the proceedings of outlawry, because at the date it was promulgated, viz. on the Monday after the Feast of St. James, 4 H. VI, and for long before, and afterwards, he was in the King's prison at Suthewerk, co. Surrey.

The proceedings, which were brought into Court by writ of error, state that Matilda, late wife of John Balterley, appeared in person at Hillary term, 4 H. VI, and appealed Thomas fitz herbard, of Norbury, gentilman, and Roger Pipe, of Burton upon Trent, yoman, and Robert Boleter, of Burton on Trent, yoman, for the death of her husband, viz. Thomas and Roger as principals and Robert as an accessory. None of the defendants had appeared, and they had been outlawed in co. Warwick. The proceedings were adjourned to Easter term, 7 H. VI. *m. 15.*

CORAM REGE. MICH., 8 H. VI.

Staff. The Venerable Father in God, J, Archbishop of York, the Chancellor, delivered into Court by his own hands a record made before the King in Chancery in these words:

Pleas before the King in his Chancery at Westminster on the Octaves of St. John the Baptist, 7 H. VI.

Staff. The King had sent a writ to the Sheriff of co. Stafford, which stated that, whereas by an inquisition taken before William Lee, of Knyghtley, late Eschaetor, 6th September, 8 H. V, it appeared that Thomas Harecourt, chivaler, was seised as of fee when he died of the manor of Elnhale, and that he had died on the 6th July last, and that Robert Harecourt was his son and heir and aged 10 years and upwards; and by another inquisition taken before the same Eschaetor on the Saturday before St. Martin the same year that Thomas Harecourt, chivaler, was seised when he died of the same manor, to him and to the heirs male of his body, and which manor one Nicholas Harecourt had given by his deed to one William Harecourt and Joan, his wife, and heirs male of their bodies, and William and Joan had issue one Thomas Harecourt, knight, who had entered as son and heir, and had issue the said Thomas Harecourt named in the above writs; and the said Thomas, son of Thomas, had entered as son and heir of the said Thomas, son of William and Joan, and had died seised as of fee tail. And by another nquisition taken before Richard Bronus, late Eschaetor of co. Oxon, on Thursday before the Feast of the Nativity of the Blessed Mary, 8 H. V, it appeared that one William de Harecourt was seised of the manor of Stanton Harecourt in co. Oxon as of fee, and by license of the King a Fine had been levied in 4 E. III between the said William Harecourt and Joan, his wife, complainants, and Nicholas de Harecourt, parson of the church of Shepeye, deforciant of the manor of Stanton Harecourt, and by which Fine the said manor had been settled on William and Joan, and the heirs male of their bodies, and failing that, on the right heirs of William. And the said William and Joan had issue the said Thomas Harecourt, knight, who had entered as their son and heir, and had issue the said Thomas Harecourt named in the above writ to the Eschaetor of co. Oxon. And Thomas, son of Thomas, had entered as son and heir, and had died seised as of fee tail.

And Thomas Asteley, armiger, had petitioned that whereas Thomas Harecourt, chivaler, named in the inquisition taken on the 6th September, and the said Thomas, son of Thomas, named in the inquisition taken on the Saturday, were one and the same person, and that long before the said Thomas, son of Thomas, held anything in the manor of Elnhale, or had taken any profits from it, a certain Thomas de Asteley, the younger, and Elizabeth, his wife, as of the right of Elizabeth, of which Elizabeth the said Thomas Asteley is son and heir, were seised of the manor of Elnhale; and the said Thomas de Asteley and Elizabeth, in 1 Ric. II being so seised, a Fine was levied in 1 Ric. II, and recorded in 2 Ric. II between Ralph de Ferrars, chivaler, and Thomas Harecourt, the father of the Thomas Harecourt named in the above writs, whose heir he was, complainant, and Thomas de Asteley and Elizabeth, his wife, deforciants of the manor of Elnhale, by which Fine the said Thomas de Asteley and Elizabeth conceded to Ralph the manor of Elnhale, to be held by the said Ralph for his life, with remainder to Thomas Harecourt, the father of Thomas, for his life, with remainder to the said Thomas de Asteley and Elizabeth, and the heirs of Elizabeth; and after the death of Ralph, the said Thomas Harecourt, the father, entered, and the said Thomas de Asteley and Elizabeth died, being seised at the time of their death of the reversion of the manor; and after the death of Thomas Harecourt, the father, the right of reversion descended to the said Thomas Asteley as son and heir of Elizabeth. And Thomas Asteley entered and held possession of the manor peaceably until the said Thomas Harecourt, son of Thomas Harecourt, removed him by force, and Thomas Asteley had claimed the said manor during all the lifetime of Thomas, son of Thomas Harecourt, and did all he could to obtain possession of it and "*ob metum mortis sue audebat personaliter accessit*," and thus Thomas Asteley as son and heir of Elizabeth was by law seised of the manor until by color of the above inquisitions, the King's father on the 24th September, in the eighth year of his reign, had granted the manor to his knight, Sir John Wilcotes, who was now deceased, the manor being in the King's hands by reason of the minority of Robert, son and heir of Thomas, son of Thomas, and by which grant the said Thomas Asteley had been expelled, to his great damage. And the King desiring to revoke and annul the said letters to John, and to restore to the said Thomas the manor, with all the profits from the date of the inquisition of the 5th September, a writ of *scire facias* was to be issued calling upon William Pope, armiger, John Barton, the younger, John Brid, yoman, Thomas Gloucestre, and William

Andrewe, the parson of Takley, and Elizabeth, late wife of John Wilcotes, knight, the executors of the will of the said John Wilcotes; and to John Blaket, knight, and Elizabeth, his wife, late wife of William Wilcotes, co-executrix of the said William Pope, John, John, Thomas, William, and Elizabeth, to appear in Chancery on the Octaves of St. John the Baptist, to shew cause why the said Letters Patent should not be revoked and the King's hand removed from the manor, and the manor restored to Thomas Asteley. Dated from Westminster 8th June, 7 H. VI. On which day none of the parties summoned appeared, and it was considered that the Letters Patent should be revoked and annulled.

Upon which the King's attorney appeared in Court and stated that the said Thomas Harecourt, chivaler, was seised when he died of the manor of Elnhale, and which manor Nicholas Harecourt, by his deed, had granted to William Harecourt and Joan, his wife, and the male heirs of their bodies; and by which grant the said William and Joan were seised of the manor and had issue Thomas Harecourt, knight, who had entered as son and heir of William and Joan, and had issue Thomas who had entered as son and heir of Thomas and had died seised of the manor as of fee tail, and he appealed to a jury. The Sheriff of co. Stafford was therefore ordered to summon a jury of 24 knights and others of the vicinage of Elnhale for this term, and Thomas Asteley appeared, and the Sheriff returned the names of 24 jurymen, none of whom had appeared. He was therefore ordered to distrain and produce them on the Quindene of St. Hillary. *m.* 28 *Rex.*

CORAM REGE. MICH., 10 H. VI.

Staff. Thomas Greswold, the King's attorney, appeared against Elizabeth, formerly wife of John Ipstones, knight, and John Bristowe, clerk, in a plea that they should permit the King to present to the church of Blymhulle, which was vacant, and of which the donation belonged to the King by reason of the custody of the land and heir of Adam Peshale, knight, deceased, who held of the King *in capite.* The defendants did not appear, and the Sheriff was ordered to distrain and produce them on the Octaves of St. Hillary. *m.* 13 *Rex.*

Staff. The Sheriff had been ordered to distrain Robert Babthorp, late Sheriff of co. Stafford, for not producing Richard, son of John Boghay, who had been in his custody *temp.* Hen. V, and who had to answer to the King for divers felonies and murders of which he had been indicted; and he now returned that Robert held nothing within his bailiwick, etc. He was therefore ordered to arrest and produce him on the Octaves of St. Hillary. *m.* 16 *Rex.*

Salop. Proceedings to estreat the recognizances of Thomas Corbet, John Esthope, Hugh Cresset, and John Leghton, of Leghton, who had found security in 100 marks each for the good behaviour of Richard Peshale, armiger, of Chetwynde, who had been indicted for divers felonies in 9 Hen. V, and had appeared in person and been bound over in a sum of 500 marks to keep the peace towards all the King's subjects, and especially towards William Hulle, of Neuport; the said Richard with 24 men, on the Wednesday after the Feast of St. Mary Magdalene 5 H. VI, having insulted, beaten, and wounded at Mere, near Neuport, William Lee, John Thikene, John Hancokson, and William Davidson. The Sheriff was ordered to levy the money on their lands and chattels. *m.* 24 *Rex.*

Staff. The Sheriff was ordered to distrain John Bagot, knight, and produce him in Court on the Octaves of St. Hillary to answer for the body of Richard, son of John Boghay, who had been in his custody when indicted, for divers felonies and murders. *m.* 16 *Rex, dorso.*

CORAM REGE. Trinity, 13 H. VI.

Staff. The suit of James Leveson against Simon Frend, of Walshale, for a trespass committed against him in conjunction with Thomas Stone, of Walshale, smyth, Roger Marshall, of Walshale, smyth, Roger Sporyour, of Walshale, lorymer, John Sporyour, of Walshale, lorymer, the younger, William Fykkes, of Walshale, lorymer, and William Wodeneford, of Walshale, lorymer, was respited till the Quindene of St. Michael unless the King's Justices of Assize should first come to Wolverhampton, etc. *m.* 12.

Staff. The suit of William, son of William de Bouweles, of Rushale, against the abbot of Hales Owayn, tenant of the manor of Rowley of Michaelmas term, 20 E. III, roll 145,[1] was brought into Court by writ of error, on the prayer of John Harpur and Alianora, his wife, daughter of William, son of Katrine, daughter of the said William, son of William, kinswoman and heir of the said William, son of William; and the record was as follows:—

Staff. William, son of William de Bouweles, of Russhale, sued the abbey of Hales Owayn for the manor of Rouley, which Laurence de Duneford had given to William de Bouwelles in frank marriage with Isabella, his daughter, and which should descend to him as son and heir of the said William and Isabella; and he stated that the said Laurence had granted the manor to William de Bouweles in frank marriage with Isabella in the time of Edward I, and they had been seised of it in demesne as of fee, etc. The abbot denied that the manor had been given in frank marriage as stated by the plaintiff, and appealed to a jury; the suit was afterwards moved by writ of *nisi prius* to be heard at Bromwych before Roger Hillary, with whom was associated John de Alrewas, according to the Statute, when a jury found in favour of the abbot.

And on the 11th July of this term John Harpur and Alianora, his wife, appeared in person, and stated that in the above record and process and judgment there was a manifest error, and prayed for a writ summoning the abbot *coram Rege;* and it was conceded, and a writ was issued summoning the abbot for the Quindene of St. Michael.

A postscript shews that the parties appeared at Hillary term, when the suit was adjourned to the following Easter term. Further postscripts shew that the suit was adjourned up to Easter term 16 H. VI. *m.* 85.

Derby. The first membrane of the Crown cases contains an indictment against Thomas Foljambe, of Walton, co. Derby, and Richard Foljambe, of Boudesall, in the same county, for a rout and riot at Chesterfield, when they had entered the church on Christmas day with a number of armed men, whilst mass was being performed, for the purpose of killing Henry Perpount, chivaler, Henry Longford, armiger, William Bradshawe, and Thomas Hasilby, and had cut off the right thumb and some of the fingers of Henry Perpount and the right thumb of Thomas Hasilby, and had shot arrows against the High Altar when the priest held the Eucharist in his hands, and had wounded Henry Perpount with an arrow in his right arm, and had beaten and wounded four of his servants named, and had wounded Henry Longford in the thigh and feloniously killed him, and had struck William Bradshawe on the head so that he died within the church, and the church had been polluted by the blood which had been shed. And that Ralph Foljambe, of Boudeshale, and others named were present on the same occasion aiding and abetting the felony.

Ralph Foljambe now appeared in person and surrendered, and was

[1] See Vol. XII, "Staff. Coll.," p. 57.

admitted to bail; and the other defendants had all been outlawed as appeared on the Roll of the previous Hillary term. *m.* 1 *Rex.*

Staff. A writ of *exigend* was issued against John Peshale, of Onn, for not appearing in answer to his bail to produce William Birmyngham, of Coventry, knight, who had been indicted for various felonies. *m.* 14 *Rex.*

DE BANCO. HILLARY, 14 H. VI.

Staff. Thomas Peshale, the executor of the will of Nicholas Peshale, sued in person Roger Lyney, of Neuport, in co. Salop, gentilman, for a debt of 10 marks. Roger did not appear, and the Sheriff was ordered to arrest and produce him on the Quindene of Easter. *m.* 70, *dorso.*

Staff. Sibil, late wife of Richard Delves, sued Stephen Ryssheton, of Eccleshale, for a third of a toft, 12 acres of land, 4 acres of meadow, 2 acres of wood, and 6 acres of moor in Eccleshale which she claimed as dower. Stephen stated she could not claim dower in the tenements, because her husband Richard was not seised of them at the date of the marriage nor afterwards, and he appealed to a jury. The Sheriff was therefore ordered to summon a jury for the Quindene of Easter. *m.* 101.

Staff. John Bate and William Piersson and Margery, his wife, sued William Neweport, armiger, for 4 messuages, 60 acres of land, and 8 acres of meadow in Stychesbroke, Elmhurst, and Curburgh; and they sued William Lychefeld, knight, for 8 acres of land and 4 acres of meadow in Curburgh; and they sued John Barre for 20 acres of land and 4 acres of meadow in Elmhurst by a writ of *formedon.* The defendants prayed a view, and the suit was adjourned to the Octaves of Holy Trinity. *m.* 101.

Bucks. William Lovell, knight, sued Nicholas Turvey for the manor of Great Craule, which he claimed by virtue of a fine levied in 5 E. III, by which the manor, with many others, was settled on John de Handlo and Matilda, his wife, and the heirs male of their bodies; and failing such, to Joan, Elizabeth, and Margaret, the daughters of Matilda, for their lives, and with remainder to John, son of John Lovell, and heirs male of his body; and William stated that John de Handlo and Matilda had died leaving no male heir, and that Joan, Elizabeth, and Margaret had died, and John, son of John Lovell, had died, and he was the male heir of John, son of John Lovell, viz. son of John, son of John, son of the said John, son of John Lovell named in the Fine. The defendant did not appear, and the plaintiff was therefore to have execution of the Fine. *m.* 102.[1]

Staff. Thomas Sprotte and Alianora, his wife, sued Agnes Bridde and Robert Bridde for a messuage in Lichefeld which Roger le Horner, of Tamworth, in 10 Ed. III, gave to Henry de Suggenhulle, chaplain, for his life, with remainder to Milisent, son of Chiistiana Snell, of Lychfeld, and to the heirs of her body; and failing such, to John, brother of Milisent, and to the heirs of his body; and failing such, to Roger le Horner, the younger, and Margery, his wife, and to their heirs, and they gave this descent from Roger le Horner and Milisent, the said John having died *s.p.*

Roger le Horner, the younger = Margery.

John.

Alianora.

[1] Another suit shews that John Lovell, the first husband of Matilda, was John Lord Lovel of Tichmarsh.

K 2

The defendants denied that they held the message, or had held it at the date of the writ; and appealed to a jury, which was to be summoned for the Octaves of Holy Trinity. *m.* 112, *dorso.*

Warw. John Chetewynde sued in person John Boteler, of Coventre, yoman, for 20 acres of wood and 20 acres of pasture in Alspathe by a writ of *quare cessavit per biennium.* John appeared in person and asked for a view, and the suit was adjourned to the Quindene of Holy Trinity. A postscript shews another adjournment to the Morrow of St. Martin. *m.* 117, *dorso.*

Leyc. William Swynfen and Alianora, his wife, sued William Marshall for a third of 3 tofts, a virgate of land, and 6*s.* 8*d.* of rent in Leyre, Cosseby, Dounton, and Hyngley which they claimed as dower of Alianora of the dotation of Henry Marshall, formerly her husband; and the defendant had not appeared. The plaintiffs were therefore to recover the dower by his default, and the Sheriff was ordered to return, by an inquisition upon oath, the amount of damage which Alianora had sustained by the detention of her dower. A postscript shews that the plaintiffs were awarded 30*s.* for the detention of the dower for two years and 31*s.* as damages. *m.* 120.

Staff. John Offeley, of Neuport, co. Salop, chaplain, and Richard Offeley, of Neuport, chapman, were attached at the suit of Hugh Willoughby, knight, for forcibly depasturing cattle on his grass at Norbury in 10 H. VI, and for which he claimed 10 marks as damages. The defendants appeared by attorney, and asked for adjournment to a month from Easter, which was granted. *m.* 130, *dorso.*

Staff. Thomas Campyon sued Thomas Nassche, of Stafford, husbondman, for forcibly depasturing cattle on his grass at Arley. The defendant did not appear, and the Sheriff was ordered to arrest and produce him at three weeks from Easter. *m.* 177, *dorso.*

Staff. Thomas Coweley, chaplain, sued Adam Coke, of Bruynton, and John Coke, of Bruynton, husbondmen, for forcibly depasturing their cattle on his corn and grass at Blymhill. The defendants did not appear, and the Sheriff was ordered to arrest and produce them on the Quindene of Easter. *m.* 232, *dorso.*

Staff. John the abbot of Byldewas sued Henry Selman, of Bruggenorth, for waste and destruction in houses at Walton which he had demised to him for a term of years. Henry did not appear, and the Sheriff was ordered to attach him for the above date. *m.* 261, *dorso.*

Salop. John Knyght, of Salop, merchant, sued John Gryffyth, of Wychenore, in co. Stafford, knight, for a debt of £40. The defendant did not appear, and had previously made default; and the Sheriff was ordered to put him into *exigend*, and if he did not appear, to outlaw him. A postscript states that the Sheriff returned that the said John Gryffyth had been exacted at three County Courts in 15 H. VI, but that no more had been held up to the date of the return. The Sheriff was therefore ordered to exact him up to five Courts, and to produce him on the Quindene of St. Hillary, 15 H. VI. *m.* 273.

Salop. The same John Knyght sued John Gryffyth, of Wychenore in co. Stafford, the younger, knight, for a debt of 20 marks. The defendant did not appear, and the Sheriff was ordered to put him in into *exigend*, and he made the same return, as in the last suit. A postscript shews that the defendant was outlawed, but afterwards, on the 10th February (17 Hen. VI), he appeared in Court and surrendered, and was committed to the King's prison in the Flete, and he then produced Letters Patent of the King pardoning the outlawry; and John Knyght was warned to appear on the following Quindene of Easter to prosecute his suit. *m.* 273.

Staff. Robert Harecourt sued Elizabeth Blaket, Thomas Blount, knight, and Elizabeth, his wife, and William Andrewe, clerk, the executors of the will of John Wilcotes, knight, for waste and destruction in houses, woods, fishponds, and gardens in Elnall which they held in custody after the death of the said John, to the disinheritance of the said Robert. The defendants did not appear, and the Sheriff was ordered to attach them for the Quindene of Easter. *m.* 399.

Staff. William Assheby sued John Hampton, of Esyngton, husbondman, John Andrewes, of Hylton, yoman, and three others named, for breaking into his close at Esyngton and depasturing cattle on his corn and grass. None of the defendants appeared, and the Sheriff was ordered to arrest and produce them on the Quindene of Easter. *m.* 399, *dorso.*

Staff. Elena, late wife of John Blount, the elder, knight, executrix of the will of the said John, sued Thomas Fouleshurst, late of Glenfeld in co. Leicester, armiger, son and heir of Thomas Fouleshurst, for a debt of 45 marks. Thomas did not appear, and the Sheriff was ordered to arrest and produce him on the above date. *m.* 399, *dorso.*

Staff. Thomas Sprot sued Robert Strelley, of Strelley in co. Notts, knight, for taking by force 10 cows and 11 oxen belonging to him from Shelfeld in the parish of Walshale, which were worth £10. Robert did not appear, and the Sheriff was ordered to distrain and produce him on the above date. *m.* 500, *dorso.*

Staff. Richard Barton, chaplain, sued John Clerke, of Repton, co. Derby, the executor of the will of Joan Mauveysin, late of Rydeware Mauveysyn, for a debt of 40*s.* John did not appear, and the Sheriff was ordered to arrest and produce him on the above date. *m.* 509.

Staff. Thomas Swynerton, armiger, sued Robert Strelley, of Strelley, co. Notts, for breaking into his close at Hylton and taking 8 cows and 6 oxen belonging to him, worth £10. Robert did not appear, and the Sheriff was ordered to distrain and produce him on the above date. *m.* 509.

Staff. John Hadyngton sued John Kynewarton, of Oldyngton, co. Stafford, husbondman, and Margery, his wife, and Richard Strawford, of Patteshulle, chaplain, for cutting down his trees at Oldyngton to the value of 40*s.*, and so cutting up his soil by their carts that he lost the profit of it for a length of time. The defendants did not appear, and the Sheriff was ordered to arrest and produce them on the above date. *m.* 509.

Staff. Robert Strelley, knight, sued John Carter, of Mavesyn Ridware, and Thomas Broun, of Pype Rideware, husbondmen, for a debt of £30; and he sued Thomas Stafford, of Alveton, yoman, and John Caumvile, of Alveton, parker, for a debt of 100*s.*; and by another writ he sued William Alyngton, of Coven, the elder, husbondman, and William Alyngton, of Coven, the younger, bailly, and Richard Taillour, of Coven, husbondman, for a debt of £20, and John Stokker, of Wolvernhampton, husbondman, for 56*s.* 8*d.* None of the defendants appeared, and the Sheriff was ordered to arrest and produce them on the above date. *m.* 509.

DE BANCO. Trinity, 14 H. VI.

Staff. Ralph Cromwell, knight, sued Robert Stokes, of Thorp, co. Stafford, gentilman, to give up to him a charter of feoffment which he unjustly detained. Robert did not appear, and the Sheriff was ordered to distrain and produce him on the Octaves of St. Michael. *m.* 163, *dorso.*

Staff. Thomas Stanley, of Elleford, armiger, sued William Adlyngton, of Coven, yoman, to render him a reasonable account for the time he was his bailiff in Coven, and receiver of his money. William did not appear, and had previously made default. The Sheriff was therefore ordered to put him into *exigend*, and if he did not appear, to outlaw him. *m.* 214.

Staff. Ralph Basset, armiger, sued Henry Atherley, of Dylvern (Dilhorn), for depasturing cattle by force on his corn and grass at Neuplace. Henry did not appear, and the Sheriff was ordered to arrest and produce him on the Quindene of St. Michael. *m.* 216.

Staff. Thomas Wolseley, executor of the will of Ralph Wolseley, sued Nicholas Ruggeley, of Dunton in co. Warwick, gentilman, for a debt of 20 marks. Nicholas did not appear, and the Sheriff was ordered to attach him for the Quindene of St. Michael. *m.* 116, *dorso.*

Staff. Simon Hadyngton sued in person Thomas Couley, of Bruynton, husbondman, in a plea that whereas he had bargained with him to sell him a horse at Bruynton, and had warranted it to be sound and fit for labour, he had sold him a horse knowing it was useless for labour and prostrated with various infirmities (*in varias infirmitates collapsum et ad laborandum impotentem*). Thomas did not appear, and the Sheriff was ordered to arrest and produce him at a month from Michaelmas. *m.* 116, *dorso.*

Staff. Thomas Webbe, of Drayton Basset, sued Ralph Orchard, of Mulwyche, yoman, and Alice, his wife, Thomas Alcock, of Leeke, yoman, and Matilda, his wife, Henry Rideyard, of Leeke, yoman, and Margaret, his wife, John of the Lowe, of Heleston, yoman, and Joan, his wife, and Henry Mosley, of Duffeld in co. Derby, yoman, for breaking into his close at Chetildon, cutting down his trees, cutting his corn and grass, and carrying away the corn, hay, and trees to the value of £40. None of the defendants appeared, and the Sheriff was ordered to arrest and produce them on the Quindene of Michaelmas. *m.* 281, *dorso.*

Staff. William Rolleston sued Ralph Bacon, of Rolleston, husbondman, for breaking into his houses at Rolleston and carrying away timber from them to the value of 40*s.* Ralph did not appear, and the Sheriff was ordered to arrest and produce him on the above date. *m.* 336.

Staff. Henry Pole sued Alexander Lytelle, of Whytyngton, laborer, for breaking into his close at Horton and cutting and carrying away trees and underwood to the value of 40*s.* Alexander did not appear, and the Sheriff was ordered as in the last suit. *m.* 336.

Staff. William Babyngton, the younger, sued in person Robert Lyngdon, of Wolvernehampton, chaplain, Hugh Bothebrook, of Wolvernehampton, chaplain, John Hunt, of Wolvernehampton, yoman, Thomas Boteler, of Fetherstone, yoman, and John Boteler, of Fetherstone, yoman, for entering his wood at Esynton and taking three young hawks worth 20 marks from a nest. The defendants did not appear, and the Sheriff was ordered as in the last suit. *m.* 336, *dorso.*

DE BANCO. HILLARY, 15 H. VI.

[*The first twenty membranes destroyed by damp.*]

Staff. William Walter sued Thomas Gifford, of Chillyngton, gentilman, John Bakeford, of Wheton Aston, husbondman, Walter Fletcher, of Penecryche, husbondman, Thomas Felton and William Felton, both of Penecryche, husbondmen, and John Hay, of Wheton Aston, husbondman, for taking by force 6 oxen belonging to him from Lapley. The defendants did not appear, and the Sheriff was ordered to arrest and produce them on the Quindene of Easter. *m.* 115, *dorso.*

Staff. The Sheriff had been ordered to summon John Kynwarton and Margery, his wife, to answer the plea of Simon Hadyngton, who claimed a messuage and 24 acres of land, 2 acres of meadow, and an acre of wood in Patteshulle, which Peter de Byspeston, the kinsman of Simon and whose heir he was, gave to John, son of William Gerrard, of Oldyngton, and Joan, his wife, and heirs of their bodies, and which should revert to Simon, as John, son of William and Joan, had died *s. p.*; and the Sheriff returned, the writ reached him too late. He was therefore ordered to summon the said John and Margery for the Quindene of Easter. *m.* 120, *dorso.*

Staff. Ralph Basset, armiger, sued Thomas Gelowe, of Leeke, for taking his horse, worth 5 marks, by force from Blore. Thomas did not appear, and the Sheriff was ordered to arrest and produce him on the above date. *m.* 155.

Staff. Richard Harecourt sued Walter Kibbulle, late of Assheby, co. Leicester, gentilman, and John Wirley, of Werneley, co. Wygorn, gentilman, and Richard Latymer, of Assheby, for taking by force from Dudley a horse belonging to him, which was worth £10. The defendants did not appear, and the Sheriff was ordered as in the last suit. *m.* 190.

Staff. Katrine Kawardyne sued Richard Jurdan, of Ingestre, yoman, for breaking into her close at Alrewych (Aldridge) and taking 2 cows worth 40*s.* Richard did not appear, and the Sheriff was ordered as in the last suit. *m.* 190, *dorso.*

Staff. Robert Darcy, Bartholomew Brokesby, Walter Kebylle, and John Bultus sued in person John Burton, fissher, John Culte, fissher, Thomas Smyth, husbondman, and William Egge, milner (all of Mere), for taking by force 6 cignets belonging to them from Mere, and worth 40*s.* The defendants did not appear, and the Sheriff was ordered to arrest and produce them on the Quindene of Easter.

Staff. John Harpur and Alianora, his wife, recovered 8 acres of land in Ruysshale, which they claimed in right of Alianora as an eschaet in a sui against John Marchall, the defendant making default. *m.* 308.

Staff. William, the Bishop of Coventry and Lichfield, sued William Smyth, of Penecryche, smith, Thomas Lyote, yoman, Henry Pery, yoman, and John Taillour, laborer (all of Penecryche), in a plea that whereas, in the Parliament of King Edward, the King's progenitor, in the third year of his reign, it had been enacted that malefactors in parks and fishponds according to their delinquency should pay substantial fines or be imprisoned for three years, and should afterwards find security for their good behaviour, the said William and the other defendants taking no heed of the said Statute (*statutum predictum minime ponderantes*) had broken *vi et armis* into his park at Brewode, and had chased and taken his wild animals without his permission. None of the defendants appeared, and the Sheriff was ordered to arrest and produce them on the Quindene of Easter. *m.* 326.

Staff. William Grevylle, knight, sued Richard Forde, of Gunstone, husbondman, for breaking into his closes at Gunstone and Chillyngton and cutting down his trees and underwood to the value of 40*s.* Richard did not appear, and the Sheriff was ordered as in the last suit. *m.* 351, *dorso.*

Staff. Ralph Smyth and Joan, his wife, sued John Welton, of Caldon, husbondman, for breaking into the close and houses of Joan at Caldon, and depasturing cattle by force on her grass. John did not appear, and the Sheriff was ordered to arrest and produce him on the Quindene of Easter. *m.* 352.

Staff. Humfrey Walker sued William Hayteley, of Casterne, Richard Bailly, of Stansope, Ralph Salt, of Wotton (all described as husbondmen), and William Bagnald, of Elkyston, laborer, for breaking into his close at Casterne, and depasturing cattle by force upon his grass and corn. The defendants did not appear, and the Sheriff was ordered as in the last suit. *m.* 352.

Staff. James Leveson sued Richard Harecourt, of Little Sardon, armiger, John Danyell, yoman, and John Cook, yoman, both of Little Sardon, for breaking into his close at Forde and taking 4 oxen, 5 cows, and 4 steers, worth £10. The defendants did not appear, and the Sheriff was ordered to distrain Richard and to arrest the others, and produce them on the Quindene of Easter. *m.* 404, *dorso.*

DE BANCO. TRINITY, 15 H. VI.

Staff. John Smyth sued John Wetton, of Caldon, husbondman, and Agnes, his wife, and Henry Lorde, of Caldon, husbondman, for breaking into his houses at Caldon and taking his goods and chattels to the value of 40*s.*, and for depasturing cattle on his corn and grass. The defendants did not appear, and the Sheriff was ordered to arrest and produce them on the Octaves of St. Michael. *m.* 51.

Staff. Robert Walker sued in person John Lovet, of Calouhill, husbondman, for breaking into his close at Calouhill (Callowhill) and depasturing cattle on his corn and grass. John did not appear, and the Sheriff was ordered as in the last suit. *m.* 51.

Staff. John Asheby sued Nicholas Waters, of Wadnesfeld, husbondman, Juliana Waters, wedowe, John Hampton, of Essington, husbondman, for breaking into his closes at Wadnesfeld and depasturing cattle on his grass and in his woods. The defendants did not appear, and the Sheriff was ordered to arrest and produce them on the Quindene of St. Michael. A postscript shews no return to the writ up to Easter. *m.* 273.

Oxon. Robert Harecourt, knight, sued Elizabeth Blakette, William Andrewe, clerk, and Thomas Blounte, knight, and Elizabeth, his wife, the co-executrix of the said Elizabeth Blakette and William, for waste and destruction in houses, woods, and gardens in Staunton Harecourt, Southleye, and Sutton, which they held in custody after the death of John Wilcotes, knight, as his executors; and he stated that King Henry, the father of the present King, had granted by his Letters Patent to the said John Wilcotes the custody of all the lands and rents and possessions which Thomas Harecourt, knight, had held of the King *in capite*, and which, owing to the minority of the said Robert, son and heir of Thomas, had come into his hands, to be held by him, together with the marriage of the heir, till the full age of the said Robert. By virtue of which Letters Patent the said John was seised of the wardship and died seised of it; and after his death the said Elizabeth Blaket and William held the same, and had caused waste by allowing a hall and 10 chambers, each worth £40, a kitchen, a *pandoximum*, a bakery, 4 stables, an oxstall, and three granges belonging to the manor house, and each worth £20, and 20 halls, 20 chambers, 20 stables, and 20 oxstalls belonging to divers messuages and cottages in Staunton Harecourt, Southlegh, and Sutton, the value of each house being £20, to remain unroofed so that the main timbers had become rotten; and by cutting down and selling from the woods 1,000 oak trees, etc. (*here follows a long account of waste in woods and fishponds*), and for which the said Robert claimed 1,000 marks as damage. The executors appeared by attorney, and asked for an adjournment till the Quindene of St. Michael, which was granted. *m.* 308.

Staff. The same Robert Harecourt, knight, sued Elizabeth Blakette and William Andrewe, the executors of the will of John Wilcotes, knight, in a plea that they, together with Thomas Blount, knight, and Elizabeth, his wife, the co-executrix of the said Elizabeth Blakette and William, had caused waste and destruction in the houses, woods, fishponds, and gardens which they held in custody of his inheritance in Enalle (Ellenhall) (*here follows the same account of the grant of the wardship as in the last suit*); and Robert stated that they had wasted the tenements by allowing a hall and 10 chambers, each worth £40, a kitchen, a *pandoximum*, a bakehouse, 4 stables, an oxstall, and 3 granges belonging to the manor house, each worth £20, and 20 halls, 20 chambers, 20 stables, and 20 oxstalls, of divers messuages and cottages in the vill of Elnall, part of the manor, the value of each house being £20, to remain unroofed, so that the main timbers had become rotten, and by cutting down in the woods 1,000 oaks, each worth 20*d*., 1,000 small oaks, each worth 8*d*., and by taking and selling from the fishponds 400 *dentrices* (pike), each worth 12*d*., 1,000 bream, each worth 16*d*., 1,500 eels, each worth 8*d*.; and by cutting down in the gardens and selling 40 pear trees, each worth 20*d*., 40 apple trees, each worth 12*d*., and 100 hazel trees (*corulos*[1]), each worth 12*d*., and for which he claimed 1,000 marks as damages. The said Elizabeth and William appeared by attorney, and the process was the same as in the last suit *m.* 308, *dorso*.

Staff. Thomas Hethe sued John Pyry, of Wyllenhale, husbondman, and Edith, his wife, and Roger Pyry, of Wyllenhale, laborer, for breaking up his soil at Wednesfeld with their carts, so that he lost the profit of it for a length of time. The defendants did not appear, and the Sheriff was ordered to arrest and produce them on the Quindene of Michaelmas. *m.* 375, *dorso*.

Staff. William Cartwryghte sued Thomas Roddesley, of Cowene, husbondman, and Richard Parker, of Cowene, husbondman, for breaking into his close at Cowene (Coven) and taking his goods and chattels to the value of £20. The defendants did not appear, and the Sheriff was ordered to arrest and produce them on the Quindene of St. Michael. *m.* 375, *dorso*.

Staff. William Lovell, knight, sued John Hemhill, of Tybyngton, husbondman, and John Merihurst, of Dudley, chapman, for breaking into his close at Tybynton (Tipton) and depasturing cattle on his grass. The defendants did not appear, and the Sheriff was ordered as in the last suit. *m.* 454.

[1] Coruli or Coryli, according to Lyttelton's Mediæval Dictionary, are Hazel trees, bearing filberts. It is clear from the text they are trees found in English orchards which bear fruit.

Staff. John Waleys sued William Salford, of Wolvernehampton, gentilman, for breaking into his close and houses at Wolvernehampton and taking his goods and chattels to the value of £40. William did not appear, and the Sheriff was ordered to distrain and produce him on the Quindene of St. Michael. *m.* 454, *dorso.*

Staff. John Sheldon sued John Baker, of Hemley, yoman, Robert Gesson, of Hemley, husbondman, William Tomson, of Hemley, and William Estman (both of Hemley, and husbondmen) for breaking into his closes at Segesley and Hemley (Himley) and depasturing cattle by force on his grass. The defendants did not appear, and the Sheriff was ordered to arrest and produce them on the Quindene of St. Michael. *m.* 454, *dorso.*

CORAM REGE. MICH., 16 H. VI.

Lanc. A writ of error to annul the outlawry of John Meverel, of Frodeswalle in co. Stafford, who, together with Sampson Meverel, of Frodeswalle, and Robert Walsale, of Frollesworth, co. Leicester, had been outlawed on an indictment for feloniously receiving at Weryngton, Isabella late servant of Andrew Salogham, of Lichefeld, who had been indicted for robbing the said Andrew, at Chorley, of five silver dishes worth £5 in 8 H. VI. John Meverel now surrendered, and the outlawry was annulled on the ground that the indictment contained no mention that the said John was of any other county than of that in which the indictment was taken, and no writ of *capias* had been issued before the writ of *exigatur*, as manifestly appeared from the Record which had been brought into Court. John Meverell also produced a general pardon from the King, dated 27 May, 15 H. VI. *m.* 5 *Rex.*

DE BANCO. HILLARY, 16 H. VI.

Salop. William Lovell sued John Radeclyf, knight, and Katrine, his wife, Geoffrey Radeclyf, knight, James Radeclyf, Richard de Barton, and John Walsh for execution of a Fine levied in 10 E. II between Hugh le Despencer, the elder, and William de Handlo, clerk, and John de Handlo and Matilda, his wife, respecting the manor and honor of Holegode, and the manors of Clya St. Margaret, Longedon, Welynton, Ardulveston, Upysston, Prestes weston, Acton Burnell, Acton Pygot, Wodeton Parva, Sutton in Cornedale, Hope boudelers, Abbeton, and Benthale, and other places and rents and advowsons of churches in co. Salop, by which Fine the above tenements, etc., were settled on John and Matilda, and heirs male of their bodies, and failing such, on the right heirs of Matilda. William claimed as right heir of Matilda, and gave this descent :—

Matilda.
|
John.
|
John.
|
John.
|
William Lovell, the plaintiff.

The defendants did not appear, and a verdict was given in favour of William Lovell. *m.* 107.

Staff. Roger Aston, knight, sued Walter Taverner, of Whityngton, husbondman, for breaking into his close at Pakyngton and depasturing cattle on his grass. Walter did not appear, and the Sheriff was ordered to arrest and produce him on the Quindene of Easter. *m.* 108, *dorso.*

Warw. Humfrey Stafford, knight, sued Robert Catesby for the manor of Harpesford, which Roger Bisshopeston and Joan, his wife, had given to Thomas de Hastyng (Hasting), chivaler, and Elizabeth, his wife, and heirs of their bodies, and which should descend to him as their heir, and he gave this descent:—

Thomas de Hastyng, Kt. = Elizabeth.
John.
John.
Matilda.
Humfrey.
Humfrey Stafford, the plaintiff.

The suit was adjourned to the Octaves of Holy Trinity. *m.* 117, *dorso.*

Staff. Memorandum that on the 14th February of this term the Justices delivered to John Bedulle, the deputy of the Sheriff of co. Stafford, a close writ addressed to the Sheriff of co. Stafford commanding him to summon twelve knights and others of the vicinage of Abbotesbromley who were not of kin to Richard de Wynynton or John de Gresley, and Margaret, his wife, to be at Westminster on the Quindene of Holy Trinity to return a verdict whether the said John and Margaret, on the Monday before the Feast of St. Laurence, 15 H. VI, had been imprisoned by one Richard Lane, and kept continuously in prison from the said Monday until the following Thursday, for all the time that a Court had been sitting at Chester, so that they could not appear in Court, by which the said Richard de Wynyngton had recovered two parts of the manor of Marchalle, which he had claimed against the said John and Margaret, by a writ of *formedon in descendere*, through the default of the said John and Margaret. *m.* 119.

Staff. William Trewbody, of Ruggeley, sued William Norman, of Ruggeley, armiger, and Nicholas Norman, of le Boldem, gentilman, for a debt of 10 marks, for which he produced their bond dated 12 H. VI. Nicholas appeared in person and William Norman by attorney, and asked that the bond might be read; and the bond was read, which stated that if the said William and Nicholas paid to the plaintiff 8 marks before the Feast of St. Martin after the date of the bond, that the bond should be of no effect. And they stated they had paid the 8 marks within the above date. The plaintiff denied this, and appealed to a jury, which was to be summoned for the Quindene of Easter. *m.* 130.

Staff. Richard Falthurst, parson of the church of Kyngeley, Robert Savage, clerk, and Ralph Basset, armiger, sued Thomas Stafford, of Alveton, gentilman, to deliver up to them a pyx containing charters and muniments, which he unjustly detained. Thomas did not appear, and the Sheriff was ordered to arrest and produce him on the Quindene of Easter. *m.* 163.

Staff. Thomas Alsop sued William Hyne, of Bromshulf, husbondman, for breaking into his close at Bromshulf (Bramshall) and depasturing cattle on his corn and grass. William did not appear, and the Sheriff was ordered as in the last suit. *m.* 163.

Staff. Humfrey Clerkeson sued Thomas Orgrave, of Abbots Bromley, yoman, and William Nevodee, late of Colton, husbondman, for breaking into his close and houses at Abbots Bromley, and carrying away goods and chattels to the value of 100*s*. The defendants did not appear, and the Sheriff was ordered as in the last suit. *m.* 163, *dorso.*

Staff. Thomas Stanley, armiger, sued Thomas Leylond, of Lichefeld, taillour, for breaking into his house at Lichefeld and insulting, beating, and wounding his servant Agnes Gresbrok, so that he lost her services for a length of time. Thomas did not appear, and the Sheriff was ordered as in the last suit. *m.* 163, *dorso.*

Staff. William Mitton, armiger, sued Thomas Jakson, of Lee, milner, for breaking into his house at Neuton and taking goods and chattels to the value of 100*s*. Thomas did not appear, and the Sheriff was ordered as in the last suit. *m.* 180.

Staff. John Bromley, prior of Ronton, sued Robert Austyn, of Stafford, taillour, and John Myghe, of Aston, yoman, for a debt of 6 marks. The defendants did not appear, and the Sheriff was ordered as in the last suit. *m.* 180.

Staff. Richard Taillour sued John Milleward, of West Bromwyche, husbondman, for breaking into his close at West Bromwyche, and depasturing cattle on his grass. John did not appear, and the Sheriff was ordered to arrest and produce him on the Quindene of Holy Trinity. *m.* 180.

Staff. William Turnour sued Margaret Burone, of Wolstanton, wedowe, John de Rowele, of Wolstanton, husbondman, Richard Beche, of Norton, husbondman, and Roger Burone, of Wolstanton, husbondman, for breaking into his close at Wolstanton and taking his goods and chattels to the value of £20, and depasturing cattle on his grass at the same place. The defendants did not appear, and the Sheriff was ordered to arrest and produce them on the Quindene of Easter day. *m.* 180.

Staff. John Gresley, knight, and Margaret, his wife, sued Thomas Makeworth, of Makeworth in co. Derby, gentilman, and Thomas Agard, of Foston in co. Derby, yoman, in a plea that each should render a reasonable account for the time they were the receivers of the money of the said Margaret. The defendants did not appear, and the Sheriff was ordered as in the last suit. *m.* 180, *dorso.*

Staff. Henry, the abbot of Roucestre, sued Robert Tomkynson, of Calton, husbondman, and John Alynforde, of Combrigge, husbondman, for breaking into his close at Swynysco, cutting down his trees and underwood, and depasturing cattle on his corn and grass. The defendants did not appear, and the Sheriff was ordered as in the last suit. *m.* 181.

Staff. Richard Falthurst, clerk, Robert Savage, clerk, and Ralph Basset sued John North, of Roucestre, yoman, and John Parker, of Denstone, husbondman, for breaking into their close at Roucestre, and cutting down their trees to the value of 10 marks. The defendants did not appear, and the Sheriff was ordered to arrest and produce them on the Quindene of Easter day. A postscript shews they had not appeared up to Hillary term, 17 H. VI. *m.* 181.

Staff. William Halle sued Roger Page, of Womburne, laborer, for breaking into his close and houses at Womburne, taking goods and chattels to the value of 40*s*., and depasturing cattle on his grass. Roger did not appear, and the Sheriff was ordered to arrest and produce him on the Quindene of Easter day. *m.* 208.

Staff. Richard Deys sued Robert Rypon, of Lychefeld, chaplain, William Fraunceys, of Allerewas, yoman, John Caldewalle, of Lychefeld, tyler, John Rideware, of Lichefeld, the younger, frankelyn, John Coppe, of Lychefeld, bochour, and William Birche, of Lychefeld, bochour, for forcibly carrying away his goods and chattels from Lychefeld to the value of 100*s.* None of the defendants appeared, and the Sheriff was ordered as in the last suit. *m.* 208.

Staff. John Grevylle, armiger, sued Richard atte fude (*sic*), of Gunstone, husbondman, for breaking into his close at Chilynton, cutting down his trees, and depasturing cattle on his corn and grass. Richard did not appear, and the Sheriff was ordered as in the last suit. *m.* 208.

Staff. John Waleys sued William Salford, of Wolvernehampton, gentilman, for breaking into his close and houses at Wolvernehampton and taking his goods and chattels to the value of 40*s.* William did not appear, and the Sheriff was ordered to distrain and produce him on the Quindene of Easter day. *m.* 208, *dorso.*

Staff. Humphrey Salewey, armiger, sued Thomas Brook, of Cannok, barker, for breaking into his close at Cannok, cutting down his underwood, and depasturing cattle on his grass. Thomas did not appear, and the Sheriff was ordered as in the last suit. *m.* 208, *dorso.*

Staff. The suit of Joan, late wife of Thomas Astley, armiger, against Robert Harecourt for dower was respited till Easter term, no jury appearing. *m.* 256.

Staff. Philip Chetewynde, knight, sued Richard Weston, of Ruggeley, yoman, for a debt of £20. Richard did not appear, and the Sheriff was ordered to arrest and produce him on the Quindene of Easter day. *m.* 368, *dorso.*

Staff. The abbot of Halesoweyn sued John Wyrley, of Honnesworth, yoman, in a plea that whereas he had taken the cattle of the said John and impounded them within his fee of Roweley for customary services owing to him, the said John had forcibly broken open the pound and carried away the cattle. John did not appear, and the Sheriff was ordered to arrest and produce him at three weeks from Easter day. *m.* 368, *dorso.*

Staff. Richard Thykebrome sued Richard Fremon, of Thykebrome, husbondman, and John Fremon, of Thykebrome, husbondman, for breaking into his close at Thykebrome and depasturing cattle on his corn and grass. The defendants did not appear, and the Sheriff was ordered to produce and arrest them on the Quindene of Easter day. *m.* 368, *dorso.*

Staff. Richard Vernon, knight, sued Thomas Makeworth, of Makeworth in co. Derby, armiger, for a debt of £10. Thomas did not appear, and the Sheriff was ordered to arrest and produce him as above. *m.* 368, *dorso.*

Staff. William Whitegreve, of Stafford, sued in person Ralph, the abbot of Burton upon Trent, for a debt of 60*s.*; and he sued John Cokkayne, of Assheburne, co. Derby, and Elizabeth, his wife, for a debt of 100*s.*, Henry Sanke, of Derby, yoman, for a debt of £7, and Richard Whyte, of Newcastle under Lyme, mercer, for a debt of 40*s.* None of the defendants appeared, and the Sheriff was ordered to summon them for the Quindene of Easter day. *m.* 389, *dorso.*

Staff. Cornelius Wyrley sued John Cook, of Little Aston-upon-Colfeld, husbondman, for breaking into his close at Little Aston, cutting down his trees, and depasturing cattle on his corn and grass. John did not appear, and the Sheriff was ordered to arrest and produce him on the Quindene of Easter day. *m.* 390.

Staff. Oliver de Chaderton sued William Bertreme, of Fulfen near Stretay, Robert Ripon, of Lychefeld, chaplain, and Lettice Cholmele, of Fulfen, servant, for breaking into his houses and close at Fulfen near Stretay, cutting down his trees, and depasturing cattle on his grass. The defendants did not appear, and the Sheriff was ordered to arrest and produce them at three weeks from Easter day. *m.* 390.

Staff. Thomas Rode sued John Rode, of Tamworth in co. Stafford, husbondman, and William Fox de la Grenes, of Tamworth in co. Warwick, yoman, for breaking into his close at Coton near Tamworth and taking his goods and chattels to the value of 40*s.* The defendants did not appear, and the Sheriff was ordered as in the last suit. *m.* 390, *dorso.*

Salop. William Lovelle, knight, of Tichemersshe, recovered the manors of Acton Reyner and Corfton from Sir John Radeclyf and the other defendants named in the former suit on *m.* 107. The pleadings shew that the manors had been formerly held by Alina, the widow of Edward Burnell, and in 8 E. III a Fine had been levied by which, after her death, they were to remain to John de Handlo and Matilda, his wife, and heirs male of their bodies, and failing such, to Joan, Elizabeth, and Margaret, the daughters of the said Matilda, for their lives; and after their deaths to remain to John, son of John Lovelle, of Tichemersshe, and heirs male of his body, and failing such, to the right heirs of Matilda, and he gave the same descent as in the former suit. *m.* 414.

Essex. By another suit the same William recovered six manors in co. Essex, seven manors in co. Surrey, including West Grenewich, Suthewerk, Bermundeseye, and Hamme near Kyngeston, Great Craule in co. Bucks, and rents in various other places. *m.* 415.

Chester. In the suit of Richard de Wynynton *versus* John de Gresley, knight, and Margaret, his wife, for two parts of the manor of Marchalle, and in which John and Margaret had complained that they had been kept in prison at Abbotsbromley by one Richard Lane whilst the suit was pending in co. Chester, and in consequence of which a verdict had been given against them, the record of the suit was returned into Court, which had been heard before Humfrey, Duke of Gloucester, the Justice of Chester at Easter term, 14 H. VI, by which it appeared that Richard de Wynynton had sued in person John de Gresley, knight, and Margaret, his wife, for two parts of the manor of Marchalle which Roger Beket, chaplain, had given, with the remaining third part to Richard de Wynynton, knight, and Agnes, his wife, and heirs of their bodies, 10 E. III, and from the said Richard and Agnes he gave this descent:—

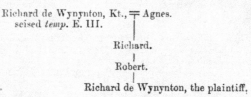

Richard de Wynynton, Kt., = Agnes.
seised *temp.* E. III.
|
Richard.
|
Robert.
|
Richard de Wynynton, the plaintiff.

The suit was continued, with several adjournments on various pleas, till Easter term, 15 H. VI, when John and Margaret called Thomas Savage, late parson of the church of Chekley, to warranty.

Richard demurred to the warranty because Thomas had never been seised of the manor before the date of the first writ, and appealed to a jury on this issue; and the Sheriff was ordered to summon a jury for the Tuesday before the Feast of St. Laurence, 15 H. VI, on which day the plaintiff appeared, and John and Margaret, being solemnly called, put in no appearance, and the Sheriff was ordered to take the two parts of the manor into the King's hands, and a day was given to the parties to hear judgment on the Tuesday after the next Feast of St. Bartholomew, on which day the parties appeared in Court, and Richard claimed a verdict by the default of the defendants.

And John and Margaret pleaded the default should not be to their injury because, on the Monday before the said Court was held, viz. on the Tuesday before the Feast of St. Laurence last past, they had been imprisoned at Abbotesbromley in co. Stafford by one Richard Lane, and had been detained there in prison from the Monday till the following Thursday, so that they could not appear in Court. Richard replied, that on the day in question the said John and Margaret were at large at Chester, and appealed to a jury on this issue. After several more adjournments, the suit was moved by writ of *recordari* into Banco, and the Sheriff of co. Stafford was ordered to summon a jury of the vicinage of Abbotsbromley for the Octaves of Holy Trinity. Richard Wynynton was under age, and the Justices of Chester had conceded that he might sue by Thomas Wynynton or by John Huxley or Thomas de Alkemontelowe. *m.* 420.

Staff. John (Sutton, of Duddeleye, and John Bredhill[1]) were summoned at the suit of the King in a plea that they should permit him to present (a fit person to the church of) King Swynford, and the King's attorney stated that (. . . . .) were seised of the (. . . . .), and the said Nicholas and Stephen, being seised of the said manor, to which the advowson was appurtenant, granted it to John de Sutton and Isabella, his wife, and heirs male of their bodies, and the said John and Isabella presented to the church one William Pykkyn, clerk, and John afterwards died, and Isabella, who survived him, being sole seised of the manor, presented to the church one John Ellesmere, clerk, in the time of King Richard II, and from Isabella the manor descended to one John, son and heir of the said John Sutton, of Dudley, and Isabella, and the said John entered and died seised of it in fee tail; and from the said John, son of John Sutton, of Dudley, the manor descended to one John Sutton, as son and heir, which John, son of John, son of John Sutton, of Dudley, entered into the manor, and died seised of it as of fee tail; and from him the manor descended to one John, as son and heir, who entered, and died seised of it as of fee tail; and from the said John, son of John, son of John, son of John Sutton, of Dudley, the manor descended to one John Sutton, chivaler, as son and heir, who entered and was seised of the manor in fee tail, and whilst so seised he married one Constance, and had issue by her the said John Sutton, knight, the defendant; and John Sutton, the husband of Constance, died seised of the manor and of other lands, tenements, and advowsons in co. Stafford, and from him they descended to the said John Sutton named in the writ as son and heir, and because the said John Sutton, chivaler, at the time of his death held the said manor of King Henry, the grandfather of the present King, *in capite* by knight's service, as appears by an inquisition taken before John Delves, then Eschaetor of the county, on the 18th September, 7 H. IV, the said

[1] The words within brackets have been added from another part of the Roll, as the Record is torn at this point.

manor, together with other lands and advowsons, were taken into the King's hands. And the said Constance afterwards sued for her dower in the King's Chancery: upon which a writ was issued to John Bagot, chivaler, the King's Eschaetor in co. Stafford, dated 24 November, 8 H. IV, to endow the said Constance out of all the said lands and tenements. By virtue of which writ John Bagot assigned to Constance, amongst other lands, the said manor of King Swynford, together with the advowson, in allocation of all the manors, lands, and advowsons of which her husband had been seised on the day he married her. And whilst Constance was so seised of the manor, one Robert Erghom, citizen and draper (*pannarius*), of London, sued the said Constance, under the name of Constance, late wife of John Sutton, knight, of Hemley (Himley), co. Stafford, wedowe, for a debt of 40*s*., and the writ being returnable at Westminster on the Quindene of St. John the Baptist, 7 H. VI, the said Constance had made default; and as the Sheriff of London had returned that she held nothing within his bailiwick by which she could be distrained, a writ of "*capias*" was issued, and the Sheriff was ordered to produce her at the Quindene of St. Michael, on which day she again made default; and another writ of *capias* was issued, returnable on the Morrow of All Souls, on which day Constance again made default; and a writ of *capias* was issued, returnable on the Octaves of St. Martin, on which day she again made default; and the Sheriff of London was ordered to exact her from Husteng to Husteng, and if she did not appear, to arrest and produce her on the Quindene of Holy Trinity; and the said Constance not having appeared at (. . . .) consecutive Courts of Husteng, had been *waiviata*, and the *waiviatura* being still in existence, and the church being vacant, it pertained to the King to present to it, and the said John Sutton and John Bredhill unjustly impeded him.

John Sutton appeared by attorney and John Bredhill in person; and John Sutton stated he could not deny that the church was vacant by the resignation of the said John Ellesmere, nor that the said Constance had been *waiviata*. It was therefore considered that the King should recover the advowson against John de Sutton, but the writ to the Bishop was postponed pending the termination of the plea between the King and John Bredhill. And the said John Bredhill stated that the said Nicholas and Stephen had been formerly seised of the manor of Swyneford Regis, to which the advowson was appurtenant, and whilst so seised had presented one Thomas Longeford, clerk, in the reign of King E. III, and had afterwards granted the manor to John Sutton, of Dudley, and Isabella, his wife, etc.—(*here follows a statement of the case, which agrees with that of the King as far as the grant of the manor as dower to Constance, the widow of Sir John Sutton in 8 H. IV, after which it proceeds to state*) that Constance whilst so seised had presented John Bredhill, her clerk, who had been canonically inducted, and he added that Constance, whilst the suit was proceeding, which had been brought against her by Robert Erghom, was residing in the parish of St. James in London, and not at Hemley as stated in the writ. John Vampage, the King's attorney, stated that on the date when the writ was sued out against Constance, viz. on the 6 June, 7 H. VI, she was living at Hemley, and appealed on this issue to a jury. After several adjournments, a postscript shews that a verdict was given in favour of John Bredhill at Hillary term 17 H. VI. *m.* 475.

DE BANCO. TRINITY, 16 H. VI.

Staff. William Bourgchier and Thomasia, his wife, sued John de Tiptoft, knight, for waste and destruction in lands, gardens, and houses, which he held in custody of the inheritance of the said Thomasia in Bitteley (Betley),

Heley, Tunstall, and Horton. John did not appear, and the Sheriff was ordered to attach him for the Octaves of St. John the Baptist. *m.* 2.

Salop. The same plaintiffs sued the same John for waste and destruction in the inheritance of Thomasia in Redecastelle, Egmondon, Whityngton in the Marches of Wales, and Neuport. John did not appear, and the Sheriff was ordered to attach him for the Octaves of St. Michael. *m.* 2.

Glouc. The same plaintiffs sued the same John for waste and destruction in Bentham. John did not appear, and the Sheriff was ordered as in the last suit. *m.* 2.[1]

Staff. Richard Harecourt, armiger, sued William Adlyngton, of Coven, husbondman, and three others, for breaking into his close at Coven and taking fish from his several fishery. The defendants did not appear, and the Sheriff was ordered to arrest and produce them on the Octaves of St. Michael. *m.* 36.

Staff. Richard Harecourt, armiger, sued Henry Boone, of Penford, husbondman, and Hugh Boone, of Penford, laborer, for breaking into his close at Great Sardon and depasturing cattle on his grass, cutting down his trees, and carrying away his goods and chattels to the value of 10 marks. The defendants did not appear, and the Sheriff was ordered as in the last suit. *m.* 36, *dorso.*

Staff. Richard Bromle sued John Smyth, the parson of Fornham, All Saints, in co. Suffolk, for beating, wounding, and illtreating him at Betly. John did not appear, and the Sheriff was ordered to arrest and produce him on the Quindene of St. John the Baptist. *m.* 52, *dorso.*

Staff. William Orme sued in person George Langeford, of Langeford (Longford) in co. Derby, gentilman, for a debt of 5 marks and 6*s.* 8*d.* George did not appear, and the Sheriff was ordered to arrest and produce him on the Quindene of St. Michael. *m.* 105, *dorso.*

Staff. Roger Aston, knight, sued in person John Fyssher, of Heywode, gentilman, and William Hexstall, of Hexstall, gentilman, for a debt of 10 marks. The defendants did not appear, and the Sheriff was ordered as in the last suit. *m.* 105, *dorso.*

Staff. Robert Holynton, the prior of St. Margaret of Calwyche, co. Stafford, and Thomas Flaket, of Calwyche, husbondman, were attached, at the suit of James Olde, for forcibly taking 10 oxen and 8 cows belonging to him at Calwyche, for which he claimed £20 as damages.

The defendants appeared in person and denied the trespass and injury, and appealed to a jury, which was to be summoned for the Quindene of St. Michael. John Bersford (Beresford), of Bersford, co. Stafford, William Corbet, of Calwyche, yoman, Roger Perpount, of Holme, co. Notts, gentilman, and Thomas Golburn, of Holme, co. Notts, yoman, became sureties to produce the said Thomas at the above date. A postscript shews no jury had been summoned up to Hillary term 17 H. VI. *m.* 106.

Staff. John Stubbes sued Robert Shepherd, of Lichefeld, chapman, and Robert Millward, of Ayton, co. Derby, yoman, for breaking into his close at Allerwas and carrying off 24 oxen worth 24 marks. The defendants did not appear, and the Sheriff was ordered to arrest and produce them on the Quindene of St. Michael. *m.* 122, *dorso.*

[1] Thomasine must have been heiress of the Audley Barony, but she is not mentioned in any of the Historical Peerages.

Staff. John Meverell, armiger, sued Ralph Wodeward, of Calton, John Cantrell, of Cantrell, John Beale, of Alstonefeld, husbondmen, and three others, for cutting down his trees and underwood at Throuley to the value of 100*s.* The defendancs did not appear, and the Sheriff was ordered to arrest and produce them on the Octaves of St. Michael. *m.* 173.

Staff. The same John sued Thomas Ellyshawe, of Botyrdon, William Homylton, of Boturdon, John Bagenald, of Botyrdon, and Thomas Wryght, late of Boturdon, husbondmen, for breaking into his house at Boturdon (Butterton on the Moors), taking timber from it to the value of 40*s.*, and for depasturing cattle on his corn and grass. The defendants did not appear, and the Sheriff was ordered as in the last suit. *m.* 173.

Staff. John Lokwode sued William Halle, of Kyngeley, yoman, and William Wodecok, of Chedylton, husbondman, for treading down and consuming his corn and grass at Kyngeley with their cattle. The defendants did not appear, and the Sheriff was ordered as in the last suit. *m.* 173.

Staff. Henry Walton sued Robert Cuyne (Coyney), of Weston Cuyne, armiger, for taking by force from Mere, near Careswalle, two horses and six oxen belonging to him, and other goods and chattels to the value of £10. Robert did not appear, and the Sheriff was ordered to distrain and produce him on the Quindene of St. Michael. *m.* 248.

Staff. William Vycars sued Nicholas Smyth, of Waterfall, husbondman, for depasturing cattle on his corn and grass at Musden. Nicholas did not appear, and the Sheriff was ordered to arrest and produce him on the Quindene of St. Michael. *m.* 248.

Staff. Richard Hewyson sued Agnes Wilkeson, of Tene, wydoue, for breaking into his close at Chedille and taking his goods and chattels to the value of 40*s.*, and for depasturing her cattle on his grass. Agnes did not appear, and the Sheriff was ordered to arrest and produce her on the Quindene of Michaelmas. *m.* 353.

Staff. John Sutton, knight, sued John Bredhulle, of Kyngeswynford, clerk, and John Balle, of London, brawederer, administrators of the goods and chattels of Constance Sutton, who it was stated had died intestate, for a debt of £40. The defendants did not appear, and the Sheriff was ordered to arrest and produce them on the Quindene of St. Michael. *m.* 432.

Staff. William Hexstalle sued Joan, formerly wife of William Birmyngeham, knight, late of Birmyngeham in co. Warwick, wedowe, for breaking into his close at Great Barre and taking away 12 oxen worth £12. Joan did not appear, and the Sheriff returned she held nothing within his bailiwick; he was therefore ordered to arrest and produce her on the Octaves of St. Michael. *m.* 432.

Staff. John Sutton, knight, sued John Bredhull, of Kingswynford, clerk, and John Balle, of London, brouderer, for breaking into his houses at Kyngeswynford, burning them down, and carrying off his goods and chattels to the value of £40. The defendants did not appear, and the Sheriff was ordered to arrest and produce them on the Quindene of Michaelmas. *m.* 433.

Staff. Thomas Stanley, armiger, sued Richard Whytelofe, late vicar of Estryngton, co. York, and Robert Bateman, prior of the Brethren of the Order of Preachers of York, for taking by force his goods and chattels from Elleford to the value of £40. The defendants did not appear, and the Sheriff was ordered to arrest and produce them on the Quindene of St. Michael. *m.* 433.

Staff. Richard Cartewryghte sued William Bronsford, of Weston upon Trent, chaplain, and Thomas Rodesley, of Coven, grome, for lying in wait at Coven for the purpose of killing him, and for beating, wounding, and illtreating him, so that his life was despaired of. The defendants did not appear, and the Sheriff was ordered to arrest and produce them on the Quindene of St. Michael. *m.* 433, *dorso.*

DE BANCO. HILLARY, 17 H. VI.

Staff. Richard Peshale, armiger, sued in person William Chayne, late of Longfeld in co. Salop, gentilman, and William Kem, late of Longfeld, servant, for breaking into his house at Patteshulle and taking goods and chattels to the value of £20. The defendants did not appear, and the Sheriff was ordered to arrest and produce them on the Quindene of Easter day. A postscript shews adjournments of the suit up to Hillary term 18 H. VI. *m.* 102, *dorso.*

Staff. William Morgan, armiger, sued William Whitemore, son of William Whitemore, of Thurstanton, for the manor of Mokleston, of which he had been unjustly disseised by the said William, son of William. The defendant appeared, and the suit was adjourned to the Quindene of Easter day. *m.* 124, *dorso.*

Staff. By another writ William Morgan sued John Clegge and John Tillesley for the same manor. The defendants appeared, and the suit was adjourned to the same date. *m.* 124, *dorso.*

Staff. Thomas Campyon sued Thomas Naysshe, of Arley, husbondman, for breaking into his close at Arley and depasturing cattle upon his grass, and ploughing up his soil so that he lost the profit of it for a long time. The defendant did not appear, and the Sheriff was ordered to arrest and produce him on the Quindene of Easter day. *m.* 153.

Staff. Philip Chetwynde, knight, sued Thomas Persale, of Onne, gentilman, William Fraunces, John Palmer, and Thomas Couper, all described as of Onne, and husbondmen, for breaking into his close at Mitton and depasturing cattle on his corn and grass. The defendants did not appear, and the Sheriff was ordered to distrain Thomas Persale and to arrest the others and produce them on the Quindene of Easter day. *m.* 153.

Staff. Henry atte Wall sued Nicholas Atkyn, of Walle, husbondman. Richard Ryssheton, and Robert Ryssheton, husbondmen, of Walle, William Lee, of Morrey, co. Stafford, and Thomas Sprot, of Lychefeld, barker, for breaking into his close at Walle, taking his goods and chattels to the value of 40*s.*, and depasturing cattle on his corn and grass. None of the defendants appeared, and the Sheriff was ordered to arrest and produce them on the Quindene of Easter day. *m.* 153, *dorso.*

Staff. Thomas Mitchale sued Richard Eyr, of Wombourne, husbondman, for breaking into his close at Wombourne and depasturing cattle on his grass. Richard did not appear, and the Sheriff was ordered as in the last suit. *m.* 153, *dorso.*

Staff. Thomas Holden sued Robert Kelyng, of Great Sutton upon Colfeld in co. Warwick, yoman, and Thomas Walker, late of Barre, yoman, for breaking into his close and houses at Barre and depasturing cattle on his corn and grass. The defendants did not appear, and the Sheriff was ordered as in the last suit. *m.* 153, *dorso.*

Staff. Thomas Barbour, of Stafford, sued Hugh Palmer, of Stafford, husbondman, and Peter Robyns, of Stafford, husbondman, for breaking into his close at Burton near Stafford and depasturing cattle on his grass. The defendants did not appear, and the Sheriff was ordered as in the last suit. *m.* 205.

Staff. Roger Draycote sued Nicholas Norman, of Boulde, gentilman, for breaking into his close at Lyes and destroying the roots of his wood with his cattle. Nicholas did not appear, and the Sheriff was ordered to distrain and produce him on the Quindene of Easter day. *m.* 205.

Staff. William, the Bishop of Coventry and Lychefeld, sued William Kempe, of Ruggeley, yoman, and Thomas Salwey, of Cank, yoman, for entering his free chase at Cank and chasing and taking his game. The defendants did not appear, and the Sheriff was ordered to arrest and produce them on the Quindene of Easter day. *m.* 269.

Staff. Philip Chetwynde, knight, sued Thomas Fyssher, of Rowelowe, executor of the will of John Coke, late of Stafford, for waste and destruction in houses in Stafford which he had demised to the said John for a term of years. Thomas did not appear, and the Sheriff was ordered to attach him for the Quindene of Easter day. *m.* 269, *dorso.*

Staff. Thomas Banastre sued Thomas Lucas, of Gnosale, laborer, for breaking into his close at Gnosale and depasturing cattle on his grass. The defendant did not appear, and the Sheriff was ordered to arrest and produce him on the Quindene of Easter day. *m.* 269, *dorso.*

Staff. William Kirkeby sued John Wyderley, of Lychefeld, bocher, William Clare, of Stretehay, husbondman, John Wryght, of Fulfen, husbondman, and two others, for breaking into his grass-land at Morwhale, depasturing cattle on it, and chasing 20 of his sheep with their dogs, so that they had been greatly deteriorated. None of the defendants appeared, and the Sheriff was ordered as in the last suit. *m.* 269, *dorso.*

Staff. John Lone sued Nicholas Leveson, of Wolvernehampton, gentilman, Clement Bate, laborer, John Congreve, laborer, William Waters, taillour, Richard Coumbar, barbour, Thomas Tayler, tyler, Roger Grene, aroughsmyth, Nicholas Botte, wever, and seven others named, all of Wolverhampton, for breaking into his close at Wednesfeld and depasturing their cattle on his grass. None of the defendants appeared, and the Sheriff had been ordered to distrain Nicholas, who had found sureties, and to arrest the others. The Sheriff now returned a sum of 12*d.* into Court as the proceeds of a distress, and he was ordered to distrain the said Nicholas again and to arrest the others, and produce them on the Quindene of Easter day. *m.* 339, *dorso.*

Staff. Thomas Coly sued John Booth, of Bruwode, husbondman, John Howghton, of Ellesmer, in co. Salop, husbondman, and Agnes, late wife of Richard Benteley, of Ellesmer, wedowe, for killing 4 oxen, 3 cows, and 3 calves belonging to him at Bruwode worth £10. The defendants did not appear, and the Sheriff was ordered to arrest and produce them on the Quindene of Easter day. *m.* 390, *dorso.*

Staff. John Barbour sued Joan, formerly wife of William Lee, of Knyghtley, widowe, to give up to him a chest (*cistam*) containing deeds and muniments, which she unjustly detained. Joan did not appear, and the Sheriff was ordered to attach her for the Quindene of Easter day. *m.* 411, *dorso.*

Staff. William Leveson sued John Barker, of Hethe, co. Stafford, husbondman, for depasturing cattle on his corn and grass at Hethe. John did not appear, and the Sheriff was ordered to arrest and produce him on the Quindene of Easter day. *m.* 411, *dorso.*

DE BANCO. TRINITY, 17 H. VI.

Staff. Robert Kelynge, late of Wolvernehampton, sued William Waturfalle, son of John Waturfalle, late of Wolvernehampton, yoman, for a debt of 10 marks. William did not appear, and the Sheriff was ordered to arrest and produce him on the Quindene of St. John the Baptist. *m.* 65, *dorso.*

Derb. Ralph Pole sued in person Thomas Holand, the prior of Bredsalpark, for the next presentation to a moiety of the church of Mogynton; and he stated that one Elizabeth Chaundos was formerly seised of the manor of Rodburne to which the advowson was appurtenant, and had presented one Henry Reve, clerk, who had been inducted *temp.* Ric. II, and from Elizabeth Chaundos he gave this descent:—

Elizabeth Chaundos, *ob. s.p.* — Alianora.
Alianora. | Elizabeth. | Ralph Pole, the plaintiff.

The prior defended his right, and produced a deed by Peter de la Pole, the father of Ralph, and Elizabeth, his wife, dated 3 H. IV, by which they granted a rood of land and a moiety of the church to one William de Dethek, knight, and his heirs, in exchange for all lands, rents, services, etc., in Rodburne which formerly belonged to Thomas de Staunton, and afterwards to John de Annesley, knight, and Isabella, his wife, and likewise for all the lands and tenements which the same William held in Dalburyleghes and Henour near Litulovere. And he stated that William, by a deed dated from Dethek, 4 H. IV, granted the same rood of land and the moiety of the church to Thomas de Wendesley, knight, Robert de Twyford magister, John Brewode, parson of the church of Rodburne, and two others; and Thomas de Wendesley died, and in 11 H. IV Letters Patent were granted to the surviving trustees giving licence to them to assign the said rood of land and moiety of the church, to the prior and convent of Bredsalpark in augmentation of the worship and prayers for the souls of William de Dethek, knight, and Alice, his wife, and children, and their ancestors, and for all the faithful departed. He also produced the Bull of Pope John XXth, dated from Bononia 15 Kalends of April, 4th year of his Pontificate, confirming the appropriation of the church.

Ralph replied that the above deeds should not prejudice him, because the advowson of the moiety of the church of Mogynton was appendant to the manor of Rodburne, and on this issue appealed to a jury. After several adjournments, a verdict was given in favour of the prior at assizes held at Derby in 18 H. VI, the jury finding that the advowson of the moiety of the church of Mogynton was not appendant to the manor of Rodburne. *m.* 119.[1]

Salop. James Levesson and Marjory Frebody sued John Lenches, of Preston, co. Salop, William Jenkenson, John Walford, John Myredon, all described as of Preston, and husbondmen, and eight others, for breaking into their close at Smethecote and depasturing cattle on their grass. None of the defendants appeared, and the Sheriff was ordered to arrest and produce them on the Octaves of St. Michael. *m.* 213.

Staff. Joan Hondesacre and Margaret Hondesacre sued David Cawardyne in a plea, that whereas after the death of Elizabeth, his wife, he held "*pro*

[1] Ralph Pole was of Neuburgh, co. Stafford, and the ancestor of the present family of Chandos Pole, of Radbourne.

indiviso" by the courtesy of England, together with the said Joan and Margaret, the manor of Rydeware Mavesyne and the advowson of the church of the same, of the inheritance of Robert Mavesyn, knight, the father of the said Elizabeth, and kinsman of the said Joan and Margaret, who were two of the heirs of the said Robert, and the said Elizabeth was the third heir, he refused to make a partition between them according to the law and custom of the Kingdom. David did not appear, and the Sheriff returned 12*d.* into Court as proceeds of a distress upon his chattels. The Sheriff, therefore, was ordered to distrain again, and produce him on the Octaves of St. Michael. *m.* 213, *dorso.*

Staff. Roger Wirley sued Juliana Golborne, of Great Barre, wedowe, for cutting down his trees and underwood at Little Barre. Juliana did not appear, and the Sheriff was ordered to arrest and produce her on the Quindene of St. Michael. *m.* 213, *dorso.*

Staff. Roger Newetone and John Wymark, *clericus*, sued John Janne, of Penne, husbondman, for breaking into their close at Penne and digging and carrying away earth from it. The defendant did not appear, and the Sheriff was ordered to arrest and produce him on the Quindene of St. Michael. *m.* 265, *dorso.*

Staff. John Griffith, knight, administrator of the goods and chattels of Thomas Griffith, late lord of Whichenoore, who, it was stated, had died intestate, sued Thomas Coton, of Coton, co. Stafford, gentilman, for a debt of £8. Thomas did not appear, and the Sheriff was ordered to distrain and produce him on the Octaves of St. Michael. *m.* 266.

Staff. John Myners, armiger, sued Ralph, the abbot of Croxdene, and William Perkyn and John Shefeld, fellow monks of the said abbot, for taking by force goods and chattels belonging to him from Tutbury, to the value of 20 marks, and 40 marks in money; and the Sheriff had been ordered to distrain the said abbot and to arrest the said William and John; and the Sheriff now returned 20*d.* into Court as proceeds of a distress upon the chattels of the abbot. He was therefore ordered to distrain again and produce him and the two monks on the Octaves of St. Michael. *m.* 312, *dorso.*

Staff. The Sheriff had been ordered to summon Elizabeth Blaket, Thomas Blount, knight, and Elizabeth, his wife, and William Andrewe, clerk, executors of the will of John Wilcotes, knight, to answer the plea of Robert Harecourt, knight, that they had caused waste and destruction in the lands, houses, gardens, etc., of which they held the custody after the death of the said John, and which were of the inheritance of Robert in Elynhale near Ecleshale. The defendants did not appear, and the Sheriff was ordered to attach them for the Octaves of St. Michael. *m.* 339.

Staff. Roger Mercer sued Cecily, prioress of the House of Black Nuns, of Brewode, for taking his goods and chattels to the value of £20 from Brewode. The defendant did not appear, and the Sheriff was ordered to distrain and produce her on the Quindene of St. Michael. *m.* 378, *dorso.*

Staff. William Holynshede sued Edmund Holynshede, of Sutton in co. Chester, grome, for breaking into his close at Wallegrange and taking his goods and chattels to the value of 40*s.* Edmund did not appear, and the Sheriff was ordered to arrest and produce him on the Octaves of St. Michael. *m.* 397.

Staff. Thomas Boughton, armiger, sued John Barnald, of Podmore, near Bromley, for breaking into his close at Podmore and cutting down his trees to the value of 100*s.* John did not appear, and the Sheriff was ordered to arrest and produce him on the Quindene of St. Michael. *m.* 411, *dorso.*

Staff. Thomas Boteler sued William Trewebody, of Ryggeley, coteler, John Eton, of Lychefeld, corviser, and John Pyper, of Grendon, co. Warwick, fuyster, for breaking into his close at Pype, killing three oxen worth 60*s*., and cutting down his trees to the value of £10. None of the defendants appeared, and the Sheriff was ordered as in the last suit. *m.* 411, *dorso.*

Staff. Sampson Erdeswyk sued William Ives, of Lynehill, husbondman, Thomas Whiston, of Pencriche, John Hille, and William Taillour, husbondmen, of Pencriche, for depasturing cattle on his corn and grass at Pencriche. The defendants did not appear, and the Sheriff was ordered as in the last suit. *m.* 411, *dorso.*

Staff. Richard Archer, armiger, sued Henry, the prior of Canwalle, for breaking into his close at Drayton-Basset, cutting down his trees and underwood to the value of 100*s*., and depasturing cattle on his grass. The prior did not appear, and the Sheriff was ordered to distrain and produce him on the Quindene of St. Michael. *m.* 411, *dorso.*

Staff. Edward Neville, lord of Bergevenny, sued John Russell, of Tamworth, husbondman, for breaking into his close at Wygington and taking his goods and chattels to the value of 40*s*. John did not appear, and the Sheriff was ordered to arrest and produce him on the Quindene of St. Michael. *m.* 475, *dorso.*

Staff. Thomas Bagote sued William Yate, of Blythebury, yoman, for breaking into his close at Blythebury and depasturing cattle on his grass. William did not appear, and the Sheriff was ordered as in the last suit. *m.* 475, *dorso.*

Staff. John Cumberford sued in person Richard Lovet, of Elleford, Henry Kyng, John Murymouth, William Robelyne, Richard Carter, and Richard Smythe, the younger, all of Elleford, husbondmen, for depasturing cattle on his grass at Wygynton. None of the defendants appeared, and the Sheriff was ordered as in the last suit. *m.* 475, *dorso.*

Staff. John Sutton sued William Galpyn, of Meylewyche, yoman, Thomas Doxsey, of James-Rushton, husbondman, and John Chaterton, of Rodeyerd, husbondman, for breaking into his close at James-Rushton and cutting down his underwood, digging in his soil, and carrying away hay belonging to him, and trees and underwood to the value of 100*s*. The defendants did not appear, and the Sheriff was ordered as in the last suit. *m.* 475, *dorso.*

CORAM REGE. TRINITY, 17 H. VI.

Derb. The King sent a close writ to the Sheriff stating that whereas it appeared by an Inquisition taken before the Eschaetor that Elizabeth Hondesacre, deceased, had been seised of the fourth part of the manor of Repyndon, and whilst so seised had married one Peter Melburne, deceased, and they had issue a son named John, who died in the lifetime of Elizabeth, and Peter retained possession of the said fourth part of the manor after the death of Elizabeth by the courtesy of England, the reversion belonging to William Frodesley *alias* Hondesacre, chivaler, and to Thomas Dyneley, as kinsmen and heirs of Elizabeth (the said Elizabeth having died without issue), viz. to William Frodesley as son of Isabella, one of the sisters and heirs of Elizabeth, and to Thomas Dyneley, as son of William, son of Alianora, another sister and heir of Elizabeth; and the said fourth part of Repyndon was held of the King *in capite* as of the honor of Chester by the service of a fourth part of a knight's fee: and afterwards, on the 18th July, 8 H. VI, the

King had committed to Thomas Dyneley and to Ralph Ingolesby the custody of a moiety of the said fourth part which Peter Melburn held of the King, the late King's father, when he died, and which had come into the late King's hand by reason of the minority of the said William Frodesley *alias* Hondesacre, and also by cause of the minorities of the daughters and heirs of William, son and heir of the said William Frodesley *alias* Hondesacre, to be held till the full age of the said heirs. And whereas now Joan and Margaret, the kinswomen and heirs of William Frodesley, viz. daughters of William, son of the said William Frodesley, had petitioned that the said William Frodesley had died on the 20th September, 5 H. VI, and that the said William, his son, had died in the lifetime of his father, and that the said moiety of the fourth part, together with the other moiety of the manor, was held of the King as of his honor of Lincoln, which is parcel of the Duchy of Lancaster by fealty in lieu of all other services, and not of the honor of Chester as stated in the Inquisitions, and that the said Elizabeth had held no other lands *in capite*, as they were prepared to prove. The King, wishing to do what was just, commanded the Sheriff to summon the said Thomas and Ralph Ingoldesby to appear in Chancery on the Morrow of the Ascension to shew cause why the Letters Patent granting the custody to them should not be annulled. And on that day the said Joan and Margaret appeared by William Rudyng, their *custos*, and the said Thomas and Ralph Ingoldesby put in no appearance. It was therefore considered that the said Letters Patent should be revoked. The King's attorney then appeared and asked for a jury to be empannelled to try whether the manor was held of the King *in capite* as of the honor of Chester or not. A postscript shews that a jury of the vicinage of Repyndon at subsequent assizes at Derby returned a verdict that the manor was not held of the honor of Chester as stated in the Inquisitions, it was therefore considered that the King's hand should be removed, and the moiety of the fourth part should be restored to the said Joan and Margaret, with all the profits and issue from the date they were expelled.[1] *m.* 23, *Rex.*

[1] The pedigree as given by the above suit and previous suits in these Collections is as follows:—

William de Handesacre, of Handsacre, co. Stafford.

Simon de Handesacre = Isabella.

Roger = Elizabeth = Peter Melburne. Roger Colmon (1st husband.)
John, *ob. s.p.*

Isabella = Laurence, son of William Forster, of Frodesley.
William Frodesley, kt., *d.* 5 H. VI.
William de Handsacre, *d. v.p.*
Joan, 17 H. VI. — Margaret, 17 H. VI.

Alianora = Richard Dyngeley or Dyneley.
William Dyneley.
Thomas Dyneley.

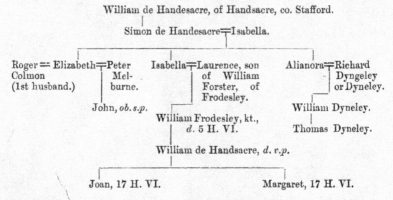

Roger Colmon, the first husband of Elizabeth, had been killed by Laurence Forster, the husband of Isabella, in 1385. Laurence Forster was afterwards killed by Sir Robert Mauveisin in 1399. The grandson of Laurence, who called himself William de Handsacre, married a daughter of Sir Robert Mauveisin. If the tradition, therefore, be true that Sir Robert Mauveisin killed Sir William Handsacre, he must have killed his own son-in-law, which is not likely. See on this subject, the note at p. 26 of Vol. XVI and the suit at p. 150 of this Volume.

DE BANCO. HILLARY, 18 H. VI.

Staff. Thomas Ferrers, armiger, Roger Aston, knight, and Hugh Wyllughby, knight, sued John Prynce, of Warwyk, yoman, for waste and destruction in houses, woods, and gardens which had been demised to him for a term of years. John did not appear, and the Sheriff was ordered to attach him for the Quindene of Easter day. *m.* 45.

Staff. Thomas Roddesley sued Henry Smyth, of Coven, husbondman, for breaking into his close at Coton and depasturing cattle on his corn and grass. Henry did not appear, and the Sheriff was ordered to arrest and produce him on the Quindene of Easter day. *m.* 197.

Staff. John Griffith, knight, sued Rees ap Thomas, late of London, armiger, for taking by force a horse belonging to him from Alderwas (Alrewas), worth £20. Rees did not appear, and the Sheriff was ordered to arrest and produce him on the Quindene of Easter day. *m.* 197.

Staff. William, the Bishop of Coventry and Lichfield, sued Thomas Pymme, of Wolvernehampton, chaplain, Henry Shawebery, of Wolvernehampton, chaplain, William Hayne, late of Wolverhampton, yoman, and William Couper, of Wolverhampton, yoman, for breaking into his park at Brewode and chasing and taking his game. None of the defendants appeared, and the Sheriff was ordered to arrest and produce them at the Quindene of Easter. *m.* 197, *dorso.*

Northumberland. John Griffith, knight, sued Roger Thornton for the manors of Witton Wyngates and Scheles, and a moiety of the manors of Stanyngton, Benasses, Tranwell, Benton, and Killingworth, which Isabella, formerly wife of Robert Somervyle, gave to Roger Somervyle and heirs of his body, from whom he gave this descent:—

Roger de Somervyle seised of the manors and tenements *temp.* E. I.
|
Philip.
|
Joan.
|
Ros, *sic* (Rhys).
|
Thomas.
|
John Griffith, the plaintiff.

The suit was adjourned to Easter term. A postscript states that on that date Roger prayed a view, and the suit was adjourned to Michaelmas term 19 H. VI, a view to be made in the interim. A further postscript shews that no view had been made up to Easter term 20 H. VI. *m.* 336.[1]

Staff. Thomas Salt, of Ricardescote, sued John de Alle, of Rycardescote, husbondman, for breaking into his several fishery at Acton Trussell and taking fish to the value of 60*s.* John did not appear, and the Sheriff was ordered to arrest and produce him on the Quindene of Easter day. *m.* 353.

Staff. John Sutton, of Duddeley, knight, sued Nicholas Waryng, of Wolvernehampton, gentilman, Thomas Colyns, of Wolvernehampton, yoman, John Bayly, of Kynfare, yoman, Thomas Hochekys, yoman, and John

[1] Sir John Griffith, the plaintiff, was lord of Whichnor and Alrewas, co. Stafford, which he had inherited from the Somervilles.

Broweland, yoman, both of Wolvernhampton, for breaking into his free chase at Pensnet and chasing and taking his game. None of the defendants appeared, and the Sheriff was ordered to distrain Nicholas, who had found sureties, and to arrest the others and produce them on the Quindene of Easter day. *m.* 353.

Staff. John Sutton, of Duddeley, knight, sued Thomas Manley, of Wylnale, gentilman, William Nichollys, of Wylnale, husbondman, Thomas Pym, of Wolvernhampton, chaplain, William Merssh, of Woddysfeld, husbondman, Henry Shawebury, of Wolvernehampton, chaplain, and William Piry, of Bylston, husbondman, for breaking into his park at Seggeley and chasing and taking his game. None of the defendants appeared, and the Sheriff was ordered to distrain Thomas Manley and William Nichollys, and to arrest the others and produce them on the Quindene of Easter day. *m.* 353.

Staff. John Sutton, of Duddeley, knight, sued John Fletcher, late of Wolvernehampton, bowyer, for breaking into his park at Wolvernhampton and chasing and taking his game. The defendant did not appear, and the Sheriff was ordered to arrest and produce him on the above date. *m.* 353.

Staff. John Sutton, of Duddeley, knight, sued Nicholas Waryng, of Wolvernhampton, gentilman, for breaking into his close at Hemley (Himley) and carrying away 200 rabbits. Nicholas did not appear, and the Sheriff was ordered to distrain and produce him on the same date. *m.* 353.

Staff. John Gresley, knight, and Margaret, his wife, sued Roger Bagnalle, of Trentham, yoman, executor of the will of Stephen Bagnall, and William Boydell, of Trentham, gentilman, and Alice, his wife, the coexecutrix of the said Roger, to give up to them goods and chattels to the value of 6 marks which they unjustly detained. The defendants did not appear, and the Sheriff was ordered to arrest and produce them on the Quindene of Easter day. *m.* 353, *dorso.*

DE BANCO. TRINITY, 18 H. VI.

Staff. John Whatcroft, Henry Frebody, Thomas Muston and Margaret, his wife, sued Richard Martyn, of Wednesbury, yoman, for breaking into their close at Grete and depasturing cattle on their grass. Richard did not appear, and the Sheriff was ordered to arrest and produce him on the Quindene of St. John the Baptist. *m.* 87.

Staff. John Whatcroft sued William Doge, of Walsale, lorymer, John Roper, taillour, William Lawe, bocher, Richard Barker, barker, John Balle, carpenter, John Sporyour, lorymer, and John Bacon, lorymer (all of Walshale), for breaking into his houses and close at Westbromwych and beating and wounding his servant John Brodeley so that he lost his services for a length of time. None of the defendants appeared, and the Sheriff was ordered as in the last suit. *m.* 87.[1]

Staff. Ralph Maynwaryng, armiger, sued Oliver Chaterton, of Fulfen, gentilman, and Alice, his wife, for burning down his house at Kele *vi et armis.* The defendants did not appear, and the Sheriff was ordered to arrest and produce them on the Quindene of St. Michael. *m.* 87.

Staff. John Barbour sued Joan Knyghtley, of Knyghtley, wedowe, to give up to him a pyx containing deeds and muniments, which she unjustly

[1] It will be seen from the number of lorymers at Walshall that the manufacture of harness and saddlery in that town is a very ancient craft.

detained. Joan did not appear, and the Sheriff was ordered to attach her for the Quindene of St. Michael. *m.* 87.

Staff. Robert Harcourt, knight, sued Sampson Erdeswyk, of Pyletenhale, gentilman, Henry Erdeswyk, of Pyletenhale, gentilman, and John Wymark, of Pencrich, chaplain, for taking *vi et armis* his goods and chattels from Pyletenhale, which were worth £10. None of the defendants appeared, and the Sheriff returned that Sampson had been distrained up to 12*d.* He was therefore ordered to distrain again, and to arrest and produce the others on the Quindene of St. Michael. *m.* 168.

Staff. Richard Wylughby sued William Colclough, of Newcastle under Lyme, gentilman, and Henry Stalynton, of Newcastle under Lyme, husbondman, for breaking into his house at Newcastle under Lyme and taking goods and chattels belonging to him to the value of 40*s.*, and 40*s.* in money. The defendants did not appear, and the Sheriff was ordered to arrest and produce them on the Quindene of St. Michael. *m* 168, *dorso.*

Staff. John Shyngilhurst sued William Bailly, of Leeke, yoman, for taking by force goods and chattels belonging to him from Leeke. William did not appear, and the Sheriff was ordered as in the last suit. *m.* 229, *dorso.*

Staff. William Cumberford sued in person John Wryght, of Tamworth, wryght, in a plea that whereas the said John had agreed to build a house for him at Cumberford within a certain time, he had not carried out his contract, and for which he claimed 40*s.* as damages. John did not appear, and the Sheriff was ordered as in the last suit. *m.* 229, *dorso.*

Staff. Thomas Blount sued Thomas Tillie, of London, souter, for taking by force goods and chattels belonging to him at Blythebury which were worth £20, and likewise £20 in money; and for beating, wounding, and illtreating his servant, John Barbour, so that he lost his services for a length of time. The defendant did not appear, and the Sheriff was ordered as in the last suit. *m.* 245.

Staff. James Assheby, of Mershton, co. Stafford, gentilman, Agnes Jamysservant Assheby, of Mershton, servant, William Honde, of Mershton, husbondman, John Baker, of Mershton, husbondman, and Richard Jamyservant Assheby, of Mershton, laborer, were attached at the suit of William Lee for taking by force 6 calves and 6 lambs belonging to him at Mershton, and worth 40*s.*, and goods and chattels belonging to him worth 40*s.* And William Lee, who sued in person, stated that on the Feast of St. Peter *ad Vincula*, 17 H. VI, they had taken 8 cartloads of hay, 3 stone of wool, 6 calves, and 6 lambs belonging to him, for which he claimed £20 as damages.

The defendants appeared, and James stated the vill of Mershton was a parish, of which one John Tilton was parish priest; and the said John Tilton, on the 1st February, 17 H. VI, had demised to him and two others the rectory of Mershton for seven years, and the calves and other things taken were the tythes of divers parishioners of the said parish, and he had taken them, as one of the fermors of the rectory, as was lawful.

William Lee replied that John Tilton had demised to him his rectory on the Vigil of the Nativity of St. John the Baptist, 17 H. VI, by virtue of which demise he was in possession of the rectory, and he appealed to a jury, which was to be summoned for the Quindene of St. Michael. *m.* 308.

Staff. Roger Draycote sued Richard Vernon, knight, Hugh Erdeswyk, Humfrey Cotes, Richard Bagot, Thomas Perkyn, parson of Blythefeld, Marjory, late wife of William Haytlees, and Nicholas Norman and Joan, his wife, for 40 acres of land and 4 acres of meadow in Lyes which Richard

Draycote, knight, had given to Philip de Draycote and Joan, his wife, and the heirs of their bodies, and from whom he gave this descent :—

Philip de Draycote, seised ═ Joan.
temp. E. I.
|
John.
|
John.
|
John.
|
Roger Draycote, the plaintiff.

The defendants admitted the claim, and Roger was to have seisin of the land. *m.* 325, *dorso.*

London. The Sheriffs had been ordered to arrest Isabella, formerly wife of John Cokayn, knight, of Polleswortb in co. Warwick, wedowe, executrix of the will of John Cokayn, late of co. Derby, knight, who had been *wayviata* in London on the Monday before the Feast of St. Matthew, 18 H. VI, at the suit of Joan Cokayn, formerly wife of John Cokayn, knight, the younger, daughter of John Daubrichcourt, the elder, knight, in a plea of debt; and Isabella, formerly wife of John Cockayn, knight, of Harlaston, co. Stafford, now appeared in person, and stated that she had been unjustly *wayved*, and greatly molested (*multipliciter inquietata*), because on the date of the original writ, viz. on the 12th January, 17 H. VI, she was living at Harlaston, and neither on that date nor ever afterwards was of Polleswortb as stated in the writ; and as it appeared to the Court that it was expedient that the said Joan should be warned before proceeding with the annulment of the *wayviaria* of Isabella, the Sheriff was ordered to summon the said Joan for the Quindene of St. Michael to shew cause, etc. And Isabella was released on the sureties of Richard Byngham, of Bateford, co. Notts, gentilman, Ralph de la Pole, of London, gentilman, Thomas Bate, of London, gentilman, and Robert Rasyn, of Notts, gentilman.

A postscript states that on that day Joan appeared, and stated that on the date of the writ Isabella was of Polleswortb, co. Warwick, and appealed to a jury, which was to be summoned for the Morrow of St. Martin. The process was afterwards transferred, by writ of *nisi prius*, to be heard at Coventry before William Ayscough, one of the Justices of the Bench, on the Tuesday before the Feast of St. Peter *in Cathedra*, 19 H. VI, when a jury stated that on the date of the writ Isabella was living at Harlaston and not at Polleswortb, and she was therefore exonerated from her *wayviaria*. *m.* 334.

Staff. William Everdon sued Nicholas atte Lowe, of Bysshbury, husbondman, and Joan, his wife, for depasturing cattle on his corn and grass at Bysshbury. Nicholas did not appear, and the Sheriff was ordered to arrest and produce him on the Quindene of St. Michael. *m.* 375.

Staff. John Beresford sued Roger Royley, of Hadekeserd, co. Stafford, husbondman, Richard Royley, of Ferneford, husbondman, James Royley, of Elcuston, husbondman, Godfrey Royley, of Waterhowses, husbondman, and six others, for taking a horse belonging to him from Hope worth 100*s*. None of the defendants appeared, and the Sheriff was ordered to arrest and produce them on the above date. *m.* 375.

Staff. John Kyngesley sued Richard Walker, of Clayton near Newcastle under Lyme, for cutting down his fences at Clayton and doing damage to the amount of £10. Richard did not appear, and the Sheriff was ordered as in the last suit. *m.* 376.

Staff. Thomas Hethe, one of the King's clerks of the Common Bench, sued in person John Couper, of Great Bloxwich, couper, for depasturing cattle on his grass at Great Bloxwich. John did not appear, and the Sheriff was ordered as in the last suit. *m.* 500.

DE BANCO. HILLARY, 19 H. VI.

Staff. Henry Sale sued Thomas Kuyheley, of Felde, carpenter, for breaking into his close at Lee and depasturing cattle on his corn and grass. Thomas did not appear, and the Sheriff was ordered to arrest and produce him on the Quindene of Easter day. *m.* 166, *dorso.*

Staff. The Dean of the King's Free Chapel of Wolvernhampton sued Nicholas Leveson, of Wolvernehampton, gentilman, to give up to him a bag containing deeds and muniments, which he unjustly detained. Nicholas did not appear, and the Sheriff was ordered to distrain and produce him on the above date. *m.* 166, *dorso.*

Staff. John Lone and William Neuporte, the executors of the will of Richard Lone, sued John Spycer, of Wolvernehampton, husbondman, and William Lone, of Wyllenhale, husbondman, for a debt of 40*s.* The defendants did not appear, and the Sheriff was ordered to arrest and produce them on the above date. *m.* 166, *dorso.*

Staff. Hugh Herdeswyk (Erdeswyk) and Thomasia, his wife, sued Peter Gooldson for waste and destruction in lands, houses, and gardens in Hyntes which they had demised to him for a term of years. Peter did not appear, and the Sheriff was ordered to attach him for the above date. *m.* 188.

Staff. James Leveson sued John Hopkyns, of Overpenne, clerk, to give up to him a pyx containing deeds and muniments, which he unjustly detained. John did not appear, and the Sheriff was ordered to arrest and produce him on the above date. *m.* 188.

Staff. James Leveson sued John Perkeshous, of Seggesley, yoman, John Perkeshous, William Elwall, Thomas Kymmon (all of Seggesley), yomen, and William Tomson, of Netherpenne, husbondman, for breaking into his close at Netherpenne and taking his goods and chattels to the value of 10 marks. None of the defendants appeared, and the Sheriff was ordered to arrest and produce them on the above date. *m.* 188.

Staff. Thomas Stanley, armiger, sued Ralph Stanley, late of Elleford, clerk, and Katrine, late wife of John Hore, of Chestre, wedowe, to give up to him two bonds, which they unjustly detained. The defendants did not appear, and the Sheriff was ordered to arrest and produce them on the above date. *m.* 188, *dorso.*

Staff. Humfrey Clerkesson sued William Stykbuk, of Colton, husbondman, John Brokhole, of Colton, laborer, and Richard Phelyp, of Blythebury, husbondman, for breaking into his close at Colton and depasturing cattle on his corn and grass. None of the defendants appeared, and the Sheriff was ordered to arrest and produce them on the Quindene of Easter day. *m.* 392.

Staff. Thomas Stele sued Thomas Watson, of Salt, husbondman, and Roger Homersley, of Salt, husbondman, for breaking into his close at Salt and depasturing cattle on his corn and grass. The defendants did not appear, and the Sheriff was ordered to arrest and produce them on the above date. *m.* 392.

Staff. John Whatcroft, of Westbromwych, sued Thomas Burgoloune, of Kyngesbromley, gentilman, and Agnes, his wife, to give up to him a pyx containing deeds and writings, which they unjustly detained. The defendants did not appear, and the Sheriff was ordered to arrest and produce them on the above date. *m.* 392.

CORAM REGE. EASTER, 19 H. VI.

Staff. The trial of John, son of Peter de Legh, late of Throweley near Altenfeld, armiger, *alias* John Legh, late of Sutton near Bosley, co. Chester, armiger, for divers felonies, was respited till the Quindene of St. Michael, unless the King's Justices holding assizes should first come to Wolverhampton on the Wednesday before the Feast of St. Margaret. *m.* 2 *Rex, dorso.*

Staff. John Bredhille, parson of the church of Kyngesswynford, appeared in Court and produced the King's pardon for all murders, felonies, etc., of which he had been indicted up to the 10th February last; dated 10th April, 19 H. VI.

The indictments had been returned into Court, and were as follows:—

1st. For the rape of Joan, the wife of Reginald Tanner, in 17 H. VI.

2nd. As accessory to the robbery of a silver patera from the church of Kyngeswynford by one Richard Ingelarowe, of Kyngeswynford, scoler, in 15 H. VI.

3rd. For entering the park of John Sutton, of Dudley, knight, at Kyngeswynford, and chasing and killing his game.

4th. For the rape of Christine, wife of John Hareward, of Kydemynstre, and robbing the said John of 40 marks in money.[1]

DE BANCO. TRINITY, 19 H. VI.

Staff. John Jolyff sued Richard Bromley, of Lichfeld, yoman, for leaving his service at Lichfeld without reasonable cause, against the Statute of King Ed. III. Richard did not appear, and the Sheriff was ordered to arrest and produce him on the Quindene of St. Michael. *m.* 19.

Staff. Robert Molyneux, armiger, sued Thomas Burgulon, of Kyngesbromley, gentilman, and Agnes, his wife, and Robert Burgulon, of Kyngesbromley, gentilman, for breaking into his houses at Pyry and taking his goods and chattels to the value of £10. The defendants did not appear, and the Sheriff was ordered to arrest and produce them on the above date. *m.* 30.

Staff. John Jolyff, clerk, sued Richard Bromley, of Lichfeld, yoman, for breaking into his close and houses at Lichefeld and taking his goods and chattels to the value of 100*s.* Richard did not appear, and the Sheriff was ordered to arrest and produce him on the above date. *m.* 30.

Midd. Henry Southwell and Joan, his wife, and Nicholas Yward (*sic*) and Elizabeth, his wife, sued Thomas Charleton, knight, and Elizabeth, his

[1] The indictments against the clergy are so numerous on the Rolls at this period, that it is probable that the invectives of John Wickcliffe against them, coarse as they were, were not very far from the truth. Even if convicted of felony, they escaped with a nominal punishment, under the plea of benefit of clergy.

wife, for a messuage, 40 acres of land, 10 acres of meadow, and 2 acres of pasture in Edelmeton and Enefeld which John Wysman, chaplain, had given to Agnes, formerly wife of John Burdeyn, late citizen and goldsmith, of London, for her life, with remainder to Gilbert, son of the said John Burdeyn and Agnes, and heirs of his body, and failing such, to Idonia, daughter of the said John and Agnes, and heirs of her body; and failing such, to Agnes, sister of Idonia, and heirs of her body; and failing such, to Joan, sister of Agnes, and heirs of her body.

The defendants called to warranty John Whytegreve, son and heir of John Whytegreve, who appeared and warranted the tenements to them; and the plaintiffs then sued the said John Whytegreve, and gave the following pedigree:—

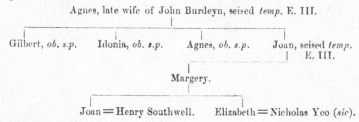

Agnes, late wife of John Burdeyn, seised *temp.* E. III.

Gilbert, *ob. s.p.* — Idonia, *ob. s.p.* — Agnes, *ob. s.p.* — Joan, seised *temp.* E. III.

Margery.

Joan = Henry Southwell. — Elizabeth = Nicholas Yeo (*sic*).

A postscript shews the suit was continued up to Hillary, 22 H. VI, without any result. *m.* 31.

Staff. Thomas Gamage, armiger, sued John Verney, dean of the Cathedral Church of St. Cedde of Lichefeld, to give up to him a pyx containing deeds and muniments, which he unjustly detained. The Dean did not appear, and the Sheriff was ordered to distrain and produce him on the Octaves of St. Michael. *m.* 71.

Staff. Philip Chetewynd, of Ingestre, knight (late armiger), sued in person John del Hulle, of Pencriche, yoman, in a plea that he should carry out a covenant made between them that he should repair and maintain a tenement situated in the market place of Pencriche for a term of 12 years, in which Ralph Brusenhulle formerly lived. John did not appear, and the Sheriff was ordered to attach him for the Quindene of St. Michael. A postscript states on that day the Sheriff made no return to the writ, and he was ordered to attach him for the Octaves of St. Hillary. *m.* 225.

Staff. Reginald Maynelle sued Robert, the prior of Calwych, for taking by force from him a bag containing £20 in money. The prior did not appear, and the Sheriff was ordered to distrain and produce him on the Quindene of St. Michael. *m.* 277.

Staff. Henry Shawe sued William Sydenhale, of Compton, husbondman, and William Wyghtwyk, husbondman, for breaking into his close at Compton and depasturing cattle on his corn and grass. The defendants did not appear, and the Sheriff was ordered to arrest and produce them on the Quindene of St. Michael. *m.* 382.

Staff. Nicholas Fynderne, of Fynderne in co. Derby, gentilman, appeared in Court on the 13th July in this term and acknowledged he owed to John Bate, clerk, £400, to be paid on the following Feast of St. Peter which is called "*ad Vincula*"; and if he failed, the money might be levied on his goods and chattels. The conditions of the recognizance were as follows: that if the said Nicholas, and Joan the wife of John Bothe, Bartholomew Brokesby, Thomas Asshby, Thomas Staunton, John Oudeby, Henry Brokesby, and

Henry Felyngley should stand to the arbitrament and judgment of William Yelverton, serjeant-at-law, and of Richard Byngham, arbitrators on the part of the said Nicholas, and Joan, Bartholomew, etc., and also of John Fortescu, the King's serjeant-at-law, and of John Chok, arbitrators on the part of the said John Bate, respecting the title and possession of 15 acres of land, 3 roods of meadow, and a moiety of a messuage in Octhorp, and upon the title and possession of the manor of Stretton en le Feld, and the advowson of the church of the same, and of all the lands and tenements, rents, etc., and other possessions formerly belonging to Margery, the daughter of John Stretton, late the wife of Aylmer Taverner, in the vills of Stretton, Okethorp, Durandesthorp, Willesley, Gopshull, Twycrosse, Appulby, Childecote, Amynton, Ednynghale, and elsewhere in cos. Derby, Leicester, Warwick, and Stafford, and likewise of all deeds and other writings, and all kinds of evidences concerning the same, and of all kinds of actions and trespasses, quarrels, demands, etc., between the said John Bate and the said Nicholas, Joan, Bartholomew, etc., then the said recognizance shall be null and void. *m.* 435.

Staff. John Bate entered into a similar recognizance. *m.* 435, *dorso.*

DE BANCO. HILLARY, 20 H. VI.

Staff. Thomas Wolseley, the executor of the will of Ralph Wolseley, sued Thomas Bloreton, of Ruggeley, cartwryght, and two others, for a debt of 40*s.*; and he sued Nicholas Ruggeley, of Dunton in co. Warwick, gentilman, executor of the will of Nicholas Ruggeley, for a debt of 4 marks. The defendants did not appear, and the Sheriff was ordered to arrest and produce them at three weeks from Easter day. *m.* 150, *dorso.*

Staff. John Northhale sued Hugh Wyldeblode, of Bednale, husbondman, for breaking into his close at Weston-under-Lusyerd and depasturing cattle on his corn and grass. Hugh did not appear, and the Sheriff was ordered to arrest and produce him on the Quindene of Easter day. *m.* 150, *dorso.*

Staff. Thomas Stanley, armiger, sued John Verney, late of Lychefeld, clerk, John Joly, of Lychefeld, clerk, William Saynt Jones, of Lychefeld, smythe, Thomas Boteler, of Longdon, yoman, Thomas Swenfen, of Swenfen, gentilman, Robert Webbe, of Edyghale, yoman, John Webbe, of Hommerwych, husbondman, John Heuster, of Lychefeld, yoman, and upwards of forty others (all tradesmen of Lichfield), for assembling together and collecting a number of unknown malefactors, and beating and wounding his servants and tenants, and so terrifying them that for fear of their lives they were unable to prosecute his business or leave the enclosure of their houses. The defendants did not appear, and the Sheriff was ordered to arrest and produce them on the Quindene of Easter day. *m.* 232, *dorso.*

Staff. Roger Aston, knight, sued Roger Mercer, of Longnor, husbondman, for breaking into his close at Longnor and depasturing cattle on his grass. The defendant did not appear, and the Sheriff was ordered to arrest and produce him on the above date. *m.* 232, *dorso.*

Staff. John, son of Thomas Cradocke, sued Thomas Colclogh, of Newcastle-under-Lyme, gentilman, to carry out the terms of a covenant made between them respecting a messuage, 30 acres of land, 8 acres of meadow, and 16 acres of pasture in Blorton which the said Thomas had demised to him for a term of 20 years. Thomas did not appear, and the Sheriff was ordered to arrest and produce him . . . . (*No date named.*) *m.* 233, *dorso.*

Staff. Richard le bard sued John Clerk, of Whytyngton, yoman, and three others, for insulting, wounding, and beating him at Wednesbury, and retaining him a prisoner there until he had made a fine with them of 6*s.* for his release. The defendants did not appear, and the Sheriff was ordered to arrest and produce them at three weeks from Easter day. *m.* 233, *dorso.*

Staff. Thomas Peshale and Isabella, his wife, sued John Aghton, of Amberton, plasterer, for taking by force goods and chattels belonging to the said Isabella at Coton. John did not appear, and the Sheriff was ordered to arrest and produce him on the Quindene of Easter day. *m.* 353, *dorso.*

Staff. Thomas Peshale and Isabella, his wife, sued William Bradshawe, of Milwiche, gentilman, and John Fernehalgh, of Milwiche, husbondman, for breaking into the close of Isabella at Coton and taking 2 cows and 6 oxen worth 5 marks. The defendants did not appear, and the Sheriff was ordered to distrain William who had found sureties, and to arrest the said John, and produce them at a month from Easter. *m.* 354, *dorso.*

Staff. Richard Cartwryght sued Richard Harecourt, of Little Saredon, armiger, Robert de Hogh, of Shareshulle, taillour, Thomas Rodesley, of Coven, husbondman, Robert Gogh, of Brewode, taillour, William Gogh, of Brewode, wever, and four others named, for beating, wounding, and illtreating him at Brewode, and taking him a prisoner to Little Saredon. None of the defendants appeared, and the Sheriff was ordered to distrain the said Richard, and to arrest the others and produce them on the Quindene of Easter day. *m.* 385.

Staff. William Hexstall sued in person Richard Harecourt, of Little Saredon, armiger, and the other defendants named in the last suit, for beating, wounding, and illtreating his servant Richard Cartewryght at Brewode, and by which he lost his services for a length of time. The process was the same as in the last suit. *m.* 385, *dorso.*

Staff. William Armeston (who sued for the King) sued Thomas Peshale, of Onne, gentilman, and (. . . . .), formerly wife of George Doryngton, executrix of the will of George Doryngton, for a debt of £12 owing to the King. The defendants did not appear, and the Sheriff was ordered to arrest and produce them on the Quindene of Easter day. *m.* 450.

DE BANCO. TRINITY, 20 H. VI.

Berks. William Trussell, knight, sued Richard Vernon, knight, for the manors of Shotesbrok and Eton Hastynges, of which Richard had unjustly disseised him. Richard stated that William could not maintain his action, because one Fulk Pembrygge was formerly seised of the manors in demesne as of fee, and had died seised of them, and they had descended to him as kinsman and heir of Fulk, *viz.* as son of Richard Vernon, knight, son of Juliana, the sister of the said Fulk. William Trussell stated that as regarded the manor of Shotesbrok, long before Fulk Pembrygge held anything in it, he had been seised of it in demesne as of fee, and had demised it to the said Fulk for his life, and after the death of Fulk, he had entered, and was seised of it until Richard had unjustly disseised him. And as regarded the manor of Eton Hastynges, a Fine had been levied in 45 E. III between William Trussell, of Cubulstone, chivaler, and the said Fulk Pembrygge and Margaret, his wife, by which Fulk and Margaret had acknowledged the said manor, with others named, to be the right of William Trussell, of Cubulstone, and for which acknowledgment the said William had granted the manor to Fulk and Margaret, and the heirs of their bodies, and failing such, to remain to the said William Trussell, of Cubulstone, and his heirs for ever. And Margaret had died without issue, and after her death, Fulk held the manor for his life, and died so seised of it; and after his death, the manor descended to William Trussell, the plaintiff, as kinsman and heir of the said William Trussell, of Cubulstone, viz. as son of Laurence, son of Warine, the brother of John, father of the said William Trussell, of Cubulstone, and he was seised of it until he had been unjustly disseised of it by the said Richard. Richard replied that Fulk Pembrygge had been seised of the said manor in demesne as of fee, and appealed to a jury. The Sheriff was therefore ordered to summon a jury for the Morrow of St. Martin.

A postscript states that a jury was empannelled at the following Easter term, and returned a verdict in favour of William Trussell, and assessed his damages at 80 marks, and his costs at 40 marks. William was therefore to recover seisin of the manors, and 120 marks.

Another postscript states that the proceedings were moved by a writ of error into the King's Court (*Coram Rege*) on the 18th May, 21 E. III, and afterwards, on the 1st May, 24 E. III, William Trussell appeared in Court in person and stated that his damages had been satisfied. *m.* 305.

Berks. William Trussell, knight, sued Fulk Vernon, armiger, for 30 messuages, 20 virgates of land, 60 acres of meadow, 200 acres of pasture, 200 acres of wood, and £20 of rent in Shotesbroke, Whitwaltham, Laurence Waltham, and Eton Hastynges, by a writ of novel disseisin. Fulk pleaded that he was not tenant of the said lands and tenements when the writ was issued, and a jury found in his favour. *m.* 306.

DE BANCO. HILLARY, 21 H. VI.

Oxon. William Lovell and Elizabeth, his wife, John Gayge and Alianora, his wife, and Richard Harecourt and Edith, his wife, sued William Cheyne, knight, and two others, for the manor of Chaldegrave, which they claimed as heirs of Philip Sentcler (St. Clair), knight, and Margaret, his wife, and they gave this descent :—

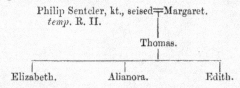

Philip Sentcler, kt., seised = Margaret.
temp. R. II.

Thomas.

Elizabeth. Alianora. Edith.

The defendants admitted the claim. *m.* 117.

Sussex. The same plaintiffs sued the same defendants for the manors of Heyghton, Brembletye, Newnham, Lampham, Exete, Britz, Helmeston, and Notbourne Sentcler, and recovered as in last suit. *m.* 118.

Staff. The abbess of Polesworth sued Margaret, late wife of Richard Myners, of Blaknalle, for a debt of 40*s.* Margaret did not appear, and the Sheriff was ordered to attach her for the Quindene of Easter day. *m.* 149.

Staff. Petronilla, late wife of William Venables, sued William de Venables, late of Careswalle, gentilman, to render a reasonable account for the time he had been the receiver of her money. William did not appear, and the Sheriff was ordered to arrest and produce him on the above date. *m.* 149, *dorso.*

Staff. John Coke sued Simon Turnour, of Gnowesale, husbondman, John Nowell, of Gnowesale, yoman, Robert Adene, Robert Calewale, and John Cartewryght, all of Gnowesale, and described as yomen, for lying in wait at Gnowesale in order to kill him, and for beating, wounding, and illtreating him. None of the defendants appeared, and the Sheriff was ordered to arrest and produce them on the above date. *m.* 149, *dorso.*

Staff. John Kyngesley sued Robert Lynley, of Newcastle under Lyme, nayler, Thomas Rancorne, corviser, Thomas Stacy, wevere, Thomas Spen, laborer, and Thomas Paver, walker, all of Newcastle under Lyme, for collecting together a number of malefactors, and lying in wait at Newcastle under Lyme in order to kill him, and for beating, wounding, and illtreating him so that his life was despaired of. None of the defendants appeared, and the Sheriff was ordered as in the last suit. *m.* 149, *dorso.*

Staff. Thomas Gresley, knight, sued John Brooke, of Blibury, husbondman, John Wolaston, vicar of Abbotesbromley, Ralph Sandbach, of Abbotesbromley, yoman, Richard Shipton, of Yoxhale, husbondman, Nicholas Clerk, of Colton, husbondman, John Hore, of Calowehille, husbondman, Thomas Hampton, of Abbotesbromley, husbondman, and Thomas Nevowe, of Pipe Ridware, gentilman, for breaking into his closes at Blibury and Morton, cutting down his trees and underwood, and depasturing their cattle on his corn and grass. None of the defendants appeared, and the Sheriff was ordered to arrest and produce them on the Quindene of Easter day. *m.* 249, *dorso.*

Staff. John Holand, knight, sued John Godefelowe, abbot of Dieulacres, Ralph Daumport, of Leeke, gentilman, Robert Frankelyn, of Leeke, yoman, Richard Glover, of Leeke, parysh clerk, and Richard Deyne, of Leeke, fletcher, for taking his goods and chattels worth £40 from Leeke *vi et armis.* None of the defendants appeared, and the Sheriff returned he had distrained the abbot up to 3*s.* 4*d.*, and the others could not be found. He was therefore ordered to distrain the abbot again, and to arrest the others and produce them on the Quindene of Easter day. *m.* 250.

Staff. John Amys sued William Ryley, of Shelton Wodhouse, husbondman, for breaking into his house and close at Shelton, and carrying away his goods and chattels to the value of £10. William did not appear, and the Sheriff was ordered to arrest and produce him on the above date. *m.* 250, *dorso.*

Staff. William Rokke sued Hugh Wyldblode, of Bedenale, yoman, for depasturing cattle on his corn and grass at Weston. Hugh did not appear, and the Sheriff was ordered as in the last suit. *m.* 266.

Staff. Thomas Weston sued Hugh Wyldblode, of Bedenale, yoman, for depasturing cattle on his corn and grass at Weston. Hugh did not appear, and the Sheriff was ordered as in the last suit. *m.* 266.

Staff. John Wylne, the prior of Repyngton, co. Derby, was sued by John Curson for depasturing cattle on his grass at Oklee. John Curson appeared in person, and stated that the prior, on the Monday before the Feast of the Nativity of St. John the Baptist, 14 H. VI, had depastured his cattle, viz. horses, oxen, cows, pigs, and sheep on his grass at Oklee, and had continued the trespass for six years afterwards, for which he claimed £20 as damages. The prior denied the trespass, and the suit was adjourned to the Quindene of Easter. *m.* 280.

Staff. The Sheriff had been ordered to distrain Humfrey Lowe, late Sheriff, to produce at this term the body of Thomas Manley, of Wyllenhale, gentilman, to answer the complaint of John Sutton, lord of Dudley, knight, that he, together with William Necheles, of Necheles, husbondman, and

John Fletcher, of Wolvernhampton, bowere, had broken into his park at Sheggeley (Sedgeley) and taken his game. Thomas did not appear, and the Sheriff was ordered to distrain the said Humfrey and produce him on the Quindene of Easter.

The proceedings state that Thomas had been exacted at the County Court at Stafford on the Thursday before the Feast of St. Margaret, and had appeared, and had been committed to prison in the custody of Humfrey Lowe. *m.* 317.

Staff. The Sheriff returned that Thomas Burgulon, of Kyngesbromley, gentilman, and Agnes, his wife, and Robert Burgulon, of Kyngesbromley, gentilman, had been exacted at five County Courts and had not appeared, but he had been unable to execute the outlawry through the default of Thomas Lokwode, Thomas Stafford, and John Burnet, the King's coroners, who had been absent from the Courts. The Sheriff was therefore ordered to put them again into *exigend*, with orders to appear on the Quindene of St. Michael. *m.* 319.

The proceedings state that the defendants had been sued by Robert Molyneux, armiger, for breaking into his house at Pery and taking goods and chattels to the value of £10.

Staff. William Coweley sued Richard Selman, of Moreton, gentilman, William Selman, of Moreton, yoman, John Selman and Henry Selman, of Moreton, yomen, for depasturing cattle by force on his corn and grass at Orslowe. The defendants did not appear, and the Sheriff was ordered to arrest and produce them on the Quindene of Easter. *m.* 376.

Staff. Thomas Wolsley sued Thomas Mytton, of Little Wyrley, husbondman, to give up to him a horse which he unjustly detained, and which was worth 40*s*. Thomas Mytton did not appear, and the Sheriff was ordered to arrest and produce him on the above date. *m.* 377.

Staff. Elizabeth Blaket, the executrix of the will of John Wilcotes, knight, and Thomas Blount, knight, and Elizabeth his wife, the co-executrix of the said Elizabeth Blaket, were summoned by Robert Harecourt, knight, for causing waste and destruction in his lands, houses, and fishponds which they held in custody after the death of the said John, of the inheritance of the said Robert in Elnalle; and Robert stated that Thomas Harecourt, his father, and whose heir he was, was formerly seised of the manor of Staunton Harecourt, co. Oxon, and of the manor of Elnalle in co. Stafford, and of other manors, lands, and tenements in divers counties, and had held the manor of Staunton Harecourt of the late King, the King's father, *in capite*, by military service, and had died so seised, leaving his son Robert under age, and the King had taken the manor of Stanton-Harecourt and Elnall into his hands by reason of the minority of the said Robert; and the King afterwards, by his Letters Patent, dated from his army before Meleyne on the 24th September, 8 H. V, had granted to the said John Wilcotes the custody of the manor of Elnall, together with other lands by the name of all the lands, rents, and possessions lately belonging to the said Thomas Harecourt, to be held till the full age of the said Robert, and rendering nothing to the King, but for which he was to maintain all the houses and fences appertaining to the said lands. And the said John had died seised of the said custody whilst Robert was still a minor, and had made a will constituting the said Elizabeth and Elizabeth his executors; and after his death Thomas Blount had held the custody of Elnall, and had caused waste by digging in two acres of land and selling 1,000 cartloads of turf each worth 8*d*., and by permitting a hall and eight chambers, each worth £40, and 20 other halls, each worth 40*s*., and 20 cowhouses, each worth 40*s*., to remain unroofed, so that the main timbers had become rotten, and by taking fish from the fishponds, viz. 200 pike, worth each 20*d.*; 200 tench, each worth 4*d.*; and 500 eels, each worth 4*d.*, and for which he claimed 300 marks as damages. The defendants appeared and asked for an adjournment till the Quindene of Easter, which was granted. A postscript shews other adjournments up to Easter, 22 H. VI. *m.* 471.

Staff. John Gresley, knight, sued Thomas Eweres, of Homerwich, yoman, for breaking into his close at Homerwiche and depasturing cattle on his corn. Thomas did not appear, and the Sheriff was ordered to arrest and produce him on the Quindene of Easter day. *m.* 477.

Staff. Robert Molyneux and Elizabeth, his wife, for themselves, as well as in the name of the King, sued Thomas Burgulon, late of Kyngesbromley, gentilman, for fabricating and publishing false documents to disturb them in the possession of their lands in Pury Hampsted, Little Barre, Honesworth, and Birmyngham. Thomas did not appear, and the Sheriff was ordered to arrest and produce him on the above date. *m.* 477, *dorso.*

Staff. The abbot of Burton upon Trent sued Thomas Hampton, of Bromley Abbots, gentilman, John Pulesdon, of Bromley Abbots, yoman, Thomas Orgrave, yoman, John Mastury, yoman, John Norman, yoman, and four others, all of Bromley Abbots, for breaking into his closes at Bromley Abbots and depasturing cattle on his grass. None of the defendants appeared, and the Sheriff was ordered to distrain Thomas Hampton, and to arrest the others and to produce them on the above date. *m.* 479.

CORAM REGE. MICH., 21 H. VI.

Staff. It had been presented before William Lee and John Harpur, Justices of the Peace in 17 H. VI, at Stafford, that John Forster, of Castelbromwych in co. Warwick, yoman, and Robert Frensshman, of the same place, grome, on the Wednesday after the Feast of St. Margaret, 16 H. VI, had feloniously killed at Hyntes in co. Stafford Thomas Ecton, gentylman, and that John Dodde, of Castelbromwych, yoman, and others were present aiding and abetting the felony, and the King for certain causes had commanded the said Indictment to be returned into this Court. And John Dodde now surrendered; and as John Forster and Robert Frensshman had been outlawed,[1] he was put on his trial, but was admitted to bail until the Saturday the Feast of St. Margaret, when the Justices holding assizes were to be at Wolverhampton. A postscript states that on that day John Dodde surrendered, and a jury found that he was not guilty. *m.* 9 *Rex*, *dorso.*

CORAM REGE. HILLARY, 21 H. VI.

Staff. It had been presented before William Lee and John Harpur, Justices of the Peace in 17 H. VI, that John Forster, of Castelbromwych, co. Warwick, yoman, and Robert Frensshman, of the same place, grome, had feloniously killed Thomas Ecton, gentilman, etc. (as before). And that William Trussell, of Castelbromwyche, yoman, Thomas Philippes, of the same place, yoman, and John Radclyff, of Kyngesnorton, co. Worcester, yoman, and others, had aided and abetted the felony. John Forster and Robert Frensshman had been outlawed, and William Trussell, Thomas Phelippes, and John Radclyffe now surrendered, and being put on their trial pleaded not guilty, and were admitted to bail. *m.* 5 *Rex.*

[1] Accessories could not be put on their trial unless the principals had been outlawed or convicted.

Derb. The King's Chancellor returned into Court an Inquisition which had been taken before William Neville, late King's Eschaetor in co. Derby, by which it appeared that Giles Swynarton, deceased, held on the day he died, in demesne as of fee tail, the sixteenth part of the manor of Repyngdon by the gift of a certain Richard Lone and John Bromley, to be held by him and the heirs of his body, the license of the King having been first obtained, and which sixteenth part was held of the King *in capite* by the service of the sixteenth part of a knight's fee ; and Ralph Basset had petitioned the King and denied the accuracy of the Inquisition, stating that the said Giles having been seised of the said sixteenth part under the name of Giles Swynerton, had granted the same under the title of 66*s.* and 8*d.* of rent in Repyndon, Melton, and Tykenhale, co. Derby, which had formerly belonged to John Swynerton armiger, and all the lands and tenements he held in the same vills which had formerly belonged to the said John Swynerton, to Thomas Assheton, of Swytheland, the younger, now deceased, and to the said Ralph under the name of Ralph Basset, of Blore, lord of Blore, to be held by them and their heirs and assigns ; and Thomas had afterwards died, so that the said Ralph had become sole seised "*per jus accrescendi*" of the said sixteenth part until he had been removed under color of the said Inquisition, and by virtue of certain Letters Patent granted to Richard Vernon, knight, and dated 16th November, 19 H. VI, etc., and the King wishing to do what was just, etc. A postscript shews that a jury, having been empannelled to try the facts, returned a verdict in favour of Ralph Basset, and the Letters Patent were annulled and seisin of the tenements granted to him. *m.* 7 *Rex.*

Staff. The Sheriff was ordered to put into the *exigend* John Marchall and to outlaw him if he did not appear, to satisfy the King for his Fine for an unjust disseisin of John Harpur and Alianora, his wife, of 8 acres of land in Ruyssale. *m.* 13 *Rex.*

DE BANCO. MICH., 22 H. VI.

Staff. Ralph Eggerton sued John White, of Hixton, husbondman, for breaking into his close and houses at Hixton and so threatening his tenants that for fear of their lives they had given up their tenancies. John did not appear, and the Sheriff was ordered to arrest and produce him at a month from Michaelmas. *m.* 112, *dorso.*

Staff. William Vernon, armiger, sued John Leche, of Lychefeld, leche, Thomas Bromley, of Lycheteld, coletter, William, son of John Faukoner, of Stretay, scolar, and three others, for entering his free warren at Walle and taking hares and rabbits, pheasants and partridges. None of the defendants appeared, and the Sheriff was ordered to arrest and produce them on the Octaves of St. Hillary. *m.* 277, *dorso.*

Staff. John Bykford sued Thomas Danyell, of Brewode, draper, for breaking into his close at Brewode and depasturing cattle on his corn and grass. Thomas did not appear, and the Sheriff was ordered as in the last suit. *m.* 278

Staff. Thomas Bokenale sued Henry Merb, of Shelton, yoman, William Pesale, of Penkylle, yoman, and Peter Hamet, late of Shelton, husbondman, for beating wounding, and illtreating his men and servants at Stoke-upon-Trent. T defendents did not appear, and the Sheriff was ordered to arrest and produ them on the Quindene of St. Hillary. *m.* 355.

Staff. Robert Harecourt, knight, sued William Gerveys, of Chatkylle, yoman, for taking by force his horse worth 40*s.* from Podmore. William did not appear, and the Sheriff was ordered to arrest and produce him on the Octaves of St. Hillary. *m.* 356, *dorso.*

Staff. Thomas Asteley sued William Baret, of Stokton, co. Salop, husbondman, for taking by force a greyhound belonging to him from Burnhill. William did not appear, and the Sheriff returned that he was hiding and wandering about in co. Salop. The Sheriff of that county was therefore ordered to arrest and produce him on the above date. *m.* 356, *dorso.*

Staff. John Lone sued John Penynton, of Mitton, husbondman, John Croftys of Stretton, husbondman, for breaking into his close at Hyde and taking by force 2 mares belonging to him worth £4. The defendants did not appear, and the Sheriff was ordered to arrest and produce them on the Octaves of St. Hillary. *m.* 482, *dorso.*

Staff. Sampson Meverell, late of Throweley, knight, John Beresford, of Beresford, the younger, gentilman, William Pursgloves, vicar of Tyddeswell, co. Derby, John Cantrell, of Alstonfeld, husbondman, John Bagnold, of Oncote, husbondman, and Thomas Wryght, of Wetton, husbondman, were attached at the suit of Ralph Basset, armiger, for treading down and consuming his hay at Throweley in stacks with their cattle; and Ralph stated that on the Feast of the Nativity of the Holy Mary, in 21 H. VI, they had come to Throweley with swords, and bows and arrows, and had consumed and trodden down with their cattle 60 cartloads of hay. The defendants appeared, and asked for an adjournment till the Octaves of St. Hillary, which was granted. *m.* 559.

Derb. Nicholas fitz Herberd, of Norbury, armiger, John Petur, of Norbury, yoman, and twelve others, described as of Norbury and Rossinton, were sued by Ralph Basset, armiger, for breaking into his close at Snelston on the Monday after the Feast of Easter, 21 H. VI, and cutting down 100 oak trees and carrying them away, with 200 cartloads of underwood. The defendants appeared, and asked for an adjournment till the Octaves of St. Hillary, which was granted. *m.* 624, *dorso.*

DE BANCO. HILLARY, 22 H. VI.

Staff. In the suit of John Sutton, lord of Dudley, against Thomas Manley, of Willenhale, for taking his deer in Sedgeley Park, Thomas now appeared, and John Sutton stated, by his attorney, that Thomas had entered the Olde parke at Seggeley on the Feast of St. Vincent, 18 H. VI, and had chased and taken from it 6 bucks and 12 does, and 8 "*humulos*," and for which he claimed 100 marks as damages. Thomas denied the injury and trespass, and appealed to a jury, which was to be summoned for the Quindene of Easter, and he was admitted to bail on the security of Robert Grey, of London, gentilman, Richard Downe, of London, gentilman, William Newport, of Lichefeld, gentilman, and John Dawinport, of Bromhale in co. Chester, gentilman. A postscript shews that the suit was moved by writ of *nisi prius* to be heard at Wolvernhampton, when a jury found that Thomas was not guilty. *m.* 101.

Derb. Thomas Bullocke, late of Erbersfeld, co. Berks, armiger, John Hyde, late of Southdenchesworth, co. Berks, armiger, and ten others, jurors in a suit between William Trussell, knight, plaintiff, and Richard Vernon, tenant of the manors of Shotesbrok and Eton Hastynges, were sued by Richard Vernon for accepting various sums of money and other gifts from William Trussell. The defendants appeared and denied the allegation, and appealed to a jury, which was to be summoned for the Quindene of Easter day. *m.* 111.

Staff. John Kyngesley, armiger, sued Richard Mosley, of Newcastle under Lyme, yoman, and six others of the same town, for lying in wait in order to kill him, and for so threatening his servants and tenants that for fear of their lives they were unable to perform their duties. The defendants did not appear, and the Sheriff was ordered to arrest and produce them on the Quindene of Easter day. *m.* 181, *dorso.*

Staff. Roger Milles, of Haywode, sued Thomas Lokon, of Huntteley, husbondman, and Christine, late wife of Richard Lokon, of Huntteley, wydowe, for depasturing cattle on his corn and grass at Huntteley. The defendants did not appear, and the Sheriff was ordered to arrest and produce them on the above date. *m.* 249.

Staff. Thomas Wulsseley, son of Ralph Wolseley, executor of the will of Ralph de Wolseley, *alias* Ralph Wolseley, sued Nicholas Ruggeley, of Dunton, co. Warwick, gentilman, executor of the will of Edith Ruggeley, executrix of the will of Nicholas Ruggeley, late of Haukesert, for a debt of £13 6*s.* 8*d.* Nicholas did not appear, and the Sheriff was ordered to arrest and produce him on the above date. *m.* 281, *dorso.*

Staff. Reginald Griffith sued Thomas Coton, of Coton, in the parish of Hambury, gentilman, in a plea that he should deliver a reasonable account for the time he was his bailiff in Draycote. Thomas did not appear, and the Sheriff was ordered as in the last suit. *m.* 282.

Staff. Richard Derewent and Edmund Derewent sued Roger Barchurdon, of Boterton, husbondman, and Thomas Olerka (*sic*), of Boterton, husbondman, for breaking into their close at Oncote and depasturing cattle on their corn and grass. The defendants did not appear, and the Sheriff was ordered as in the last suit. *m.* 282.

Staff. William Repyngton sued Alan Moton, of Stapilton, co. Leicester, armiger, for counterfeiting his seal and attaching it to a bond for £100, by reason of which he had been greatly vexed by divers writs, and for which he claimed £40 as damages. Alan did not appear, and the Sheriff was ordered as in the last suit. *m.* 282, *dorso.*

Oxon. A suit respecting an alleged illegal distress in Chestreton shews that William de la Pole, Earl of Suffolk, was married to Alice, the daughter and heir of Thomas Chawcers, armiger.[1] *m.* 335.

Middlesex. Richard Vernon, of Harlaston in co. Stafford, knight, was summoned by William Trussell, knight, in a plea that he should pay him 120 marks which he unjustly detained; and William stated (*here follows an account of the plea in 20 H. VI respecting the manors of Shotesbroke and Eton Hastynges, which William had recovered against Richard, with* 120 *marks damages*), and Richard had obtained a writ of error on the 4th June, 21 H. VI, by which the suit had been transmitted to be heard again Coram Rege, and which suit was now in progress, and in consequence of which Richard had refused to pay the above damages. Richard Vernon appeared by attorney and asked for an adjournment to the Quindene of Easter, which was granted. A postscript shews a further adjournment to the Octaves of Holy Trinity. *m.* 403.

Staff. Thomas Danyell sued John Bykford of Brewode, husbondman, for breaking into his close at Brewode and depasturing cattle by force on his corn and grass, and for so threatening him tha for fear of his life he was unable to leave the enclosure of his dwelling house. John did not appear, and the Sheriff was ordered to arrest and produce him at a month from Easter. *m.* 414.

[1] See notes to Suffolk, p. 306, Vol. VII of the new Peerage, respecting the identity of this Thomas Chaucer.

CORAM REGE. Hillary, 24 H. VI.

Staff. The King sent a close writ to the Sheriff stating that if John Buffrey entered into security to prosecute his claim, he was to summon a jury of twenty-four of the vicinage of Netherpenne for Easter term to return a verdict if the said John had unjustly disseised John Duddeley of his freehold in Netherpenne, and respecting which the said John Buffrey had complained that the jury in a suit of novel disseisin which had been taken before the King's Justices, Sir William Yelverton and Sir Richard Byngham, at Stafford, had delivered a false judgment. *m.* 21.

Staff. Roger Aston, knight, sued Richard Parker, of Wythynton, in a plea that whereas the said Richard had covenanted to rebuild a house for him at Wythyngton, he now refused to complete his bargain. Richard did not appear, and the Sheriff was ordered to arrest and produce him on the Quindene of Easter day. *m.* 24, *dorso.*

CORAM REGE. Trinity, 24 H. VI.

The Venerable Father in Christ, John, the Archbishop of Canterbury, the King's Chancellor, delivered into Court the following record of a suit in Chancery :—

Staff. It appeared by an inquisition taken at Burton upon Trent on the Tuesday before the Feast of the Annunciation, 24 H. VI (March, 1446), before Humfrey Blount, the King's Eschaetor, that Richard Delves, armiger, deceased, was seised amongst other lands, when he died, of the manors of Knotton, Apedale, Hilderstone, and 8 messuages and 4 carucates of land in Audeley, Chesterton, Rugges, and Delves, in demesne as of fee, and that the manors of Knotton and Apedale were held of the King *in capite* as of his honor of Tutbury, viz. the manor of Knotton by fealty, and the service of rendering to the King and to his heirs the third part of the value of the manor annually, and the manor of Apedale by services unknown ; and that John Delves was brother and nearest heir of the said Richard, who had died leaving no issue, upon which one Ralph Egerton had appeared in Court and stated that 2 messuages of the said 8 messuages and half a carucate of land of the four carucates said to be in Audeley, Chesterton, Rugges, and Delves, were in Audeley, and that another messuage and another half carucate of land were in Chesterton, and that the said messuage and half carucate of land in Chesterton had been from time out of memory parcel of the manor of Apedale, and that 5 messuages and 3 carucates of land, the residue of the 8 messuages and 4 carucates, were in Delves and formed the manor of Delves, and were known by that name, and none of the land was in Rugges ; and as regarded the manors of Knotton, Apedale, and Hilderstone, and the said messuages and carucates of land excepting the 2 messuages and half carucate of land in Audeley, one Thomas Hunt, the elder, of Newcastle under Lyme, long before the death of the said Richard Delves, was seised of the entire manors of Knotton, Apedale, Hilderstone, and Delves, and whilst so seised, by his deed, which Ralph produced in Court, and which was dated from Apedale on the Tuesday before the Feast of St. George the Martyr, 7 H. VI, had granted them to the said Ralph and to a certain John Delves and Margaret, his wife, Edmund Basset, and William Lee, with other lands under the name of his manors of Apedale, Knotton, Hilderstone, Whitmore, Dymmysdale, Honford, Little Clayton, and Delves, to be held by them and the heirs of the body of John Delves ; and John Delves and Edmund afterwards died and the said William and Margaret survived them and were seised of the manors by the *jus accrescendi*; and Margaret afterwards took for a husband one John Gresley, knight; and John Gresley and Margaret, by their deed which Ralph produced, and which was dated the 9th November, 20 H. VI, remitted and quit-claimed to the said Ralph and to William all their right and claim which they had in the manors of Knotton, Apedale, Hilderstone, and Delves, amongst other lands, under the names of the manors of Clutton and Apedale, and in all other lands and tenements which had lately belonged to John Delves, the husband of Margaret, in co. Stafford; by virtue of which release the said Ralph and William Lee became seised; and William Lee afterwards died, and Ralph survived and was seised of the said manors until, under colour of the above inquisition, he had been expelled, and he prayed that the King's hand might be removed from the said manors of Knotton, Apedale, and Hilderstone, and from the 5 messuages and 3 carucates of land in Delves, and from the said messuage and half carucate of land in Chesterton.

Upon which John Vampage, the King's Attorney, stated that the said Richard was seised of all the above tenements in demesne as of fee when he died, and asked for a jury of twenty-four knights and others.

The Sheriff of co. Stafford was therefore ordered to summon a jury for this term, and Ralph Egerton appeared by his attorney, and the Sheriff returned the names of the jury, none of whom appeared, and he was ordered to distrain and produce them on the Quindene of St. Michael. A postscript shews that the process was continued for several terms, and the suit was eventually moved by writ of *nisi prius* to be heard at Lychefeld on the Wednesday after the Feast of St. Peter in Cathedrâ 26 H. VI, when a jury found in favour of Ralph. It was therefore considered that the King's hand should be removed, and that Ralph should be restored to the possession of the tenements together with all profits and issues from the date of his removal. *m.* 23 *Rex.*

The Venerable Father in Christ, J, the Archbishop of Canterbury, and Chancellor, delivered with his own hands the record of a suit in Chancery, as follows:—

Staff. It appeared by a certain inquisition taken at Burton upon Trent on the Tuesday before the Feast of the Annunciation, 24 H. VI, before Humfrey Blount, the King's Eschaetor, that Richard Delves, armiger, deceased, was seised on the day he died of the manor of Crakemersshe, and that John Delves, his brother, was his nearest heir, and that the said manor was held of the King as of his honor of Tutbury, and upon which the said John Delves and Elena, his wife, had appeared by their attornies, and stated that long before the death of the said Richard a certain John Bulkeley and William Wall, chaplain, had been seised of it amongst other tenements in demesne as of fee, and by their deed, which the said John and Elena produced in Court, and which was dated from Crakemersshe on the Feast of the Invention of the Holy Cross, 19 H. VI, had enfeoffed in it the said John Delves and Elena under the names of John Delves, son of John Delves, and Elena, his wife, daughter of Ralph Eggerton, to be held by them and the heirs of their bodies, and by virtue of which deed the said John and Elena had been in possession until removed under colour of the above inquisition, and they prayed that the King's hand might be removed.

John Vampage, the King's Attorney, appeared on the part of the Crown, and claimed that the said Richard Delves had died seised of the manor in demesne as of fee, and asked for a jury as in the last case. The same process was followed as in the previous suit, and a jury at Lichfield found in favour of John Delves and Elena, who recovered seisin of the manor with all profits and issues from the date of their expulsion. *m.* 24 *Rex.*

DE BANCO. Trinity, 24 H. VI.

Northampton. Elizabeth Chetewyne sued William Zouch, knight, lord of Seymour Toteneys and Haryngworth, for a sum of 10 marks, the arrears of an annual rent of 4 marks which he owed to her; the suit was adjourned to Michaelmas term, and a postscript shows further adjournments up to Michaelmas term, 25 H. VI. *m.* 123.

Staff. Reginald Gryffyth sued Thomas Coton of Hambury, gentilman, to render to him a reasonable account for the time he was his bailiff in Draycote. Thomas asked for an adjournment which was granted to the Quindene of St. Michael. *m.* 218.

Derb. John, son of John Savage, knight, sued Richard Peshale, son and heir of Matilda, late wife of John Savage, knight, for 15 messuages, 3 tofts, 130 acres of land, 7 acres of meadow, 8 acres of pasture, 200 acres of wood, and a moiety of a fourth part of 200 acres of heath in Repyndon, Moleton, Tykenhale, Staynstone and Twyford, as his right and inheritance, and he stated one John Daniell, knight, his ancestor was seised of the tenements in demesne as of fee, temp. E. 2, and from the said John the right descended to one Margaret as daughter and heir, and from Margaret to one John Savage, knight, as son and heir, and from John Savage to the plaintiff as son and heir.

Richard denied the seisin of John Daniell and called to warranty Richard Beke, who was to be summoned for the morrow of All Souls. *m.* 405.

Derb. By another writ the same John Savage sued Richard Peshale, for moiety of the manor of Dore near Norton, and gave the same plea, and Richard called Richard Beke to warranty. *m.* 405.

Staff. By a third writ John Savage sued Richard Peshale for the advowson of the church of Chakley (Chekley), and stated that John Danyell, knight, had been seised of the advowson temp. E. 2, and had presented one John Beke his Clerk, who had been admitted and instituted on his presentation and from John Danyell he gave the same descent as before. Richard denied the seisin of John Danyell and called Richard Beke to warranty. *m.* 405, *dorso.*

Staff. By a fourth writ John Savage sued Richard Peshale for the manor of Russheton Spencer, and 20 acres of land, and 1,000 acres of moor in Corneford, and gave the same descent as before from John Danyell, knight, viz.:

John Danyell, Kt.
|
Margaret.
|
John Savage, Kt.
|
John Savage, the plaintiff.

Richard denied the seisin of John Danyell and called Robert Haydok to warranty, who was to be summoned for the morrow of All Souls. *m.* 405, *dorso.*

DE BANCO. HILLARY, 25 H. VI.

Staff. William Hexstall and John Maryes sued John Massy of Crosley, Co. Chester, gentilman, William Massy of Crosley, gentilman, John Massy of Walton-near-Stone, gentilman, Thomas Bromswerd of Crosley, husbondman, Peter Francheman and Hamon Francheman of Crosley, labourers, for so threatening their tenants at Bydulf, that for fear of their lives or mutilation of their limbs they had given up their tenancies so that they had lost their rents and services for a length of time. The defendants did not appear, and the Sheriff was ordered to arrest and produce them on the Morrow of the Purification. *m.* 19, *dorso.*

Staff. Henry Overton sued the same defendants as in the last suit for breaking into his close at Bydulf and taking 13 steers, 2 colts and 2 mares worth £10. None of the defendants appeared and the Sheriff was ordered as in the last suit. *m.* 79.

Staff. John Lane sued William Wyghtwyke of Wyghtwyke, husbondman, for depasturing cattle by force on his grass at Wyghtwyke. William did not appear, and the Sheriff was ordered to arrest and produce him on the Quindene of Easter Day. *m.* 161, *dorso.*

Staff. Thomas Boteler, the elder, sued Richard Halsey of la Walle, husbondman ; Hugh Colyns of Chorley, husbondman ; Nicholas Campedone of Longedon, husbondman ; John Bromley of Chorley, husbondman ; and Roger Sprot of Asshemerbroke, husbondman, for breaking into his close at Longedon, and depasturing cattle on his corn and grass. The defendants did not appear and the Sheriff was ordered as in the last suit. *m.* 179.

Staff. The suit of Nicholas fitz William and Margery his wife alias Margery Makerell, complainants ; *versus* Thomas Okore (Okeover) late of Notyngham, Squyr, in a plea of debt was respited till the Quindene of Easter Day through defect of a jury. *m.* 179.

Staff. William Shirley and Joan his wife, formerly wife of John Botte of Asshebourne, sued John Botte of Denstone, for a third of 4 messuages, and 4 virgates of land in Denstone which they claimed as dower of Joan. John did not appear and the dower claimed had been taken into the King's hands. A day was given to the parties to hear judgement at three weeks from Easter. *m.* 235, *dorso.*

Staff. Robert Harecourt, knight, sued John Boteler of Chebsey, husbondman ; Thomas Blest, husbondman, and Richard Aleyn, husbondman, both of Chebsey ; for taking fish from his several fishery at Little Brycheford, to the value of £10. The defendants did not appear, and the Sheriff was ordered to arrest and produce them at the above date. *m.* 263.

DE BANCO. MICH., 25 H. VI.

Staff. Roger Holbeche sued Joan, formerly wife of Henry Beaumont, knight, of Wednesbury, wydowe, executrix of the will of Henry Beaumont, knight, for a debt of £16 10*s.* 6½*d.* Joan did not appear, and the Sheriff was ordered to attach her for the morrow of All Souls. *m.* 90, *dorso.*

Staff. Elizabeth, late wife of Richard Delves, sued John Delves for a third of the manors of Bukenale and Fenton, and of 16 messuages, 6 cottages, 40 acres of land, an acre of meadow, an acre of wood, and 2*s.* 10*d.* of rent in Bukenale and Fenton, Newcastle-under-Lyme, Betteley, and Chesterton, which she claimed as dower.

John stated that she was not entitled to dower as she had never been lawfully married to the said Richard, which he was prepared to prove. Elizabeth replied that she had been lawfully married to Richard at the Parish Church of St. Mary atte Hill of Chester. As the question belonged to the ecclesiastical court, a writ was sent to the Bishop of Coventry and Lichfield, the Diocesan, to convoke the parties before him and return his Inquisition by his Letters Patent on the Octaves of St. Hillary.

A postscript shows that the process was continued up to Michaelmas term, 26 H. VI, when Elizabeth failed to appear and the suit was dismissed. Up to that date the Bishop had made no return to the writ. *m.* 106, *dorso.*

Staff. In the plea in which Reginald Gryffyth sued Thomas Coton of Coton near Hambury, gentilman, to render an account for the time he was the Bailiff of Reginald at Draycote, viz., for a year in 8 H. VI. Thomas now appeared and denied he had ever acted as the Bailiff of Reginald and appealed to a jury, which was to be summoned for the Octaves of St. Hillary. A postscript shows no jury had been empanelled up to Michaelmas 26 H. VI. *m.* 183.

Derb. On the Roll of the term of Holy Trinity 24 H. 6, Roll 405, it was contained as follows, *Derb.* John son of John Savage, knight, had appeared before the Court of John the Cardinal Archbishop of York, John the Archbishop of Canterbury, Robert the Bishop of London, William the Bishop of Lincoln, and six other Bishops named, William the Marquis of Suffolk, Henry Earl of Northumberland, John Viscount Beaumont, Walter Lord Hungerford, Ralph Lord Cromwelle, Ralph Lord Seudeley, John Somersett Clerk, and six other Clerks named, Edmund Hungerford, knight, John Beauchamp, knight, James Fenys, knight, Edward Hulle, knight, John Sauntlo, armiger; John Hampton, armiger; John Noreys, armiger; William Tresham, armiger; John Vampage, armiger; and Richard Alred, armiger[1]; and sued Richard Peshale son and heir of Matilda late wife of John Savage, knight, for a moiety of the manor of Dore near Norton as his right by the King's open writ of right. And the cause on the petition of the said John son of John Savage, asserting he had not had full right in the Court of Robert Strettey, then Sheriff of co. Derby, had been moved to this Court by the King's writ to be heard on the Octaves of Holy Trinity, on which day John son of John sued Richard Peshale for the said moiety and stated that his ancestor John Danyell, knight, had been seised of it in demesne as of fee, in the reign of King Edward II, and from the said John the right descended to one Margaret as daughter and heir, and from Margaret to one John Savage, knight, as son and heir and from the said John son of Margaret, to this John son of John Savage, knight, the plaintiff as son and heir.

And the said Richard defended his right and had called to warranty Richard Beke and Richard now appeared, and John son of John Savage then sued the said Richard Beke and repeated his plea as above.

And the said Richard Beke the tenant by the warranty denied the seisin of John Danyell and offered to defend his right by the body of his freeman Nicholas son of John Barker who was present in Court and if any ill should befall him *quod absit* he was prepared to defend it by another etc.

[1] This Court appears to have consisted for the most part of the king's household.

And John son of John stated that Richard Beke unjustly disputed his right and he repeated his plea and stated he was ready to prove it by his body or in any other way the Court should think fit, and if any ill should befall him then by the body of Richard son of Robert Proudlove, upon which the said Nicholas son of John Barker and Richard son of Robert Proudlove were asked if they were prepared to proceed to a duel, as waged above and they said they were—and the said Nicholas son of John waged himself to defend (*dat vadium defendendo*) and the said Richard son of Robert waged himself to prove *dat vadium disrationando* and the "vadimonium" being given according to custom the said John son of John Savage and Richard Beke were asked if they knew of any reason why the duel should not take place and they answered they did not. It was therefore considered that a duel should be fought.

And Richard son of Robert Proudlove found pledges for the duel, viz. John Nedeham and Thomas Duncalf.

And the said Nicholas son of John Barker found as pledges "de duello,' John Savage, armiger, the elder, and Giles de Bothe, and a day was given to the parties on the Octaves of St. Martin, and they were informed that each should produce at that date their champions competently and sufficiently armed, as was necessary to proceed to the duel, *quod uterque eorum habeat hic tunc pugilem suum armaturi competenti sufficiente prout decet munitum ad proficiendum duellum predictum*, and that in the meantime their bodies should be in safe custody. On which day the said John son of John Savage, knight, appeared by his attorney with his champion competently armed and Richard Beke being solemnly called up to the fourth day put in no appearance. It was therefore considered that the said John son of John Savage, knight, should recover seisin of the moiety of the manor claimed for ever. And that Richard Peshale should be compensated for the land of Richard Beke to the same value. *m.* 409.

Derby. By a similar process John son of John Savage, knight, recovered against the same Richard Beke called to warranty by Richard Peshale 15 messuages, 3 tofts, 138 acres of land, 7 acres of meadow, 8 acres of pasture, 200 acres of wood and the moiety of a fourth part of 200 acres of heath in Repyndon, Moleton, Tykenhale, Staynston and Twyford. *m.* 410.

Staff. In the same way, and by the same process John son of John Savage, knight, recovered the advowson of the church of Chekley against the same Richard Beke, called to warranty by Richard Peshale. *m.* 413.

Staff. Margery, late wife of Robert Berdemore, sued John Berdemore for a third of 4 messuages, 300 acres of land, 40 acres of meadow, 100 acres of pasture, 100 acres of wood, and 40*s.* of rent in Wiston, Farlegh and Chedulle (Cheadle) as his dower. John appeared by attorney, and asked for a view of the tenements.

Margery pleaded that John could not claim a view, as Robert Berdemore, her husband, had died seised of the tenements in demesne as of fee. John denied this and appealed on this issue to a jury which was to be summoned for the Octaves of St. Hillary. *m.* 414, *dorso.*

Suff. (*sic*), but should be *Staff.* On the Roll of Michaelmas term, 24 H. VI, it was thus contained. John, son of John Savage, knight (*militis*) sued Richard Peshale, the son and heir of Matilda, late wife of John Savage, knight, for the manor of Russheton Spencer, and 20 acres of land, 1,000 acres of moor in Corneford, as his right and inheritance by the King's writ of "*precipe in capite*" and he stated that one John Danyelle, knight, his ancestor had been seised of the said manor tempore Edward II, and from John Danyelle he gave the same descent as in previous suits. Richard appeared by attorney and denied the seisin of John

Danyelle and called to warranty Robert Haydok, who was to be summoned for the morrow of All Souls. *m.* 411.

Norf. (*sic*). On the Roll of Trinity term, 24 H. VI, it was thus contained *Staff.* John, son of John Savage, knight, had sued in the court of Humfrey, Duke of Buckingham,[1] Richard Peshale, son and heir of Matilda, late wife of John Savage, knight, for 21 messuages, 356½ acres of land, 18½ acres of meadow, 347 acres of pasture, 2 acres of wood, 200 acres of moor, and 2*s.* 10*d.* of rent, and the moiety of the fourth part of an acre of meadow in Tene (Tean), as his right by the King's open writ of right; and the cause on the prosecution of John, son of John Savage, knight, asserting that he had not had full right (*plenum rectum*) was removed from the said court to be heard before John Griffith, knight, the Sheriff of co. Stafford, and from thence on the petition of the same John, son of John, it was moved into this court, and John stated that one John Danyelle, knight, had been seised of the said tenements and rent in demesne as of fee in the time of King Edward II, and from this point he gave the same descent as in previous suits. Richard defended his right and called to warranty Richard Beke who was to be summoned for the Morrow of All Souls. *m.* 417.

Staff. On the Roll of Trinity term, 25 H. VI, Roll 424, it was thus contained. *Staff.* John, son of John Savage, knight, had sued in the court of Hugh Erdeswyk, armiger, Richard Peshale, son and heir of Matilda, late wife of John Savage, knight, for 20 marks of rent from the manor of Draycote by the King's open writ of right (*per breve domini Regis de recto patens*), and the cause on the petition of John, son of John Savage, knight, asserting he had not had full right (*plenum rectum*) had been moved to be heard in the county before John Griffiths, knight, the Sheriff of co. Stafford, and from thence on the petition of John, son of John Savage, knight, it had been moved into this court, and John, son of John, stated that one John Danyelle, knight, his ancestor had been seised of the said rent in his demesne as of fee and right in the reign of Edward II. From the said John he gave the same descent as in previous suits.

Richard Peshale defended his right and called to warranty Richard Beke; and John, son of John Savage, knight, then sued Richard Beke, and repeated his plea.

(The process is the same as before, each party produced a champion and battle was waged (*radiatum*) between them, but at the last moment Richard Beke put in no appearance and John Savage therefore recovered seisin of the rent claimed, and Richard Peshale was to be compensated by Richard Beke.) *m.* 418.

Warw. The appeal of Henry Roos, of Clyfton Camvyle, co. Stafford, from the verdict of a jury of the vicinage of Grendon, in a suit brought against him by Robert Chetylton in a plea of trespass came before the court, and the record of the former suit was read as follows. Hillary 24 H. VI, Roll 501. *Warw.* Henry Roos, of Clyfton Camvyle, yoman, was attached at the suit of Robert Chetylton, for taking by force from Grendon, 4 oxen and 4 cows belonging to him worth 5 marks on the 12th January, 24 H. VI, and for which he claimed £10 as damages.

Henry pleaded that the action would not lie against him because one Philip Chetewynde, knight, was formerly seised of the moiety of the manor of Grendon called Chetwynd's manor in co. Warwick, in demesne as of fee, in which the alleged trespass was said to have taken place, and held the said moiety of John Stanley, armiger, as of his manor of Clyfton Camvyle in co. Stafford, viz., by homage, fealty and a scutage of 40*s.*, when the

[1] Humfrey, Earl of Stafford, had lately been created Duke of Buckingham. The suit was in his Court as superior lord of Tean.

King's scutage of 40*s.* was levied; and Philip died and the said moiety descended to one John Chetewynd who was of full age, being 40 years old and more, as his cousin and heir of Philip, viz., as brother of Richard, the father of the said Philip; and as 100*s.* for the relief of the said John Chetewynd, after the death of Philip, had not been paid to John Stanley, the said Henry acting as bailiff of the said John Stanley, had taken the oxen and cows in the name of distraint, as was lawful.

Robert admitted that the said Philip was seised of the said moiety, in demesne as of fee, and held it of John Stanley, but he stated that Philip by his deed which he produced in court and which was dated 23rd January, 17 H. VI, had granted the said moiety to John Hampton, armiger, William Purfrey, armiger, Simon Melborne, Rector of Grendon, and Robert Whitgreve, of Stafford, gentilman, under the name of his manor of Grendon in co. Warwick, together with the advowson of the church of Grendon and also all his other lands and tenements which he held in the vills of Dorden and Warton in co. Warwick, and the said John, William, Simon, and Robert being so seised of the tenements had granted them to the said Philip and to Joan, then his wife, and to the heirs male of their bodies and failing such, to remain to the right heirs of Philip; and Philip died without leaving any male issue, and Joan then held the moiety and the advowson and was sole seised in demesne as of fee tail, and was still alive.

Henry denied the feoffment of the said John Hampton, William, Simon, and Robert, and stated the manor and advowson had descended to John Chetewynde, and he appealed to a jury which was to be summoned for the Quindene of Easter, on which day the Sheriff made no return and the suit was afterwards moved by writ of *nisi prius* to be heard before the Justices of Assize at Warwick, when a jury found in favour of Robert and assessed his damages at 6*s.* 8*d.*, and his costs at 13*s.* 4*d.*

And the said Record having been read, Henry stated that the jury had made a false oath when they found that the said Philip had enfeoffed the said John Hampton, William, Simon, and Robert, and they had also sworn falsely when they said that the plaintiff had sustained any damage, and this he was prepared to prove by a jury of 24. A postscript shows that after several adjournments of the suit through defect of a jury, a verdict was given in favour of the first jury, at the Assizes held at Warwick on the Monday before the Feast of St. Margaret, 26 H. VI.[1] *m.* 426.

Staff. William Cumberford sued in person John Myners, of Uttoxhater, the younger, gentilman, and Ralph de la Ward, of Uttoxhater, yoman, for beating wounding, and illtreating his servant John Clerk at Lokkesley, and so threatening him that for fear of his life or mutilation of his limbs he was afraid to leave the enclosure of his house, and by which he had lost his services for a length of time. The defendants did not appear and the Sheriff was ordered to distrain the said John and to arrest Ralph and produce them on the Quindene of St. Hillary. *m.* 575, *dorso.*

Warw. John Thurstone, Master of the College of the Chapel of Corpus Christi in the Parish Church of Pulteney, London, was summoned by Thomas Shukburgh in a plea that he should permit him to present a fit person to the church of Napton, and Thomas stated that one Adam de Napton, knight, was formerly seised of the manor of Napton to which the advowson was appurtenant and had presented one Robert Napton, clerk, in the time of Edward III, and Adam had afterwards granted the manor to Adam, son of Adam, son of the said Adam de Napton, knight,

[1] Sir Philip de Chetwynd died in 1444. The deeds mentioned in the above suit are printed in the "Chetwynd Chartulary," pp. 314 and 316 of Vol. XII "Staffordshire Collections."

and to the heirs of his body. And the said Adam, son of Adam, son of Adam, had issue, Joan and Thomasine, and they made partition; and Joan had issue one William, who had issue Thomas Shukburgh, the plaintiff. The defendant stated that Richard, late Earl of Arundelle and Surrey, was seised of the advowson of the church of Napton, and had presented to it one Richard Tyso, in the reign of King Richard II, and afterwards King Richard, by his Letters Patent dated 8th February, 8 Ric. II, had granted license to the said Earl to grant the advowson to Richard the master of the College of St. Laurence, of Pulteney, London, in exchange for a house (*hospitium*) in the City of London, which had formerly belonged to John de Pulteney called Pulteneysyne, and which was held of the King by a burgage tenure, and the Master also produced the bull of Urban IV the Pope, sanctioning the annexation of the Parish Church of Napton to the said College.

Thomas replied that the advowson was appurtenant to the manor of Napton and appealed to a jury.

A postscript shows that a jury at Warwick in 26 H. VI, found in favour of the Master of the College, and the suit was dismissed. *m.* 626.

Staff. In the suit of John, son of John Savage, knight, *versus* Richard Peshale for the manor of Rushton Spencer, and 1,000 acres of moorland in Corneford, and in which Richard Peshale had called Richard Beke to warranty, a duel was waged as in the other suits. Richard Beke not appearing, after the duel had been waged, John, son of John Savage, recovered the manor and moor, and Richard Peshale was to be compensated by Richard Beke. *m.* 628.

Staff. The same process was followed in the suit of the same John, son of John Savage, knight, *versus* Richard Peshale for 22 messuages, 356½ acres of land, 18½ acres of meadow, 347 acres of pasture, 2 acres of wood, 200 acres of moor, and 2*s.* 10*d.* of rent and the moiety of the fourth part of an acre of meadow in Tene. Richard Beke did not appear after the duel had been waged, and the tenements and rent were adjudged to John, son of John Savage, knight, for ever.[1] *m.* 636.

DE BANCO. EASTER, 25 H. VI.

Staff. Roger Bromley and Agnes, his wife, sued William Chaldon, of Chaldon, husbondman, for fabricating false documents and muniments respecting lands and tenements belonging to them in Whitmore, with a view of disturbing their title and possession in the said lands. William did not appear, and the Sheriff was ordered to arrest and produce him on the Octaves of St. John the Baptist. *m.* 40.

Staff. John Wodnot sued Robert Cuny (Coyney) of Weston Cuny near le Meere, yoman, for taking by force two mares belonging to him worth 60*s.* from Weston Cuny juxta le Meere. Robert did not appear, and the Sheriff returned he held nothing within his Bailiwick. He was therefore ordered to arrest and produce him on the Octaves of Holy Trinity. *m.* 96.

Staff. John Chetewynd sued in person Thomas Lyttylton and Joan, his wife, for two parts of 13 messuages, 2 carucates and 5 virgates and a half of land, 40 acres of wood, and 40*s.* of rent in Rowele, Rugge, and Breredon, and two parts of the manors of Mutton, Ingestre, and Gretewych excepting a mill in Ingestre as his right by a writ of *formedon in discendere.* Thomas

[1] The verdict of a Great Assize in a writ of right, or the result of a duel in a writ of right could not be disturbed, there being no appeal from the action.

appeared in person, and Joan by attorney, and they asked for a view, and a day was given to the parties on the Quindene of St. Michael. A postscript states that on that day the parties appeared, and the Sheriff returned that no one had come in the part of John to shew the lands etc. which he claimed, and the suit was adjourned to the Quindene of St. Hillary, *m.* 103.

Staff. Robert Qwytgreve, of Stafford, armiger, *alias* Robert Whitgreve, armiger, sued Agnes Draycote, late wife of John Draycote, of Draycot, on *les mores*, wydowe, for a debt of 5 marks. Agnes did not appear, and the Sheriff was ordered to attach her for the Quindene of Holy Trinity. *m.* 379.

CORAM REGE. TRINITY, 25 H. VI.

Staff. Memo. that on the 28th June of this term Robert Molyneux and Elizabeth, his wife, appeared in person *coram Rege* and delivered a bill against Robert Burgulon, late of Kyngesbromley, now in the custody of the Marshal, in which they complained that the said Robert on the 10th August, 23 H. VI, had fabricated a false deed, by which one Robert Burgulon, the great grandfather of the said Robert Burgulon, had granted to one Nicholas Leveson 3 messuages, 358 acres of land, 43 acres of pasture, 78 acres of wood, and 56*s.* of rent in Piry, Little Barre, and Honnesworthe in co. Stafford, and another false deed by which James Leveson, son and heir of the said Nicholas, had released and quit-claimed to Thomas Burgulon, the father of the said Robert Burgulon, late of Kyngesbromley, all his right and claim in the said lands and tenements, with a view of destroying and disturbing the possession and title of the said Robert Molineux and Elizabeth, his wife. Robert Burgulon appeared in person and denied the injury, and appealed to a jury, which was to be summoned for the Tuesday after the Feast of St. John the Baptist. *m.* 24, *dorso.*

Staff. It had been presented before Richard Byngham and his fellow Justices at Lychefeld, in 24 H. VI, that Robert Burgulon, late of Tutbury in co. Stafford, gentilman, otherwise called Robert Burgulon, late of Kyngesbromley, yoman, with many other malefactors, had insulted Thomas Phippon, of Brokhous, on the Saturday after the Feast of the Annunciation, 24 H. VI, and had robbed him of divers fishes, viz. :—roches, perches, and tenches to the value of 10*s.* And it had also been presented before John Harper and his fellow Justices of the Peace of co. Stafford, that the said Robert, with many other robbers and malefactors unknown, had laid in wait at Theffesoke, near Hillewode in co. Stafford, and had beaten and wounded John Gregory, chapman, so that his life was despaired of, and had robbed him of £3 in money, and that Robert Johnson, late of Kyngesbromley, who had been hanged at Abbots Bromley, before his death had confessed in presence of William Burton, one of the coroners of the county, that he had committed the said felony in company with the said Robert and John Burgulon, and that the said Robert, on the Friday after the Feast of St. James, 24 H. VI, had laid in wait at Theffesoke, near Bassets Crosse in co. Stafford, with other robbers and malefactors unknown, arrayed in manner of war, had robbed John Gregory, chapman, of £3 2*s.* in money; and which indictments the King, for certain reasons, had commanded to be returned into this Court, and Robert Burgulon now surrendered and pleaded he was not guilty, and he was admitted to bail. A postscript shews that the case was ultimately transferred to be heard at Lichfield on the Wednesday after the Feast of St. Peter *in Cathedrâ*. *m.* 7 *Rex.*

DE BANCO. MICH., 26 H. VI.

Staff. Humfrey Swynerton, armiger, sued Mayhowe Breton, of Swynerton, gentilman, for cutting down his trees and underwood at Swynerton to the value of £40. The defendant did not appear and the Sheriff states he held nothing, etc. He was therefore ordered to arrest and produce him on the Octaves of St. Hillary. *m.* 291, *dorso.*

Staff. Thomas Stikebuk sued William Birche, of Lichefeld, Bocher, for breaking into his close at Fulfen, and taking 7 cows and 11 steers worth 100*s.* William did not appear, and the Sheriff was ordered to arrest and produce him on the above date. *m.* 291, *dorso.*

Staff. Robert Kynnardesay sued Robert Lowe, of Bromshulf, clerk, for breaking into his close at Loxley and cutting down his trees to the value of £10. The defendant did not appear, and the Sheriff was ordered as in the last suit. *m.* 312.

Staff. Ralph Basset, armiger, sued John Berysford, of Berysford, gentilman, William Pursgloves, vicar of the church of Tyddeswalle, co. Derby, and John Bagenhall, of Onecote, husbondman, for depasturing cattle on his corn and grass at Grendon and Musdene. The defendants did not appear, and the Sheriff was ordered to distrain John Berysford, and to arrest the others and produce them on the Octaves of St. Hillary. *m.* 374, *dorso.*

Staff. Richard Hille sued John Egynton, of Rodbaston, yoman, for breaking into his close at Penkeryche, and cutting down his trees and carrying away goods and chattels belonging to him to the value of £20. John did not appear, and the Sheriff was ordered to arrest and produce him on the Quindene of St. Hillary. *m.* 456.

Staff. Nicholas Leveson sued William Cokes, late of Walsall, Coryour, and Nicholas Barbour, late of Walsale, barbour, for taking fish from his several fishery at Wodenesfeld to the value of 100*s.* The defendants did not appear, and the Sheriff was ordered to arrest and produce them on the Octaves of St. Hillary. *m.* 460.

Staff. John Walwene, of Denstone, husbondman, sued John Maryot, late of Bydulf, gentilman, *alias* John Bydulf, of London, gentilman, for a debt of 40*s.* The defendant did not appear, and the Sheriff was ordered to arrest and produce him on the Octaves of St. Hillary. *m.* 597.

Staff. John, the Archbishop of Canterbury, sued Ralph Basset, late of Blore, armiger, Richard Basset, of Tuttebury, gentilman, Richard Meverell, late of Blore, gentilman, William Thornbury, late of Blore, yoman, John Canterell, of Alsfeld, yoman, Roger Assheton, of Wetton, yoman, John Goples, of Stansop, yoman, Richard Tippyng, of Greetyate, yoman, and William Goold, of Grendon, yoman, for breaking into his closes and houses in Throweley and Froddeswalle. The defendants did not appear, and the Sheriff was ordered to distrain Ralph and to arrest the others, and produce them on the Quindene of St. Hillary. *m.* 597, *dorso.*

Staff. Sampson Meverell, knight, sued Thomas, the prior of Tuttebury, William Lee, of Malefeld, William Elson, of Alton, and Edmund Elson, late of Assheborne, yomen, for taking by force 12 oxen and 4 cows belonging to him worth £12 at Throweley, and for taking and impounding without reasonable cause 1,080 sheep from the same place. The defendants did not appear, and the Sheriff was ordered to distrain the prior and to arrest the others and produce them on the above date. *m.* 619.

CORAM REGE. MICH., 26 H. VI.

Staff. Memo. that on the 4th November in this term, Matthew Delahay appeared in person before the Court and brought a certain bill against John Griffith, knight, who was in the custody of the Marshal, and by which bill Matthew complained that on the 3rd May, 25 H. VI, the said John had taken *vi et armis* from Blakenale 4 horses worth £20, 8 mares called stod-mares worth 40 marks, and 2 colts worth 10 marks, and for which he claimed £100 as damages. John appeared in person and denied the injury and appealed to a jury, which was to be summoned for the Tuesday after the 18th of St. Hillary. *m.* 9.

Staff. Pardon for John Lache, late of Lichefeld in co. Stafford, synger, who had been indicted for lying in wait in order to kill Nicholas Boteler in 23 H. VI, and for beating, wounding, and ill-treating the said Nicholas so that his life was despaired of. *m.* 3 *Rex.*

Staff. A jury had been summoned at Easter to return a verdict between the King and Ralph Egerton, as to whether Richard Delves, armiger, deceased, had been seised, amongst other lands when he died, of the manors of Knotton, Apedale, and Hilderstone, of a messuage and half a carucate of land in Chesterton, and of five messuages and three carucates of land in Delves in co. Stafford, in demesne as of fee, as appeared in a certain inquisition, which had been taken before Humfrey Blount, the King's Eschaetor, and the suit had been respited till this term, unless the King's Justices came first to Wolvernehampton on the Tuesday after the Feast of St. Mary Magdalene, and afterwards at the day and place named, a jury had been empannelled, of which William Brachowe, Thomas Maweley, of Denstone, Cornelius de Wereley, Richard Thikbrome, of Thikbrome, Thomas Brette, of Newcastle under Lyme, William Wolrych, the elder, of Werestone, Ralph Macclesfeld, John Unet, of Holdyche, Nicholas Snede, of Bradwall, William Bolde, of Enstone, and John Fernehalghe, the younger, of Shaldeford, appeared and were sworn, and John Alymun, of Mulwych, and William Clerk, of Bukenale, likewise appeared, and were removed as they were found to be suspicious "*eo quod suspectuosi inveniebantur,*" and as some of the jury did not appear the suit was respited till the Morrow of All Souls. *m.* 6 *Rex.*

Staff. A jury had been summoned at Easter between the King and John Delves, brother of Richard Delves, armiger, deceased, and Elena, his wife, to return a verdict whether the said Richard was seised when he died of the manor of Crakemersshe as appeared from an inquisition taken before Walter Blount, the King's Eschaetor, and the suit had been respited till this term unless the King's Justices should first come, etc. (as in the last suit), and on the day named John Delves and Elena, his wife, appeared in person before the Justices at Wolverhampton; and the jury having been summoned, some of them, viz. Ralph Orchard, of Mulwyche, William Wolryche, of Berestone, William Boydell, of Trentham, John Urset, of Holdyche, Ralph Byschton, of Byschton, William Bolde, of Enstone, Thomas Lokwode, William Delf, of Dilrone, John Berdesmore, of Froghole, Roger Trubshawe, of Strongeshulle, and William de Bradshawe appeared and were sworn in. And Roger Hoens, of Hanyate, and John Aleyne, of Mylwyche, likewise appeared, but being suspicious, were removed from the panel, and some of the jury did not appear, the suit was therefore respited till the Morrow of All Souls. *m.* 7 *Rex.*

Staff. A pardon for Madoc ap Griffith, late of Wechenore, yoman, *alias* called Walsheman for feloniously killing Richard Edward, late of Barton under Nedewode, in 25 H. VI. *m.* 27 *Rex.*

Staff. On the Monday after the Feast of the Epiphany, 25 H. VI, it had been presented at Stafford, before John Harpur and his fellow Justices of the Peace, that Rys ap Madoc, late of Whechenore, yoman, *alias* called Walsheman *alias* called gentilman Diowe Duy, late of the same place, yoman, *alias* called Walsheman, and Madoc ap Griffith, of the same place, yoman, *alias* called Walsheman, on Sunday the Feast of the Circumcision, 25 H. VI, had feloniously killed at Barton under Nedewode Richard Edward, late of Barton, and that John Griffith, of Whechenore, knight, and others, had aided and abetted them, and that the said Rys, Diowe, and Madoc on the day named had come to the house of Richard Edward and called to him saying they wished to speak to him; and on his coming to them, pretending they had divers matters of which to speak to him, the said Rys took him amicably by the arm, placing his arm in his, and in this way, whilst pretending to speak amicably with him on the part of the said John Griffith, the said Rys suddenly stabbed Richard to the heart with a certain gestrum "*cum quodam gestro.*"

And that John Griffith on the Sunday before Christmas day had procured at Whechenore the said Rys, Diowe, and Madoc to commit the felony.

John Griffith, knight, now appeared and surrendered, and stated he was not guilty, and appealed to a jury. As the principals had not been convicted or outlawed, he was admitted to bail.

A postscript shews that he afterwards received the King's pardon dated 20th December, 26 H. VI. *m.* 22 *Rex, dorso.*

N.B.—At membranes 2 *Rex* and 25 *Rex* of this Roll will be found the trials for high treason of the servants of Humfrey, late Duke of Gloucester. The Duke had been arrested shortly after the meeting of the Parliament of this year, and had been found dead in his bed a fortnight afterwards. His servants were tried for attempting to deliver from prison Eleanor, the wife of the Duke, and for designing to place the Duke on the Throne. The Duchess had been confined for life in 1441, ostensibly for making an image of wax representing the King and melting it before a slow fire; but the real reason of her confinement seems to have been the licentiousness of her conduct.

The servants brought to trial were William Bokeland, armiger, Thomas Wylde, gentilman, Richard Middleton, armiger, Thomas Herberd, armiger, Arthur de Cursy, armiger, Richard Nedehan, yoman, and Sir Roger Chamberleyn, knight. The first named was acquitted, but the Court party were determined to obtain a verdict, and probably changed the jury, for all the others were convicted and the usual sentence was passed upon them. They were all hanged at Tyburn, then cut down, stripped naked, a knife passed over their naked bodies, and then pardoned. The King's pardon states in each case that they were to be *tracturus et suspensus, et dispoliatus de vestura sua usque ad denudationem corporis sui et tactus cum cultello.* The whole proceeding strongly reflects the barbarity of the age and the cruelty exercised against political enemies after the advent of Margaret d'Anjou to England.

CORAM REGE. HILLARY, 26 H. VI.

Warw. The suit of Thomas Littleton and Joan, his wife, against John Chetwynd, late of Merydon, came before the Court again on an appeal brought by John against the verdict of a local jury.

The process had been continued *coram Rege* till Michaelmas term, 26 H. VI, when it had been moved by a writ of *nisi prius* to be heard in the county before the Justices of Assize at Warwick, where a jury found that

John Chetwynd was guilty of the trespass and injury laid to his charge, and had assessed the damages of the plaintiffs at £20, and their costs at £20, of which Thomas and Joan had remitted £10. A postscript shews that the suit was carried on for many years, but no result is shown on the Rolls. *m.* 76, *dorso.*

Staff. Richard Tempulle, of Blakenhale, co. Stafford, gentilman, who had been indicted for abetting the murder of Richard Edward at Barton under Nedewode, surrendered at this term, and as the principals had not been convicted or outlawed, he was admitted to bail. *m.* 4 *Rex.*

Leyc. The Sheriff was ordered to put into *exigend* Christofor Draycote, late of Draycote in the Morys, co. Stafford, gentilman, *alias* of London, gentilman, and William Sandebache, late of London, soudrour, and if they did not appear, to outlaw them, and if they appeared to produce them *coram Rege*, on the Octaves of St. Hillary, to answer for certain felonies and murders of which they had been indicted. *m.* 19 *Rex.*

Derby. It had been presented before the Justices of the Peace at Beuraper, in 26 H. VI, that Sampson Meverell, late of Tiddeswelle in co. Derby, knight, and others, on the Sunday before the Feast of the Conversion of St. Paul, 26 H. VI, at Thorp, with many other persons unknown to the number of at least forty persons, had assembled in a riotous manner armed with jacks, salets, swords, and bows and arrows, with a view of killing John Southeworth, the vicar of the church of Ilum, and had insulted and threatened him that they would kill him unless he was willing to give up the society and service of Ralph Basset ; and unless he would demise to the said Sampson all the tithes of Throweley which belonged to the church of Ilum, and to which the said vicar refused to consent, because he had previously demised the same tithes to Ralph Basset ; and because the said vicar refused the demand of the said Sampson Meverell, knight, and the others at Thorp, had feloniously robbed him of 8 marks of lawful money, and through fear of death he had been forced to make a general release of the tithes to the said Sampson. And the King for certain reasons had commanded the above indictment to be heard and terminated in this Court. Sampson Meverell now surrendered and stated he was not guilty, and appealed to a jury, which was to be summoned for three weeks from Easter day, and Sampson was admitted to bail. A postscript states that a jury at Michaelmas term found that he was not guilty. *m.* 23 *Rex, dorso.*

DE BANCO. MICH., 27 H. VI.

This Roll has no heading, the first five membranes being destroyed.

Staff. Gerard Ryngeley sued William Hendelowe, of Swynford, Regis, yoman, for taking fish from his several fishery at Tybyngton (Tipton). William did not appear, and the Sheriff was ordered to arrest and produce him on the Octaves of St. Hillary. *m.* 19, *dorso.*

Staff. Robert Cuny (Coyney) sued Thomas Clayton, of Badeley, carpenter, for breaking into his park at Weston Cuny and taking 4 oxen, worth 4 marks, and for cutting down his trees and underwood. Thomas did not appear, and the Sheriff was ordered as in the last suit. *m.* 19, *dorso.*

Staff. Ralph Basset, armiger, sued John, the Abbot of Dieulacres, Sampson Meverell, late of Throweley, knight, Isabella, his wife, Nicholas Moungomery, late of Cubley, co. Derby, armiger, Thomas Meverell, late of Throweley, gentilman, William Rufford, late of Grendon, clerk, John Holys, of Moseley, gentilman, John Berford, of Berford, gentilman, John Stathom, late of Throweley, yoman, William Londesdale, late of Throweley, yoman, and four others named, for breaking into his houses and closes at Flore (*sic*), (Blore) and taking 12 oxen and 12 cows worth 20 marks, and for insulting and beating his servants so that he lost the services of one Ralph his servant, for a length of time. None of the defendants appeared, and the Sheriff was ordered to distrain the said abbot and Sampson, and to arrest the others and produce them at the above date. *m.* 64, *dorso.*

Staff. Thomas Mollesley sued William Leveson, of Wollerhampton, armiger, for a debt of 29 marks, and he sued John Holt, of Aston, near Birmyngham, co. Warwick, armiger, for a debt of 20 marks, and John Gardner, of Tunstall, yoman, for a debt of 46*s.* 8*d.* The defendants did not appear, and the Sheriff was ordered to distrain the said William and to arrest the others and produce them on the Quindene of St. Hillary. *m.* 286.

Staff. Ralph Eggerton sued John Wyllys, of Walshale, yoman, for breaking into his close at Bentley, and cutting down his trees and underwood, and depasturing cattle on his grass. John did not appear, and the Sheriff was ordered to arrest and produce him on the Octaves of St. Hillary. *m.* 286.

Staff. John Bernard, of Beanbrugge, in co. Salop, Mulleward, sued Joyce Gatacre, of Gatacre, co. Salop, wedowe, John Gatacre, of Gatacre, co. Salop, armiger, John Corbett, late of Longnore, co. Salop, gentilman, and four others named, in a plea that by a conspiracy between them, they had caused him to be indicted for feloniously receiving at Beanbrugge in 17 H. VI, one John Bernard, clerk, knowing that he had stolen an ox belonging to Joyce Gatacre, in consequence of which he had been taken and detained in prison until acquitted by the Justices at Ludlowe in 26 H. VI. None of the defendants appeared, and the Sheriff was ordered to arrest and produce them on the Octaves of St. Martin. *m.* 350.

Staff. William, the Bishop of Coventry and Lichfield, sued John Justice, of Cannok, Milward in a plea that whereas he had had the multure of all corn of all tenants and residents within his manor of Cannok at his mill at Cannok from time out of memory, the said John had carried corn of his men and tenants of Cannok to the mill of Humfrey Salwey in the same bill, and for which the Bishop claimed £40 as damages. John did not appear, and the Sheriff was ordered to arrest and produce him on the Quindene of St. Hillary. *m.* 350, *dorso.*

Staff. John Wither sued Henry Molyley and Agnes, his wife, for waste and destruction in lands, houses, gardens, woods, etc., which they held in Ilum, as dower of Agnes of the dotation of John Wyther her former husband and which were of his inheritance. The defendants did not appear, and the Sheriff was ordered to distrain and produce them on the Octaves of St. Hillary. *m.* 453.

DE BANCO. TRINITY, 27 H. VI.

Staff. William Mitton, armiger, sued William Adlyngton, of Brommesgrove, co. Worcester, yoman, and John Tummon, of Woldebury, co. Salop, husbondman, for breaking into his close at Penkerege and taking his goods and chattels to the value of 10 marks. The defendants did not appear, and the Sheriff was ordered to arrest and produce them on the Quindene of Michaelmas. *m.* 19.

Staff. John Heywode sued William Burnley, of Whitmore, yoman, William Damport, of Whitmore, yoman, and Margaret, his wife, John Damport, of Whitmore, yoman, John Damport, of Merton, co. Chester, yoman, William Wyse, of Staundon, yoman, William Smyth, of Mere, yoman, and John Whitmore, of Mere, yoman, for breaking into his close at Kele and taking three horses, worth £4, belonging to him and goods and chattels to the value of 40*s.* None of the defendants appeared, and the Sheriff was ordered to arrest and produce them on the Octaves of St. John the Baptist. *m.* 19, *dorso.*

Staff. Robert Cuny (Coyney) sued William Warylowe, of Normecote Graunge, yoman, Ambrose Bydyk, of Stone, yoman, and Nicholas Roe, of Stone, yoman, for breaking into his close and houses at Weston Cuny and taking his goods and chattels to the value of £10 and for so threatening his tenant William Wolryche, that he had given up his tenancy, and he had lost his rent and service for a length of time. The defendants did not appear, and the Sheriff was ordered as in the last suit. *m.* 19, *dorso.*

Staff. William Gough, of Brewode, wever, John Standiche, of Brewode, husbondman, and Robert Gough, of Tonge, co. Salop, taillour, were attached at the suit of Richard Cartwright for beating, wounding and illtreating him at Brewode on the 10th Sept. 21 H. VI, and detaining him in prison there for three days, and for which he claimed £20 as damages.

The defendants denied the injury and trespass, and appealed to a jury which was to be summoned for the Quindene of St. Michael. A postscript shews that no jury had been impanelled up to Hillary term, 28 H. VI. *m.* 291, *dorso.*

Staff. Thomas, the Prior of Tuttebury, William Lee, of Malefeld, yoman, William Elson, of Alton, yoman, and Edmund Elton, of Asshebourne, co. Derby, yoman, were attached at the suit of Sampson Meverell, knight, for taking by force on the 12th May, 25 H. VI, 12 oxen, and 4 cows belonging to him and worth £12 from Throweley, and for impounding 1,080 sheep for a day against the law and custom of England, and for which he claimed £100 as damages. The defendants appeared by attorney and the Prior denied the trespass and injury, and appealed to a jury. And as regarded the taking of 2 oxen and 4 cows; the other defendants stated that long before the assumed trespass, the king had been seised of the Honor and manor of Tuttebury in co. Stafford in demesne as of fee and that he and all his ancestors in the said honor, from time out of memory had been seised of a certain annual rent of 5*s.* from the manor of Throuley, and when the said rent was in arrear, the king and his ancestors had always levied distraints in the said manor, and the present king before the trespass complained of, viz., on the 26th February, 23 H. VI, at a Parliament held at Westminster, and with the authority of the said Parliament had assigned to Margaret the Queen of England his consort, the said manor and honor, and all fees, advowsons, lands and tenements belonging to it, as her dowry, and because 5*s.* of the said rent was in arrear at Michaelmas 25 H. VI, after the assignment of the Honor to the Queen, the said William, William and Edmund acting as Bailiffs of the Queen, had taken 2 oxen and 4 cows, which were grazing within the manor of Throwley as a distraint, as was lawful.

Sampson replied that the cattle had been taken without reasonable cause and appealed to a jury, upon which the defendants stated that without the King and the Queen they could not maintain their plea, and asked for the assistance of the Court so that the King and Queen might be advised before the issue of the writ of "venire facias" and the suit was adjourned to the Quindene of St. Michael. A postscript shews repeated adjournments of the suit up to Easter, 29 H. VI. *m.* 307.

Staff. William Rufford, late of Grendon, clerk, and John Bersford (Beresford), of Bersford, gentilman, were attached at the suit of Ralph Basset, armiger, in a plea that they together with John the Abbot of Dieuleucres, Sampson Meverell, late of Throweley, knight, and Isabella his wife, Nicholas Mountgomery, late of Cubley, co. Derby, armiger, Thomas Meverell, late of Throweley, gentilman, John Holys, of Moseley, gentilman, John Stathome, late of Throweley, yoman, William Londesdale, late of Throweley, yoman, and from others named, had broken into his close at Blore, on the Friday before the Feast of St. Barnabas, 26 H. VI, and had taken 12 oxen, 12 cows, worth 20 marks, and had so beaten his servants John Hudde, John Baxdonden, and John Cole, that he had lost their services for 6 months afterwards, for which he claimed £40 as damages.

The defendants appeared and denied the trespass and injury and appealed to a jury, which was to be summoned for the Quindene of St. Michael. *m.* 321.

CORAM REGE. TRINITY, 27 H. VI.

Staff. William Aleyn, late of Stubbylane, yoman, Ralph Henley, abbot of Burton upon Trent, Thomas Norton, monk of Burton upon Trent, and William Stapenhyll, a monk of Burton upon Trent, were attached to answer the appeal of Joan, late wife of William Cowper, for the death of her husband.

Joan appeared in person, and stated that on the Tuesday after the Feast of the Translation of St. Thomas the Martyr, 26 H. VI, the said William Aleyn, who now appeared, together with Robert Curteys, John Courte, Robert Careless, Roger Plummer, and others named who had not appeared, had laid in wait, with malice aforethought, and the said William, with a two-handed sword, had struck William Cowper on his right thigh causing a mortal wound of which he afterwards died, and that the said abbot, Thomas Norton and William Stapenhylle, had knowingly received the said William Aleyn, Robert Curteys, and the others named, after the felony.

The defendants denied the felony, and appealed to a jury. And the abbot stated that Joan was a native of the Abbey, as of the right of his church of St. Mary of Burton, appurtenant to his manor of Burton, and saving his rights, he pleaded not guilty and appealed to a jury; and William Aleyn took exception to the writ, because on the date of the writ he was living at Draycote in co. Stafford, and was never resident at Stubbylane; and as regards the felony he pleaded not guilty, and appealed to a jury, which was to be summoned for the Octaves of St. Martin; and the abbot, and Thomas Norton, and William Stapenhulle were admitted to bail, Richard Vernon, of Hadden, co. Derby, knight, John Gryffyth, of Whychenore, knight, Godfrey Hylton, of Chanton, co. Southampton, knight, and John Mathewe, of London, armiger, standing security for them. A postscript states that on the Octaves of St. Martin, Joan appeared, and the Marshal of the Court stated that William Aleyn had escaped from his custody. The Sheriff was therefore ordered to put the said William into *exigend*, and to outlaw him if he did not appear. The process was continued till the following Hillary term, when all the defendants appeared but Joan put in no appearance; and her appeal was dismissed. The process was continued at the suit of the King until 29 H. VI, when the abbot and Thomas Norton, and William Stapynhill appeared in Court and produced the King's pardon dated 5th June, 29 H. VI. *m.* 72.

Warw. It had been presented on the Tuesday before the Feast of St. Margaret, 26 H. VI, at Warwick, before William Ferrers, knight, John Rous, Thomas Huggeford, and William Donyngton, who had been assigned by Letters Patent to hear the case, that Richard Taillour, of Boseworth, co. Leicester, yoman, and other servants of Robert Harcourt, late of Stanton Harcourt, knight, designing the death of Humfrey Stafford, knight, and of Richard Stafford, armiger, the eldest son of the said Humfrey, on the Wednesday before the Feast of Corpus Christi, 26 H. VI, in the High Street, of Coventre, at the time of the Fair and Market, had collected many other malefactors to the number of at least sixty persons, armed and arrayed in the manner of war, with salades, jakkes, swords and bills, by the procurement and abetment of Lady Joan Harecourt, late of Boseworth, widowe, and had laid in wait to kill and murder the said Humfrey Stafford and Richard Stafford, and had insulted, beaten, and wounded the said Humfrey, and had feloniously killed and murdered the said Richard Stafford and William Sharpe, his servant. And that the said Richard Taillour, and other servants of Robert Harcourt, with many other malefactors arrayed in manner of war, with salades and *diploidis* defensible, long swords and short pollaxes, gleyves and daggers on the same day had beaten and wounded Humfrey Stafford, knight, Richard Beauchamp, armiger, William Sye, John More, John Hansbury, William Hanbury, Ralph Jowkes, John Marteyn, John Manchestre, Richard Manchestre, and Alexander Hunte, servants of the said Humfrey, and had left Humfrey Stafford insensible and nearly dead, so that his life was despaired of. And which indictment the King, for certain reasons, had commanded to be brought up and heard and terminated in this Court.

And Richard Taillour was now brought to the bar of the Court by the Sheriff of co. Warwick, and being questioned stated that he was not guilty, and appealed to a jury which was to be summoned for a month from St. Michael, and in the meantime the said Richard was admitted to bail. *m.* 19 *Rex.*[1]

DE BANCO. HILLARY, 28 H. VI.

Staff. Margaret, late wife of John Hampton, armiger, and Bevis Hampton, armiger, the son of the said John, executors of the will of the said John Hampton, sued Joyce, late wife of Leonard Stapulton, armiger, of Sesencote, co. Gloucester, wedowe, the executrix of the will of John Grevelle, armiger, for a debt of £100.

Joyce did not appear and the Sheriff was ordered to arrest and produce her on the Octaves of the Purification. A postscript shews adjournments of the suit up to 30 H. VI. *m.* 95.

Staff. Robert Peutrere sued Robert Burnell, of Coventre, co. Warwick, Peutrere, for taking from him by force John George his apprentice, from Lychefeld.

The defendant did not appear, and the Sheriff was ordered to arrest and produce him on the Quindene of Easter. *m.* 95, *dorso.*

Staff. John Talebot, knight, and Ralph, the abbot of the Monastery of the Blessed Mary of Crokysdene, sued John Romsoure, of Greteyate

[1] By other writs Humfrey Stafford, armiger, appealed Roger Kyngesbury, of Tredyngton, co. Worcester, David Taillour and others for the death of Richard Stafford his brother. See *coram Rege*, Easter and Trinity, 27 H. VI, and Hill, 28 H. VI.

Smythymon, William Stoke, of Romsoure, husbondman, John Romsoure, the son of James Romsoure, of Romsoure (Ramsor), husbondman, in a plea that each of them should render a sum of £60 which they unjustly detained. The defendants did not appear, and the Sheriff was ordered to arrest and produce them on the above date. *m.* 232.

Staff. John Gryffith, knight, sued John Bertram, of Strethay, husbondman, and William Brid, of Alrewas, husbondman, for breaking into his close at Alrewas, and cutting down his trees and taking his goods and chattels to the value of £20. The defendants did not appear, and the Sheriff was ordered as in the last suit. *m.* 232.

Staff. John Hampton, armiger, and Bevis Hampton, armiger, sued the Mayor and County (Comitatus) of Plymmouth, in co. Devon, for a debt of £20. The defendants did not appear, and the Sheriff returned they held nothing within his Bailwick. He was therefore ordered to arrest and produce them on the Quindene of Easter. *m.* 253, *dorso.*

Staff. John Cokayne, of Asshburne, co. Derby, armiger, William Cokayne, of Asshburne, gentilman, Thomas Mouner, of Asshburne, yoman, John Smyth, of Asshburne, Corvyser, Thomas Chamberleyn, of Assheburne, Corvyser; and 37 others named of co. Derby, Ralph Madeley, of Denstone, co. Stafford, yoman, Richard Tiddeswalle, of Mathefeld, co. Stafford, yoman, John Shirard, of Wetton, yoman, John Smyth, of Mathefeld, yoman, John Dorwer, of Mathefeld, husbondman, John Smyth, of Calton, husbondman, Thomas Smyth, of Calton, husbondman, James Mellour, of Hope, co. Stafford, yoman, and Richard Lout, of Stansop, laborer, were attached at the suit of Ralph Basset, for breaking into his close at Blore, on the Thursday before the Feast of All Saints, 28 H. VI, and burning 40 cartloads of peas, 20 cartloads of hay, to the value of £10 and taking two "armulasas" of a black color, 2 bows and 1,000 arrows to the value of £20, and for beating and wounding his servant Adam Baxtondene so that he lost his services for a length of time. John Cokayne and William Cokayne and the other defendants appeared by attorney and denied the trespass and injury, and appealed to a jury and as regarded the beating of Adam Baxtondene they stated that the said Adam with many other malefactors and disturbers of the king's peace, had attacked the said defendants on the day named at Thorp, in co. Derby, and had followed them from Thorp to Blore continually insulting them, and they had beaten him in self defence and in consequence of his insults, and they appealed to a jury, which was to be summoned for the Quindene of Easter Day. After several adjournments through defect of juries, the cause was moved by writ of *nisi prius* to be heard at Stafford before the Justice of Assize on the Friday after the Feast of St. James, 30 H. VI, when a jury found that John Cokayne, William Cokayne, John Smyth, of Assheburne, William Derby and Thomas Chamberleyn, were guilty of the assault and trespass, and they assessed the damages of Ralph Basset at £80 and his costs at £20 upon which Ralph stated he did not wish to prosecute the other defendants, "*Radulphus Basset fatetur se ulterius nolle prosequi versus predictos Thomam Mouner, etc., placitum suum.*" *m.* 318.

Staff. William Wynneshurst and Isabella, his wife, sued Thomas Nothale for a third of a messuage and virgate of land in Bisshebury, which they claimed as dower of Isabella of the dotation of Thomas Pyry her former husband. Thomas Nothale did not appear, and the Sheriff was ordered to take the dower claimed into the king's hands, and to summon him for three weeks from Easter Day. A postscript shews that the Sheriff had made no return to the writ up to Easter term, 29 H. VI. *m.* 347.

CORAM REGE. EASTER, 28 H. VI.

Staff. William Trussell, knight, appealed against the verdict of an assize of novel disseisin which Richard Vernon, knight, had arraigned against him respecting tenants in Kybbylstone, Acton, and Hales, and which had been heard at Tuttebury before Richard Byngeham, Ralph Poolle, Thomas Blount, knight, and William Mountforth, knight, on the Wednesday before Michaelmas Day, 27 H. VI.[1] The record of the assize was brought into Court and read as follows :—

Richard Vernon appeared in person and complained that William Trussell had unjustly disseised him of 100 messuages, 30 tofts, 3 water-mills, 60 carucates of land, 30½ virgates of land, 400 acres of meadow, 400 acres of wood, 400 acres of pasture, and £20 of rent. William Trussell appeared in person, and stated that as regarded £9 of the rent, he had never been in seisin of it, and if that was decided against him, he pleaded that Richard had never been in seisin of the rent, and if that was given against him he denied the disseisin, and put himself on the assize; and as regarded 40 messuages, 10 tofts, one of the mills, 30 carucates and 20 virgates of land, 100 acres of meadow, 200 acres of wood, and 200 acres of pasture, claimed by Richard, and 20*s.* of rent out of the £11 of rent, the residue of the tenements as specified in the bill, these were parcel of the manor of Kybbylstone, and 30 messuages, 10 tofts, one of the mills, 20 carucates and 6 virgates of land, 160 acres of meadow, 100 acres of wood, and 100 acres of pasture specified in the bill, and likewise £8 out of the £11 of rent, were parcel of the manor of Acton, and 30 messuages, 10 tofts, a mill, 10 carucates and 4½ virgates of land, 40 acres of meadow, 20 acres of wood, and 100 acres of pasture, as well as 40*s.* out of the said rent of £11, were in the vill of Hales, and were parcel of the moiety of the manor of Hales in co. Stafford ; and as regarded the said 40 messuages, 10 tofts, one of the mills, and 30 carucates and 8 virgates of land, 99 acres of meadow, 200 acres of wood, 200 acres of pasture, and 16*s.* 1*d.* of rent in Kybbylstone ; William Trussell stated an assize would not lie, because a certain William Mosse, parson of Langeporte, and two others named, on the Tuesday in the week of Lent, 4 H. IV, had arraigned an assize of novel disseisin against Alured de Lathebury, knight, Fulk de Pembrugge, knight, and Thomas de Appulby, respecting tenements in Cubblestone, complaining that they had disseised them of the manor of Cubblestone ; and the jury had found that William Trussell, knight, was formerly seised of the manor, and had issue John and William (the younger), and William (the elder) died, and John entered as son and heir, and after his death William entered as son and heir of John, and had issue Katrine, who had issue Elizabeth, and Katrine died in the lifetime of her father, and the said William, son of John, died seised of the manor, and after his death Elizabeth entered as his kinswoman and heir, and died seised of it, and after her death the said Fulk and one Margaret, then his wife, entered as in right of Margaret, who was kinswoman and heir of Elizabeth, viz. daughter of William, brother of John, father of William, father of Katrine, the mother of Elizabeth ; and Fulk and Margaret levied a Fine in 15 R. II, viz. between Walter Blount, knight, and Thomas Beek, knight, and John Brette, clerk, complainants, and the said Fulk and Margaret, and John de Grendon, deforciants of the said manor, by which the deforciants acknowledged the manor to be the right of the said Walter, Thomas and John Brette, and the said Walter, Thomas, and John Brette afterwards, on the 5th December, 15 R. II, granted the manor to the said John de Grendon for his life, with

[1] William Ayscough, Thomas Stanley, and Robert Whitgreve were likewise assigned to take the assize, but did not attend.

remainder to Fulk and Margaret, and their heirs for ever; and John de Grendon died, and Fulk and Margaret then entered, and Margaret died, and after her death, Fulk by his deed dated from Tongg on the Tuesday after the Feast of the Exaltation of the Holy Cross, 2 H. IV, granted the manor to the said William Mosse, Robert and Walter Swan, and to one John Walton, vicar of Hales, now deceased: and the said Alured and Thomas de Appulby afterwards entered into possession claiming as kinsmen and heirs of the said Elizabeth, asserting that a certain Margaret Sulney, the grandmother of Alured, and great-grandmother of Thomas de Appulby, whose heirs they were, to have been daughter of the said John Trussell, when she was not his daughter, but daughter of a William Trussell, of Noteworthy in co. Northampton, and had removed the said William Mosse, Robert and Walter Swan from the manor, but whether such removal was a disseisin in law they were ignorant; and being asked by the Justices whether the removal was *vi et armis* or not, they replied that it was; and being asked if all the defendants had taken part in the removal, they replied that Alured and Thomas de Appulby took part in it, but not Fulk, and they assessed the damages at £100. And the said William Mosse, Robert and Walter Swan, became seised of the manor by virtue of this judgment.

And William Trussell further stated that Fulk de Pembrugge, on the date of the original writ of the said assize against him and Alured and Thomas de Appulby, and ever since had been tenant of the manor of Cubbleston, and the said manor and the manor of Kybbylstone were one and the same manor, and the tenements respecting which William Trussell was now pleading were parcel of the same manor, and Robert Say died, and William Mosse and Walter Swan became seised, as survivors, and by their deed, which was dated from Cubblestone on the Monday after the Feast of the Purification, 10 H. IV, granted the manor to one Fulk Pembrugge, of Tonge, knight, and Isabella, his wife, and to the heirs of their bodies, and failing such, to remain to William Trussell, the defendant, under the name of William Trussell, son of Laurence Trussell, and Margery, his wife, and to his heirs, and Fulk died thus seised of the manor as of fee tail, leaving no issue by Isabella, and Isabella survived him and died seised, and the said Margery afterwards died, and after their deaths William Trussell, the defendant, entered by virtue of the remainder, and was seised until the said Richard claimed the manor as kinsman and heir of Fulk Pembrugge, of Tong, viz. as son of Richard, son of Juliana, sister of the said Fulk, under the supposition that Fulk had died seised in demesne as of fee simple, and one David Donner had then expelled him as he was prepared to prove, and he prayed for judgment whether, under these circumstances, an assize would lie between him and Richard Vernoun; and as regarded 2 virgates of land of the said 30 carucates and 20 virgates of land in the vill of Kybbylstone the residue, as well as regarded the moiety of all the said tenements in the vill of Hales, besides a carucate of land of the said 10 carucates $4\frac{1}{2}$ virgates of land in the same vill, William Trussell stated an assize would not lie between him and Richard Vernon, because long before Richard held anything in the said $2\frac{1}{2}$ virgates of land, William Mosse, the parson of Langeport, Robert Say, the parson of Eton, Walter Swan, the parson of Ayleston, and John Walton, vicar of Halys, were seised of them as of fee, and whilst so seised Fulk de Pembrugge, knight, to whom Richard was kinsman and heir, viz. brother of Juliana, the mother of Richard, father of the said Richard Vernon, the plaintiff, by a deed which William Trussell produced in Court dated from Tonge, co. Salop, on the Monday after the Feast of the Exaltation of the Holy Cross, 3 H. IV, had remitted and quit-claimed to the said William Mosse, Robert, Walter, and John all his right and claim to them under the names of the manors of Halis, Cublestone, Acton-Trussell and Tonge, and all lands and tenements, rents and services and revenues which they held by the grant of the said Fulk; and afterwards Robert Say and John Walton died, and William Mosse and Walter survived them, and held the said two virgates and a half by the "*jus accrescendi*," and William Trussell now held the *status* of the said William Mosse and Walter; and as regarded an acre of meadow of the said 100 acres of meadow in Kybbylstone, the residue, William Trussell stated that an assize would not lie, because Fulk de Pembrugge, knight, was seised of it in demesne as of fee, and demised it with other lands to one Hugh de Bradbury for a term of six years beginning in 1 H. IV; and Fulk, by a deed dated from Tong in 2 H. IV, granted it to William Mosse, Robert Say, John Walton, and Walter Swan, with other lands, under the name of Fulk's manor of Cublesdon, and Robert Say and John Walton died, and the said William Mosse and Walter remained in possession, and were seised as of fee, and William Trussell now held their *status* in the tenements, and Richard Vernon claiming the land under colour of the deed of feoffment made to him and his heirs by the said Fulk de Pembrugge, had entered into possession, and had been expelled by one David Donner on the part of William Trussell; and as regarded a rent of 3*s*. 11*d*., &c. (*here the same plea is repeated*).

And as regarded an acre of land of the said lands and tenements in the vill of Acton, William Trussell stated that an assize would not lie, because one William Trussell, of Cublesdon, knight, took to wife one Isabella, daughter of Warine de Maynwaryng, and they had issue William Trussell and Warine Trussell, knights, and they died, and William, son of William, had issue Margaret, and died, and Margaret was seised of the said acre of land in demesne as of fee and died leaving no issue, and after her death William Trussell, the defendant, entered as her heir, viz., as son of Laurence, son of the said Warine, brother of William, the father of the said Margaret, and William entered, and was seised of it, until Richard Vernon, claiming it under colour of a deed of feoffment made to him and his heirs by the said Margaret, had entered and expelled him, and Richard had been removed by one Thomas Everdon, whose possession William Trussell now defended.

And as regarded 20 acres of land of the said 20 carucates and 6 virgates of land in Acton, William stated an assize would not lie between him and Richard, because long before the said Richard held anything in them, a Fine had been levied, in 45 E. III, between William Trussell, of Cublesdon, chivaler, complainant, and the said Fulk de Pembrugge, under the names of Fulk de Pembrugge, knight, and Margaret, his wife, deforciants of the said 20 acres of land, with other lands, under the name of the manor of Acton-Trussell, by which Fine the tenements had been settled on the said Fulk and Margaret, and the heirs of their bodies, and failing such, to revert to the said William Trussell, of Cublesdon, knight, and his heirs for ever, and he now held the *status* of the said William Trussell, of Cublesdon.

And as regarded a carucate of land of the said 20 carucates and 6 virgates of land in Acton, and a carucate of land in Halys, William stated an assize would not lie between him and Richard, because long before Richard held anything in the tenements, a Fine had been levied, in 6 R. II, between John Grendon, the younger, and William Blemehulle, complainants, and the said Fulk de Pembrugge, to whom Richard was kinsman and heir (viz. as brother of Juliana, mother of Richard, the father of the said Richard Vernon) under the name of Fulk Pembrugge, chivaler, and Margaret, his wife, deforciants of the said 2 carucates of land amongst other lands, by the name of the manor of Acton-Trussell, and a moiety of the manor of Sherrevehalis in co. Stafford, by which Fine, Fulk and Margaret acknowledged the said tenements to be the right of John Grendon, and for which acknowledgment the said John Grendon and William Blemehulle granted them to Fulk and Margaret, and the heirs of their bodies, and failing such, to revert to the said John Grendon and William Blemehulle, and the heirs of John. And John had issue Elena and Margaret, and died at Tong during the lifetime of the said Fulk and Margaret. And Elena had issue Elizabeth, Alice, Elizabeth, and Joan, and she died, and Fulk and Margaret had died leaving no issue; and after their deaths the said Margaret, the daughter of John Grendon, and the said Elizabeth, Alice, and Elizabeth, and Joan, as kinswomen and heirs of John Grendon, had entered and were seised in demesne as of fee, and William Trussell stated he now held the *status* of the said Margaret, Elizabeth, Alice, Elizabeth, and Joan, etc., etc. (*here follow some other pleadings of the same kind, but containing no new facts*).

Richard Vernon stated in reply that as regarded the said 40 messuages, 10 tofts, a mill, 30 carucates and 18 virgates of land, 99 acres of meadow, 200 acres of wood, 200 acres of pasture, and 16*s.* 1*d.* of rent in Kybbylstone, the said Fulk Pembrugge, of Tonge, knight, was sole seised in demesne as of fee when he died, and he died leaving no issue, and after his death the tenements descended to him as kinsman and heir of the said Fulk, viz. as son of Richard, son of Richard, son of Juliana, sister of the said Fulk, and he had entered and was seised of them until the said William Trussell had unjustly disseised him. Richard repeated the same plea in all the other cases quoted.

The jury at Tuttebury had found a verdict in favour of Richard, stating that the said Richard was seised of the tenements as of his freehold until William Trussell had disseised him *vi et armis*, and they assessed his damages at £2,080.

The Record having been read, Richard Vernon asked that William Trussell should specify the articles in which the jury of the assize had delivered a false judgment, and William stated that the jury had sworn falsely in all the articles, and this he was prepared to prove by a jury of 24. The Sheriff was therefore ordered to produce a jury for the Quindene of Holy Trinity, etc. A postscript shews that the suit was carried on for several terms after this date, but with no result. *m.* 28.[1]

Staff. Sampson Meverell, knight, John Pole, of Shene, Robert Cuny (Coyney), armiger, John Borghton, armiger, John Horwode, of Compton, armiger, John Thykbrome, of Thykbrome, William Selmon, of Moreton, Thomas Madeley, of Denstone, Roger Fowke, of Brewode, Thomas Shore, of Burton, Thomas Kegworth, of Lychefeld, and John Fraunceys, of Alderwas, were attached to answer to the King, as well as to William Trussell, knight, for a misdemeanour; and William Trussell appeared in person, and stated that whereas in the Parliament of 34 & 35 E. III it had been ordained that if any juror of an assize or inquisition should take money from either party to an assize he should pay ten times as much as he had received, and if any juryman had not sufficient to satisfy the Fine, he should suffer one year's imprisonment, the said Sampson, John, etc., who had been jurors in a certain assize of novel disseisin which Richard Vernon had arraigned before William Ascogh, Richard Byngeham, Ralph Poolle, Thomas Blount, knight, William Mountforth, knight, Thomas Stanle, and Robert Whitgreve, and which had been heard at Tottebury on the 7th June, 26 H. VI, had accepted divers sums of money, viz. each juryman 100*s.* for food, and pocket money to

[1] The following dates will help to elucidate this plea:—William Trussell, the father of Margaret Pembrugge, died 20 July, 1363, leaving Margaret, his daughter and heir, then aged fourteen. She was already the wife of Fulk de Pembrugge. (Inq. p. m., 37 E. III, No. 69.)

William Trussell, the nephew of the above William, was dead in 1379-80, leaving his grand-daughter Elizabeth his heir, then aged eight. (Chester Inq., 3 R. II, No. 1.) She died shortly afterwards, when Margaret succeeded to the family estates.

Margaret Pembrugge died *circa* 1399 (Inq., 22 R. II, No. 102), and Fulk de Pembrugge died *circa* 1409 (Inq., 10 H. IV, No. 45). *Ex inf.* Mr. Charles Bridgeman.

the value of 13*s*. 4*d*., and other gifts at Lychefeld against the Statute and in contempt of the King.

The defendants appeared and denied the injury, and a day was given to the parties on the Quindene of Holy Trinity. A postscript states that on that day all the parties appeared in person, and the defendants denied that they had received any money or gifts as stated by William Trussell, and appealed to a jury, which was to be summoned for the Octaves of St. Michael. *m*. 33.

Salop. Richard de Vernon, late of London, knight, was *in misericordiâ* for several defaults (*of appearance*). The said Richard and John Broun, late of Coldnorton in co. Stafford, armiger, were attached at the suit of William Trussell, knight, to answer to him as well as to the King for a conspiracy and the fabrication of false documents to destroy and disturb the title and possession of the said William in lands and tenements in Cubleston, Acton, and Hales in co. Stafford, and Shyrevhales (Sheriff Hales), in co. Salop. And William stated that the said Richard and John, on the 5th December, 25 H. VI, had promulgated a false deed, dated from Tonge, 4th August, 7 H. IV, respecting the manors of Cublestone and Acton, a moiety of the manor of Hales in Cublestone, Acton and Hales in co. Stafford, a moiety of the manor of Shyrevhale in co. Salop, and the manor of Blaken in co. Chester, in which it was contained that William Mosse, the parson of Langeport, Walter Swan, parson of Pembrugge, and Robert Say, the parson of Eton, had released and quit-claimed to Fulk Pembrugge, knight, all their right and claim in the said manors, etc., and in the manor of Gyldemorton in co. Leicester, which they held by the feoffment of the said Fulk, and which deed was dated from Tonge on the Tuesday after the Feast of the Exaltation of the Holy Cross, 2 H. IV, in contempt of the King, and to the grievous damage of the said William, and for which he claimed £1,000 as damages. Richard and John appeared by attorney and denied the injury, and appealed to a jury, which was to be summoned for the Octaves of Holy Trinity. A postscript shews no jury had been empannelled up to many adjournments of the Court. *m*. 43.

CORAM REGE. MICH., 29 H. VI.

Staff. A writ was sent to the Sheriff, Humfrey Swynarton, armiger, to cause proclamation to be made that all the persons named in a petition to Parliament made by Ralph Basset, of Blore, should appear *coram Rege* at this term to answer the complaints made against them, dated from Leicester 26th May, 28 H. VI. The petition had been transmitted to the Justices assigned to hear pleas *coram Rege*, and was in these terms :—

"Mekely besechith Rauff Basset Squier, that whereas John Cokayn of Assheburne in the Schire of Derby Squier, Thurstan Vernon late of Haddon in the same schire Squier, William Cokayn of Assheburne of the same schire Gentilman with other malicious persones to the noumbre of xxx whos names are contayned in a sedelle to this bille annexid, with grete multitude of riottous people unknowen, with force and armes arraied with jakkes, salettes, bowes, arrowes, swordes, gleyves and boklers and other manere of wepon defensive come the Thursday next before the fest of Alhalowene in the yere of the regne of oure soveraine lord the Kyng xxviii. to a place of youre seid besecher called Blore in the schire of Stafford to the entent to have murdred, slayn, maymed and beton youre seid besecher, his tenaunts and his servaunts, and for to brenne his howse, and leied sege to his place and there brennyd a stake of his heye and a stake of his peise, and had not John Curboun, Richard Bagot, and Henry Bradburne with others heryng of his grete riot and route come thider to the entent for to se pees kept and for to entrete them to go thens thei hadde brennyd the place of youre seid besecher, and his brother Richard Basset and other divers of his tenaunts the which were at that tyme within the seid place, and so at the request and at the instaunce of the seid John Curboun, Richard Bagot and Herry Bradburne the seid misgoverned and riottous persones were intretide to go thence and so thei dide, but thei wold not leyng be intredit but for the nyghte thenne next folowying and on the Fryday next aftur youre seid besecher heryng of this grete riott come home to his seid place in grete feere and drede of his life thei makyng uppon hym grete assautes and beton divers of his servaunts that is to sey Adam Baxtondon and other threthnyng and manassyng hym to slee and to brenne so that youre seid besecher dare not in no wyse be at home in his one house which shuld be his grete defence and tuicion so he is likly to be undowne on lasse than he may purvayed of remedie, wherefore please it to youre wysdomes theese premisses to consider and thereupon to pray the oure soveraine lorde to consider and ordeyne that be the assent of his lordis spirituelle and temporelle in this present parlement assembled and by the auctorite of the same parlement that a writ of proclamation may be had oute of the chauncery of oure seid soveraine lord, directed to the Shirreff of Staffordshire for the tyme beyng commaundyng hym to proclayme in two countees to be holden in the same shire next aftur the delivraunce of the same writte to hym made that the seid misgoverned and riottes persons and every of them may be solempnedly calde to come to appere before the Justices of oure soveraine lorde in his Benche at the Quinzisme of Seint Michell next comyng to answere to the seid orrible riottes, wronges, assautes, trespasses and oppressions after the discretion of the seid Justice," etc., etc., etc.

The names on the schedule annexed were :—

Thomas Gilbert, of Tyddeswalle, co. Derby, yoman.
Nicholas Coterell, late of Bakewell, co. Derby, yoman.
William Foxlate, of Monyasshe, co. Derby, yoman.
William Londesdale, late of Throwley, co. Stafford, yoman.
Ralph Maddeley, late of Denstone, co. Stafford, yoman.
John Smyth, of Mathefeld, co. Stafford, yoman.
Richard Teddeswalle, of Mathefeld, co. Stafford, yoman.
John Shirard, of Wetton, co. Stafford, yoman.
James Miloure, of Hope, co. Stafford, yoman.
Thomas Meverell, late of Trouley, co. Stafford, gentilman.
Richard Lout, of Stansop, co. Stafford, laborer.
Thomas Chamberleyn, of Assheburne, co. Derby, yoman.
Christofer Stokedale, of Thorp, co. Derby, yoman.
Robert Stokedale, of Thorp, co. Derby, yoman.
Robert Careles, late of Tyddeswalle, co. Derby, yoman.
John Stathom, late of Derby, yoman, and 14 others.

Ralph Basset appeared in person, but none of the defendants appeared, and the Sheriff was ordered to make a return of the damage which had been caused to the said Ralph on the oath of a jury of the vicinage of Blore, and to return it into Court on the Octaves of St. Martin. A postscript states that on that day Ralph appeared, and the Sheriff returned that he had made an inquisition on the oath of the jurymen at Chedull, on the Thursday after the Feast of All Saints, 29 H. VI, by which it appeared that the said Ralph had sustained damage to the amount of 390 marks, and they assessed his costs at 10 marks, and as the Court was not prepared to give judgment (*et pro eo quod curia hic de judicio in premissis reddendo nondum avisatur*) a day was given to Ralph on the Octaves of St. Hillary, on which day Ralph appeared and *pro eo quod curia hic de judicio*, etc. (*as before*) a day was given to him on the Morrow of St. John the Baptist, on which day Ralph appeared and *pro eo*, etc. (*as before*). N.B.—The same form was used every term up to the end of the reign, Ralph Bassett appearing in person at every term. *m.* 21.

Staff. John Berisforde, late of Berisforde, the younger, gentilman, and John Cowaderey, late of Ilum, yoman, were attached by their bodies to answer the appeal of Agnes, late wife of John Taillour, for the death of her husband.

Agnes appeared in person, and stated that the said John Taillour was at Chedull in co. Stafford on the Feast of St. Laurence the Martyr, 26 H. VI, about the third hour of the day, when John Berisford and John Cowaderey, who were now in Court, together with Thomas Meverell, late of Throwley, gentilman, William Londesdale, late of Throwley, yoman, James Mellour, late of Hope, co. Stafford, yoman, Richard Lout, late of Stansop, laborer, Robert Starkey, late of Fossebroke, yoman, and six others named, and whom she would have appealed for the same death if they had been present, had laid in wait with malice aforethought, and Thomas Meverell had struck her husband on the right side of the head with a staff, causing a mortal wound of which he had died, and the said William Londesdale had likewise struck her husband on the head with a staff, causing a mortal wound, and James Mellour and Robert Starkey had done the same, and Richard Lout had struck him with a dagger on his right arm, causing a mortal wound of which he would have died if he had not been killed by the others, and the said John Beresford and John Cowedery, as well as four others named, servants of the said Thomas Meverell, had feloniously received and maintained them after the felony. John Beresford and John Cowedery appeared in person and denied the felony, and put themselves on the country (i.e. *appealed to a jury*) which was to be summoned for the Octaves of the Purification, and Thomas Meverell, William Londesdale, James Mellour, Richard Lout, and Robert Starkey, the principals, had been outlawed; and Sampson Meverell, of Throweley, knight, Henry Punt, of Rodburne, co. Derby, gentilman, Humfrey Haskyth, of Rodburne, gentilman, and John Staley, of Throweley, yoman, stood bail to produce the other defendants at the above term. A postscript shews that after many adjournments through defect of a jury, the case was ultimately heard before the Judges of Assize at Stafford, when a jury found they were not guilty, and assessed the damages of each of them at 20*s*. The record says that the jury "*assident dampna ipsius Johannis occasione falsi appelli infra specificati ut in captione et imprisonamento corporis sui necnon et pro infamio, misis, laboribus et expensis suis inde habitis et factis ad viginti solidos.*" *m.* 24.

Staff. Agnes, formerly wife of John Hert, appeared in person and appealed William Vernon, late of Nethershaile (Nether Seal) in co. Leicester, armiger, and Hugh Davenport, of Rydeware Mavesyn, gentilman, John Malpas, of Rideware Mavesyn, wever, John Slyngesby, late of Milton, co. Derby, yoman, John Bromley, of Burton upon Trent, karvour, and 60 others, described as of Nether Seal, Chilcote, Over Appulby, Burton on Trent, Edmyngale, Rideware Mavesyn, Pipe Rideware, Brerdon, Hampstall Rideware, and Curborowe, for the death of her husband, viz. the said John Bromley, John Malpas, and John Slyngesby as principals, and the others as accessories. None of the defendants appeared, and the Sheriffs of co. Stafford, Derby, and Leicester were ordered to put them into *exigend*, and if they did not appear to outlaw them, and if they appeared to arrest and produce them at a month from Easter. *m.* 33, *dorso.*

Derb. Ralph Basset, of Maynil Langley, co. Derby, armiger, Robert Shawe, of Colond, co. Derby, gentilman, Humfrey Walker, of Casterne, co. Stafford, gentilman, John Suthworth, vicar of Ilum, Richard Torpyng, of

Greteyate, co. Stafford, yoman, William Sonde, parson of Bloure, co. Stafford, William Golde, of Grendon, co. Stafford, yoman, Nicholas Bagnald, of Oneote, co. Stafford, yoman, William Vigorys, late of Musden, co. Stafford, yoman, were attached to answer the complaint of Sampson Meverell, late of Tyddeswalle, co. Derby, knight, that by a conspiracy formed by them at Monyasshe they had caused him to be indicted, in 26 H. VI, for robbing the said John Southworth of 8 marks of money and to be arrested and lodged in the prison of the Marshalsea until he had been acquitted *coram Rege*, on the Morrow of St. Martin, 28 H. VI, and for which he claimed £400 as damages.

The defendants appeared by attorney and denied the injury, and appealed to a jury which was to be summoned for the Octaves of St. Hillary. *m*. 39.

Staff. and Warw. The petition of Thomas Ferrers, the younger, esquyer, Gilbert Faldryng, and Hugh More, servaunts of the said Thomas, made to Parliament in 28 H. VI, was returned into Court to be heard and determined. The petition was as follows :—

"To the right wyse and discrete commons in this present parlement assembled shewyth to your wyse discretions Thomas Ferrers the younger, Squyer, Gilbert Faldryng and Hugh More servaunts of the same Thomas, That where upon Michallmesse evenin last passed weren in Goddis peas and the Kynges our soveraigne lord yn the felde of the towne of Colshille in Arderne in Warrewikshire there come one Thomas Hexstall Gentilman, Thomas Cotys of the Co. of Stafford Gentilman Richard Emme of Tamworth in the Co. of Warwick, Fuyster, Hugh Colman of Tamworth co. Stafford, Souter, William Banastre, of co. Stafford yoman, John Ballard of co. Stafford yoman, John Baker of Wolvernehampton yoman (and others named) gydred to theym other mysgoverned people to the nombre of 80 persons riotours arraied in rioutouse wyse, distourbours of the Kings peace, ayens his corone and dignite with force and armes that is to sey Jackes, salettes, bowes, arowes, swerdes, bokelers, daggers and other wepons defensible by the sturryng excityng, procuryng and comaundement of the said Richard Emme and Hugh Colman and than and there assaute made to the seide Thomas Ferrers, Gilbert, and Hugh More, and theym thenne and there bete, wounded and theym and everyone of theym then and there foule mahemyd and there theym lefte for dede and the said mysdoers, styrrers, exciters procurers and comaunders herewith alle nat content of theyre insanable malice continuyng in thaire seid riote the seid Soneday come to the seid towne of Tamworth yn the seid shyre of Warrewik arraied in maner beforeseide and than and there assauted the castelle of Thomas Ferrers the elder Squyer to the entente to have slayne hym yf they might have goten the same castelle with the same assaute the saide misdoers contynuyng yit in their seid malice ageyne the seid Thomas Ferrers the elder and Thomas Ferrers the younger and their servaunts, please it your right wyse discretions the premisses tenderly to considere and theruppon to pray the King our soveraigne lord by the advys of his lordes spirituelle and temporelle in the present parlement assembled and by the auctorite of the same to ordeyne and establisshe that severalx writtes of proclamations may be direct to the Shreves of Warwikshire and Staffordshire charging the same Shreves of Warrewickshire to make open proclamation in Coventre Warwick, Colshulle and Thamworth, in the same shire and the seid shryef of Staffordshire to make open proclamation in Lychefeld Burton upon Trente Stafford and Tamworth in the same shire that the seid misdoers and every one of them appere in the Kinges Courte before the Justices of the Pleas before the Kyng to be holden assigned at the XV me of Seynt John next comyng there to answere to the premisses and to such matters as by the seid Thomas Ferrers the younger, Gilbert and Hugh More then shall be put ageyns them," etc., etc.

And Thomas Ferrers Gilbert Faldryng and Hugh More now appeared in person, and none of the defendants appeared and the said Thomas Gilbert and Hugh then prayed that damages might be adjudicated for the said riots and transgressions, and the Sheriff of co. Warwick was commanded to return the damage sustained by each of the plaintiffs separately on the Quindene of St. Hillary. A postscript states that on that day the Sheriff returned that by a inquisition made before him it appeared that the said Thomas had sustained damage to the amount of £120 and that each of the others had sustained damage to the extent of £20. It was therefore considered that the Plaintiffs should recover those damages against the said Thomas Hexstall and the other defendants. A late postscript states that afterwards, on the 8th May, 33 H, VI, Thomas Ferrers and the other plaintiffs appeared in person and stated that their damages had been satisfied. *m.* 43.

Staff. Derb. The petition of Philip Oker (Okeover), armiger made to Parliament in 28 H. VI, was returned into Court to be heard and determined, the Sheriffs of cos. Stafford and Derby having been previously commanded by writs dated 2nd July, 28 H. VI, to cause public proclamation to be made in their respective counties that all the defendants named in the petition should appear in Court at this term to answer to the said Philip for the riots and transgressions of which he had complained.

The petition of Philip was in these words.

To the Kyng our most dowted soveraine lord:—Sheweth unto your Highnes your humble besecher Philip Oker Squier that where your seid besecher and his auncestres of tyme that no mynde is, have peasible byn possessed and seised in and of the maner of Oker, with a parke adjoynyng therto and other appurtenaunces in the County of Stafford there one John Cokeyne Squier hath riottesley diverse tymes as wel be nyghtes as by dayes with grete nombre of riotes poeple the seid parke of your seid besecher huntyd and distroyed and on the Wedynsday next after the fest of all Halowene laste paste William Cokyn of Assheburne in the County of Derby Squier brother to the seid John and by his comaundement assembled to hym divers misdoers and riottes persones to the nombre of a C persones some of whose names were conteyned in a cedelle to this bylle annexed arraied with jackes, salettes, sperys, bowes and arrowes and with other wepens of defence in weye of warre and riottsnes come to the seid maner, and there and than brake up the dores, baywyndowes and other wyndowes of the seid maner with fournes, trestille and tabulle dormant and brende them there and by the seid fyre rostyd parcele of the seid dere takyn in the seid parke in dyspyte of your seid besecher and there huntyd and destroyed the seid park and brake downe the palys thereof your seid besecher thanne beyng at the parlement at London in the service of Edward Gray lord Ferrers of Groby, and after that wone Thurstan Vernon of his grete malice and maliciouse purpose and William Cokyn by the comaundement of the seid John Cokyn with the foreseid mysdoers and riottes persons arrayed in the maner as it is before rehersed of whom dyvers namys been conteyned in the seid cedulle to this bille annexed on the day of the conception of our lady laste passed come to the seid park and there and than huntyd alle the day and drowen down the moste parte of the pale of the seid park there then kylled all the dere there ynne to the nombre of 120 and lafte in the seid park but 5 dere alyve and so it is utelye destroyed to the grete hurte and utterly shame and undoying of your seid besecher withoute your Highness provided a remedeye in this partie, Wherefore please it your high and habundaunt grace the premisses tenderly to considere and by the assent of your lordes spirretuelle and temporelle in this present parlement assembled and by the auctoritie etc, (as in the petition of Thomas Ferrers on the last page)."

The names on the Schedulle annexed to the bill are over 70 in number, but with few exceptions are all tenants in Asshebourne and other places in Derbyshire, the Staffordshire names on it are William Londesdale late of Throwley, yoman, Ralph Madeley, of Denstone yoman, John Mathefeld, yoman, Richard Tiddeswelle, yoman, John Shirard, of Wotton, yoman, James Mellour, of Hope, yoman, Richard Lout of Stanhope yoman, John Smyth of Calton, husbondman, Thomas Smyth of Calton husbondman, Robert Curteys late of Falde yoman, and John Bradshawe, late of Burton upon Trent yoman, Philip Oker appeared in person, but none of the defendants appeared and Philip then prayed that damages might be adjudicated to him for the trespass and injury he had sustained, and the Sheriff of co. Stafford was ordered to return the amount of the damage on the oath of a jury of the vicinage of Oker on the Quindene of St. Hillary. A postscript states that on that day Philip appeared in person and it was shewn that he had sustained damage to the amount of 395 marks, and that his costs amounted to 5 marks. It was therefore considered that the said Philip should recover 400 marks from the defendants. And the Sheriffs of cos. Stafford and Derby were ordered to arrest them. *m.* 74.

CORAM REGE. HILLARY, 29 H. VI.

Middlesex. Thomas Wolsley, late of Wolsley, co. Stafford, gentilman, was attached at the suit of Thomas Luyt, for taking his goods and chattels at Enfeld, *vi et armis* to the value of 6 marks. Thomas Luyt appeared in person and stated that on the 10th March, 26 H. VI, Thomas Wolsley had taken by force a gold ring, a pair of "bonges, a girdle of silk *harnesiata* with silver belonging to him from Enfeld, and for which he claimed £10 as damages. Thomas Wolsley appeared by attorney, and the suit was adjourned to Easter term. A postscript shews adjournments up to Hillary term, 30 H. VI. *m.* 48.

Warw. Process to annul the outlawry of Robert de Harcourt, late of Stanton Harcourt, co. Oxon, knight.

The original Indictment against him was returned into Court, which stated that it had been presented on the Tuesday before the Feast of St. Margaret, 26 H. VI, at Warwick before William Ferrers, knight, John Rous and others, Justices of the Peace, that Robert Harecourt, late of Stanton Harcourt, knight, and William Massy, late of Stanton Harcourt, gentilman, and other servants of Robert, designing the death of Humfrey Stafford, knight, and of Richard Stafford, the eldest son of the said Humfrey, on the Wednesday before the Feast of Corpus Christi, 26 H. VI, had laid in wait in the High Street of Coventry, etc. (as before) by the procurement and abetment of the Lady Joan Harcourt, late of Bosworth, wydowe, and had wounded and illtreated the said Humfrey and had killed and murdered Richard Stafford and William Sharpe, the servant of the said Richard.

Robert Harcourt had not appeared and had been outlawed on the Monday after the Feast of SS. Peter and Paul, 27 H. VI; and at the present term, viz., on the 12th February, 29 H. VI, Robert Harcourt surrendered and was committed to the Marshalsea, and being brought before the Court, he stated there was a manifest error in the promulgation of the outlawry against him, because on the Monday when he was outlawed, and both before and afterwards he was in the King's prison in the Castle of Chester, within the ward of the said Castle and in the custody of Thomas Stanley, knight, the Constable of the said Castle, so that he could not surrender himself to answer to the Indictments and as it was testified to the Court by many trustworthy persons that the said Robert was in prison as he stated, he was admitted to bail on the sureties of Edward Langeford, of Bradfeld, co. Oxon., armiger; Walter Blount, of London, armiger; Richard Harcourt, of Northleye, co. Oxon., armiger, and Thomas Lynde, of London, armiger; and the Sheriffs of cos. Warwick, Leicester, Oxford, and Stafford, were ordered to return into court an extent of the lands held by Robert in those counties on the following Easter term; on which date the Sheriffs returned he held no lands in those counties, and a day was given to him on the following Trinity term, and he was admitted to bail on the sureties of William Vernon, of Haddon, co. Derby, armiger, and the said Richard Harecourt, Edward Langford, and Thomas Seynt Barbe, armiger; and at Trinity term the King's attorney appeared and stated that the outlawry should not be annulled, because on the day it was promulgated the said Robert was at large and not in prison, and asked that the question might be decided by a jury of the vicinage of Chester, and because the said Castle is within the County Palatine of Chester, and the men of that county could not be summoned out of the county. A mandate was sent to the Justice of co. Chester to summon a jury of twenty-four of the vicinage of the ward of the Castle, and to return their verdict on the Quindene of St. Hillary, and Robert was admitted to bail on the sureties of Ralph Radclyffe, of Ekylston, co. Lancaster, knight; John Harecourt, of Elinhale, co. Stafford, armiger; John Nowers, of Takley, co. Oxon, armiger; and William Brounyng, of Saresdene, co. Oxon, armiger. A postscript states that on that day Thomas Stanley, knight, returned that a jury had been assembled at Chester on the Tuesday after the Feast of the Epiphany, 30 H. VI, and had found that the said Robert Harecourt, on the Monday in question was in the King's prison in Chester Castle. It was therefore considered that the outlawry promulgated against him should be revoked and annulled, but that he should answer to the appeal arraigned against him by Humfrey Stafford, the brother and heir of the said Richard. *m.* 8 *Rex.*

Warwick. Process to annul the outlawry promulgated against the same Robert Harecourt for lying in wait at Coventry with a large body of men arrayed as for war, on the Wednesday before the Feast of Corpus Christi, 26 H. VI, and assaulting Humfrey Stafford, knight; Richard Beauchamp, armiger, and William Lye, John More, and other servants of the said Humfrey, at Coventre, and leaving the said Humfrey insensible and nearly dead and so that his life was despaired of; the proceedings are the same as in the last suit, and the outlawry was annulled on the same ground. *m.* 9 *Rex.*

Warw. Process to annul an outlawry of the same Robert, which had been promulgated against him for not appearing to answer the appeal of Humfrey Stafford, armiger, for the death of his brother Richard.

The plea of Hillary term, 27 H. VI, was put in, which stated that William Massy, of Stanton Harecourt, gentilman, John Slyndon, of the same place, yoman, John Hattefelde, of the same place, yoman, Roger Kyngesbury, of Tredyngton, co. Worcester, yoman, Robert Botley, of Stratford-upon-Avon, taillour, David Taillour, late of Wycombe, co. Bucks, taillour, and Joan Harecourt, late of Boseworth, co. Leicester, wedowe, alias Dame Joan Harecourt, of Boseworth, wedowe, with many others named, were attached by their bodies to answer the appeal of Humfrey Stafford, together with Robert Harecourt, late of Stanton Harcourt, knight, John Aleyn, of the same place, yoman, John Harecourt, late of Eccleshale, co. Stafford, armiger, John Farnlagh, alias Fernehalgh, late of Hulcote, co. Stafford, yoman; and many others named (who had not surrendered), for the death of Richard Stafford, his brother; and Humfrey stated that his brother Richard was in the peace of God and of the King at Coventry on the Wednesday before the Feast of Corpus Christi, 26 H. VI, when the said William, John and the others named who were present in Court, as well as the said Robert Harecourt, John Aleyn and the others named who had not surrendered, and whom he would have appealed for the same death if they had been present, feloniously laid in wait at the hour and place named, and Robert Harecourt, with a two-handed sword, had struck the said Richard on the head, causing a mortal wound of which he had died the same day; and the said William Massy had struck Richard with a two-handed sword on his left arm, causing a mortal wound; and Roger Kyngesbury had struck him with a sword on the head, causing a mortal wound; and Robert Botley had struck him with a two-handed sword on his right arm; and the said David had struck him in the back with an arm called a custelle, causing a mortal wound; and the said Hugh Taillour had struck him with a dagger in the stomach, causing a mortal wound; and he accused the others of aiding and abetting the felony, or knowingly receiving the principals after the felony had been committed.

Robert Harecourt now surrendered and was committed to the Marshalsea (the process was the same as in the previous suits), the outlawry was revoked and annulled, but he was to answer for the felonies arraigned against him elsewhere.[1] *m.* 34 *Rex.*

DE BANCO. HILLARY, 29 H. VI.

Staff. Ralph Basset, armiger, sued Sampson Meverel late of Throweley, knight, for a debt of 48 marks. Sampson did not appear, and the Sheriff was ordered to distrain and produce him on the Quindene of Easter Day. *m.* 19.

Staff. Humfrey Walker sued Sampson Meverell, late of Throweley, knight, and Isabella his wife for breaking into his close at Casterne, together with William Rufford of Grendon, clerk, William Londesdale of Throweley, laborer, Edmund Elton, of Assheburne, co. Derby, Robert Harryson of Calton, laborer, Thomas Throweley, late of Throweley, gentilman, and depasturing cattle *vi et armis* on his wheat and grass. None of the defendants appeared, and the Sheriff was ordered to distrain and produce them on the above date. *m.* 19, *dorso.*

Staff. Ralph Basset, armiger, sued Sampson Meverelle, late of Throweley, knight, and Isabella his wife, and John Beresford, of Beresford, gentilman, for breaking into his close at Blore, and carrying off 12 oxen and 12 cows, worth 20 marks, and for beating, wounding and illtreating his men and servants, so that he lost their services for a length of time. The defendants did not appear, and the Sheriff was ordered to distrain and produce them

[1] The feud between the two families of Stafford and Harecourt continued for many years, and Sir Robert Harecourt was eventually slain by the Staffords in 11 E. IV. At Michaelmas term, 11 E. IV, Margaret, late wife of Robert Harecourt, Kt., appealed William Stafford, the Bastard, of Grafton, in co. Worcester, Thomas Stafford, late of Grafton, armiger, Humphrey Stafford, late of Grafton, armiger, Richard Leveson, late of Wolverhampton, armiger, John Salford and Richard Salford, late of Wolverhampton, gentilmen, Henry Hancokes, late of Compton in Tetenhall, yoman, Hugh Molle, late of Codsale, yoman, and about 150 others, 16 of whom are described as of Wolverhampton, for the death of her husband, William Stafford; John Schaylle, late of Evesham, and Richard Reynold, late of Kedemynster, were appealed as principals, and the others as accessories.

Sir Robert Harecourt was a Knight of the Garter and high in the King's favor. In 4 E. IV, the King had granted to him for his great and laudable services at the Siege of Alnewick, and for the custody of the said castle afterwards, a sum of £300 ('Pell Issues' 4 E. IV, No. 495).

on the above date. A postscript states that on that day the Sheriff made no return to the writ, and he was ordered to distrain and produce them on the Octaves of Holy Trinity. *m.* 849, *dorso.*

Staff. John Bermyngham, clerk, the Dean of the King's Free Chapel of Wolvernehampton, sued William Taillour of Wolvernehampton to render an account for the time he was his Bailiff in Wolvernehampton. William did not appear, and the Sheriff was ordered to arrest and produce him on the Quindene of Easter day. *m.* 164, *dorso.*

Staff. John Burghton sued Richard Oles of Chorleton, husbondman, Richard Chelton, of Chorleton, husbondman, Stephen Bromley of Chorleton, husbondman, William Chelton, James Bowelond, John Lysotte, all of Chorleton, husbondmen, and Richard Chesterton, of Pedmore, husbondman, for breaking into his closes at Burghton and Pedmore and cutting and carrying away turf to the value of 40*s.* and for destroying the roots of his wood in the same places with their cattle. None of the defendants appeared, and the Sheriff was ordered to arrest and produce them on the above date. *m.* 239.

Staff. William Frebody sued John Haukes, of Westbromwych, husbondman, for breaking into his close at Westbromwych and cutting down his trees and underwood. John did not appear, and the Sheriff was ordered to arrest and produce him on the above date. *m.* 246.

Staff. Richard Vernon, late of London, knight, was attached at the suit of William Burley, and Thomas Lyttelton, for entering by force into the manor of Cubleston, which William Trussell, knight, had demised to them for a term, and ejecting them *vi et armis*, and the plaintiffs stated that William Trussell, on the vigil of Michaelmas, 25 H. VI, had conveyed the manor to them for a term of 10 years, and they had occupied it until the said Richard on the 6th August, 28 H. VI, had entered the manor and ejected them *vi et armis*, for which they claimed 500 marks damages.

Richard denied having used any force, and stated that he had arraigned an assize of novel disseisin against the said William Trussell, respecting his freehold in Kybbylston, Acton and Hales before Richard Byngham and other Justices, assigned to take assizes at Tuttebury at Mich. 27 H. VI, in which he had complained that the said William had unjustly desseised him of 100 messuages, 30 tofts, 3 water mills, 60 carucates, 30 virgates and a half of land, 400 acres of meadow, 400 acres of wood, 400 acres of pasture, and £20 of rent, and which messuages tofts, etc., formed the manor of Cublestone and the said assize had remained over till the following Easter. (*Here the former proceedings are detailed at length until a verdict was given for Richard by which he had recovered the manor and had occupied it according to the judgment of the Court.*)

The plaintiffs stated that they should not be precluded from their action because William Trussell had not unjustly disseised Richard Vernon of the tenements, and they appealed to a jury, which was to be summoned for the Quindene of Easter Day. A postscript shews that at Easter term a writ of *nisi prius* was issued, transfering the suit to be heard at Stafford, on the Friday after the Feast of St. James, when Richard made default and a verdict was delivered in favor of the plaintiffs, and their damages were assessed at £100. And as the Justices wished to consult respecting the effect of the two judgments before execution, the case was adjourned to Westminster on the Octaves of St. Hillary, 30 H. VI. No judgment had been delivered up to Michaelmas 31 H. VI. *m.* 303.

Staff. Roger Homersley sued Thomas Stele, of Salt, husbondman, for breaking into his close at Salt, and taking goods and chattels belonging to him to the value of 40*s*. Thomas did not appear, and the Sheriff was ordered to arrest and produce him on the Quindene of Easter Day. A postscript states that on that day the Sheriff made no return, and he was ordered to produce him on the Octaves of St. Michael. *m.* 306.

Wygorn. A writ of *capias* addressed to the Sheriff of co. Worcester to arrest Humfrey Stafford, late of Grafton, knight, Thomas Bordel, of Arowe, armiger, Humfrey Stafford, late of Grafton, armiger, Richard Beauchamp, of Grafton, gentilman, John Aldeberd of Pershore, gentilman, John More, alias Jenyn More, of Bromsgrove, gentilman, Thomas Clarendon, late of Cokhill, Hanbury, gentilman, John Seye, alias William Sye, late of Grafton, gentilman, and upwards of 90 others, described as yomen of Bromsgrove, Evesham and other places in Worcestershire, and to produce them before the Kings Justices assigned to hear and determine divers felonies and trespasses at Oxford on the Monday the Feast of St. Anne, to answer for divers felonies of which they had been indicted. And if they could not be found within his bailiwick to cause public proclamation to be made summoning them to appear before the said Justices on the date named. Dated from Oxford, 9th Jan., 29 H. VI.

Staff. Thomas Ferrers of Tamworth, the elder, armiger, was attached, at the suit of Humfrey Duke of Buckingham, for beating, wounding and illtreating his men and servants at Tamworth, together with Thomas Ferrers, late of Tamworth, the younger, armiger, John Ferrers, late of Tanworth, armiger, and five others named, and the Duke by his attorney stated that on the Saturday before the Feast of St. Mathew, 28 H. VI the defendants had beaten and wounded his servants, Richard Emme and Hugh Colman, at Tamworth, so that out of fear of death or mutilation of their limbs they had been unable to transact his business for 30 weeks or leave the enclosure of their houses, and for which he claimed £200 as damages.

Thomas Ferrers, the elder, appeared by attorney and denied the accusation, and stated that Hugh Colman was not a servant of the Duke. The Duke repeated his plea, and appealed to a jury which was to be summoned for three weeks from Easter Day. A postscript shows that the process was moved by writ of *nisi prius*, to be heard at Stafford on the Friday after the Feast of St. James, when a jury found that Thomas Ferrers was guilty of the trespass, and that Hugh Colman was the servant of the Duke, and they assessed the Duke's damages at £40, and his costs at £20; but as the Justices wished to consult respecting the effect of the verdict, the case was adjourned till Whitsuntide again. No judgment had been delivered up to Michaelmas, 31 H. VI. *m.* 325.

Staff. Edmund Vernon and Joan his wife, and Hugh Davenport and Margaret his wife, were summoned at the suit of John Cawardyne in a plea that whereas the said John, Edmund, Joan, Hugh, and Margaret held *pro indiviso* the manor of Maveseyn Rydware, and the advowson of the church of the same manor of the inheritance formerly belonging to Robert Mavesyn, knight, the grandfather of the said John, Joan, and Margaret, whose heirs they were; the said Edmund, Joan, Hugh, and Margaret would not permit a partition of the manor to be made between them; and John stated that whereas he and the said Edmund, Joan, Hugh, and Margaret held the manor and advowson of the said manor of the inheritance of the said Robert, grandfather of John, Joan, and Margaret, viz., father of Elizabeth, the mother of John; and of Margaret, the mother of the said Joan, and Margaret, those heirs they were, of which manor and advowson a moiety ought to belong to him in severalty, and another to the said Edmund, Joan, Hugh, and Margaret, so that each of them could approve of his purparty at his will; the defendants refused to permit a partition to be made according to the law and custom of the kingdom.

The defendants admitted the claim of John, and the Sheriff was ordered to go in person to the manor, taking with him twelve free and legal men of the vicinage; and on their oath, and in presence of the parties, if they wished to be present, to make a partition of the manor between them, so that a moiety might be assigned to the said John Cawardyn as his purparty, to be held by him in severalty, and another moiety be assigned to the said Edmund, Joan, Hugh, and Margaret, as the purparty of the said Joan and Margaret, to be held also in severalty; and to return the inquisition into court on the Octaves of Holy Trinity. A postscript shews that the Sheriff had made no return up to Michaelmas, 31 H. VI.[1] *m.* 355.

Wygorn. Thomas Lyttylton sued in person John Kampage and Thomas Swyney for two parts of three messuages in Worcester, and which, together with a third part of the same messuages which one William Pullesdon had held (and who had made default of appearance at a previous hearing), they had no entry except by one Robert Nelme, who had unjustly disseised Thomas Heuster, the father of Thomas Lyttylton, and whose heir he was.

The defendants appeared by attorney and defended the suit, and asked for an adjournment to the Quindene of Easter Day, which was granted. A postscript shews another adjournment up to the Octaves of St. Michael. *m.* 376 *dorso.*

CORAM REGE. Easter, 29 H. VI.

Staff. The appeal of Agnes, late wife of John Taillour, against John Beresford, of Beresford, gentilman, for the death of her husband, was respited till the Quindene of St. Michael, unless the King's Justices assigned to take the assizes in the county should first come to Stafford on the Friday after the Feast of St. James. *m.* 29.

Staff. Fines and Amercements:—

From John Cokayne, of Assheburne, armiger, as a fine for a trespass committed against Ralph Bassel, armiger, *vi et armis*, and against the King's peace, of which he had been convicted *coram Rege* by authority of the Act of Parliament passed at Leicester. 100*s*.

From William Cokayne, of Assheburne, gentilman, for the same 40*s*.; eighteen others were fined from 30 to 40*s*. each for the same trespass.

Staff. From John Cokayne, of Assheburne, armiger, as a fine on the occasion of divers trespasses, riots, insurrections, and conspiracies, of which he had been indicted, and on which he had put himself on the King's grace. 40*s*.

From William Cokayne, of Assheburne, gentilman, for the same, 2 marks. Fifty others were fined 1 mark each for the same trespass.

[1] See suits at pp. 149 and 151 of this volume. The descent from Sir Robert Mauveisin is shown to be as follows:—

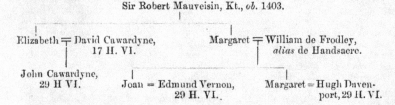

Sir Robert Mauveisin, Kt., *ob.* 1403.

Elizabeth = David Cawardyne, 17 H. VI. — Margaret = William de Frodley, *alias* de Handsacre.

John Cawardyne, 29 H VI. — Joan = Edmund Vernon, 29 H. VI. — Margaret = Hugh Davenport, 29 H. VI.

DE BANCO. MICH., 30 H. VI.

Staff. Margaret, late wife of Roger Swynshed, and Thomas Swyneshed, the executors of the will of Roger Swyneshed, sued Thomas Pykkyn, late of Mere, yoman, for taking by force goods and chattels belonging to them to the value of 40*s.* Thomas Pykkyn did not appear, and the Sheriff was ordered to arrest and produce him on the Quindene of St. Hillary. *m.* 19, *dorso.*

Staff. James Lee, armiger, sued John Page, late of Aston, near Stone, for breaking into his close at Aston, near Stone, and so threatening his men and servants that, for fear of their lives, they had given up their tenancies and service. John did not appear, and the Sheriff was ordered to arrest and produce him on the Octaves of St. Hillary. *m.* 19, *dorso.*

Staff. Richard Curson, armiger, sued John Wright, of Barre, in the parish of Allerwych (Aldridge), carpenter, for breaking into his close and houses at Alrewas. John did not appear, and the Sheriff was ordered to arrest and produce him on the above date. *m.* 167.

Staff. John Jolyff sued John Freman, late of Lychefeld, chaplain, for taking by force goods and chattels belonging to him from Lychefeld to the value of £20 and £20 in money. The defendant did not appear, and the Sheriff was ordered to arrest and produce him on the Octaves of St. Martin. *m.* 167.

Staff. John Lone sued John Fyssher, of Wolvernehampton, to render a reasonable account for the time he was the receiver of his monies. The defendant did not appear, and the Sheriff was ordered to arrest and produce him on the Quindene of St. Hillary. *m.* 389, *dorso.*

Staff. William Rugge, of Rugge, co. Salop, gentilman, was attached at the suit of Roger Rugge, of Seysdon and Henry Rugge, of Brereton, for taking by force goods and chattels belonging to them at Tresulle on the 10th August, 29 H. VI, viz., six cartloads of wheat and ten cartloads of rye (*siliginis*). William stated that the plaintiffs could not maintain the action against him because they were villein tenants of his manor of Rugge in co. Stafford (*sic*). The plaintiffs replied that they were freemen, and appealed to a jury which was to be summoned for the Octaves of St. Martin. A postscript shews that the suit was removed by writ of *nisi prius*, to be heard before the Justices of Assize on the Friday after the Feast of St. James at Lychefeld, when a jury found in favour of the plaintiffs, stating that they were of free condition and not villein tenants of William, and they assessed their damages and costs at 20*s.* The plaintiffs subsequently remitted their damages. *m.* 408.

Staff. Roger Draycote, armiger, sued Richard Felip, of Teyne, yoman, William Pakeman, of Teyne, yoman, Richard Rawelyn, of Teyne, husbondman, Richard Birkys, of Teyne, husbondman, John Grene, of Teyne, husbondman, Thomas Broune, of Teyne, husbondman, John Felip, of Teyne, husbondman, John Torkynton, of Teyne, yoman, and Margaret Buknalle, of Teyne, wedowe, for forcibly depasturing cattle on his corn and grass at Teyne, and causing damage to the amount of £10. The defendants did not appear, and the Sheriff returned they held nothing within his bailiwick by which they could be attached; he was therefore ordered to arrest and produce them on the Octaves of St. Hillary. *m.* 470.

Staff. John Knyght sued Richard Collettys, of Billerbroke, husbandman, for breaking into his close at Billerbroke, and taking three oxen, worth 60*s*. Richard did not appear, and the Sheriff was ordered as in the last suit. *m.* 471, *dorso.*

Staff. William Aldewynkylle, John Grysley, armiger, and John Curson, armiger, executors of the will of Elena, formerly wife of John Holand, knight, executrix of the will of John Holand, knight, sued William Rokeby, late of Erith in co. Hunts, yoman, for a debt of £40. The defendant did not appear, and the Sheriff was ordered to arrest and produce him on the Quindene of St. Hillary. *m.* 532, *dorso.*

Staff. John Littelton and Joan, his wife; William Leg and Margaret, his wife; William Ruggeley and Alice, his wife; William Trussell, the younger, and John Brace sued Richard Vernon, late of London, knight, and John Chapman, of Sherevehales, yoman, in a plea that whereas it had been ordained in the Parliament of 5 Ric. II, that no one should make an entry into any lands or tenements except in cases when entry was given by law, by main force (*manu forte*), nor with a multitude of men; the said John Chapman, together with the said Richard, who was now dead, had entered into a moiety of the manor of Sherevehales, when no entry had been given to them by law, to the contempt of the King and to the great injury of the plaintiffs. The defendants did not appear, and the Sheriff now returned that Richard Vernon was dead, and that the said John Chapman could not be found. He was therefore ordered to arrest and produce the said John on the Quindene of St. Hillary. *m.* 535.

DE BANCO. MICH. 31, H. VI.

Staff. Robert Cuny (Coyney), armiger, sued Thomas Buknale of Buknale, yoman, for taking by force 5 oxen belonging to him, worth 5 marks, from Dylryne (Dilhorn). Thomas did not appear, and the Sheriff was ordered to arrest and produce him on the Octaves of the Purification. *m.* 19, *dorso.*

Staff. It appeared from the Roll of Hillary term, 30 H. VI, *m.* 352, that William Ballard, parson of the church of Swynerton, had been summoned by Thomas, the prior of the Monastery of St. Wolphad the Martyr, of Stone, in a plea that he should render to the Priory 9 marks, the arrears of an annual rent of 40*s*., and the prior appeared in person and stated that he and his predecessors from time out of memory had been seised of the said rents by the hands of the parson of the church of Swynerton. William appeared by attorney, and stated that he had found the parson of the church exonerated from the said rent at the date of his institution, and he could not charge the church with it without the consent of Humfrey Swynarton, the patron, and of William, the Bishop of Coventry and Lichfield, the ordinary, and he asked for the assistance of the Court to compel the attendance of the said patron and ordinary, and a day was given to the parties in the Quindene of Easter Day, and the Sheriff was ordered to summon the patron and ordinary for that date. And the process had been continued till this term, when the patron and ordinary, being solemnly called, put in no appearance, and it was therefore considered that the said William should defend the action, and he then pleaded that the Prior and Convent had not been seised of the annual rent continuously, and appealed to a jury which was to be summoned for the Quindene of St. Hillary. *m.* 119.

Derb. Nicholas Fitzherbert, armiger, sued John Bothe, armiger, for the manor of Asshe, which Thomas, son of William fitz Herbert, of Somersalle, had given to William fitz Herbert, of Norbury, and Edeka his wife, and to the heirs of the bodies of William and Edeka his wife, and which should descend to him by the form of gift, and he gave this descent.

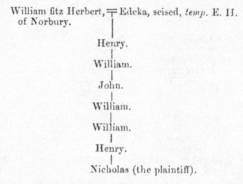

William fitz Herbert, of Norbury. = Edeka, seised, *temp.* E. II.
|
Henry.
|
William.
|
John.
|
William.
|
William.
|
Henry.
|
Nicholas (the plaintiff).

John Bothe admitted the claim, and Nicholas was to recover seisin.

N.B.—The above pedigree is taken from the original writ, but there is a discrepancy between it and the "narratio" of the suit, thus the latter states "Et de ipsis Willelmo filio Herberti de Norbury et Edeka descendit jus etc. cuidam Henrico ut filio et heredi. Et de ipso Henrico descendit jus etc. cuidam Willelmo ut filio et heredi. Et de ipso Willelmo descendit jus etc. cuidam Johanni ut filio et heredi. Et de ipso Johanne descendit jus etc. cuidam Willelmo ut filio et heredi. Et de ipso Willelmo filio Willelmi filii Johannis descendit jus etc. cuidam Henrico ut filio et heredi. Et de ipso Henrico filio ejusdem Willelmi filii Willelmi descendit jus etc. isti Nicholao qui nunc petit ut filio et heredi."[1] *m.* 333.

Staff. Ralph Basset, armiger, and William Beck, clerk, were summoned at the suit of John Etryngham, the Master of the House of the College of St. Michael of Cambridge, in a plea that they should permit him to present a fit person to the church of Chedele (Cheadle), which was vacant, and he stated that one Henry Granby, late master of the House, had been

[1] Owing to this discrepancy I referred the question of the pedigree to Major Fitz Herbert of the Hall, Somersal Herbert, and he informs me that "the pedigree should undoubtedly run as follows: William, Henry, John, William, William, Henry, Nicholas. There are many authorities which shew that John was son of Henry and not of William. Perhaps the most decisive is to be found in the 'Placita de Quo warranto' of 4 E. III. John was summoned to prove his right to free warren. He stated that King Henry, great grandfather of the present king had granted free warren to William FitzHerbert of Norbury, his grandfather, and to his heirs for ever, and from William the right descended to Henry as son and heir, and from Henry to himself as son and heir.

"The original grant of free warren was dated 4th September, 36 H. III, and included free warren in Ash."

Major Fitz Herbert likewise gives the following dates, which may help to throw light on the pedigree:

Thomas Fitz Herbert of Somersal was lord of Twycross in 1240, and was dead before 1279.

William Fitz Herbert was Sheriff of co. Derby in 1264, and his son Henry acted under him as Sub-Sheriff.

seised of the advowson, as in right of his House, and had presented to it one William Yewdale, who had been admitted and instituted in the time of King Henry, the grandfather of the King, and the church was now vacant by his resignation, and the said Ralph and William Beek, unjustly impeded his presentation, for which he claimed £100 as damages.

The defendants pleaded that the church was not vacant, it having been filled by the said William Beek, on the presentation of Ralph, and William had been in full possession for six months before the Master's writ had been issued.

The Master denied that the church had been filled for six months before the issuing of his writ, which was dated 23rd March, 30 H. VI, and offered to prove this in any way the Court thought fit. As the question belonged to the ecclesiastical courts, it was referred to the Bishop of Coventry and Lichfield, who was requested to return on the Quindene of St. Martin, whether the church had been filled for six months or not, before the issue of the Master's writ, on which date the parties appeared, and it was shewn that the Bishop had died on the Saturday the Feast of St. Katrine in this term, upon which the Master prayed for a writ to J. the Archbishop of Canterbury and Primate of All England, which was granted and made returnable on the Quindene of St. Hillary.

A postscript states that on that date Ralph Basset and William Beek relinquished their plea, and judgment was given in favour of the Master. The Master then asked that his damages might be assessed, and a writ was sent to the Sheriff commanding him to return the amount of damage at a month from Easter. A further postscript shews that the Sheriff had made no return to the writ up to Michaelmas term, 33 H. VI. *m.* 447.

Staff. John Hampton, armiger, sued William Lowe, of Enfeld, armiger, to give up to him two bonds which he unjustly detained. William did not appear, and the Sheriff was ordered to attach him for the Octaves of St. Hillary. *m.* 477 *dorso.*

Staff. Beatrice, late wife of John Tytley, sued John Ecton, of Blore, husbondman, for breaking into her close at Whyternehurst, and depasturing cattle on her corn and grass. John did not appear, and the Sheriff was ordered to arrest and produce him on the Quindene of St. Hillary. *m.* 478.

Staff. In the suit of John Cawardyn versus Edmund Vernon, and Joan his wife, and Hugh Davenport, and Margaret his wife, the Sheriff returned into Court the partition of the manor of Rydeware Mauvesyn, which had been made between the parties, excepting the advowson of the church and the mill. The partition had been made by Thomas Asteleye, the Sheriff, on the 12th May, 30 H. VI. The site of the manor house and park was assigned to John Cawardyne. The Sheriff's return covers both sides of the membrane, and contains a great number of local names. *m.* 412.

Leys. Edward Gray, knight, sued John Gresley, late of Drakelowe, co. Derby, armiger, and Senchia Curson, late of Croxhale, co. Derby, wedowe, for abducting from Lutterworth, Thomas Curson, son and heir of John Curson, who was under age, and whose marriage belonged to him. The defendants did not appear, and the Sheriff had been ordered to distrain John and to arrest the said Senchia, and to make enquiry respecting the heir. And the Sheriff now returned he had distrained John by his chattels to the amount of 40*d.* and that neither Senchia nor John Curson could be found within his bailiwick. He was therefore ordered to arrest Senchia if she could be found, and to produce the defendants on the Quindene of St. Hillary. *m.* 425.

Staff. John Hampton, armiger, alias John Hampton, armiger, *pro corpore Regis*[1] sued John Attewode, of Codsale, yoman, for a debt of £14. The defendant did not appear, and Sheriff returned he held nothing, etc. He was therefore ordered to arrest and produce him on the Quindene of St. Hillary. *m.* 478.

CORAM REGE. MICH., 31 H. VI.

Staff. An assize of novel disseisin arraigned by Richard Vernun, knight, against William Trussell, knight, respecting tenements in Kybbylstone, Acton, and Hales, was brought before the Court on an appeal by William Trussell against William Vernon, armiger, the son and heir of the said Richard.

The Record of the former assize, taken at Tuttebury in 27 H. VI, was read as before, and William then took exception to the writ on a technical point, pleading he was not tenant of the tenements named at the date of the original writ of attaint, and if that point was given against him, he pleaded that the jury of the assize had given a good and legal verdict, and he put himself on a jury of 24. The Sheriff was therefore ordered to summon a jury of 24, for the morrow of All Souls. A postscript shews that no jury had been assembled up to Michaelmas, 34 H. VI. *m.* 35.

Staff. A writ of replevin addressed to the Sheriff commanded him to return the cattle of Humfrey Walker, which had been unjustly taken by Richard Bagot, armiger, dated 20th June, 30 H. VI, and if Humfrey entered into securities to prosecute his claim he was to summon the said Richard to appear in Court on the morrow of the Purification, to answer for the unjust detention of the cattle.

A postscript shews that on that date the Sheriff made no return to the writ, and it was testified that Richard was the Sheriff "*datum est curie hic intelligi, quod predictus Ricardus Bagot est Vicecomes Comitatus predicti, per quod idem Humfridus de deliberatione catallorum suorum et responseo in hac parte habendo multipliciter retardatus extitit.*" The Sheriff was therefore ordered as before, but no return was made to the writ up to Trinity term, 32 H. VI, when the record terminates. *m.* 43.

Oxon. It had been presented in 28 H. VI at Wodestock, before Dru Barantyne, William Marmyon, and John Ledeyard, Justices of the Peace, that whereas Humfrey Stafford, of Grafton, in co. Wygorm, knight, and Thomas Bordet, of Arowe, in the same county, armiger, with the purpose of killing and murdering Robert Harecourt, knight, had assembled together with Richard Becham (Beauchamp), of Grafton, gentilman, and upwards of 100 more named, and several other malefactors and disturbers of the peace to the number of at least 300, armed and harnessed in manner of war, on the Friday before the Feast of the Invention of the Holy Cross, 28 H. VI, at Felde, within the forest of Whichwode, co. Oxon, by the abetment or procurement of the said Humfrey Stafford, and Thomas Bordet, and from thence had gone by night to the manor of Robert Harecourt, called Staunton Harecourt, and at the break of day following had attacked the said Robert and his servants whilst at their devotions, and had driven them into the church tower of Staunton Harecourt, when perceiving that they could not draw the said Robert from the tower owing to its strength they had besieged the church and the village of Staunton Harecourt with a great

[1] John Hampton, of Stourton, was an Esquire in the Household of the King. At this date they were called Esquires of the Body of the King.

army for six hours, and had shot more than 1,000 arrows at the said Robert, proclaiming that unless he left the tower they would burn the church and him within it, and because Robert refused to do this they had burnt a great part of the church, by which the crucifix on the altar and other ornaments of the church had been completely destroyed; and then, finding they could not kill the said Robert, they robbed him of 7 horses, each worth 40*s.*, and of saddles and bridles and other chattels worth £40, and had beaten, wounded and illtreated his servants William Massy, William Dely, and Matthew Sawyer.

It had also been presented that whereas Humfrey Stafford, late of Grafton, co. Wygorm, knight, Thomas Burdet, of Arowe, co. Wygorm, armiger, Humfrey Stafford, of Grafton, armiger, Richard Beauchamp, of Grafton, co. Worcester, gentilman, Thomas Clarendon, late of Cokhill Hanbury, co. Worcester, gentilman, and more than 100 others named with many other malefactors and disturbers of the peace had assembled at le Felde, in the forest of Whichewode (etc. as before), with a view of killing and murdering Robert Harecourt, knight.

Then follows the coroner's inquest on the body of William Massy, who had been killed, it was stated, by one John Monke on the same occasion, who had wounded him with an arrow in the right thigh, and owing to which wound the said William had languished from the Saturday till the following 8th June, on which day he died.

Then follows the proceedings of a special Commission, consisting of Richard Byngham, Dru Barantyn, William Marmyon, and others to enquire into certain riots and trespasses within co. Oxon, committed by Humfrey Grafton son and heir of Humfrey Stafford, of Grafton, knight, and which sat at Oxford on the Wednesday after the Feast of St. Fides, 29 H. VI, before which it was presented that Humfrey Stafford, of Grafton, son and heir of Humfrey Stafford, of Grafton, knight, John Trussell, late of Byllisley, co. Warwick, armiger, Richard Beauchamp, late of Grafton, co. Worcester, gentilman, and upwards of 60 others named, with many others to the number of more than 200 men had assembled in manner of war at Feld in the forest of Wykelwode, co. Oxon, by the procurement of Thomas Burdet, and (*etc., as before, but with the addition of a detailed list of the household goods and chattels of Robert Harecourt which had been taken, and which is very curious*) and which indictments the King for certain causes had commanded to be brought up and terminated in his Court.

And at this term the said Humfrey Stafford, armiger, John More, alias Jenyn More, William Fyton, John Monke and 16 others of the defendants appeared, and surrendered and were committed to the Marshalsea, and being brought before the Court they produced Letters Patent by which the King had pardoned them, and which were dated 23rd November, 29 H. VI. *m.* 3 *Rex.*

Staff. The Sheriff was ordered to put into the *exigend* William Trussell, knight, and if he did not appear to outlaw him; and if he appeared to produce him coram Rege to answer for his redemption and fine for a disseisin of Richard Vernon, knight, of tenements in Kibbelstone, Acton, and Hales. *m.* 20 *Rex.*

Derb. It had been presented before John Rolstone, one of the coroners of the county, on the vigil of Xmas, 28 H. VI, at Assheburne, on a view of the body of Thomas Mane that David Trigg, late of Blore, in co. Stafford, laborer, together with Philip Okove, late of Blore, armiger, Richard Basset, late of Blore, gentilman, Thomas Hochynes, late of Blore, yoman, Ralph Philyp, late of Mapulton, co. Derby, yoman, William Webster, of Ilom, John Torald, of Ilom, husbondman, Oliver Dethyk, late of Blore, yoman, John Suthworth, vicar of Ilom, Thomas Pyott, of Chedulle Grange, yoman,

John Shelton of Blore, yoman, William Aleyn, late of Blore, servant, Henry Forde, late of Blore, yoman, Henry Lorde, of Caldon, yoman, and 40 others named, on the Saturday the Feast of St. Nicholas, 28 H. VI, armed and arrayed in manner of war, with bows and arrows, swords, jakkes, palets, daggers and other arms, had assaulted the said Thomas Mane at Mapulton, co. Derby, and the said David had shot him with an arrow on the left thigh, causing a mortal wound of which he had died on the Tuesday before Xmas following, and that the others had been present aiding and abetting the felony, and which Indictment the King for certain causes had commanded to be brought up and terminated in this Court.

And David Trigg now surrendered and was committed to the Marshalsea, and being brought up before the Court he produced the King's pardon, dated 23rd June, 30 H. VI, for the said felony, and having found sureties to keep the peace, he was discharged, and it was ordered that the process against the other defendants should cease. *m.* 32 *Rex.*

Staff. The Sheriff was ordered to put into *exigend* William Cokkayne, of Asshebourne, co. Derby, gentilman, John Sherard, of Wetton, yoman, and seven others named, and if they did not appear to outlaw them, and if they appeared to produce them *coram Rege* at a month from Easter day and to make their fine and redemption on account of their trespass and contempt both against Philip Oker and the King, committed against the Statute, "*de malefactoribus in parcis et warrennis.*" *m.* 26 *Rex, dorso.*

Staff. Derb. It had been presented in the week of Pentecost, 29 H. VI, at Stafford before Sampson Meverell, knight, Justice of the Peace, that John Stathom, late of Throwley, co. Stafford, yoman, John Fychet of the same place, laborer, and Thomas Wyder of the same place, laborer, on the Friday before the Feast of St. Barnabas, 25 H. VI, had feloniously taken at Blore 12 oxen worth £8 and 12 cows worth £6, of the goods and chattels of Ralph Basset, armiger, and that John Beresford of Beresford, co. Stafford, gentilman, and John Staley, late of Throwley, yoman, on the same day had aided and abetted and knowingly received them afterwards.

It had also been presented before John Curson and John Tunsted, Justices of the Peace at Benreper, on the Monday before the Feast of the Purification, 26 H. VI, that Sampson Meverell, late of Tiddeswall, co. Derby, knight, John Staley of Tiddeswalle, yoman, on the Sunday before the Feast of the Conversion of St. Paul, 26 H. VI, at Thorp, with many other malefactors unknown, to the number of at least 40 persons, had riotously laid in wait, armed with jakkes, salets, swords, bows and arrows, and with long "*rostris*" to kill John Southworth, vicar of Ilum, and had assaulted, etc. (as before).

It had also been presented on the Thursday in the week of Easter, 27 H. VI, at Stafford, before John Harpur and his fellow Justices of the Peace, that Thomas Meverell, late of Throweley, co. Stafford, gentilman, and others, on the Feast of St. Laurence, 26 H. VI, had laid in wait at Huntley, in co. Stafford, in order to kill John Taillour, and had assaulted and feloniously killed him. And it had been also presented, on a view of the body of John Taillour of Huntley, on the Feast of St. Laurence, 26 H. VI, before Thomas Lokwode, one of the Coroners of the County at Chedulle, that William Londesdale, late of Throweley, yoman, James Mellour of Hope, yoman, Richard Lout of Stansop, laborer, and Robert Starke, late of Fossebroke, yoman, had laid in waite on the above day and place, and that William Londesdale had struck the said John Taillour with a staff on the head, causing a mortal wound of which he had died, etc. (as before), and that Thomas Meverell, late of Throweley, gentilman, and John Beresford, late of Beresford, the younger, had knowingly received the said William Londesdale, Richard Lout, and Robert Starke at Chedulle after the felony. And it had also been presented (here follow two other indictments against John

Staley, John Stathom and others for stealing cattle, and which Indictments the King had commanded to be brought into this Court to be terminated, and John Beresford, John Staley, Sampson Meverell and Thomas Meverell now appeared and surrendered and were committed to the Marshalsea, and being brought before the Court, they produced Letters Patent of the King pardoning them for the above offences, dated 30 October, 31 H. VI. *m.* 8 *Rex, dorso.*

Staff. It had been presented at Stafford in 28 H. VI, before Sampson Meverell, knight, and his fellow Justices of the Peace that John Broun, late of Coldenorton, in co. Stafford, armiger, on the 5th December, 25 H. VI, had fabricated at Stone a false deed, which purported that William Mosse, Parson, of Langport, Walter Swan, Parson, of Pembrigge, and Robert Say, Parson, of Eton, had remitted and quitclaimed to Fulk Pembrigge, knight, all their right and claim in the manor of Cublestone and Acton and a moiety of the manor of Hales, with a view of disturbing and destroying the possession and title of William Trussell, knight, in the said manors. And which Indictment the King had commanded to be brought up to be terminated in this Court.

And John Broun now surrendered and stated he was not guilty, and appealed to a jury, which was to be summoned for the morrow of St. Martin. A postscript shews that the process was continued till Michaelmas, 32 H. VI, when it was moved to be heard by the Justices of assize on the Friday after the Feast of St. James at Lichefeld, when a jury found that he was not guilty. *m.* 1 *Rex, dorso.*

CORAM REGE. EASTER, 31 H. VI.

Staff. The Venerable Father in Christ J. Cardinal and Archbishop of Canterbury delivered with his own hands into Court the following Record of a suit in his Chancery.

Pleas before the King in Chancery, 30th November, 30 H. VI. It appeared by an Inquisition taken at Penkridge, co. Stafford, 20th October, 30 H. VI, before Thomas Bate, late the King's Escheator, that Thomas Hawton was formerly seised of the manor of Derlaston, near Stone, which was worth 4 marks, and 84 acres of land, 8 acres of meadow, 10 acres of wood, and 16 acres of waste, in Annysley, in co. Stafford, in his demesne, as of fee, which were worth annually 20*s.*, and died so seised, leaving no issue. And after his death the said manor and tenements descended to one John Hawton, his brother and heir, and that the said John was a natural idiot "*fatuus naturalis*," in consequence of which the custody of the said manor and tenements belonged to the King during the idiotcy of the said John, and which Inquisition was returned into Chancery for certain reasons.

Upon which, viz., on the 30th November of this term, Richard Fyton, armiger, appeared in Court and stated that under cover of the above Inquisition, he had been removed and expelled from the tenements, and they had been unjustly taken into the King's hands; and he stated that the said Thomas Hawton had been seised of them in demesne as of fee, under the name of Thomas de Howeton, son of William de Howeton, of Derlaston, near Stone, and had enfeoffed in them in 5 H. VI, Hugh Erdeswyk, armiger, Robert Marchall, of Aston near Stone, and William Clerk, of Stone, and Robert Marchall had died; and the said Hugh and William survived him, and were seised of the tenements *per jus accrescendi*, and whilst so seised the said Hugh had enfeoffed Laurence

Fyton, knight, John Duncalf, and John Bosdon, clerks, and the said William Clerk, by a deed dated on the Saturday after the Feast of the Annunciation, 11 H. VI, had released and quitclaimed all his right in the same tenements to the same Laurence, John Duncalf and John Bosdon, under the name of the manor of Derlaston, near Stone, and all his lands and tenements, rents and services in Derlaston and Annysley, co. Stafford; and John Bosdon died so seised, and after his death the said Laurence and John Duncalf held the manor and tenements "*per jus accrescendi*," and whilst so seised had enfeoffed Robert Hewester, Parson, of Boseworth, and the said Robert whilst seised of them by his deed dated on the Monday after the Feast of St. George, 22 H. VI, had demised the tenements to the said Laurence for his life with remainder after his death to the said Richard Fyton, son of Laurence Fyton, and to the heirs male of his body, and failing such, to the right heirs of the said Laurence. And the said Laurence being so seised had surrendered to Richard Fyton all his *status* in the said manor and lands, by virtue of which surrender Richard Fyton was seised of them in his demesne as of fee tail, and was in peaceable possession of them until he had been removed by virtue of the above Inquisition, and he prayed that the King's hand might be removed.

Upon which William Notyngham, the King's attorney, stated that Thomas Hawton had died seised of the said manor and tenements, and asked that the truth might be enquired into by a jury. The Sheriff of co. Stafford was therefore commanded to summon a jury of 24, to appear *coram Rege* on the Quindene of Easter. A postscript states that the process was adjourned to Michaelmas, 32 H. VI, unless the Justices of Assize should first come to Lychefeld on the Friday after the Feast of St. James, on which day a jury found a verdict that the said Thomas Hawton did not die seised of the said manor and tenements as alleged by the King's attorney. It was therefore considered that the King's hand should be removed, and that Richard Fyton should be restored to the possession of the tenements, with all issues and profits from the date when they had been taken into the King's hands. *m.* 34 *Rex.*

Staff. The Sheriff was ordered to put into the *exigend* Agnes, late wife of John Hert, and if she did not appear to "*waive*" her, and if she appeared, to produce her upon the Octaves of St. Martin to make her fine and redemption with the King, for not prosecuting her appeal against John Bromley, of Burton-upon-Trent, karver, and others for the death of her husband. *m.* 19 *Rex, dorso.*

Staff. The same process was followed in the case of Joan, late wife of William Couper, who had not followed up her appeal against Ralph Hanley, the Abbot of Burton-upon-Trent, and others for the death of her husband. *m.* 17 *Rex, dorso.*

DE BANCO. MICH., 32 H. VI.

Staff. Isabella Creghton, Prioress of the House of White Nuns, of Brewode, was sued by John Lone for unjustly taking his cattle. John did not appear and was plaintiff. The suit was therefore dismissed, and the cattle were to be restored to the Prioress. A postscript states that on the 23 October of this term, a writ was sent to John Stretehay, the Sub-Sheriff, to that effect, and that on the 24 January, 32 H. VI, John Lone appeared in Court and asked for a writ to the Sheriff (. . .) the delivery of the cattle, and it was granted to him returnable in the Quindene of Easter. A further postscript shews that no return to the latter writ had been made by the Sheriff up to Hillary term, 33 H. VI. *m.* 106, *dorso.*

Staff. John Stretehay recovered a messuage and 10 acres of land and 12 acres of pasture in Stretehay by a writ of formedon against William Forster—the latter making default. *m.* 149.

Staff. Aleanora, formerly wife of Humfrey Stafford, kt., recovered a third part of the manor of Chebsey as dower—a suit against Humfrey Stafford of Grafton, armiger—the latter making default. *m.* 149, *dorso.*

Staff. Thomas Stafford, clerk, sued William Beke, late of Lychefeld, chaplain, John Grene, of Theyne, yoman, and Thomas Walle, of Chedelle, yoman, for breaking into his close at Chedelle, and taking 50 lambs worth 40*s.* The defendants did not appear, and the Sheriff was ordered to arrest and produce them on the morrow of St. Martin. *m.* 150.

Staff. In the suit of Joan, formerly wife of William Mountfort, knight, against Baldwin Mountford, knight, and Joan, his wife, in which the first-named Joan claimed dower from lands in Walshale, Weddesbury, and Bescote. The Sheriff returned that the plaintiff had not found any sureties for the prosecution of the suit, and therefore nothing had been done in the matter. And Joan, formerly wife of William, now appeared in Court, and found the requisite sureties, viz., William Haloughton and William Slynt. The Sheriff was therefore ordered to summon the said Baldwin and Joan, his wife, for the Octaves of St. Martin. *m.* 150, *dorso.*

Staff. Nicholas Waryng, armiger, sued Thomas Cokkes, late of Stoke Priors, co. Stafford, and Isabella, his wife, late wife of Richard Frebody, for a debt of £39 19*s.* 4*d.* The defendants did not appear, and the Sheriff was ordered to arrest and produce them on the Quindene of St. Hillary. *m.* 180, *dorso.*

Staff. Thomas Pykkyn and Margery, his wife, sued John Chyderplawe, of London Glasyer, William Yeus, of Congreve, yoman, and Margery, his wife, and John de Rowelegh, of Woolstanton, husbondman, for a forcible entry into two messuages, 100 acres land, and 20 acres of meadow in Bydulf and Caverswalle against the statute of 5 Ric. II. The defendants did not appear, and the Sheriff was ordered to arrest and produce them on the morrow of St. Martin. *m.* 273.

Staff. Richard Wyneshurst sued John Bylston, of Wolvernehampton wever, Cecily Bereward, of Wulvernehampton, wydowe, and Thomas Tymiakulle, of Wulvernehampton, taillour, in a plea that in concord with Thomas Baker, of Wulvernehampton, baker, and Margaret, his wife, they had abducted Joan, his wife, from his house at Wulvernehampton with goods and chattels belonging to him. The defendants did not appear, and the Sheriff was ordered as in the last suit. *m.* 273, *dorso.*

Staff. William Wylde, the younger, sued Thomas Swynerton, late of Elmesthorpe in co. Leycester, yoman, for breaking into his close at Hales and taking four oxen worth 40*s.* Thomas did not appear, and the Sheriff was ordered to arrest and produce him on the Octaves of St. Martin. *m.* 274, *dorso.*

Staff. John Hasard, Richard Fox, Nicholas Offeley, Richard Grene, Nicholas Bernard, Roger Offeley, all described as of Hopton, husbondmen. John Carter, and William Hall, of Knyghtley, husbondmen, were attached at the suit of Richard the Prior of St. Thomas the Martyr, near Stafford, for breaking into the close of the Prior at Bromehurst, on the 7 June, 31 H. VI, for which he claimed £40 as damages.

The defendants stated that from time out of memory, there had been a high road through the middle of the close in question for all the King's lieges, either on foot or on horseback from the vill of Hopton to the vill of Stafford, until the Prior had put up a gate and fastened it with a lock, and they had broken open the gate and entered the close in order to pass through it as was lawful.

The Prior stated that he was seised in demesne as of fee in right of his Priory of the close, and from time out of memory there had been a footpath between the two vills above-named, but he and his predecessors had always fixed gates, and kept them locked for the enclosure of the close, excepting at the footpath where they had placed styles (*scansilia*) in the pathway for the convenience of persons passing that way. And a style existed at the date of the trespass of which he complained.

The defendants repeated their plea and appealed to a jury which was to be summoned for the Octaves of St. Martin. A postscript shews the process was moved by writ of *nisi prius*, to be heard at Stafford before the Justices of assize on the Monday after the Feast of St. James, 33 H. VI, when a jury found in favour of the Prior, stating that there was no right of way for horses through the close in question, and they assessed the Prior's damages at 13*s.* 4*d.* *m.* 315.

Staff. John Squyer, of Stircheley, co. Salop, yoman, was attached at the suit of Ralph Busshebury for breaking into his close at Wolvernehampton, and depasturing cattle on his grass on the Monday after the Feast of St. Andrew, 31 H. VI, for which he claimed £40 as damages. John stated that the close in question was the sole and free tenements of (blank), and he was acting as their servant. Ralph appealed to a jury what was to be summoned for the Octave of St. Hillary. A postscript shews no jury had been empanelled up to Easter, 34 H. VI. *m.* 350, *dorso.*

Staff. Amise, formerly wife of John Bowghey, sued James Bowghey, of Whitemore, gentilman, for a third of 24 messuages, 300 acres of land, and 200 acres of pasture in Whitemore, Bukenalle, Fenton, and Audesley (Audley), which she claimed as dower. James asked for an adjournment to the Quindene of St. Hillary, and a day was given to him on that date with the assent of Amise. A postscript shews that the suit was adjourned again to the Quindene of Easter Day. *m.* 413.

Staff. The Sheriff had been ordered to put into *exigend*, John Cokayne, of Asshebourne, armiger, and if he appeared to produce him at this term to answer Thomas Asteley, the Sheriff of co. Stafford in a plea of debt of 40*s.* And the Sheriff now returned that the said John had been exacted for the fourth time at the Court held on the Thursday the vigil of St. Matthew, 32 H. VI, on which day he had appeared and had surrendered, and he was now in prison, but he was so ill and detained by such infirmities that he could not be produced in Court without fear of death. The Sheriff was therefore ordered to produce him on the Quindene of St. Hillary. *m.* 495, *dorso.*

Staff. Thomas Stanley, armiger, sued Thomas Wilcokson, of Lichefeld, chaplain, and Richard Martyn, of Whytyngton, parysshe clerk, for entering his free warren at Elford, and chasing and taking his rabbits. The defendants did not appear, and the Sheriff was ordered to arrest and produce them on the Quindene of St. Hillary. *m.* 498.

Staff. Elizabeth, formerly wife of Thomas Leukenore, knight, sued Edward Doyle (Doyley), armiger, for a third part of the manor called Leukenore's manor in Ronton, formerly called Doyle manor in Ronton, Bylynton, Careswelle, Sesteford, Coton, Mulnemese, and Brycheford, which she claimed as dower.

Edward pleaded he could not render the third part claimed, because he was not the tenant of the manor, nor was tenant at the date of the writ.

Elizabeth stated her writ should not be quashed on that account, for the said Thomas Leukenore after her marriage with him had demised the manor to Edward Doyle for his life, and that Edward, after the death of Thomas and up to the date of the issue of the writ, viz., 1 November, 31 H. VI, had held the manor, and that after the death of Thomas, Edward had made a feoffment of the manor to divers persons unknown to Elizabeth, by fraud and collusion with a view of depriving her of her dower, and that her writ was issued within a year and a day after the death of her husband, and therefore Edward as tenant of the land was answerable.

Edward denied that he, on the date of the writ or ever afterwards, had received the profits of the manor, and he stated that the demises mentioned by Elizabeth were made by Thomas Leukenore long before he married the said Elizabeth, and that long after the demise of the manor made to him by Thomas, he had been seised of the manor in demesne during the lifetime of Thomas, and whilst so seised he had demised it to one John Harecourt during the lifetime of Thomas to be held for the life of Edward, by virtue of which demise the said John had held the manor during the lifetime of Thomas, and was still in possession of it.

Elizabeth replied that Edward was tenant of the manor at the time of the death of her husband Thomas, and appealed to a jury which was to be summoned for the Morrow of All Souls. A postscript shews no jury had been summoned up to the following Easter term. *m.* 564.

Staff. John Trevilian, armiger, Roger Stokley and Thomas Gardyner, had sued in the court of Margaret the Queen of England of her Honor of Tuttebury, Thomas Blount, knight, and Walter Blount, armiger, for the manor of Falde by the King's open writ of right; and the cause had been moved into the county of Stafford on the appeal of the plaintiffs, asserting that they had not full right in the said Court, and from thence it had been brought into this Court on the petition of the plaintiffs; and the said John, Roger, and Thomas now sued the said Thomas Blount and Walter, for the said manor which they claimed as their right and of which they had been seised in the time of the present King, and they offered to prove their right, etc.

And Thomas Blount and Walter defended their right and called to warranty Thomas Broun the younger, of Tuttebury, who appeared and warranted the manor to them; upon which the said John, Roger, and Thomas Gardyner sued the said Thomas Broun, and repeated their plea as before; and Thomas Broun as tenant by the warranty denied the right of the plaintiffs, and put himself on a great assize. The plaintiffs then asked for a license "*inde interloquendi*" which was granted to them. They afterwards appeared in Court and Thomas Broun put in no appearance and judgment was given in favour of the plaintiffs, who were to have seisin of the manor. *m.* 613.

London. Isabella Tregornowe, of London, wedowe, was summoned at the suit of Richard Leukenore, armiger, to give up to him a pyx containing deeds and muniments, one of which was a deed by which Anne, formerly wife of John Roger late of Brianeston in co. Dorset, armiger, had granted to the said Richard, under the name of Richard, son of Thomas Leukenore, knight, the cousin of the said Anne, an annual rent of £20 to be received by the said Richard from all her lands and tenements in co. Southampton, and the said Richard stated he had accidentally lost (*casualiter amisit*) the pyx in London, in the parish of St. Andrew in Holborn, in the Ward of Faryngdon-Without on the Vigil of Pentecost 30 H. VI, and it had come into the possession of the said Isabella who had refused to give it up, and for which he claimed £100 as damages.

And the same Isabella had been likewise summoned by John Audeley, armiger, to give up to him a pyx containing deeds and muniments which she unjustly detained, and he repeated the same story of its loss as Richard Leukenore and claimed damages.[1]

Isabella now appeared by her attorney and stated that the pyx named in the two suits was one and the same pyx. And ever since she had found it, she had been prepared to give it up to the person whom the Court should consider entitled to possess it. And she was ready to give it up at the present time and she asked that the two claimants should sue one another for the pyx in Court. A day was therefore given to them for that purpose. (*Here the record stops.*) *m.* 658.

DE BANCO. MICH., 33 H. VI.

Roll in bad condition, first two membranes missing.

Staff. John Harpur of Ruysshale, sued Thomas Shelfeld of Walshale, chaplain, for breaking into his close and house in Ruysshale. Thomas did not appear and the Sheriff was ordered to arrest and produce him at a month from Michaelmas. *m.* 19.

Staff. Margery Shalcrasse, widow, sued Hugh Sherard of Shendon, yoman; Isabella Bentlye of Brokhous, widow, and John Bentlye of Brokhous, husbondman for breaking into her close and that of John Shalcrosse at Brodcooke and cutting down their trees and taking goods and chattels belonging to them to the value of 100*s.* The defendants did not appear, and the Sheriff was ordered to arrest and produce them on the Octaves of St. Hillary. *m.* 19.

Staff. John Gresley, knight, and William Bukkenale, sued John Madeley of Newcastle under Lyme, yoman; Nicholas Bratte of Dymmesdale, yoman; Richard Swetnam of Wolstanton, husbondman; Thomas Turnemore of Shelton; John Kydde of Shelton, William Lovot of Clayton, Robert Poynton of Sheprigge; Richard Lovot of Clayton; Thomas Kendale of Sheprigge, all described as husbondmen; Hugh Orchard, of Hanford, yoman, and six others named, for breaking into their houses at Stoke, and taking goods and chattels to the value of £20. None of the defendants appeared and the Sheriff was ordered to arrest and produce them on the Octaves of St. Martin. *m.* 19.

Staff. Agnes, late wife of Richard Weston, John Smyth and William Wode, executors of the will of Richard Weston, sued Richard Tyler of Brereton, laborer, for a debt of 4 marks, and they sued Richard Waklen, husbondmen, late of Hixton, for a debt of 100*s.*, and John Egyngton, of Penkrich, husbondman, and Simon Colman of Canke, yoman, for a debt of 40*s.* None of the defendants appeared, and the Sheriff was ordered to arrest and produce them on the Morrow of All Souls. *m.* 19, *dorso.*

Staff. The Warden or Dean, and Canons of the College of St. George within the Castle of Wyndesore, sued William Elysaunder, Parson of the church of Leye, for a debt of £10, the arrears of an annual rent of 6*s.* 8*d.*, which he owed to them. William did not appear, and the Sheriff was ordered to attach him for the Quindene of St. Hillary. *m.* 97.

Staff. John Curson of Ketlyston, armiger, sued William Trussell of Elmesthorp, knight, for a sum of 40 marks, the arrears of an annual rent

[1] John Audeley in his plea makes no mention of the deed of Anne Roger, but states he lost the pyx in the same place.

of 10 marks which he owed to him. William did not appear, and the Sheriff returned he had distrained him up to 10*s*. He was therefore ordered to distrain again and produce him on the Octaves of St. Hillary. *m.* 97.

Staff. William Attelbourgh sued John Doune, late of Loxley, husbandman, for so threatening his tenant at Loxley, Henry Higgeson, that for fear of his life he had given up his tenancy. John did not appear, and the Sheriff was ordered to arrest and produce him on the above date. *m.* 98.

Staff. John Stretehay recovered a messuage—10 acres of land, and 12 acres of pasture in Stretehay—in a suit against Alice, late wife of John Clerkson, through the default of the defendant. *m.* 98, *dorso.*

Staff. The Sheriff was ordered to distrain Robert Aston, armiger, late Sheriff of co. Stafford, to produce John Cokayne of Asshebourne, armiger, who had surrendered at the County Court, held on the Thursday, the vigil of St. Matthew 32 H. VI. to answer to Thomas Asteley, late Sheriff of the County in a plea for a debt of 40*s*. The Sheriff returned he had distrained the said Robert up to 10*s*. He was therefore ordered to distrain again and produce him on the Quindene of St. Hillary. *m.* 98, *dorso.*

Staff. The Sheriff was ordered to distrain the following members of a jury summoned to return a verdict in the suit of Robert Cuny (Coyney) armiger, versus Thomas Buknale of Buknale, yoman, in a plea of trespass, and produce them on the Octaves of St. Hillary. viz.

John Pulesdon of Bromley, Abbots; Robert Lambard, of the same; Ralph Byssheton of Byssheton; Thomas Hampton of Byssheton; John Smyth of Ruggeley; Ralph Nevowe of Ruggeley; Ralph Vicars of Careswalle; William Delf of Dilron; Richard Turnehare of Fossebroke; Richard Pakeman of Fossebroke; Edmund Turnehare of Fossebroke; John Trubshawe of Strongshulf; Robert Russell of Cornbrigge; John Northo of Roucester; Robert Verney of Marchynton; John Kay of Kyngeston; William Lovot of Calowhylle; John Frogot of Calowhylle; William Norman of Westwode; Hugh Shawe of Feld; John Muchehale of Muchehale; John Knyght of Netherpenne; Thomas Hethe of Bysshebury; William Smyth of Penkeriche; William Wyot of Stone; Thomas Pulesdone of Salt; John Cook of Overton; William Bolde of Enstone; Thomas Adderley of Kyngeleye; and John Unet of Holedyche. *m.* 110.

Staff. Robert Grevelle, and Alice his wife, sued James Assheby, for a third of 6 messuages in Esyngton, as the dower of Alice of the dotation of Nicholas Assheby, her former husband, James asked for a view and the suit was adjourned to the Octaves of St. Hillary. *m.* 120, *dorso.*

Staff. William Lee, late of Russhale, yoman, was attached at the suit of John Harpur, armiger, for breaking into his house at Russhale, on the Wednesday before the Feast of the Nativity of the Blessed Virgin, 31 H. VI, and carrying away £52 in money.

William appeared in person and denied the trespass and injury, and appealed to a jury, which was to be summoned for the morrow of St. Martin. A postscript states that the process was continued till Michaelmas term, 34 H. VI, when it was moved by writ of *nisi prius* to be heard before the Justices of Assize at Lichefeld, on the Monday, after the Feast of the Epiphany, when a jury found that the said William was guilty, and they assessed the damages and costs of John at £58 13*s.* 4*d.* *m.* 121.

Staff. Thomas Lyttylton, and Joan his wife, sued Richard Cokette, for the next presentation to the free chapel of Ingestre. Richard did not appear, and had been distrained, and failed to appear again. Thomas and Joan were therefore to recover the advowson. And the Sheriff was ordered to return by Inquisition upon oath, whether the chapel was vacant or not. And if the six months had expired, and what the chapel was worth annually. And to return the inquisition into Court on the Octaves of St. Hillary. *m.* 124.

Staff. John Brumley, knight, William Hexstall, armiger, Hugh Hexstall, clerk, and Roger Clerk, sued Thomas Danyell, of Brewode, draper, for breaking into their closes at Wetmore, near Brewode, and depasturing cattle on their grass. Thomas did not appear, and the Sheriff was ordered to arrest, and produce him on the Octaves of St. Hillary. *m.* 240, *dorso.*

Staff. Thomas Arblaster the elder, armiger, and Henry Lynby, sued Walter Blount, of Aylwardby, co. Derby, armiger, executor of the will of John Gresley, knight, late of Colton, for a debt of £8 8*s.* Walter did not appear, and the Sheriff returned he held nothing within his Bailiwick. He was therefore ordered to arrest and produce him on the above date. *m.* 241.

Staff. John, Earl of Shrewsbury[1], sued Ralph Basset, late of Blore, armiger; William Basset, late of Blore, gentilman; Richard Basset, late of Blore, gentilman; Humfrey Walker, late of Blore, gentilman; Oliver Dethyk, late of Blore, yoman; Henry Ford, late of Blore, yoman; Simon Walle of Thornebury, yoman; Thomas Walle of Chedulle, yoman; William Heuster of Chedulle, yoman; John Berdemore of Froghole, yoman; William Berdemore of Froghole, yoman; William Fox of Chedulle, colyer; and John Asshenhurst, late of Blore, yoman; for entering his park at Alveton, and taking his game. None of the defendants appeared, and the Sheriff was ordered to distrain the said Ralph Basset, William Basset, Richard Basset, and Humfrey, and to arrest the others, and produce them on the Quindene of St. Hillary. *m.* 243.

Staff. James Morton sued John Cotes, for a moiety of the manor of Wilbrighton, in which the said John had no entry, except by a disseisin, which John Stafford had unjustly made of James Morton, his grandfather. And he stated that his grandfather James, was seised of the said moiety, in demesne as of fee, temp. Hen. V, and from James the right descended to one Thomas, as son and heir, and from Thomas to the plaintiff, as son and heir. John appeared by attorney, and stated he could not render the moiety to James, as he was not tenant of it, nor was tenant at the date of the writ. James replied that on the date on which the writ was sued out, viz. on the 28th November, 32 H. VI, John was tenant of the moiety, and he appealed to a jury which was to be summoned for the Octaves of St. Hillary. *m.* 316.

Staff. Hugh Wrottesley, armiger, sued William Hamulton of Butterton, husbondman, for breaking into his close at Butterton, digging in his soil, and carrying away earth to the value of 40*s.* And for depasturing cattle on his grass, and consuming it to the value of £10. William did not appear, and the Sheriff was ordered to arrest, and produce him on the Quindene of St. Hillary. *m.* 344, *dorso.*

[1] John, Earl of Shrewsbury, was the son of the famous Talbot, who had been killed in 1453, at Chastillon near Bordeaux. His mother was Maud, Baroness Furnival, senior co-heir of the Barony of Verdon, through whom he had come into possession of Alton.

Staff. Nicholas Norman and William Whitby, sued William Alsop, late of Haughton, husbondman, for a debt of 20 marks, and they sued John Kaye, late of Kyngestone, yoman, and William Mason, late of Ruggeley, husbondman, for a debt of 40*s*. The defendants did not appear, and the Sheriff was ordered to arrest and produce them on the Quindene of St. Hillary. *m.* 387.

Staff. Richard Bagot, armiger, sued Thomas Colelogh of Newcastle under Lyme, gentilman ; Richard Coklogh of Chelles, yoman ; Roger Cokelogh of Colclogh, co. Stafford, yoman ; and Roger Knyght of Bedulle, yoman, for a debt of £40. The defendants did not appear, and the Sheriff was ordered to arrest and produce them on the Quindene of St. Hillary. *m.* 396.

Staff. Richard Gaylard, and Margery his wife, sued Margery, formerly wife of William Hayteley, for waste and destruction in lands, houses, woods, and gardens, which she held of the inheritance of Margery, the wife of Richard in Uttoxater. The defendant did not appear, and the Sheriff was ordered to attach her for the Quindene of St. Hillary. A postscript shews that the Sheriff had made no return to the writ up to Michaelmas, 34 H. VI. *m.* 493.

Leyc. The Sheriff had been ordered to summon John Harpur, of Russhale, for this term to answer Nicholas Ovy (*sic*), and Anne his wife, John Wyslove, and Isabella his wife, and Thomas Halton, in a plea that he should give up to them, 10 messuages, 9 virgates of land, 30 acres of meadow, 20 acres of pasture, and 52*s.* of rent in Thedyngworth and Carleton-Curly, which Robert de Ernesby, had given to Theobald Trussell, knight, and Katrine his wife, and heirs of the body of Theobald, and which after the death of the said Theobald, and Katrine, and of John, son and heir of Theobald, and of Philippa, daughter and heir of John, and of Elizabeth, one of the daughters of the said Philippa, should descend to the said Anne, and Elizabeth, the other daughters of the said Philippa, and to Thomas the son of the said Elizabeth, the cousins and heirs of the said Philippa. And the Sheriff returned, the writ reached him too late, and he was ordered to summon him for a month from Easter. *m.* 530.

Staff. Thomas Lyttylton sued in person, Alexander Benet of Ruggeley. William Couper of Ruggeley, William atte Knolle of Ruggeley, Robert Bowyer of Ruggeley, and William Walker of Ruggeley, all described as yoman, for cutting down his trees and underwood at Brereton, to the value of 40*s*. The defendants did not appear, and the Sheriff was ordered to arrest and produce them on the Octaves of St. Hillary. *m.* 624.

CORAM REGE. TRINITY, 33 H. VI.

Staff. Charles Nowelle sued William Haukes, of Wednesbury, husbondman, in a plea that whereas he had impounded within his fee of Wednesbury, certain cattle belonging to him for customs and services owing to him, the said William had broken into his pound *vi et armis*, and carried away the cattle. William did not appear, and the Sheriff was ordered to arrest and produce him on the Quindene of St. Michael. *m.* 29.

Staff. The Sheriff had been ordered to produce in Court, James Leveson, late of Willenhale, to answer as an accessory to the death of Thomas Gery, of which he had been appealed by Elizabeth, late wife of Thomas, and Elizabeth now appeared in person, and the Sheriff returned that the said James had been arrested by his predecessor, Richard Bagot, late Sheriff of the County, who had not delivered his prisoner over to him. The Sheriff was therefore ordered to distrain the said Richard to produce the said James at three weeks from Michaelmas. A postscript shews that no further steps had been taken in the matter up to Easter term 34 H. VI. *m.* 29.

Oxon. The Venerable Father in God, T. Archbishop of Canterbury, the King's Chancellor, delivered with his own hands into Court, the record of a suit heard before the King in his Chancery, as follows :

It appeared by an Inquisition taken at Wodestok, co. Oxford, 4th April, 30 H. VI, before John Pury, then the King's Eschaeter for the County, that in 18 E. III, a fine had been levied by William de Shareshulle, chivaler, and Dionisia his wife, by which the manor of Barton Odo had been settled on the said William, and Dionisia for their lives, and that the manor of Roulesham, which John, son of William Foliot, then held for his life, should remain after the death of John, to the said William and Dionisia for their lives, and after the deaths of William and Dionisia, the said manors should remain to William, son of the said William, and to Joan his wife, and to the heirs of the body of William, son of William, and failing such should remain to the right heirs of William de Shareshulle, chivaler. By virtue of which fine, William, son of William and Joan, entered the manors after the deaths of William de Shareshulle and Dionisia, and of John, son of William Foliot, and were seised in demesne as of fee tail, and they had issue, Elizabeth, and Elizabeth entered as heir of William, and had issue Joan Legh, and Joan entered as heir of Elizabeth, and died seised of the manors and left no issue, and after her death, the manors should remain to Richard Beaufo, armiger, and to Joan, the wife of John Dynham, knight, as cousins and heirs of the said William de Shareshulle, knight, viz., to the said Richard, as son of John, son of Elizabeth, son of Agnes, daughter of the said William de Shareshulle, knight, and to the said Joan, wife of John Dynham, as daughter of Lucy, another of the daughters of the said Agnes, daughter of William de Shareshulle, knight, inasmuch as the said William, son of William, died leaving no issue (*sic*), and the said manor of Barton was held by the King as of the honor of Walyngford, by knight's service, and the manor of Roulesham was held of the King as of the same honor.

And it also appeared that the said William de Shareshulle, knight, the elder, was lately seised of the manor of Derneford in the same county, which was held of the King, as of the same honor. And he had granted the manor to William de Shareshulle, the younger, and to the heirs of his body, and failing such to remain to Agnes, daughter of the said William, the elder, and heirs of her body. By which grant William de Shareshulle, the elder, was seised of the manor in demesne as of fee tail, and had issue Elizabeth, and Elizabeth entered as heir of William, and had issue the said Joan, who had entered as her heir, and had died leaving no issue, in consequence of which the said manor should remain to Richard Beaufo, and to Joan, the wife of John Dynham, as cousins and heirs of Agnes, viz., to Richard, as son of John, son of Elizabeth, one of the daughters of Agnes, and to Joan, as daughter of Lucy, another of the daughters of Agnes, and that Richard at the date of the Inquisition was aged 30 years and more, and Joan was aged 24 years and more. And on the 21st February, 33 H. VI, the said John Dynham, knight, and Joan his wife, appeared and complained that by virtue of the above Inquisition they had been unjustly removed from the manors of Barton Odo, Roulesham, and Derneford, and they stated that the said Richard Beaufo was not cousin and heir of William de Shareshulle, the elder, nor was Joan, the wife of John Dynham, a daughter of Lucy, and as regarded the manors of Barton and Roulesham they stated that Richard Webbe, the vicar of Albryghton, was seised of them long before the said Joan Lee held anything in them, and whilst so seised, he had granted them, with others to the said Joan Lee, under the name of Joan Lee, late wife of William Lee of Knightley, to be held by her for her life, with remainder after her death to John Dynham, knight, and to Joan his wife, and the heirs of Joan, and Joan Lee was seised of the manors by virtue of the said grant, and after her death, John Dynham, and Joan his wife, had entered and were seised of them until they had been removed under order of the above Inquisition. And as regarded the manor of Derneford they stated that the said Joan was not daughter of the said Lucy, and that the said Richard Webbe was seised of the manor before Joan Lee held anything in it, and whilst so seised had granted it to the said Joan Lee, under the name of Joan Lee, late wife of William Lee of Knyghtley to be held for her life with remainder to the said John Dynham, knight, and Joan his wife, and to the heirs of Joan. And Joan Lee had died so seised of the manor, and after her death John Dynham, and Joan his wife, had entered and were seised of it until they had been removed by the above Inquisition, and they prayed that the hand of the King might be removed.

The King's attorney then asked for a jury to state whether the said Joan Lee had died seised of the manors as of fee tail or not, and the Sheriff of co. Oxford was ordered to summon a jury for this term. The suit was afterwards adjourned to Michaelmas term unless the Justices of Assize should first come to Oxford on the Tuesday after Michaelmas, on which latter date a jury was empanelled and returned a verdict that Joan Lee had not died seised of the said manors in demesne as of fee tail. It was therefore considered that the King's hand should be removed, and that the said John Dynham, and Joan his wife, should be restored to the possession of the manors with all issues from the date from which they had been expelled. *m.* 8. *Rex.*

DE BANCO. HILLARY, 34 H. VI.

Staff. Thomas Knyghtley sued John Somerford of Somerford, gentilman, for breaking down his millpool "*gurgitem*" at Brewode. John did not appear, and the Sheriff returned 12*d.* as proceeds of a distress. He was therefore ordered to distrain again and produce him on the Quindene of Easter Day. A postscript shews adjournments of the writ up to Michaelmas, 35 H. VI. *m.* 19, *dorso.*

Staff. John FitzHugh, the executor of the will of Alice Ruggeley, sued Robert Ruggeley of Shenstone, gentilman, for a debt of 6 marks. Robert did not appear, and the Sheriff returned he had distrained him up to 16*d.* He was therefore ordered to distrain again and produce him on the Quindene of Easter Day. *m.* 77, *dorso.*

Staff. John Huntyngdon sued Richard Rous of Breredon, husbondman, for breaking into his close at Breredon and depasturing cattle on his corn and grass. Richard did not appear, and the Sheriff was ordered to arrest and produce him on the above date. *m.* 77, *dorso.*

Staff. Richard Colwych, the Prior of St. Thomas the Martyr, near Stafford, sued John Staunford of Staflord, yoman, to render a reasonable account for the time he was his bailiff in Penford, Drayton, and Apeton. John did not appear, and the Sheriff returned he had distrained him up to 12*d.* He was therefore ordered to distrain again and produce him on the above date. *m.* 77, *dorso.*

Staff. Thomas Lyttylton sued in person Agnes Weston of Ruggeley, wedowe, in a plea that whereas he had taken certain chattels belonging to her by Henry Rugge, his servant, as a distress within his fee of Brereton, for customs and services owing to him as was lawful; the said Agnes had forcibly removed them. Agnes did not appear, and the Sheriff was ordered to arrest and produce her on the above date. *m.* 78. *dorso.*

Staff. Richard Congreve, armiger, sued Thomas Erdyngton of Erdyngton, co. Warwick, knight, and Henry Juce (or Ince), clerk, late of Little Saredon, the executors of the will of Alianora, formerly wife of Richard Harcourt, armiger, in a plea that they should give up to him a chest (*cistam*) containing deeds and muniments which they unjustly detained. The defendants did not appear, and the Sheriff was ordered to arrest and produce them on the Quindene of Easter Day. *m.* 80, *dorso.*

Staff. Robert Taillour of Stafford, Taillour, was attached at the suit of Elizabeth Whitgreve for breaking into her house at Stafford on the 21st June, 33 H. VI, and taking her goods and chattels, viz.: three dinner tables "*tabulas mensales*," 6 *mansoria*, called mangers, 6 "*prasepia*," 3 "*stamia*," called in English Stondyngbenches, 6 "*formulas*," and 100 "*asseres*," called pentes bordes to the value of 40*s.*, and for which she claimed 100*s.* as damages. Robert appeared by attorney and denied the trespass and injury, and appealed to a jury which was to be summoned for the Quindene of Easter Day. *m.* 114.

Staff. Thomas Whitgreve, Prebendary of the Prebend of Collewych, sued John Mollesley, late Billestone, armiger, for a debt of 6 marks. John did not appear, and the Sheriff was ordered to distrain and produce him on the above date. *m.* 114.

Staff. Thomas Stanley, armiger, sued William Rose of Allerwas, yoman, for breaking into his close at Allerwas and taking 8 steers and 7 heifers worth 100*s.* William did not appear, and the Sheriff was ordered to arrest and produce him on the Quindene of Easter Day. *m.* 171.

Staff. John Gresley, knight, Hugh Wrottesley, armiger, and John Moy sued John Knyght of Byllerbrok, yoman, for breaking into their close at Billerbrok, and depasturing cattle on their grass. The defendant did not appear, and the Sheriff was ordered to arrest and produce him on the Quindene of Easter Day. *m.* 171, *dorso.*

North. Thomas Jolyff sued William Saundyre of Burgo Sancti Petri (Peterborough), yoman, and two others, for breaking into his close at Peterborough and depasturing cattle on his corn and grass. The defendants did not appear, and the Sheriff was ordered to distrain William, who had found bail, and to arrest the others and produce them on the Quindene of Easter Day. *m.* 247.

Staff. Agnes Malley, the lady of Westbromwych, sued John Clerk, late of Tybton, gentilman, for a debt of £20. John did not appear, and the Sheriff was ordered to attach him for the above date. *m.* 247.

Staff. Agnes, formerly wife of John Hamton, sued John Couper of Netherton, yoman, and Richard Couper of Pipe Ridware, yoman, for breaking into her close at Hamstall Rydware, insulting, beating, and wounding her, and taking a horse, 6 oxen, 2 cows and 80 sheep worth £12, and other goods and chattels to the value of 100*s.* The defendants did not appear, and the Sheriff was ordered to arrest and produce them on the above date. *m.* 247.

Staff. John Myners, the elder, sued Gregory Neuport, the parson of Hanbury, for a debt of 60*s.* Gregory did not appear, and the Sheriff was ordered as in the last suit. *m.* 247.

Staff. Agnes, formerly wife of John Hamton, administratrix of the goods of John Hamton, late of the parish of Hamstall Rydware, who it was stated had died intestate, sued John Bradwall of Birmyngeham, drover, and William Eyton, of Hondesworth, drover, for a debt of £10. The defendants did not appear, and the Sheriff was ordered as in the last suit. *m.* 248.

Staff. John Knyght sued Richard Colet of Byllerbrok, husbondman, for depasturing cattle on his grass at Byllerbrok (Billbrook). Richard did not appear, and the Sheriff was ordered as in the last suit. *m.* 248.

Staff. Thomas Lyttylton, and Joan his wife, sued Richard Rous of Brereton, husbondman, for breaking into their close at Brereton and depasturing cattle on their grass. Richard did not appear, and the Sheriff was ordered as in the last suit. *m.* 248.

Staff. William Deykyn, the elder, sued John Kynthall of Wodehous, husbondman, and Richard Webbe of Wodehous, husbondman, for breaking into his close and houses at Yedyhale, and depasturing cattle on his grass. The defendants did not appear, and the Sheriff was ordered as in the last suit. *m.* 249.

Staff. John Verney, dean of the cathedral church of Lichfield, John Stanley of Pipe, armiger, John Chetwinde, and Edward Colt of Lichefeld, draper, executors of the will of John Jolyff, late Canon Residentary of Lichfield, sued Richard Rokeby, late of Creek, co. Northampton, yoman, Robert Robert, *alias* Robert Fermour, late of Creek, husbondman, and Thomas Rokeby, late of Creek, yoman, for a debt of £80 and 10 marks. The defendants did not appear, and the Sheriff was ordered as in the last suit. *m.* 250.

Staff. Roger Whitmare (*sic*), and Margaret his wife, sued William Litholle of Storeton, husbondman, for breaking into his close and houses at Compton, and depasturing cattle on his grass. William did not appear, and the Sheriff was ordered as in the last suit. *m.* 250.

Staff. William Cumberford and Thomas Cumberford sued William Walker of Lichefeld, Walker, for depasturing cattle on their grass at Thomynhorm (Tamhorn). William did not appear, and the Sheriff was ordered as in the last suit. *m.* 250.

Staff. Edmund Mulso, knight, John Mulso, the elder, and John Mulso, the younger, sued Robert Moton, knight, and Elizabeth, his wife, for the manor of Chetell, and £10 12*s.* of rent in Chetell, as their right and inheritance by the King's writ of right, because Robert Grey, armiger, the capital lord of the fee, had remitted his right (of holding the plea) to the King.

Robert and Elizabeth defended their right and called to warranty Thomas Gerveys, who accepted the warranty. The plaintiffs then sued Thomas Gerveys as tenant by the warranty, and stated they had been seised of the said manor and rent in the time of the present King and offered to prove their right, etc.

Thomas defended his right and put himself on a great assize, but he afterwards made default and the plaintiffs recovered the manor and rent. *m.* 335, *dorso.*[1]

Staff. John Wotton sued Thomas Nowell for a messuage in Wotton, in which Thomas had no entry, except by an intrusion after the deaths of John Nowell, and Katrine his wife, to whom John Wotton had demised the tenement for their lives. Thomas defended his right, and the suit was adjourned at his request to the Quindene of Easter Day. A postscript shews other adjournments up to Easter Day 35 H. VI. *m.* 507, *dorso.*

CORAM REGE. MICH., 35 H. VI.

Staff. On the Thursday in the Feast of Pentecost 34 H. VI, it had been presented before Sampson Meverell, knight, and his Fellow Justices of the Peace, that John Cokkys, the younger, late of Ennveld in co. Stafford,

[1] These suits by a writ of right in the Lords Court seem to be collusive.

yoman, Thomas Cokkys, late of Weddesbury, yoman, Henry Jurdon, late of Alveley, co. Salop, husbondman, and John Cokkys, the elder, ate of Enneveld, co. Stafford, husbondman, with many other malefactors and disturbers of the peace, to the number of more than 40, had assembled on the Friday before the Feast of St. George 34 H. VI, at le Lee in co. Stafford, armed with swords, clubs, bows and arrows, with coats of mail, doublets, steel caps and other defensible arms, and had broken into the close and houses of Nicholas Waryng at that place, and had shot arrows at him and had taken him into custody by main force, whilst John Cokkys, the younger, Thomas Colyns, Henry Jurdon, John Cokkys, the elder, and other malefactors had feloniously ravished Elena Roger, the servant of the said Nicholas, and which indictment, the King, for certain causes, had commanded to be terminated in this Court. And at this term, viz., on the Tuesday in the Quindene of St. Michael, the said John Cokkys, Thomas Cokkys, Henry Jurden, and John Cokkys surrendered and were committed to the Marchalsea, and being brought before the Court, pleaded that they were not guilty and put themselves on the country, and the Sheriff was ordered to summon a jury for the Quindene of St. Hillary, and they were admitted to bail on the security of Ralph Wolseley of London, gentilman, John Mokkelowe of London, gentilman, and John Transall of London, barbour. And on that day the said John Cokkys, and the other defendants appeared and the Sheriff returned the names of twenty-four jurymen, none of whom were present. He was therefore ordered to distrain, and the process was continued but respited till a month from Easter 36 H. VI, unless the Justices holding Assizes should first come to Stafford on the Wednesday before the Feast of St. Gregory the Pope, on which day the said Thomas Colyns, Henry Jurden, and John Cokkys, the elder, appeared and John Cokkys, the younger, made no appearance, and a jury being empanelled found they were not guilty, and Ralph Wolseley, one of the pledges of John Cokkys, the younger, stated that he was dead, and as it was testified by others worthy of credit that the allegation of the said Ralph was true, it was considered that the process against John Cokkys, the younger, and his sureties should cease. *m.* 2, *Rex.*

Derb. On the Monday after the Feast of St. Mark 33 H. VI, it had been presented at Derby on a view of the body of Roland Blount, then lying dead and killed; on the oath of twelve jurymen, that Henry Curson of Ketlestone, in co. Derby, gentilman, John Damport of Derby, armiger, Thomas Penystone of Ketlestone, yoman, and John Savage of Dubrigge, yoman, on the Friday after the Feast of Easter 33 H. VI, with many other malefactors unknown, armed with swords, clubs, langdebeeffes, glaives, and other arms defensible, had laid in wait at Derby, in order to kill the said Roland, and had assaulted him, and the said Henry Curson with an arm, called a glaive, had struck the said Roland on the head causing a mortal wound of which he had instantly died, and the said John Damport had struck the said Roland on the head with a sword, causing a mortal wound, of which he would have died if he had not died of the blow delivered by the said Henry, and the said Thomas Penyston had struck the said Roland on the head with a certain arm called a "fuste" and caused a mortal wound, etc., and the said John Savage had struck Roland with a sword on the head, causing a mortal wound, of which he would have died, etc. (as before), and that after the said felony and murder, the said Henry Curson, John Damport, Thomas and John Savage had fled and they had no goods nor chattels.

And that John Jeer, *alias* John Anker Jeer, *alias* John Anker of Derby, patemaker, on the same day had laid in wait with the other malefactors and had struck the said Roland Blount on the head with a club, causing a mortal wound, of which he would have died, etc. (as before), and the said John Jeer had instantly fled and had no goods or chattels. And which indictment the King, for certain causes commanded to be heard and terminated in this Court.

And at this term the said Henry Curson, John Damport, Thomas and John Savage, and John Jeer, were brought before the Court and pleaded they were not guilty and put themselves on the country. The Sheriff was therefore ordered to summon a jury for the Octaves of St. Hillary and in the meantime the prisoners were admitted to bail. *m.* 8, *Rex.*

Staff. The Sheriff was ordered to put into *exigend* John Vernon of Haddon, co. Derby, armiger, and if he did not appear to outlaw him; and if he appeared to arrest and produce him *coram Rege* at a month from Easter, to answer for divers transgressions of which he had been indicted. *m.* 17, *Rex.*

Warw. Thomas Porter of Eyneshan, co. Oxford, yoman, a servant of Robert Harecourt, late of Staunton Harecourt, co. Oxford, who had been indicted with many others for an assault upon Sir Humfrey Stafford, and for killing Richard Stafford, the son and heir of Sir Humfrey, at Coventry, in 26 H. VI, surrendered at this term and produced the King's pardon. *m* 23, *Rex.*

Staff. It had been presented before John Harpur, and his fellow Justices of the Peace at Stafford, that William Radeclyff of Elvaston, co. Derby, yoman, Ralph Radclyff, late of the same place, yoman, John Thornes, late of the same place, yoman, and Edmund Radclyff, late of the same place, yoman, on the Monday after the Feast of St. Thomas the Martyr, 32 H. VI, had come to Lichfield with others unknown, and had entered the close of John Atwell, and broken into his house, and had abducted by force, Alice, the daughter of Robert Strangulford, and carried her into co. Derby, and that Walter Blount of Elvaston, armiger, John Agard of Foston, co. Dudley, yoman, and Richard Yate of Scropton, co. Derby, and others, had knowingly received and entertained them afterwards at Burton, in co. Stafford, and which indictment the King, for certain reasons, had commanded to be brought up and terminated in this Court.

And Walter Blount, John Agard, and Richard Yate, now appeared, and surrendered, and were committed to the Marshalsea, and being brought before the Court, they pleaded that the indictment was not sufficient in law, and prayed they might be released, and the indictment having been viewed by the Court, they considered it was insufficient, and the prisoners were released. *m.* 25, *Rex, dorso.*[1]

CORAM REGE. EASTER, 35 H. VI.

Staff. Robert Harecourt, knight, sued Thomas Astley, late of Pateshulle, armiger, Richard Beaufo, late of Hylton, armiger, and Richard Congreve, late of Little Sardon, gentilman, in a plea of trespass. The defendants did not appear, and a day had been given to them at this term by their *essoins* after they had been attached. The Sheriff was therefore ordered to distrain and produce them on the Quindene of Holy Trinity. *m.* 13.

Staff. Elena Roggers appeared in person, and appealed John Cokkys, the younger, late of Enneveld (Enville), yoman; Thomas Robyns, late of Wadesbury, yoman, and John Cokkys, the elder, late of Enneveld, husbondman, and Henry Jurden, late of Alveley, co. Salop, husbondman, in a plea of rape. The defendants did not appear, and the Sheriff was ordered to arrest and produce them on the above date. *m.* 13, *dorso.*

[1] Robert Strangulford was in custody at this date for killing one, Simon Iden at Derby, and Henry Curson of Ketulston and three others named on *m.* 8, were indicted as accessories to the felony.

Staff. Joan, late wife of Robert Boughey, appeared in person and appealed William Guddeman, late of Burton upon Trent, laborer, Robert Wade, of the same place, Payntour, Henry Ryde, Bocher, John Blythe, Payntour, and Nicholas Guddeman, Payntour, all of Burton upon Trent, for the death of her husband. None of the defendants appeared, and the Sheriff was ordered to arrest and produce them on the Octaves of Holy Trinity. *m.* 72.

Staff. John Savage of Clyfton, co. Chester, the elder, armiger; John Savage of Maxfeld, co. Chester, the younger, armiger; and Peter Dombylle of Great Barewe, co. Chester, gentilman, were attached at the suit of Humfrey Swynarton, late of Swynarton, in co. Stafford, gentilman, in a plea that by a conspiracy between them they had caused the said Humfrey to be arrested and lodged in the gaol at Chester, for robbing one Richard de Bekyngton of a horse worth 19*s.* 8*d.* at Assheton, near Torpurley, on the Friday before the Feast of St. Laurence, 32 H. VI, and by reason of which he had been detained in the gaol, until acquitted by Sir Thomas Stanley, knight, and his Fellow Justices, on the Friday after the Feast of St. Bartholomew, 32 H. VI, and for which he claimed £400 as damages (*the record stops here*). *m.* 86.

CORAM REGE. MICH., 36 H. VI.

Staff. Proceedings to annul the outlawry of Thomas Meverel of Throwley, who had been indicted with others for the death of John Taillour. The process shews that two of the defendants, John Cowederay, of Ilum, yoman, and John Beresford of Beresford, co. Stafford, gentilman, had been acquitted at assizes held at Stafford in 29 H. VI. The outlawry of Thomas Meverel was annulled owing to errors in the process. *m.* 7, *Rex.*

Derb. Margaret Dethyk of Newehall, Wedowe; Thomas Dethyk, late of Newehalle, armiger; John Dethyk, late of Newehall, gentilman; Thomas Dethyk of Uttoxhather, co. Stafford, armiger, and William Tykkylle, late of Aston upon Trent, co. Stafford, gentilman, were attached at the suit of Richard Dalman, William Dalman, Hugh Dalman, and John Dalman for taking their goods and chattels, viz. 4 quarters of wheat, 6 quarters of peas, and 6 quarters of barley, at Newehalle, on the Feast of the Nativity of St. John the Baptist, 35 H. VI, for which they claimed 100*s.* as damages.

The defendants stated that the plaintiffs were villein tenants of Newehall, of which manor the defendants were seised, and they had taken the plaintiffs' goods as was lawful. The plaintiffs replied they were freemen and appealed to a jury which was to be summoned for the Morrow of All Souls. A postscript shews the process was continued and moved by writ of *nisi prius* to be heard at Derby before Sir Ralph Pole, one of the Justices of the King, when a jury found that the plaintiffs were freemen, and assessed their damages at 20*s.*, and their costs at 13*s.* 4*d.* *m.* 33.

APPENDIX.

The following suits should have appeared in Volume XVI, but were overlooked at the time that volume was in preparation.

EDITOR.

CORAM REGE. HILLARY, 15 RIC. II.

Thomas, the Archbishop of York, the King's Chancellor, delivered into Court the following record of a plea taken in Chancery on the Quindene of St. Michael. 15 R. II.

Staff. The King had sent to Edward de Acton, his escheator, in co. Stafford, his close writ in these words :—

Whereas we have understood that John Salesbury, knight, deceased, whose lands had been forfeited, had enfeoffed certain persons in divers lands and tenements to the use of the said John, and which should have come into our hands by reason of the forfeiture of the said John, you are therefore commanded to make inquisition into the same and return it into our Chancery under your seal. Dated 10th March. 13 R. II.

By virtue of which writ the said Edward sent the following inquisition—taken at Chebbesey on the oath of Robert Deken, Thomas Muleward, Alan de Hilcote, John de Horton, William de Slyndon, John de Grafton, and six others named, who stated that John de Salesbury was seised in his demesne as of fee of the manor of Walton near Chebbesey, and had enfeoffed in it Nicholas de Salesbury, clerk, his brother, on condition that the said Nicholas should re-enfeoff the said John Salesbury and Joan, his wife, and the heirs of their bodies, and failing such, the manor was to remain to the right heirs of John, and they said that the said Nicholas was seised of the manor to the use of the said John Salesbury and in no other manner.

And they said that John Salesbury long before the said feoffment, had granted to one John Purcell an annual rent of 11 marks to be received from the same manor, and that the manor was worth nothing beyond the said 11 marks, and that Nicholas had occupied the manor since the date of the forfeiture of the said John. Dated the Tuesday before the close of Easter. 13 R. II.

And as it did not appear from the above inquisition whether the manor had been taken into the King's hands or not, another writ was sent to the escheator directing him to take the manor into the King's hands, and to answer for the issues of it. Dated 13th June. 13 R. II.

Upon which John Giffart appeared in person in the King's Chancery and stated that John Salesbury on the 16th June, 6 R. II, had enfeoffed Nicholas Salesbury, clerk, of the said manor of Walton near Chebbesey as stated above, but long before the forfeiture of the said John he had sued the said Nicholas by a writ of formedon in Banco, for the said manor, and which writ was returnable on the Quindene of St. Hillary. 10 R. II.

And the writ stated that Stephen de Bromley, parson of the church of Blemenhulle, and Walter le Brere, chaplain, had granted the manor to Edmund Giffart and Agnes, his wife, and to the heirs of the bodies of Edmund and Agnes, and which manor after the death of Edmund and Agnes, should descend to him as their son and heir, and the process was continued in Banco, the said Nicholas having pleaded that the said Stephen and Richard had not granted the manor as stated by John Giffart, and both he and Nicholas had appealed to a jury. And afterwards, whilst the suit was still pending, the King had issued his Letters Patent, dated 18th Nov., 13 R. II, which recited that whereas the said John Salesbury, knight, on the 16th June, 6 R. II, had enfeoffed the said Nicholas Salesbury in the said manor in fee simple, and in consequence of the forfeiture of the said John Salesbury, and of the ordinance of Parliament made in 11 R. II, the King should have all the lands and tenements and possessions held for the use of the said John, and the King willing to do a special grace to the said Nicholas, and for £80 of money paid to the King's Clerk, John de Hermesthorp for the use of the King, the King had ratified and confirmed the status which the said Nicholas held in the manor of Walton near Chebbesey. And the process being continued between John Giffart and Nicholas, it was moved by a writ of *nisi prius* to be heard before the justices of assize in co. Stafford, when a jury found that the said Stephen de Bromley and Richard le Brere had granted the manor to Edmund Giffard and Agnes, his wife, as stated by John Giffart, by which verdict the said John Giffart had been in peaceable seisin of the manor until removed by the King's escheator, and he prayed for restitution of the manor, and of the mesne profits from the date when he had been expelled.

The King's attorney opposed the application on the ground that by the Act of Parliament, the manor had come into the King's hand, and the writ of formedon had been quashed by it. And being asked by the Court if he had anything else to bring forward against the claim, he stated that long before the King's Letters Patent confirming the status of Nicholas in the manor, and before the verdict given in the suit "*de forma donationis*" the manor had been taken by the escheator into the King's hands. John Giffart denied this, and both parties appealed on this issue to a jury.

A postscript states that the suit was moved by writ of *nisi prius* to be heard at Stafford before John Hulle, the King's Justice, with whom was associated Nicholas de Stafford, chivaler, according to the statute, when a jury found in favour of John Gyffart. It was therefore considered that John Gyffart should have restitution of the manor with mesne profits from the date of his removal. *m.* 18 Rex.[1]

[1] See the suit between John Giffard and Nicholas Salesbury at p. 9 of Vol. XV of these collections. The verdict was delivered in the spring of 13 Ric. II, and the writ to the Escheator to take the manor into the King's hands was dated the 13th June, 13 Ric. II. Sir John Salisbury was one of the five knights of the King's household who were put to death by the Duke of Gloucester in 1388.

CORAM REGE. TRINITY, 2 H. IV.

Edmund, the Bishop of Exeter, the King's Chancellor, delivered into Court the following record of a Plea taken in the King's Chancery.

Staff. The King sent his close writ to the Sheriff of co. Stafford, stating that whereas by a fine levied in 14 R. II, between William de Shareshulle, knight, and Margaret, his wife, complainants, and Richard Fauley, clerk, deforciant of the manors of Patteshulle, Shareshulle, Great Sardon and Little Sardon, and of two parts of the manors of Covene and Brinsford, the said manors, etc., had been settled on William and Margaret, and the heirs of the body of William, and failing such, on Richard Harecourt and Margaret, his wife, and the heirs of their bodies, and it appeared by an inquisition taken before William Banastre, late escheator, that a fine was levied in 18 E. III, by which the manor of Patteshulle had been settled on William, son of William de Shareshulle and Joan, his wife, and the heirs of the body of William, son of William, and by another fine levied 18 E. III, the manor of Shareshulle had been settled on the same William, son of William and Joan, and the heirs of their bodies. By which fines the said William, son of William and Joan, were seised of the said manors, and had issue William Shareshulle, chivaler, and Elizabeth, and after their deaths the said manors descended to the said William Shareshulle, knight, viz., the manor of Patteshulle, as son and heir of the said William, son of William, and the manor of Shareshulle, as son and heir of the said William, son of William and Joan, and it likewise appeared that the said William, son of William, held on the day he died, viz., to him and to the heirs of his body the manors of Great Sardon and Little Sardon, and two parts of the manors of Covene and Brinsford, and after his death, the said William Shareshulle, knight, had entered as his son and heir into the said manors, and held them all his life, and that the manors of Patteshulle, Shareshulle, Great Sardon and Little Sardon, and two parts of the manors of Coven and Brinsford included lands which were held of the King *in capite*, viz., 6 acres of land called Rydyngfeld, 4 acres of wood called Rudyngefeldesmore, and an acre of meadow which were parcels of the manor of Shareshulle, and were held of the King *in capite* by knights' service, and the said William de Shareshulle, chivaler, died on the 17th of May last, leaving no issue, and that the said Elizabeth had died and had left three daughters, viz., Joan, Margaret, and Katrine, and Joan had a daughter named Joan, now the wife of William Lee, and the said Margaret had two daughters, viz., Isabella and Joyce, and had died, and the said Katrine, now the wife of Roger Wililey, and Joan, the wife of William Lee, both of full age, and the said Isabella and Joyce being under age, are the kinswomen and heirs of the said William de Shareshulle, chivaler.

And now *ex parte* the said Richard Harecourt it had been shewn that whereas the said 6 acres of land, 4 acres of wood, and an acre of meadow are held of the Earl of Stafford and not *in capite*, and the manor of Patteshulle named in the inquisition and in the fine were one and the same place, and that he had entered the said manors and the two above-named parts of the manor after the death of William Shareshulle, chivaler, by virtue of the remainder named in the fine, and had held them peaceably until and under color of the inquisition, they had been granted by Letters Patent to John Ikelington, clerk, and John Colle, clerk, and he had been expelled, and he now petitioned that the said Letters Patent might be annulled, and that he might be restored to the possession of the said manors—the King therefore wishing to do what was just, commanded the Sheriff to summon the said John Ikelyngton and John Colle, for the Quindene of Easter Day, to shew cause why the said Letters Patent should not be annulled. Dated from Westminster, 8th March, 2 H. IV. On which day the said John and John did not appear, but William Ludyngton, the King's attorney, appeared for the King and stated that the 6 acres of land called Rudyngfeld, and the 4 acres of wood and an acre of meadow, parcels of Shareshulle were held of the King *in capite* by knights' service, in consequence of which, the King rightly held the custody of the said manors, etc., and he appealed to a jury. The Sheriff was therefore ordered to summon a jury of the vicinage for the Quindene of Holy Trinity.

A postscript shews that the cause was afterwards removed by writ of *nisi prius* to be heard at Stafford, when a jury found that the 6 acres of land, and the 4 acres of wood and acre of meadow above-named, were held of the Earl of Stafford and not *in capite* of the King. It was therefore considered that the said Letters Patent should be annulled, and possession of the tenements given to Richard Harecourt with all profits and issues from the date of his expulsion. *m.* 23, *Rex.*

INDEX.

VOL. III. NEW SERIES.

INDEX.

A.

Abney, Geo., 25.
Abnoll, Gt., 26.
——— Lit., 26.
Abone, Parke, 52.
Acre, 116.
Acton, 6, 104, 188, 192, 200, 207, 208, 210.
——— Trussell, 30, 189, 190.
——— Burnell, 138.
——— Reyner, 142.
——— John, abbot of Bordesley, 123.
——— Edw. de, 226.
Adbaston, 59.
Adderley, Rich., arm , 23, 57.
——— ——— Ellen, w. of, 57.
——— Will., 60.
——— Thom., of Kyngeleye, 216.
Addyes, Thom., 25.
Adene, Rob., 163.
Adlyngton, Will., of Coven, 134, 145.
——— ——— ——— of Bromsgrove, 183.
Admaston, 29, 30.
Adye, Franc., 63.
Agard, Thom., of Foston, co. Derby, 140.
——— John ——— ——— 224.
——— Will., 26.
——— Humph., 57.
——— Hen., 62.
Agardsley, 26, 42, 52, 55.
Alan, Rob., son of, 111, 112, 113.
Albryghton, 219.
Alcock, Thom., 58.
——— Thom., of Leeke, 134.
——— ——— Matil., w. of, 134.
——— John, 66.
Aldersey, John, 3.
Aldewynkylle, Will., 204.
Aldriche, Aldridge, *and see* Allerwich, 135, 203.
——— Rog., 16, 18.
——— Geo., 16.
——— ——— Thom., w. of, 16.
——— Jam., 59.
——— ——— Margy., w. of, 59.
Aleyne, John, 180, 198, 199.
Aleyne, Will., of Stubbylane, 185.
——— Will., of Blore, 209.
Allatt, John, 56, 58.
——— ——— Anne, w. of, 56.
——— ——— Margt., w. of, 58.
——— Rog., 59.
——— ——— Margt., w. of, 59.
Allerwich, 6, 23, 25, 35, 38, 42, 46.
Allyn, Nich., 12.
——— John, 14, 49.
——— ——— Agnes, w. of, 49.
——— Will., arm., 16.
——— Rich., 172.
Almount, Rich., 11, 58.
——— ——— Alice, w. of, 11.
Almyngton, 60.
Alport, Rich., 70.
——— ——— Eliz., w. of, 70.
——— Will., 70.
Alrewas, 141, 153, 187, 191, 203, 221.
——— John de, 130.
Alsager, Will. de, 106.
——— ——— Adam, s. of, 106.
Alsop, Thom., 139.
——— Will., 218.
Alstonfield, 7, 11, 29, 42, 68, 146, 167, 179.
Alton, 179, 184, *and see* Alveton.
Alveton (Alton), 4, 16, 24, 27, 28, 133, 139, 217.
Alymun, John, of Mulwych, 180.
Alynforde, John, of Combrigge, 140.
Alyngton, Will., of Coven, 133.
Amerton, 41.
Amerye, Ralph, 16, 20.
——— Will., 20, 39.
——— ——— Mary, w. of, 39.
Ampe, John, 55.
——— ——— Sarah, w. of, 39.
Amys, John, 163.
Ancott (Oncote), 32.
Anderton, Jam., arm., 60.
Andrewe, Will., clerk, 136, 137.
Andrewes, John, of Hilton, 133.
Anker, John, of Derby, patemaker, 223.
Annesley, John de, kt., 149.
——— ——— Isab., w. of, 149.
Ansley, 17, 33, 47, 210, 211.
Ansted, John, 50.

Apedale, 169, 170, 180.
Appulby, Thom. de, 188, 189.
Arblaster, Thom., arm., 62, 65, 217.
Archbolde, Rich., 63.
Archer, Rich., arm., 151.
Arden, Amb., arm., 27, 35.
—— Sam., 48.
—— —— Mary, w. of, 48.
—— John de, 92.
—— —— Margt., w. of, 92.
Arderne, Will., of Merston, 124.
Arley, 132, 147.
Armeston, Will., 161.
Armitage, 36, 66.
Arowe, 201, 207, 208.
Arundel, Thom., E. of, 16.
—— —— Alathea, w. of, 16.
—— Rich., E. of, 177.
Ascalon, 116.
Ascogh, Will., 191.
Asheby, 135.
—— Will., 133.
—— John, 136.
—— James, 155, 216.
—— Thom., 159.
Ashemores, 67, 68.
Ashforde, Thom., 50.
—— —— Joan, w. of, 50.
Ashley, 9, 56, 60.
—— John, 14.
—— Thom., 15.
Ashmerbroke, 26, 172.
Aspinall, Franc., 41, 62.
—— —— Kath., w. of, 41, 62.
—— Thom., 62.
Aspley, 55, 82, 98, 99.
—— Simon de, 80, 81, 88.
—— —— John, s. of, 88.
—— —— Nich., s. of, 80, 81, 100, 101.
—— —— —— Avice, w. of, 80.
—— —— —— Will., s. of, 81.
—— —— —— —— Dorea., w. of, 81.
—— Steph. de, 81, 82, 84, 98, 101.
Asshe, 205.
Assheburne, co. Derby, 141, 179, 184 187, 192, 196, 202, 209, 216.
Assheton, Thom., of Swytheland, 166.
—— Rog., of Wetton, 179.
—— Ralph, arm., 60.
Asteley, Thom., arm., 128, 141, 167, 206, 216.
—— —— Joan, w. of, 141.
—— Thom., the younger, 128.
—— —— Eliz., w. of, 128.
—— Thom., the Sheriff, 213.
—— Thom., of Pateshulle, 224.
Aston, 15, 18, 34, 39, 46, 115, 140, 183.
Aston upon Trent, 225.
—— in Hales, 20.
—— near Doxey, 24.
—— —— Stone, 65, 66, 203, 210.
—— Little, 12, 142.
—— Walt., kt., 17, 21, 29, 30, 36, 38, 41, 48, 53, 54, 62, 64, 67.
—— —— Gert., w. of, 21, 36, 38, 41, 62, 67.
—— Walt., gent., 41, 57, 63, 64.
—— —— Joyce, w. of, 57, 63.
—— Will., 21, 54.
—— Edw., 21.
—— Edw., kt., 53.
—— Thom., 21.
—— Gilbt. de, 106.
—— Geof. de, 106.
—— Rob. de, 88, 216.
—— Rog., kt., 139, 145, 153, 160, 169.
Astyn, John, 4, 38, 48.
—— —— Kath., w. of, 49.
Atherley, Hen., of Dilhorne, 134.
Atkyn, Nich., of Walle, 147.
Attelbourgh, Will., 216.
Atwood, Hen., 22.
—— Walt., 123.
Audeley, 31, 34, 46, 60, 105, 169, 213.
—— Barony, 145.
—— Liulf de, 75, 103.
—— —— Liulf, s. of, 103.
—— —— —— Rog., s. of, 103.
—— —— —— Adam, s. of, 99, 102, 103, 105.
—— —— —— —— Hen., s. of, 99, 103, 104.
—— —— —— —— —— Jam. de, s. of, 104.
—— —— —— —— Adam, s. of, 99, 103.
—— —— —— —— Will., s. of, 103.
—— —— Ralph, s. of, 103.
—— Emma, w. of Adam, 102, 105.
—— Hen. de, 85, 103, 104.
—— Nich. de, 86, 87, 90, 91.
—— —— Katr., w. of, 86, 87.
—— Hugh, elder, 91, 92, 83.
—— —— younger, 91.
—— James, 91, 92, 104.
—— —— James, s. of, 91.
—— Margy., de, 105.
—— John, arm., 215.
Austen, James, 22.
—— John, 58.
—— —— Susan, w. of, 58.
—— Thom., of Birmingham, 125.
—— Rob., of Stafford, 140.
Awcocke, John, 36.
Aylwardby, co. Derby, 217.
Ayton, co. Derby, 145.

B.

Baban, Thom., 92.
——— ——— Margt., w. of, 92.
Babingtons, the, 17.
——— Zach., D.L., 5.
——— ——— Thom., w. of, 5.
——— Will., 5.
——— Will., the younger, 134.
Babthorp, Rob., 129.
Bache, Will., 45.
——— Thom., 45.
Backhouse (Chamberlyn), Franc., 21.
——— Rob., 21.
——— Rob. del, 94.
——— ——— Agnes, w. of, 94.
Bacon, Matt., 19.
——— ——— Eliz., w. of, 19.
——— Ralph, of Rolleston, 134.
——— John, 154.
Badeley, 4, 67, 182.
——— Thom., 34, 106.
——— John, 9, 34.
Badenale, Rob. de, 103, 104.
Badham, Thom., 13.
——— ——— Franc., w. of, 13.
Badkin, Will., of Fulford, 88.
Badlesmere, Sir Barth. de, 88.
Bagnald, 27.
——— Nich., of Oncote, 195.
——— Thom., 4, 65.
——— Will., of Elkyston, 136.
——— John, of Botyrdon, 146.
——— John, of Oncote, 167, *and see* Bagnall.
Bagnall, 5.
——— Rog., 154.
——— Steph., 154.
——— John, of Oncot, 179.
Bagot, Ant., 12, 62.
——— Hervey, 99, 116.
——— ——— Milis., w. of, 116.
——— John, kt., 127, 129, 144.
——— Thom., 151.
——— Rich., arm., 155, 192, 193, 207, 218.
Bagshawe, Arth., 8.
——— ——— Cecil., w. of, 8.
——— Nich., 9.
Bailly, Rich., of Stansope, 135.
——— Will., of Lecke, 155, *and see* Baly *and* Baylie.
Bakeford, John, of Wheaton Aston, 135.
Baker, John, 30.
——— ——— Cecil., w. of, 30.
——— John, of Hemley, 138.
——— John, of Mershton, 155.
——— John, of Wolverhampton, 195.
——— Griffin, 69.
——— Edw., 69.
Bale, Matt., 25.
Ball, Thom., 12.
——— John, 146.
Ballard, John, 195.
——— Will., parson of Swinnerton, 204.
Balsters, the, 17.
Balterley, 50, 60.
——— John, 127.
——— ——— Matil., w. of, 127.
Baly, Will., 92.
Banester, Geo., 54.
——— Thom., 148.
——— Will., 195, 228.
Barantyne, Dru., 207.
Barboure, Geo., 20.
——— Rich., 35.
——— Nich., 35.
——— Nich., of Walsall, 179.
——— John, 148, 154.
——— Anne, widow, 42.
——— Thom., of Stafford, 148.
Barchurdon, Rog., 168.
Bard, Rich. le, 161.
Bardeley, 44.
Baret, Will., 167.
Barkeley, Rob., arm., 69.
Barker, Phil. le, of Eccleshale, 97.
——— ——— Will., s. of, 97.
——— John, of Hethe, 148.
Barlaston, 32.
Barnald, John, of Podmore, 150.
Barnefilde, Rich., arm., 37.
Barnesby, Will., 8.
——— ——— Isab., w. of, 8.
Barnett, John, 24.
Barre, 203.
——— Great, 18, 23, 25, 35, 38, 46, 146, 147, 150.
——— Perrie, 27, 41, 50, 66, 150, 165, 178.
——— John, 131.
Barton under Needwood, 5, 24, 181, 182.
——— Odo, manor of, 219.
——— John, the younger, 128.
——— Rich. de, 138.
Bartram, Will., 31, 37.
——— ——— Eliz., w. of, 37.
Bassets Cross, 178.
Bassett, Rich., 179, 193.
——— Rich., of Blore, 208, 217.
——— Will. ——— ——— 217.
——— Ralph, 134, 135, 139, 140, 166, 167, 179, 182, 185, 187, 192, 193, 194, 199, 202, 205, 206, 217.
——— Edm., 169.
——— Walt., 10, 11, 20, 38, 45.
——— ——— Sconso., w. of, 11, 20.
——— Edw., arm., 11.
——— ——— Jane, w. of, 11.

Baswiche, 30.
Bata, Matt., 61.
——— ——— Eliz., w. of, 61.
Bate, Humph., 24.
——— John, 48, 131, 160.
——— Clem., 148.
——— Thom., 156.
Bateford, 156.
Bateman, Rob., 58.
——— Hugh, 58.
Batkyn, Humph., 26.
Baxter, Rich., 49.
——— Rob., of Lichfield, 124.
Bayles, Thom., 33.
Baylie, Thom., 17.
——— Rich., 17.
——— ——— Margt., w. of, 17.
——— Hugh, 18.
——— ——— Margt., w. of, 18.
——— Steph., 55.
——— Ralph, 58.
——— John, of Kynfare, 153.
Beale, John, of Alstonefeld, 146.
Beanbrugge, co. Salop, 183.
Beardmore, John, 12, 24, 31.
——— ——— Margt., w. of, 24.
——— Anne, 29.
——— Thom., 40.
——— *see also* Berdmore.
Beardsmore, John, of Froghole, 186.
Beauchamp, Rich., arm., 186, 198, 201, 207, 208, *and see* Bellocampo.
Beaufo, Rich., arm., 219, 224.
Beaumont, Hen., kt., 172.
——— ——— Joan, f. w. of, 172.
Becham, *see* Beauchamp.
Bedel, Steph. le, of Eccleshale, 97.
——— ——— Rob., s. of, 97.
——— John, 139.
Bednall, 30, 61, 163.
——— Will., 125.
——— John, of King's Bromley, 126.
Bedulle (Biddulph), 218.
Beeche, 6, 106, 115.
——— Thom., 10.
——— John, 12.
——— Will., 19.
——— Rich., 140.
Beek, Will., hosier, 125.
——— Will., clerk, 205, 206.
——— Will., of Lichfield, chap., 212.
——— John, clerk, 171.
——— Rich., 171, 173, 174, 177.
——— Thom., kt., 188.
Beffcotte, 34.
Beke, *see* Beek.
Bekyngton, Rich. de, 225.
Belcher, Ellen, widow, 5.
——— Will., 62.
Bellocampo, A. de, 74.
Benasses, 153.
Bennett, Jam., 18, 59.
Benreper, 209.
Bentham, 145.
Bentley, 19, 138, 183.
——— John, 15, 62.
——— Isab., of Brokhous, 215.
Benton, 153.
Berdmore, Rob., 174.
——— ——— Margy., f. w. of, 174.
——— John, 4, 174.
——— Humph., 18.
——— ——— Barb., w. of, 18.
——— *see also* Beardmore.
Berford, 183.
Bergevenny, Edw., lord of, 151.
Berington, Rich., arm., 44.
Berisforde, 22, 145, 167, 179, 185, 193, 199, 202, 209, 225.
——— John, 42, 145, 156, 167, 179, 183, 185, 193, 199, 202, 209, 210, 225.
Berkeley, Maurice, de Gaunt, 118.
Berks, 167.
Bermondsey, 142.
Bernard, John, of Beanbrugge, 183.
——— Nich., 212.
Bertram, John, of Strethay, 187.
Bertreme, Will., of Fulfen, 142.
Beryhill, 33.
Bescote, 212.
Bett, Rob., 17.
Betteley, 29, 60, 144, 145, 173.
Beumeys, Hugh de, 104.
——— ——— Isab., w. of, 104.
Bevell, Lawr., 52.
Bevile, Ralf de, 103, 104.
Bickford, Walt., 53.
——— Joan, widow, 53.
——— Eliz., 53.
Biddulph, *see* Bedulle *and* Bydulf.
Biggenhall, 34.
Bignoll ende, 60.
Bilbrook, *see* Billerbroke.
Bill, Rob., 64.
——— Rich., 64.
——— ——— Eliz., w. of, 64.
Billerbroke, 204, 221, 222.
Billington, 44, 213.
Bilston, 68, 221.
Birche, John, the younger, 15, 65.
——— Thom., the elder, 25.
——— Will., of Lichfield, 179.
Birchenfeld, 52.
Birkys, Rich., of Teyne, 203.
Birmingham, 125, 146, 155, 221.
——— Will., of Coventry, kt., 125, 131, 146.
——— John, Dean of Wolverhampton, 200.
Bishton, 30, 180, 216.

Bishton, Ralph, 180, 216, *and see* Byspeston.
Bissell, Thom., 31, 37.
—— —— Margt., w. of, 31, 37.
—— Will., 34.
—— —— Elean., w. of, 34.
Bisshebury, 187.
Bisshopeston, Rog., 139.
—— —— Joan, w. of, 139.
Blackehaughe, 52.
Blackwood, 27.
Blakemere, John, of Weston-under-Lesyord, 125.
Blaket, John, kt., 129.
—— Eliz., 129, 133, 136, 137, 150, 164.
Blaknall, 162, 180, 182.
Blest, Thom., 172.
Blibury, 163.
Blithbridge, 44.
Blithe, water of, 69.
Blithefeld, Thom., pars. of, 155.
Bloomer, Thom., 3.
—— —— Isab., w. of, 3.
Blore, 60, 135, 166, 179, 183, 187, 192, 193, 195, 199, 206, 208, 209, 217.
—— heathe, 60.
—— Ralf de, 75.
—— Will., pars. of, 195.
Bloreton, 160.
—— Thom., of Rugeley, 160.
Blount, Thom. Pope, kt., 7, 30.
—— Thom., kt., 133, 136, 137, 150, 155, 164, 188, 191, 214.
—— —— Eliz., w. of, 133, 136, 137, 150, 164.
—— John, kt., 133.
—— —— Elena, f. w. of, 133.
—— Humf., 169, 170, 180.
—— Walt., kt., 188, 198, 214.
—— Walt., of Aylwardby, arm., 217.
—— Walt., of Elvaston, 224.
—— Roland, 223, *and see* Blunt.
Bloxwich, 43, 50.
—— Little, 17.
—— Great, 53, 157.
Blumenhull, *see* Blymhill.
Blunt, Edw., 47.
Blymhill, 27, 129, 132.
—— church of, 123.
—— Steph. de Bromley, pars. of, 227.
Blythbury, 30, 151, 155, 163.
Blythford, 30.
Bobington, 50, 51, 125.
Boghay, John, 129.
—— —— Rich., s. of, 129.
Bokeland, Will., arm., 181.
Bokenale, Thom., 166.
Bold, Ralph, 54.
Bold, Ralph, Parnell, w. of, 54.
—— Will., of Enstone, 180, 216.
Boldem, 139.
Boleter, Rob., of Burton, 127.
Bolton, John, 9, 15.
—— —— Alice, w. of, 15.
—— Geo., 58.
Bonehill, 19.
Bonus, Thom., 57.
—— —— Joan, w. of, 57.
Boone, Hen., of Penford, 145.
—— Hugh —— —— 145.
Booth, Geo., kt., 60.
—— John of Bruwode, 148.
Bordel, Thom., of Arowe, arm., 201, 207, 208.
Bordesle, Abbot of, 123.
Borghton, John, arm., 191.
Bosson, Edw., 29.
Bosworth, 186, 197, 198.
—— Rob., pars. of, 211.
Boteler, John, of Coventry, 132.
—— Thom., 134, 151, 160, 172.
—— John, of Fetherstone, 134.
—— John, of Chebsey, 172.
—— Nich., 180.
Boterley, *see* Balterly.
Bothe, John, 159, 205.
—— —— Joan, w. of, 159.
—— Giles de, 174.
Bothehall, 52.
Botley, Rob., 199.
Bott, Edw., 47.
—— Robt., 47.
—— John, of Denstone, 172.
Botteslowe, 4.
Boturdon, 146, 168.
Boudesall, 130.
Boughey, Geo., 11.
—— —— Alice, w. of, 11.
—— Rob., 225.
—— —— Joan, f. w. of, 225, *and see* Boghay *and* Bowghey.
Boughton, Thom., arm., 150.
Boulde, 148.
Bourgchier, Will., 144.
—— —— Thoma., w. of, 144,
Bouthes, 52.
Bouweles, Will. de, of Rushale, 130.
—— —— Will., s. of, 130.
Bower ende, 31.
Bowers, 6.
Bowes, Jerome, kt., 65.
—— John, 65.
Bowghey, John, 213.
—— —— Amise, f. w. of, 213.
—— James, of Whitemore, 213.
Bowman, John, 68.
Bowyer, Will., arm., 24, 38, 46, 47.
—— Rich., 41.
—— Thom., 62.

Bowyer, Rob., of Rugeley, 218.
Boydell, Will., 154, 180.
——— ——— Alice, w. of, 154.
Boylson, Hen., 36.
Boylston, John, 5, 20, 25, 66.
——— ——— Eliz., w. of, 5, 20, 66.
Boys, Rich. de, 78.
——— ——— Basil, w. of, 78.
Brace, John, 204.
Brachowe, Will., 180.
Brackley, Will., 61.
Bradborne, Will., arm., 25, 61.
——— Hen., 192, 193.
Bradbury, Hugh de, 190.
Braddock, 44, *see also* Brodoke.
Bradley, 68, 69.
——— Humph., 32.
——— Denis, 32.
——— ——— Judith, w. of, 32.
——— Rich., 33.
——— Bened., 38.
——— ——— Jane, w. of, 38.
——— Thom., 55.
Bradnappe, 6, 38, 47, 48, 53, 54.
Bradshawe, Chris., 5.
——— Rich., 5.
——— ——— Eliz., w. of, 5.
——— Isab., 44.
——— John, 44.
——— John, of Burton, 197.
——— Ellen, 44, 58.
——— Will., 130, 161, 180.
Bradwall, 34, 102, 180.
——— John, 221.
Bramshall, 139, *and see* Bromshulf.
Branston, 29.
Bratte, Nich., of Dymmesdale, 215.
Bredhill, John, 144, 158.
Bredhulle, John, of Kyngeswynford, 146.
Bredsalpark, Thom., prior of, 149.
Breewood, 23, 43, 49, 136, 148, 153, 161, 166, 168, 184, 191, 217, 220.
——— John, pars. of Rodburne, 149.
——— Cecil., prioress of House of Black Nuns of, 150.
Brembletye, 162.
Brendwoode, 8, 10, 26, 37, 59.
Brere, Walt. de, 227.
Breres, Edm., 28.
Brereton, 36, 66, 177, 203, 218, 220, 222.
——— Ralph, kt., 27.
Brerewood, 36.
Breton, Nich., arm., 42, 43, 45.
——— ——— John, s. of, 42, 43.
——— ——— ——— Nich., s. of, 42, 43.
Breton, Edw., 42, 43, 45.
Breton, Mayhowse, of Swinnerton, 179.
Brett, Thom., 34, 180.
Brianeston, co. Dorset, 214.
Brid, John, 128.
——— Agnes, 131.
——— Rob., 131.
——— Will., 187.
Bridgeford, 213.
——— Great, 15, 67.
——— Little, 6, 15, 24, 32, 46, 67, 172.
Bridgenorth, 123.
Brierley, 3.
Brindley, Robt., 3, *and see* Brundley *and* Bryndelegh.
Brinley, John, 53.
Brinsford, 67, 68, 228.
Brinton, 26, 27, *and see* Bruynton.
Britz, 162.
Broadheade, 51.
Broadoke, 56, *see also* Brodoke.
Brocke, Ant., 35, 50.
——— ——— Anne, w. of, 50.
——— Hen., 35, 50.
——— ——— Joan, w. of, 50.
Brockhous, 52, 178, 215.
Brockhurst, Rob., 6.
——— ——— Alice, w. of, 6.
Brockton, 30.
Brodcooke, 215.
Brodoke, 22, 28, 44, 56.
Brodrepp, Rich., arm., 67.
——— ——— Mary, w. of, 67.
Brokesby, Barth., 135, 159.
——— Hen., 159.
Brokhole, John, 157.
Brome, Reg., arm., 43.
Bromehurst, 212.
Bromley, 124.
——— Abbots, 26, 31, 32, 37, 40, 45, 139, 140, 143, 165, 216.
——— ——— John, vicar of, 163.
——— King's, 14, 20, 41, 57, 62, 126, 158, 164, 165, 178.
——— Bagottes, 31, 40, 45, 55.
——— Gerardes, 60.
——— Pagettes, 66.
——— Hurst, 60.
——— Sir Rob. de, 78.
——— Will. de, 89.
——— ——— John, s. of, 89.
——— John, 140, 166, 172.
——— John, kt., 217.
——— John, of Burton, 194, 211.
——— Rich., 145, 158.
——— Thom., of Lichfield, 166.
——— Rog., 177.
——— ——— Agnes, w. of, 177.
——— Steph., of Chorleton, 200.
——— Steph. de, parson of Blymhill, 227.

Bromsgrove, 183.
Bromshulf, 179.
——— Little, 20, 64, *and see* Bramshall.
Bromswerd, Thom., of Crosley, 172.
Bromwych, co. Warwick, 124.
Brooke, Will., 20, 60.
——— John, 50.
——— Thom., 141, 163.
Broughall, 15.
Broughton, Brian, 9.
——— Edw., 20, 64, *and see* Burghton.
Brouyng, Will., of Saresden, 198.
Broweland, John, 153, 154.
Browne, Rich., 7, 20.
——— Rob., 9.
——— Will., 9, 51.
——— Thom., 16, 22, 58, 65.
——— Thom., of Pype Ridware, 133.
——— Thom., of Teyne, 203.
——— John, of Coldnorton, 210.
Bruggenorth, 132.
Brun, Rich., 83.
Brundley, Rich., 4.
Brunner, John, 34.
Brusenhulle, Ralph, 159.
Bruynton, 132, 134.
Bryerley, 19.
Bryndelegh, Rich. de, of Wystanton, 126.
——— John de ——— ——— 126.
Bucke, Franc., 50.
Buckingham, Humph., Duke of, 175, 201.
Bucknall, 12, 21, 67, 173, 180, 204, 213, 216.
——— Eves, 9.
——— Thom., 12, 204, 216.
——— Will., 13, 215.
——— ——— Margt., w. of, 13.
——— Margt., of Teyne, 203, *and see* Bokenale.
Bucks, co., 131, 142.
Buffray, Will., lord of Womborne, 17.
——— ——— John, s. of, 17.
——— ——— ——— Jane, d. of, 17.
——— John, 169.
Bulkley, Will., arm., 15.
——— John, 170.
Bulleyn, Rob., 46.
Bullock, Rob., 54.
——— ——— Joan, w. of, 54.
——— Thom., of Erbersfeld, 167.
Bultus, John, 135.
Burbury, Will., 11.
Bures, Adam de, 78.
——— ——— Alditha, d. of. 78.
——— ——— Felic., d. of, 78.
Burghton, 200.
——— John, 200.
Burgilon, Sim., 83.
——— Rog. de, 84, 86, 95.
——— Thom., 158, 164, 165, 178.
——— ——— Agnes, w. of, 158, 164.
——— Rob., elder, 178.
——— Rob., younger, 158, 164, 178.
——— Ralph, 89.
——— John de, 92, 93, 95.
Burie, Thom., 44.
——— ——— Eliz., w. of, 44.
Burley, Will., 200.
Burne, Thom., 36.
——— ——— Margt., w. of, 36.
Burnell, Edw., 142.
——— ——— Alina, w. of, 142.
——— Rob., 186.
Burnes, John, 15.
Burnett, John, 17, 164.
——— ——— Jane, w. of, 17.
——— Thom., 17, 32, 35, 39, 45, 58, 63.
——— ——— Alice, w. of, 32.
——— ——— Kath., w. of, 35.
——— ——— Rob., s. of, 17.
——— ——— ——— Thom., s. of, 17.
——— Margt., Maud, Agnes, 17.
Burnhill, 167.
Burnley, Will., of Whitmore, 184.
Burone, Margt., 140.
——— Rog., 140.
Burslem, 67.
Burston, 66.
Burton-on-Trent, 7, 9, 11, 29, 33, 44, 64, 127. 148, 194, 197, 211.
——— Thom., arm., 13.
——— ——— Kath., w. of, 13.
——— Edw., arm., 13.
——— ——— Eliz., w. of, 13.
——— John, fissher, 135.
——— Ralph, abbot of, 141, 185, 211.
——— Abbot of, 165.
——— Will., 178.
Bushbury, 7, 12, 13, 23, 63, 68, 156.
——— Ralph, 213, *and see* Bisshebury.
Butler, Hen., 24, 37.
Butterton, 9, 10, 65, 78, 89, 117, 146, 217, *and see* Boturdon.
Button, John, 45.
——— ——— Walt., s. and h. of, 45.
Bydulf, 172, 179, 212.
——— John, of London, 179.
Bydulk, Amb., of Stone, 184.
Bykford, John, 166, 168.
Byllerbrok, 222, *see also* Billerbroke.
Byllisley, co. Warwick, 208.
Bylston, John, of Wolverhampton, 212.

Byngham, Rich., of Bateford, 156, 160, 188, 191.
Byrche, John, 12.
Byrde, John, of Lichfield, mercer, 125, 126.
Byron, *see* Burone.
Byspeston, Pet. de, 135.

C.

Caldmore, 47.
Caldon, 8, 15, 20, 52, 136.
Caldwall, Will., 33.
——— ——— Eliz., w. of, 33.
——— John, 141.
Caldwich, 28, *and see* Colwych.
Calewale, Rob., 163.
Callengewood, Rich., 42.
Callowhill, 136, 163, 216.
Calton, 20, 28, 140, 146, 187, 197.
Campedone, Nich., 172.
Campyon, Thom., 132, 147.
Cannock, 30, 37, 43, 68, 69, 124, 141, 148, 183, 215.
——— forest, 30, 36, 54, 68.
Canterbury, John, Archb. of, 173, 179.
Cantrell, John, of Cantrell, 146.
——— John, of Alstonfeld, 167, 179.
Canwall, Hen., prior of, 151.
Careless, Rob., 185.
Careswall, 22, 26, 28, 33, 44, 49, 58, 126, 162, 212, 213.
Carlett, John, 34.
Carter, Thom., 27.
——— John, of Mavesyn Ridware, 133.
Cartwright, Franc., 11.
——— ——— Anne, w. of, 11.
——— Rowland, 25.
——— ——— Alice, w. of, 25.
——— Edw., 45.
——— Thom., 52.
——— ——— Anne, w. of, 52.
——— Will., 137.
——— Rich., 147, 161, 184.
Casterne, 27, 136, 194, 199.
Castle, 44.
——— Paryshe, 33.
Castlebromwych, 165.
Catesby, Rob., 139.
Cauldon, 55, *and see* Caldon.
Caumvile, John, of Alveton, 133.
Caverswall, *see* Careswall.
Cawardyne, John, 201, 206, *and see* Cowardyne *and* Kawardyne.
Chackill, 55, 60, 166.
Chaddersley, 102.
Chadderton, Oliv. de, 142.
Chadwick, John, 26, 38, 57, 60.
——— John, Joyce, w. of, 60.
——— Nich., 29.
Chaldegrave, 162.
Chaldon, 177.
——— Will., 177.
Chaloner, Hen., of Dulverne, 126.
Chamberleyn, Sir Rog., 181.
Chamberlyn (Backhouse), Franc., 21, 32.
——— ——— Rob., 21.
Chancellor, Thom., the King's. 226.
——— Edm. ——— ——— 228.
Chanton, 185.
Chapman, John, 13, 52, 53, 204.
——— ——— Thoma., w. of, 52.
——— Rich., 13, 52.
——— ——— Mary, w. of, 52.
Charleton, Thom., kt., 158.
——— ——— Eliz., w. of, 158, *and see* Cherleton.
Charnes, 55, 79, 84.
——— Reg. de, 78.
Charteley, 26.
Chaterton, John, 151.
——— Oliv., of Fulfen, 154.
——— ——— Alice, w. of, 154.
Chatkulum, Thom. de, 78.
——— ——— Sarra, w. of, 78.
——— Nich. de, 78.
——— ——— Avice, w. of, 78.
Chatterley, Rich., 36.
——— ——— Dory., w. of, 36.
Chatwall, 46.
Chaucer, *see* Chawcers.
Chaundos, Eliz., 149.
Chawcers, Thom., arm., 168.
Chayne, Will., of Longefeld, 147.
Cheadle, *see* Chedull *and* Chetell.
Chebsey, 8, 10, 47, 61, 66, 172, 212, 226.
Checkley, 10, 14, 16, 32, 41, 63, 67, 143, 171, 174.
——— banke, 67.
Chedull, 14, 22, 23, 28, 29, 30, 31, 34, 39, 45, 49, 51, 52, 56, 58, 61, 65, 146, 174, 194, 205, 212, 222.
——— Grange, 208.
Chedulton, 22, 23, 27, 56, 134, 146.
Chelderhey end, 26.
Chell, 102, 103, 104, 105, 107.
——— Great, 86, 102, 105, 106.
——— Rob., 85, 106, 107.
——— Hen. de, 88, 1 8.
——— Rich. de, 88, 104, 105, 107.
——— Pavia, widow, 104.
——— Margy., 105.
——— Will. de, 108.
——— Hugh de, 108.
Chelton, Rich., of Chorleton, 200.

Cherleton, John de, 85, 90, 106.
——— Will. de, 85, 106.
——— ——— Will., s. of, 85, 106.
——— Walt. de, 113.
Chesterfield, 18, 130.
Chesterton, 46, 168, 169, 173, 180.
——— Rich., of Pedmore.
Chetell, 222.
Chetelton, Rich. de, 86, *and see* Chetylton.
Chetwind, 129.
——— manor, 175.
——— Walt., 12, 45, 56, 88.
——— ——— Elean., w. of, 12.
——— Will., kt., 56.
——— Phil., kt., 141, 147, 148, 159, 175.
——— John, 56, 66, 67, 132, 176, 177, 181, 182, 222.
——— Rich., 176.
Chetwood, Rich., kt., 6.
Chetwyne (Chetwynd), Thom., 21, 32.
——— Eliz., 171.
Chetylton, Rob., 175.
Chewte, Phil., 15.
Cheyne, Will., kt., 162.
Chillington, 43, 135, 141.
Chippingdale, John, Doctor of Laws, 24.
Chistlyn Hay, 43, 68.
Chok, John, 160.
Cholmondelegh, Rob. de, of Edlaston, 126.
Chorleton, 9, 84, 85, 200.
——— Simon de, 84.
——— ——— Rob., s. of, 84.
Chorley, 8, 26, 138, 172.
Clanford, 21.
——— Grange, 15.
Claro, Will. of Stretehay, 148.
Clarendon, Thom., of Cokhill, 208.
Clarke, John, 32, 37, 59.
——— ——— Eliz., w. of, 32, 37.
——— Rich., 32, 37.
——— Will., 48.
——— Ant., 67.
Clayton, 93, 156, 215.
——— Little, 169.
——— Thom., of Badeley, 182.
Clegge, John, 147.
Clemson, Thom., 68.
Clerk, Thom., 6.
——— John, 24.
——— ——— Jane, w. of, 24.
——— John, of Repton, 133.
——— John, of Whittington, 161.
——— John, of Tybton, 221.
——— Nich., of Colton, 163.
——— Will., of Bukenale, 180.
——— Will., of Stone, 210.
Clerkeson, Humph, 140, 157.
Cliffe, Thom., 47.
——— Lawr., 47.
Clifton, 65, 66, 225.
——— Camvile, 175.
Cloughton (alias Ufton), 5.
Clove, Rog., 123.
Clowdewood, 9.
Clowes, Thom., 34, 54.
——— ——— Eliz., w. of, 34.
——— Lawr., 34.
——— ——— Margt., w. of, 34.
——— Will., 43.
——— Robt., 51.
Cluloe, Will., 60.
Clutton, 170.
Cocker, John, 47, 48.
Cocknage, 37.
Codsall, 13, 199.
Cokayne, John, of Asshburne, 187, 192, 196, 202, 213, 216.
——— Will. ——— ——— 187, 192 196, 202, 209.
——— John, 141.
——— ——— Eliz., w. of, 141.
——— John, kt., 156.
——— ——— Isab., f. w. of, 156.
——— John, the younger, kt., 156.
——— ——— Joan, f. w. of, 156.
Coke, Adam, of Bruynton, 132.
——— John ——— ——— 132.
——— John, 163.
——— John, of Stafford, 148.
——— Edw., kt., Chief Justice, 46.
Cokes, Will., of Walsall, 179.
Cokkes, Thom., of Stoke Priors, 212.
——— ——— Isab., w. of, 312.
Cokkys, John, 224.
——— John, the younger, 222, 224.
Cooke, Thom., 10, 62.
——— Will., 41, 62.
——— John, 130, 142.
Cookes, Hen., 35.
——— John, 62.
——— ——— Ellen, w. of, 62.
——— Samson, 62.
Cookeslande, 6, 12, 15, 32, 46.
Cokenegge, Geof. de, 106.
Cokette, Rich., 216.
Cokhill, Hanbury, 208.
Coklogh, Rich., 218.
——— Rog., 218, *and see* Colclough.
Colborne, Rob., 125, 126.
——— ——— Eliz., w. of, 125.
——— Anne, 23.
Colclough, 218.
——— Barth., 36.
——— John, 65.
——— Will., 155.
——— Thom., 160, 218.
Coldnorton, 8, 192, 210.
Cole, Edw., 49.

Cole, Hen., 46.
——— John, 49.
Colet, Rich., of Byllerbrok, 222.
Colle, Rich., clerk, 229.
Colleman, Rich., courtholder, 126.
Collettys, Rich., of Billerbroke, 204.
Collinson, Will., 44.
Colmon, Rog , 152.
——— Hugh, of Tamworth, 195, 201.
——— Simon, of Canke, 215.
Colmore, Thom., 43.
——— ——— Eliz., w. of, 43.
Colond, co. Derby, 194.
Colseley, 41, 69.
Colt, Edw., 222.
Colton, 29, 30, 140, 157, 163, 217.
——— church, 30.
——— tithes, 30.
Colwych, 26, 29, 30, 62, 145.
——— priory of St. Margt. of, 145.
——— Rob., prior of, 159.
——— Thom., preb. of, 221.
——— Rich., 220.
Coly, Thom., 148.
Colyns, Thom., 153.
——— Hugh, of Chorley, 172.
Comberford, 42, 43, 45, 155.
——— Thom., 21.
Combridge, 63, 67, 140.
Compson, James, 32.
Compton, 159, 191, 199, 222.
Comslowe, 52.
Congreve, Rich., arm., 221, 224.
——— John, 148.
Consall, 26.
Cooper, John, 5.
Copenhall, 46.
Copwood, Jane, 16.
——— Will., 26.
——— ——— Geo , s. and h. of, 26.
——— Bassett, 26.
Corbett, Will., 13, 17.
——— Will., of Colwich, 145.
——— Judith, widow, 51, 52, 56.
——— Thom., 129.
——— John, of Longnore, 183.
Corfton, 142.
Cornbrigge, 216.
Corneford, 171, 174, 177.
Cosseby, 132.
Cotes, Rob. 83, 84.
——— Will., 84.
——— Humf., 155.
——— John, 217, *and see* Cotys.
Coton, 36. 42, 43, 45, 68, 142, 150, 153, 161, 168, 213.
——— near Hambury, 173.
——— Will., 125.
——— Thom., 150, 168, 171, 173.
Cotton, 4, 15, 21, 24, 25, 66, 68.
——— Walt., 7, 59.
Cotton, Edw., arm., 9.
——— Will., 10, 17, 37, 59.
——— ——— Margt., w. of, 17.
——— Thom., 37, 59.
——— ——— Franc., w. of, 59.
——— Geo., 49.
Cotwalton, 33.
Cotys, Thom., 195.
Coucher, Rich., coucher, 125, 126.
Couper, John, of Lichfield, couper, 126.
——— Thom., of Onne, 147.
——— John, 157.
——— John, of Netherton, 221.
——— Will., 153.
——— Rich., of Pipe Ridware, 221.
Courte, John, 185.
Coven, 67, 68, 133, 134, 137, 145, 147, 153, 161, 228.
Coventry, 125, 131, 132, 186, 197.
——— and Lichfield, Bishops of, *see* Lichfield.
Cowan, Will., 40.
——— ——— Margt., w. of, 40.
Cowarderey, John, of Ilum, 194, 225.
Cowardyne, Dav., 149.
Cowene, *see* Coven.
Cowlep, 34.
——— Will., 164.
——— Thom., of Bruynton, 134.
Cowop, Thom,, 69.
——— Rich., 69.
Cowper, John, 36, 61.
——— Geo., 50.
——— Rob., 50.
——— James, 51.
——— Thom., 63, 65, 67.
——— ——— Margt., w. of, 65.
——— Will., 185.
——— ——— Joan, f. w. of, 185.
Coxe, Rich., 23, *and see* Cokkes *and* Cokkys.
Coxon, Anne, widow, 26.
Coyney, Thom., elder, 9.
——— Thom., younger, 9.
——— John, 37.
——— Rob., of Weston Coyney, 146, 177, 182, 184, 191, 204, 216.
Cradocke, Walt., 5.
——— Edw., 9.
——— Geo., 22, 28, 30, 32, 43.
——— Matt., 32, 46.
——— Thom , 160.
——— ——— John, s. of, 160.
Crakmersh, 7, 37, 59, 63, 67, 170, 180.
Craule, Gt., 131, 142.
Creek, co. Northamp , 222.
Creghton, Isab., prioress of Brewode, 211.
Creighton, 59.
Cresset, Hugh, 129.

Cresswalle, 27, 33, 34.
Crich, Geo., 9.
——— ——— Jane, w. of, 9.
Cricheley, Edw., 38.
——— Thom., 38.
Crichlowe, Geo., 42.
Crick, Rob., 222.
Croftys, John, of Stretton, 167.
Crompton, Thom., arm., 33, 37, 49.
Cromwell, Ralph, kt., 134.
Crosley, 172.
Crosse, Robt., 12.
——— ——— Eliz., w. of, 12.
——— Will., 35.
——— ——— Agnes, w. of, 35.
Crosswey, John, 68.
——— ——— Rich., s. of, 68.
——— ——— ——— Anne, w. of, 68.
Croxdene, Ralph, abbot of, 150, 183.
Croxhale, co. Derby, 206.
Crusader, Old, Effigy of, 117.
Cubleston, *see* Kebbulston.
Cubley, co. Derby, 182, 185.
Culvert, 65.
Cumberford, John, 151.
——— Thom., 222.
——— Will., 155, 176, 222, *and see* Comberford.
Cuny, *see* Coyney.
Cupper, John, 54.
Curboun, John, 192, 193.
Curburrowe, 5, 20, 27, 41, 55, 57, 131.
——— Darvell, 57.
——— Somerfield, 57.
Curson, John, 163, 204, 206, 209, 215.
——— ——— Thom., s. and h. of, 206.
——— Rich., arm., 203.
——— Senchia, of Croxhale, 206.
——— Hen., of Ketlestone, 223, 224.
Cursy, Arth. de, arm., 181.
Curteys, Rob., 185, 197.
Curtler, John, 22.

D.

Daddesley (Dodsleigh), 23.
——— Leas, 23.
Dalman, Rich., 225.
——— Will., 225.
——— Hugh, 225.
——— John, 225.
Damefield, 20.
Damport, Hugh, 124.
——— Will., of Whitmore, 184.
——— ——— Margt., w. of, 184.
——— John, of Whitmore, 184.
——— John, of Merton, 184.
Damport, John, of Derby, arm., 223, 224.
Danvers, Dan., 37.
Danyell, John, kt., 136, 171, 173.
——— Thom., of Brewode, 166, 168, 217.
Darbye, Will., 5.
——— ——— Margy., w. of, 5.
——— Edm., 49.
Darcy, Rob., 135.
Darlaston, 54, 98.
——— Alina, lady of, 73.
——— Petron., of, 98, *and see* Derlaston *and* Dorlaston.
Dashfen, Humph., 28.
——— ——— Joyce, w. of, 28.
——— Rose, widow, 28.
Daubrichcourt, John, kt., 156.
——— ——— Joan, d. of, 156.
Daumport, Ralph, of Leeke, 163.
Davenport, John, arm., 9.
——— Hugh, of Mavesyn Ridware, 194, 201, 206.
——— ——— Margt., w. of, 201, 206, *and see* Damport *and* Daumport.
Davidson, Will., 129.
Dawes, Will., 14, 57.
Dayken, Rich., 26.
Deken, Rob., 226.
Delahay, Matt., 180.
Delf, Will., of Dilron, 180.
Delfehowses, 52.
Delves, 169, 170, 180.
——— John, 89, 124, 169, 170, 173, 180.
——— ——— Margt., w. of, 169, 170.
——— ——— Elena, w. of, 170, 180.
——— Rich., 131, 169, 170, 173, 180.
——— ——— Sibil, f. w. of, 131.
——— ——— Eliz., f. w. of, 173.
Denstone, 144, 172, 179, 180, 187, 191, 193, 197.
Derby, co., 126, 130, 133, 140, 141, 145, 149, 159, 163, 167, 179, 182, 184, 185, 187, 192, 194, 195, 196, 198, 206, 208, 209, 217, 223, 224.
Derewent, Rich., 168.
——— Edm., 168.
Derington, 15, 21.
Derlaston, near Stone, 210, 211.
Derneford, manor of, 219, 220.
Dernesiawe, *see* Dorslow.
Despencer, Hugh le, the elder, 138.
Dethek, Will. de, 149.
——— Oliv., of Blore, 208, 217.
——— Margt. of Newehall, 225.
——— John ——— ——— 225.
——— Thom. ——— ——— 225.
——— Thom., of Uttoxeter, 225.
Devereux, John de, 86.
Deykyn, Will., 222.

Dayne, Rich., Leek, 163.
Deys, Rich., 14
Dicken, Chris., 13.
——— John, 28.
——— ——— Jane, w. of, 28.
Dieulacres, John, abbot of, 163, 182, 185.
Digby, John, 61.
Dilhorn (Dilron), (Dulverne), 16, 20, 22, 26, 28, 31, 33, 34, 44, 49, 58, 59, 66, 126, 134, 180, 204.
Docksie, Thom., 34.
Dodde, John, 165.
Dodington, *see* Derington.
Dodsley, 67, *see* Daddesley.
Doge, Will., 154.
Dolphyn, Thom., 4.
——— ——— Alice, w. of, 4.
Dombylle, Pet., 225.
Donyngton, Will., 183.
Dorden, 176.
Dore, near Norton, 171, 173.
Dorington, Rich., 6.
——— Franc., 6, 56.
——— ——— Franc., s. of, 6.
——— Matt., 6.
——— Geo., 161.
Dorlaston, 14, 69.
——— Humph., 11.
——— ——— Chris., w. of, 11, *and see* Darlaston.
Dorslow, 74, 75, 77, 81.
——— Petron. de, 73, 75.
——— Gamel de, 75.
——— Thom. de, 79.
——— Rog. de, 80.
Dorwer, John, of Mathefeld, 187.
Doune, John, arm., 34.
——— John, of Loxley, 216.
Dounton, 134.
Downes, Will., 43.
——— ——— Joan, w. of, 43.
Doxeye, 15.
——— Thom., of James Rushton, 151.
Doyley, Edw., arm., 213, 214.
——— manor, 213.
Draffgate, Will., 42.
Drakeford, Rich., 11, 13, 30, 51.
Drakelowe, co. Derby, 206.
Draycott, 12, 22, 28, 36, 51, 58, 63, 171, 173, 178, 182.
——— Will., 8.
——— John, 52.
——— ——— Anne, w. of, 52.
——— John, of Draycott, 178.
——— ——— Agnes, f. w. of, 178.
——— Chris., 182.
——— Rog., 148, 155, 156, 203.
——— Rich., kt., 155, 156.
——— Phil. de, 156.
Draycott, Phil. de, Joan, w. of, 156.
——— ——— John, s. of, 156.
Draynton, 62.
Drayton, 60.
——— Bassett, 19, 134, 151.
——— Great, 60.
——— Little, 60.
Drover, Will., of Birmingham, hostler, 125.
Dudley, 137, 143, 153, 154, 158, 163, 167.
——— Thom., 4.
——— Edw., Lord, 68.
——— John, 169.
Dudson, Elias, 26.
——— ——— Franc., w. of, 26.
Dulrigge, 223.
Duncalf, John, 51, 211.
——— ——— Joyce, w. of, 51.
——— Will., 51.
——— Thom., 174.
Dunsclev, 24.
Dunston, 5.
Dunton, co. Warwick, 134, 160, 168.
Duredent, Bishop, Walt., 111.
Dutton, John, 50.
Duy, Diowe, 181.
Dyminysdale, 169, 215.
Dyngeley, Rich., 152.
——— ——— Will., s. of, 152.
——— Thom., 151, 152.
Dynham, John, kt., 219, 220.
——— Joan, w. of, 219, 220.

E.

Ealy, 36.
Eardley, John, 9.
——— ——— Alice, w. of, 9.
Ebroicis, *see* Devereux.
Eccleshall, 14, 25, 39, 54, 55, 59, 61, 77, 79, 80, 82, 83, 84, 86, 88, 90, 91, 94, 97, 131, 198.
Ecton, Thom., 165.
——— John, of Blore, 206.
Edlaston, co. Cheshire, 126.
Edward, Rich., 181, 182.
Edynghale, 160.
Egerton, John, kt., 6, 52, 55.
——— Ralph, arm., 16, 34, 166, 169, 170, 180, 183.
——— ——— Eliz., w. of, 16.
——— ——— Elena, d. of, 170.
——— Rich., kt., 34.
——— Will., 124.
Egmondon, 145.
Egynton, John, of Rodbaston, 179.
Ekylston, co. Lanc., 198.
Elaston, 28.
Elde, Rich., 15.

Elford, 134, 146, 151, 213.
Elkyn, John, 59.
——— ——— Margt., w. of, 59.
Elkyston, 136.
Ellenhall, 67, 128, 129, 133, 137, 164, 198.
Ellyshawe, Thom., of Botyrdon, 146.
Elmehurst, 26, 27, 37, 41, 55, 57, 59, 65, 131.
Elmesthorpe, co. Leic., 212, 215.
Elson, Will., of Alton, 179, 184.
——— Edm., of Assheborne, 179.
Elton, Edm. ——— ——— 181.
Elvaston, 224.
Elwall, Will., 157.
Elysaunder, Will.,parson of Seye, 215.
Emme, Rich., of Tamworth, 195, 201.
Endesor, Chris., 11.
——— Will., 45.
Endon, 15, 52.
Enfeld, 25, 28, 68, 197, 206.
Engleton, 36.
Englondfeild, 27.
Ensore, Anne, widow, 36.
Enstone, 180, 216.
Enville, 222, 224, *and see* Enfeld.
Erbersfeld, co. Berks, 167.
Erdeswyk, Hugh, 124, 155, 157, 175, 210.
——— ——— Thom., w. of, 157.
——— Rob., of Great Sandon, 124.
——— Samp., 151, 155.
——— Hen., 155.
Erdington, Will. de, 99.
——— Thom., of Erdington, kt., 125, 221.
Erghom, Rob., of London, 144.
Ernefeild, 24.
Ernesby, Rob. de, 218.
Esington, 43, 50, 63, 133, 134, 136, 216.
Espley (Aspley), Steph. de, 84.
Esthope, Jno., 129.
Estman, Will., of Hemley, 138.
Eston, 83.
Ethell, Jno., 6, 8, 31.
——— ——— Kath., w. of, 8, 31.
Ethershawe, Edw., 48.
——— ——— Martha, w. of, 48.
Etingsall, 21.
Eton Hastynges, 161, 162, 167.
——— Jno., of Lichfield, corviser, 151.
——— Rob., parson of, 210.
Everard, Jno., 13. 25, 48, 50, 57, 61.
——— ——— Bridget, w. of, 13, 48, 50, 57, 61.
Everdon, Edw., 36.
——— Will., 156.
Eves, 14, 29.
Eweres, Thom., of Homerwich, 165.
Exete, 162.
Exeter, Edm., Bishop of, 228.
Eyr, Rich., of Wombourne, 147.

F.

Faldryng, Gilbt., 195.
Falthurst, Rich., parson of Kyngeley, 139.
Farley, 28, 64, 174.
Farwell, 8, 26.
Fauld, 25, 58, 66, 197, 214.
Fauley, Rich., clerk, 228.
Fawkener (Sawyer), David, 25.
Felip, Rich., of Teyne, 203.
——— Jno. ——— ——— 203.
Felton, Thom., 135.
——— Will., 135.
Felyngley, Hen., 160.
Fenton, 65, 173, 213.
——— Ralph, 23.
——— Vivian, 4, 35, 50.
Ferneford, 156.
Fernyhaughe, 15.
——— Will., 15, 19, 31, 52.
——— Joice, w. of, 15.
——— Jno., 52.
——— Jno., of Hulcote, 198.
——— Jno., of Tamworth, 201.
——— Jno., of Milwich, 161.
——— ——— ——— Shaldeford, 180.
Ferrers, Ralph de, chiv., 128.
——— Thom., arm., 153.
——— Thom., the younger, 195, 196, 201.
——— ——— ——— elder, 201.
——— Will., kt., 186, 197.
——— lord of Groby, 196.
——— Jno., kt., 53.
——— Edm., kt., of Bromwyche, 124.
Fetherston, 67, 68, 134
Fevre, Adam le, of Swinnerton, 83.
Fewkes, Robt., 54.
Feyre, Thom., 11, 12.
——— ——— Alice, w. of, 12.
Field, 23, 67, 157.
Fisher, Will., 4.
——— John, of Heywode, 145.
——— John, of Wolverhampton, 203
——— Thom., of Rowelowe, 148.
Fisherwick, 27, 31, 49, 57.
Fitzherbert. Edw., arm , 6.
——— Ralph, 14, 15.
——— ——— Griselda, w. of, 14, 15.
——— Ant., arm , 55.
——— Will., of Somersalle, 205.
——— ——— Thom., s. of, 205.
——— Will., of Norbury, 205.
——— ——— Edeka, w. of, 205.
——— ——— Hen., s. of, 205.
——— ——— ——— Will., s of 205.

Fitzherbert, John, s. of above Will., 205.
—— —— Will., s. of, 205.
—— —— —— Will., s. of, 205.
—— Hen., s. of above Will., 205.
—— Thom., of Norbury, 127.
—— Rich. —— —— 167, 205.
Fitz Alwin, Simon, 81, *and see* Herbert.
Fitz Eelen, Rob. (of Swynnerton), 111, 112, 113.
Fitz Griffin, Gamel, 75.
Fitz Hugh, John, 220.
Fitz Odo, Ralph, of Hodnet, 83.
—— Ernald, 75.
Fitz Orm, Rob., 98.
—— —— Alina, d. of, 98.
—— Ralph, 102, 103.
—— —— Emma, d. and h. of, 102, 105.
Fitz Payne, Rob., 115.
Flackett, Hen., 63.
—— Thom., 67.
—— —— Eliz., w. of, 67.
Flaket, Thom., of Calwyche, 115.
Fleeminge (alias Greene), Will., 41.
Fletcher, John, of Lichfield, fletcher, 126.
—— Walt., of Pencrich, 135.
—— John, of Wolverhampton, 154, 164.
Flore, 183.
Flosbroke, 126.
Flyer, Ralph, 7, 20.
—— —— Margy., w. of, 7.
Foale, 67.
Foderley, 65.
Fodon, Thom., 35.
Foliot, Will., 219.
—— —— John, s. of, 219.
Foljambe, Thom., of Walton, 130.
—— Rich., of Boudesall, 130.
—— Ralph, 130.
Forbrige, 33, 64.
Forde, 136.
—— Rich., 28, 58.
—— —— Anne, w. of, 58.
—— Rich., of Gunstone, 136.
Fornham, John, parson of, 145.
Forster, Will., 152, 212.
—— —— Laur., s. of, 152.
—— John, of Castelbromwych, 165.
Fortescu, John, 160.
Fossebrook, 16, 20, 22, 26, 33, 34, 36, 44, 49, 58, 66, 194.
Foster, Rob., 6, 12, 24, 49.
—— —— Margt., w. of, 49.
—— Ant., 16.
Foston, co. Derby, 140, 224.
Fotherley, 19, *and see* Foderley.
Fouleshurst, Thom., of Glenfeld, 133.
Fowke, Rog., arm., 43, 54.
—— —— Kath., w. of, 43.
Fowke, Rog., Mary, w. of, 54.
—— Rog., of Brewode, 191, *and see* Fewkes.
Fowlar, Walt., arm., 47.
—— —— Edw., s. and h. of, 47.
Fox, Rich., 212.
—— Will., de la Grenes, 142.
—— Edw., 10, 38.
—— —— Eliz., w. of, 38.
—— Rich., 23, 32.
—— —— Eliz., w. of, 32.
—— Thom., 38.
—— Hen., 38.
Foxall, John, 7.
Foxewcist, 27.
Frankelyn, Rob., of Leeke, 163.
Fraunceys, Will., of Alrewas, 141, 147.
—— John —— —— 191.
Frebody, Ralph, of Bobyngton, 125.
—— Mary, 149.
—— Hen., 154.
—— Will., 200.
—— Rich., 212.
Freford, 27.
Fremon, Rich., of Thickbrome, 141.
—— John —— —— 141.
—— John, of Lichfield, chap., 203.
Frend, Simon, of Walsall, 130.
Frensshman, Rob., 165.
Frithe, 8.
Frodeley, 152.
Frodesley, Will., chiv., 151, 152.
—— Joan and Margt., 149, 152.
Frodeswall, 138, 179.
Froghole, 180.
Frogot, John, of Callowhill, 216.
Fulfen, 27, 142, 148, 154, 179.
Fulford, 18, 22, 28, 34, 44, 59, 66, 88.
Fulwood, John, 21, 41.
—— —— Matil., w. of, 41.
—— Rich., 21, 41.
—— —— Anne, w. of, 21, 41.
Fykkes, Will., of Walsall, 130.
Fynderne, 159.
—— Nich., 159.
Fynney, Will., 31.
—— John, 34.
Fysbroke, 28.
Fyton, Will., 208.
—— Laur., 211.
—— —— Rich., s. of, 211.

G.

Galey, 11.
—— Haye, 36.
Gallymore, Ralph, 16.
—— John, 63.
Galpyn, Will., 151.
Gamage, Thom., arm., 159.

Gamull, Thom., 31.
Garbett, John, 35, 63, 64.
——— Will., 35, 38, 39, 58.
——— ——— Eliz., w. of, 35, 38.
Gardner, John, of Tunstall, 183.
Gardyner, Thom., 214.
Garsall (Garingshall), 46, 54, 58.
Gatacre, 183.
——— Eliz., widow, 6.
——— Joyce, 183.
——— John, 183.
Gaveston, Piers, 90.
Gayge, John, 162.
——— ——— Alion., w. of, 162.
Gaylard, Rich., 218.
——— ——— Margy., w. of, 218.
Gayton, 33, 49.
Gebertsley, 39.
Gelowe, Thom., of Leeke, 135.
Gentille, John le, the Bishop's steward, 97.
Gerard, Thom., Lord, 56, 60.
——— Will., of Oldyngton, 135.
——— ——— John, s. of, 135.
——— ——— ——— Joan, w. of, 135.
Gervies, Thom., arm., 55, 222.
——— ——— Dory., w. of, 55.
——— Will., of Chatkylle, 166.
Gery, Thom., 218.
——— ——— Eliz., f. w. of, 218.
Gesson, Rob., of Henley, 138.
Gest, Rich., 31.
——— John, 31.
Gibbyns, Rich., 19.
——— ——— Ellen, w. of, 19.
Giffard, Walt., arm., 43.
——— Thom., of Chillington, 135.
——— John, 226.
——— Edm., 227.
——— ——— Agnes, w. of, 227.
Gilbert, Thom., 8.
——— John, 39.
Gill, John, 66.
——— ——— Eliz., w. of, 66.
——— Ralph, 66.
——— ——— Grace, w. of, 66.
Gloucester, Thom., 128.
——— Humph., D. of, 181.
Glover, Thom., 29.
——— Rich., of Leeke, 163.
Gnosall, 46, 67, 148, 163.
Godefelowe, John, abbot of Dieulacres, 163.
Gogh, Rob., of Brewode, 161.
——— Will. ——— ——— 161.
Godwyn, Edm., 66.
——— Edm., Joan, w. of, 66.
——— John, 66.
Golborne, Juliana, of Great Barre, 150
Golburn, Thom., of Holme, 145.
Goldsmith, John, of Tamworth, 127.
Goodwyn, Alex., 32.
——— John, 33.
——— ——— Anne, w. of, 33.
——— Hen., 36.
Goold, Will., of Grendon, 179, 195.
Gooldson, Pet., 157.
Goples, John, of Stansop, 179.
Gorsoforthe Green, 21.
Gorsticott, 54.
Gorwey, Thom., 42.
Goscott, 43, 47.
Gospell, 24.
Gouche, Hen., 23.
——— John, 23.
Goughe, Rog., 36.
——— ——— Mary, w. of, 36
——— Will., of Brewode, 184.
——— Rob., of Tonge, 184.
Gouldthorne, 68.
Grafton, 199, 200, 207, 208, 212.
——— Humph., 208.
——— John de, 226.
Grasebrook, *see* Gresbroke.
Gratwich, 7.
Gravener, John, 46.
Gray, Edw., kt., 196, 206.
——— Ambr., arm., 51.
——— ——— Margt., w. of, 51.
——— Geo., arm., 51.
Greaves, Thom., 62.
Greene, 21.
——— Nich., 56.
——— Godfrey, 56.
——— Will., 14, 41, 61, 65.
——— Hen., 15, 65.
——— John, 20, 49.
——— John, of Theyne, 203, 212.
——— Jam., 39.
——— Rich., 212.
Greetyate, 179, 186, 195.
Gregg, John, 30.
Gregory, John, 178.
Grendon, 175, 176, 179, 182, 185, 195.
——— Simon, rector of, 176.
——— John de, 188, 189.
——— Ralph de, 97.
Grenwich, West, 142.
Gresbroke, Hugh, 38.
——— ——— Margt., w. of, 38.
——— Agnes, 140.
Gresley, Thom., kt., 29, 30, 163.
——— ——— Mary, w. of, 30.
——— ——— Geo., s. and h. of, 29.
——— ——— ——— Susan, w. of, 30.
——— Simon, arm., 20, 64.
——— Engen. de, 73, 98, 100, 102.
——— ——— Alina, w. of, 73, 102.
——— ——— Petron., d., of 73, 98, 99, 100.

Gresley, John de, 139, 140, 142, 154, 165, 170, 204.
——— ——— Margt., w. of, 139, 140, 142, 154, 170.
——— John, of Drakelowe, arm., 206.
——— John, kt., 215, 217, 221.
Greswold, John, of co. Warwick, 125.
——— Thom., King's Attorney, 129.
Grete, 154.
Gretewych, 177.
Gretton, 27, 42.
Grevylle, Will., kt., 136.
——— John, arm., 141, 186.
——— Rob., 216.
——— ——— Alice, w. of, 216.
Grey, Hen., kt., 16.
——— ——— Eliz., w. of, 16.
——— Rob., arm., 222.
Griffin, Sir Geof., 103.
Griffith, John, kt., 132, 150, 153, 175, 180, 181, 185, 187.
——— ——— kt., the younger, 132.
——— Reg., 168, 171, 173.
——— Madoc ap, 181.
——— Thom., 150.
Groby, 196.
Grosvenor, Thom., 21.
——— ——— Rob., s. of, 21.
——— Will., 21.
——— Walt., 44.
——— ——— Ellen, w. of, 44, *and see* Gravenor.
Grove, Phil., 3, 20.
——— ——— Anne, d. and h. of, 20.
——— Hen., 4.
——— Edw., 4.
——— ——— Anne, w. of, 4.
——— Rich., 5, 55.
——— Humph., 28.
——— ——— Eliz., w. of, 28.
Gryffyth, *see* Griffith.
Gryn, 10.
Grynley, 26.
Guddeman, Will., 225.
Guldene, Ormus de, 102.
——— ——— Rob., s. of, 102.
——— ——— Ralph, s. of, 102.
——— ——— ——— Emma, d. and h. of, 102.
Gunstone, 136, 141.
——— Rich. atte fude of, 141.
Gybons, Humph., 13.
Gyldemorton, co. Leic., 192.
Gyles, Will., of London, grocer, 126.

H.

Hadden, co. Derby, 185, 192, 198, 224.
Hadekeserd, 156.
Hadley, Rich., 34.
Hadyngton, John, 133.
——— Simon, 134, 135.
Hales, 37, 60, 188, 189, 192, 200, 207, 208, 212.
——— moiety of manor of, 210.
Halfeheade, 61.
Halghton, Thom. de, 90.
——— Will., 212.
Hall, John, 13, 53.
——— ——— Joan, w. of, 13.
——— Thom., 51.
——— ——— Ellen, w. of, 51.
——— Gerv., 53.
——— Will., 140.
——— Will., of Kyngeley, 146.
Hallywell, 34.
Halmore ende, 60.
Halsey, Rich., of la Welle, 172.
Hambury, 168, 171, 173.
Hamerwiche, 37, 160.
Hamet, Pet., of Shelton, 166.
Hamme, near Kyngeston, 142.
Hammersley, *see* Homersley.
Hamond, Edm., 16.
——— Will., 16.
Hamptede Pury, Hamptead Perry, 165.
Hampton, 123.
——— John, of Esyngton, 133, 136, 173, 176.
——— John, arm., 186, 187, 206, 207, 221.
——— ——— Agnes, f. w. of, 221.
——— Thom., of Abbot's Bromley, 163, 165.
——— Thom., of Bishton, 216.
——— Bevis, 186, 187.
Hamulton, Will., 217.
Hanbury, 12, 25, 36, 54, 58, 70, 221.
——— Will., 186.
Hanchurch, 88.
Hancocke, Geo., 13.
——— Hen., 199.
Hancockson, John, 129.
Handlo, John de, 131, 138, 142.
——— ——— Matil., w. of, 131, 138, 142.
——— ——— Joan, Eliz., Margt., drs. of, 131, 142.
——— Will. de, 138.
Handsacre, 14, 16, 41, 66, 152, 178.
——— Will. de, 151, 152.
——— ——— Simon, s. of, 152, *and see* Hondesacre.
Handsworth, 13, 18, 27, 31, 39, 41, 44, 141, 165.
Hanford, 169, 245.
Hanley, 9, 35, 50.
——— Nich., 126.
——— Ralph, 211.
Hanmett, Rich., 33.

Hansbury, John, 186.
Hardwick, 66.
Harbourne, *see* Horborne.
Harecourt, Stanton, 128, 136, 137, 164, 186, 197, 198, 207.
——— Walt., kt., 47.
——— ——— Dory., w. of, 47.
——— Rob., arm., 47, 67.
——— Rob., 127, 133, 136, 137, 141, 150, 155, 199, 224.
——— Rob., kt., 164, 166, 172, 183, 197, 198, 199, 207, 224.
——— ——— Margt., w. of, 199.
——— Will., 128, 129.
——— ——— Joan, w. of, 128, 129.
——— Lady Joan, widow, 186, 197, 198
——— Humph., arm., 68.
——— ——— Bridg., w. of, 68.
——— Nich., 128, 129.
——— Thom., 128, 129, 136, 164.
——— ——— Thom., s. of, 129.
——— Rich., 135, 136, 145, 161, 162, 198, 221, 228, 229.
——— ——— Edith, w. of, 162.
——— ——— Alianora, f. w. of, 221.
——— Margt., 228.
——— John, of Elinhale, 198.
——— John, of Eccleshall, 198.
Harington, Edm., 61.
Harlaston, 156, 168.
Harley Eves, 12.
Harpesford, 139.
Harpur, John, kt., 9, 11.
——— John, 130, 135, 165, 166, 178, 181, 203, 215, 216, 218, 224.
——— ——— Alian., w. of, 130, 135, 166.
Harrison, Rich., 3.
——— ——— Ellen, w. of, 3.
——— John, 29, 42, 47.
——— ——— Joan, w. of, 29.
——— Edm., 38.
——— Thom., 39, 42.
——— ——— Anne, w. of, 42.
Harrold, Franc., 5.
Harryes, Rich., 51.
Harvy, Franc., arm., 14.
——— Thom., 22, 28.
——— Rog., 25, 31.
——— Sebas., 33.
——— ——— Mary, w. of, 33.
——— Edw., 54.
——— Will., 54.
——— Mary, 54.
Hasard, John, 212.
Haselour, 15.
Hasilby, Thom., 130.
Haskyth, Humph., 194.
Hasselwood, 60.
Hastang, John de, 90.
Hastang, Thom. de, 139.
——— ——— Eliz., w. of, 139.
Hasterley, Thom., 50.
Hastinges, Walt., arm., 22, 28.
Hatchett, Humph., 50.
Hatchley, 39.
Hatfeilde, Thom., 31, 60.
——— John, 198.
——— Leon., 60.
——— ——— Kath., w. of, 60.
——— Leon., the younger, 60.
——— ——— Jane, w. of, 60.
Hatherton, 36, 67, 68.
Hatton, 6, 18, 23.
——— Steph. de, 113.
Haughton, 21, 52, 59, 218, *and see* Halghton *and* Hawton.
Haukesert, 168, *and see* Hadekeserd.
Haule (Hawley), John, 53.
Hauley, Nich., 123.
Hawe, Geo., 53.
Hawkes, Hillary, 11, 12.
——— John, 15, 65.
——— ——— Anne, w. of, 15, 65.
——— John, of Westbromwich, 200.
——— Will., 62, 218.
Hawkesyard, *see* Haukesert.
Hawnton, 22, 65, 66.
Hawrden, 54.
Hawton, Thom., 210, 211.
——— John, 210.
——— Will. de, 210.
Hay, John, of Wheaton Aston, 135.
Haydok, Rob., 171.
Hayes, John, 17.
——— ——— Margt., w. of, 17.
——— Sylv., 23, 62.
Hayne, Will., 153.
Hayteley, Will., of Casterne, 136, 218.
——— ——— Margy., f. w. of, 218.
Haytlees, Will., 155.
——— ——— Margy., w. of, 155.
Hayton, 51.
——— James de, 85, 106.
Healey, 60, 145.
Heathcote Grange, 15.
Heathe, 67, 68, 148.
Heaton, 40.
——— John, 48.
——— Ralph, 48.
Heckley, 45.
Heleston, 134.
Helmeston, 162.
Hemhill, John, of Tibbington, 137.
Hemley, 138, 144, 154.
Hendelowe, Will., of King's Swinford, 182.
Henley, Rich., 8.
——— Ralph, abbot of Burton, 185.
Henney, Will., 36.
——— John, 36.

Henshawe, Rich., 20, 58.
—— —— Eliz., w. of, 58.
—— Thom., 28.
Herberd, Nich. fitz, of Norbury, arm., 167.
—— Thom., arm., 181.
Hermesthorp, John de, 227.
Hert, John, 194.
—— —— Agnes, f. w. of, 194.
Herts., co., 17.
Hethe, John, draper, 125.
—— Thom., 137, 157.
Hethehowse Grange, 67.
Hetly, 55.
Heuster, John, 160.
—— Thom., 202.
—— —— Thom., s. of, 202.
Heveningham, Walt., arm., 65.
Hewester, Rob., parson of Bosworth, 211.
Hewyson, Rich., 146.
Hextall, 15, 145.
—— Will., 145, 146, 161, 172, 217.
—— Thom., 195.
—— Hugh, clerk, 217.
Heyghton, 162.
Heynes, Mich., 64.
Heytley, 62.
Heyton, 19, 43.
Heywood, 145, 168.
—— Great, 29.
—— Little, 66.
—— John, 184.
Hicks, Babt., kt., 33.
Higgens, Rich., 50.
Hilcote, Alan de, 226.
Hilcott, 61.
Hilderston, 18, 20, 58, 60, 62, 169, 170, 180.
Hill, 8, 34, 46.
—— House, 46.
—— Rich., 5, 179.
—— Walt., 47.
—— —— Ellen, w. of, 47.
—— Edw., 63, 64.
—— —— Margy., w. of, 64.
Hillary, Sir Rog., 17.
Hillewode, 178.
Hilton, 50, 67, 68, 78, 87, 89, 93, 133, 224.
—— Abbey of, 104.
—— Godfrey, of Chanton, 185, *and see* Hulton.
Himley, *see* Hemley.
Hixon, 20, 41, 62, 64, 166.
Hochekys, Thom., 153.
Hochynes, Thom., of Blore, 2 8.
Hockin, John, 63.
—— —— Dory., w. of, 63.
Hodnet, 83.
—— Odo de, 83.
Hodnet, Rich. de, 83.
Hodgettes, Will., 13, 65.
—— —— Joan, w. of, 13.
—— Nich., 13.
Hoens, Rog., 180.
Hogh, Rob. de, of Shareshull, 161.
Holbeche, Rog., 172.
Holden, Geo., 31, 32.
—— —— Kath., w. of, 32.
—— Thom., 147.
Holdyche, 180, 216.
Holegode, manor and honor, 138.
Holland, Gabriel, 14.
—— Rich., clerk, 24.
—— —— Alice, w. of, 24.
—— Thom., 149.
—— John, kt., 163, 204.
—— —— Elena, f. w. of, 204.
Hollins, John, 23, 49.
Hollys, Will., 42.
—— —— Mary, w. of, 42.
—— Hugh, 42.
—— John, 42, 182, 185.
—— Geo., 42.
Holme, 44, 145.
—— Will., 43.
—— Rich., 43.
Holte, John, 7.
—— John, of Aston, 183.
Holynshede, Will., 150.
—— Edm., 150.
Holynton, Rob., prior of St. Margt. of Colwich, 145.
Homersley, Rob., 56.
—— Thom., 56.
—— Rog., 200.
Homerwich, 43, 165.
Homylton, Will., of Boturdon, 146.
Honde, Will., 155.
Hondesacre, Joan, 149, 152.
—— Margt., 149.
—— Eliz., 151, 152.
—— Will., chiv., 151, 152.
—— —— Simon, s. of, 152.
—— *see* Handsacre.
Hondesworthe, 13, 18, *see also* Handsworth.
Honnesworth, *see* Handsworth.
Hood, John, 64.
Hooley, James, 43.
Hope, 156, 187, 193, 194, 197.
Hopkis, Rich., 11.
Hopkyns, John, of Overpenne, 157.
Hopton, 33, 69, 212, 213.
Hopwas, 19, 42, 43, 45.
Horborne, 22.
Hord, Rich., of co. Salop, 125.
Hore, John, 157, 163.
—— —— Katr., w. of, 157.
Horecrosse, 23.
Horner, Rog. le, of Tamworth, 131.

Horner, Rog. le, of Tamworth, the younger, 131.
——— ——— Margy., w. of, 131.
Horsebrooke, 53.
Horsley, John, 6, 42.
Horton, 13, 27, 40, 42, 57, 134, 115.
——— Lowe, 34.
——— Will., 69.
——— John de, 226.
Horwode, John, of Compton, arm., 191.
Houlden, Geo., 40.
Howe, Edw., 40.
Howndhill, 12.
Huggeford, Thom., 186.
Hulcote, 198.
Hulle, John del, of Pencrich, 152.
——— John, King's Justice, 227.
Hulme, Will., 29, 41.
Hulton, 21, 67.
Hunt, Thom., 169.
——— Alex., 186.
——— Rob., 24.
——— Will., 53.
——— John, 134.
Huntbach, John, 54.
——— Mary, 54.
——— Steph. de, chaplain, 100.
Huntingdon, Hen., E. of, 22, 28, 44.
——— ——— Eliz., w. of, 22, 28.
——— John, 220.
Huntington, 30.
Huntley, 45, 52, 168, 209.
Hurdman, John, 58.
Hurt, Thom., 52.
——— Elean., 59.
Hussey, Rich., kt., 4, 44.
——— Rob., arm., 44.
Hyde, 167.
——— John, of Southdencheswortb, 167.
Hyne, Will., of Bromshulf, 139.
Hynts, 10, 11, 19, 20, 38, 45, 157.
——— Thom., 6.

I.

Ikelington, John, clerk, 229.
Illesley, Geo., 19.
Ilum, 183, 194, 208, 225.
——— John, vicar of, 182, 194, 208, 209.
Ince, Hen., of Little Saredon, 221.
Ingestre, 33, 34, 135, 159, 177.
——— free chapel of, 216.
Ingleton, 43.
Ingoldesby, Ralph, 152.
Ipstones, 27, 42.
——— John, kt., 129.
——— ——— Eliz., f. w. of, 129.
Isewall, 78, 82, 85, 89, 91, 92, 93, 97, 105, 107.
——— Steph. de, 82, 83, 84, 105, 106.
——— ——— Rog., s. of, 106.
——— John de, 87, 93, 94, 95, 97, 107.
——— ——— John, s. of, 93.
Ives, Will., of Lynehill, 151.

J.

Jackson, Hen., 7.
——— ——— Anne, w. of, 7.
——— Thom., 12.
——— ——— Franc., w. of, 12.
——— Phil., 54.
——— Rob., 61.
——— Lawr., 68.
——— Thom., of Lee, 140.
James, Will., 49.
——— ——— Mary, w. of, 49.
——— (Strynger), Will., 6.
——— ——— Thom., 6.
——— Edw., 36.
——— ——— Isab., w. of, 36.
Janance, Rog., 29.
Janne, John, 150.
Jarvis, Alex., 3, 11.
——— ——— Eliz., w. of, 11.
Jasson, Simon, 29, 44.
Jayler, Thom., hostler, 125, 126.
Jeer, John, 224.
Jeffreye, Humph., 7.
Jelyff, Thom., 221.
Jem, Humph., 48.
——— Rich., 48.
Jesson, Geo., 41.
——— ——— Elean., w. of, 41, *and see* Jasson.
Jevon, Rich., 56, 65.
Joceran, Robt., 98.
Jodrell, John, 31.
Johns, Thom., 40.
Johnson, Rob., of Kingsbromley, 178.
——— Geo., 47.
——— ——— Ellen, w. of, 47.
Jolyff, John, 158, 160, 203, *and see* Jelyff.
Jones, Walt., 23.
——— Anne, 23.
Joneston, Rob. de, 78.
——— Will. de, 94.
Jowkes, Ralph, 186.
Jukes, Thom., 31.
——— ——— Eliz., w. of, 31.
Jurden, Humph., 24.
——— Thom., 35, 38.
——— Will., 38, 46.
——— Rich., of Ingestre, 135.

K.

Kawardyne, Katr., 135.
Kegworth, Thom., of Lichfield, 191.
Kele, 154, 184.
Kellett, Alf., 46, 54.
——— Franc., 54.
Kelsall, Will., clerk, 31.
Kelyng, Rob., of Great Sutton, 117, 149.
Kempe, Geo., 66.
——— Will., of Rugeley, 148.
Kent, Rich., 10.
——— ——— Emotta, w. of, 10.
——— Rog. de, 88.
Ketlestone, 223.
Ketylston, 215.
Kevenall, 33.
Kibbulle, Walt., of Assheby, 135.
Kibbulstone, 33, 104, 161, 162, 188, 189, 190, 191, 192, 200, 207, 208, 210.
Killingworth, 153.
Kilvart, Rob., 69.
——— ——— Eliz., w. of, 69.
Kinfare, 153.
Kingesbury, Rog., 199.
Kingesley, 12, 22, 28, 31, 44, 56, 130.
——— John, 124, 126, 156, 163, 168.
Kingeston, 26, 142.
Kinson, 41.
Kirkeby, Will., 148.
Kneyghton, 15, 34.
Knight, John, 7, 9, 30, 204, 216, 221, 222.
——— ——— Agnes, w. of, 9.
——— ——— Joan, w. of, 30.
——— Will., 65.
——— Rog., of Bedull, 218.
Knightley, 46, 67, 127, 148, 154.
——— Joan, 154.
——— Sir Rob. de, 78.
——— Thom., 220.
Knighton, near Adbaston, 46.
——— Will. de, 124.
Kniveton, Will., arm., 27, 40.
——— Jane, 27, 40.
Knotton, 34, 92, 94, 109, 170, 180.
——— Rob. de, 92.
——— ——— Agnes, w. of, 92.
Knowle, 60.
——— ende, 60.
Knutton, 88, 93, 95.
——— Ralph de, 75, 103.
——— ——— John, s. of, 103
Kuybeley, Thom., of Felde, 157.
Kydde, John, of Shelton, 215.
Kymmon, Thom., 157.
Kynaston, Thom., arm., 52.
Kynder, Franc., 23.
Kynewarton, John, of Oldyngton, 133.
Kyngesnorton, 165.
Kynges Swynford, 24, 25, 32, 143, 144, 146, 158.
Kynnardesay, Rob., 179.
Kynnersley, John, 14.
——— Ant., arm., 44, 69.
——— ——— Franc., s. of, 69, *and see* Kynnardesay.
Kynston, 7, 30.
Kynthall, John, of Wodehous, 222.
Kynver, 24, 28, 123.
Kynwarton, John, 135.
——— ——— Margy., w. of, 135.
Kynwaston, 11.

L.

Lache, John, of Lichfield, 180.
Lacon, Rowland, arm., 10.
——— ——— Ellen, w. of, 10.
——— Franc., kt., 10, 41, 46, 59, 69.
——— ——— Margt., w. of, 46.
——— Will., arm., 41.
——— Thom., 57.
——— ——— Thoma., w. of, 57.
Lagon, Rich., 92.
Lampham, 162.
Lancaster, Thom., E. of, 87, 88, 90, 93.
Lane, John, 172.
——— Thom., 41.
——— Rich., 139, 142, 143, *and see* Lone.
Langeford, Geo., of Langeford, 145.
——— Edw., 197, 198, *and see* Longeford.
Langeley, Hen., 57.
——— Isab., w. of, 57.
Langett, 27.
Langham, Rob., arm., 124.
Langport, Will., parson of, 210.
Langton, Will., 20.
——— John, clerk, 20, 57.
——— ——— Matil., w. of, 57.
——— Walt. de, 91.
Lapley, 135.
Lathebury, Alur. de, kt., 188.
Lathropp, Thom., 23.
——— ——— Mary, w. of, 23.
Latoner, Will., of Lichfield, 125.
——— ——— Alan, w. of, 125.
Latymer, Rich., of Assheby, 135.
Lawley, Will., co. Salop, 125.
Lawnder, Jam., 54.
——— Robt., 58.
Lawrance, John, 40.
Lea, 62.
Leche, John, of Lichfield, 166.
Lee, 157, 223, *see also* Leighe.

Lee, Will., 129, 147, 148, 155, 165, 169, 170, 179, 184, 216, 228.
——— ——— Joan, w. of, 148, 228.
——— Rich. du, 106.
——— Jam., arm., 203.
Leeke, 5, 6, 8, 27, 34, 38, 42, 47, 69, 134, 135, 155, 163.
Leekefrithe, 8, 34, 60.
Lees, 31.
——— Hill, 7.
Leg, Will., 204.
——— ——— Margt., w. of, 204.
Legh, Joan, 219.
Leghton, 129.
——— John, 129.
Leic., co., 133, 135, 138, 168, 186, 192, 194, 197, 198, 212, 215.
Leighe (Lee), 10, 23, 41, 67, 69, 140, 157, 223.
——— Pet., 60, 158.
——— ——— John, s. of, 158.
——— Thom., 25, 52.
——— ——— Kath., w. of, 52.
——— John, 25.
——— Urian, kt., 34.
——— Edw., kt., 35, 38, 46, 54.
——— ——— Anne, w. of, 35, 38, 46, 54.
——— Hen., arm., 35, 38, 46, 54.
——— Franc., kt., 52, 55.
——— Will., of Knightley, 127.
Leighton, Eliz., widow, 21, *and see* Leghton.
Lemeseye, Pet. de, 88.
Lenches, John, 149.
Leukenore, Thom., kt., 213, 214.
——— ——— Eliz., f. w. of, 213, 214.
——— manor, 213.
——— Rich., arm., 214, 215.
Leverych, John, of Lichfield, souter, 126.
Leveson, Walt., kt., 3, 8, 18, 23, 46, 64, 67, 68.
——— ——— Anne, w. of, 23, 67.
——— Thom., 3, 67.
——— John, 8, 18.
——— Jam., 130, 136, 149, 157, 218.
——— Nich., of Wolverhampton, 148, 157, 179.
——— ——— James, s. and h. of, 178.
——— Will., of Wolverhampton, 183.
——— Will., 123, 148.
——— Rich., of Wolverhampton, 199.
Leycroft, 26, 37.
Leylond, Thom., of Lichfield, 140.
Licett, Geo., 55.
Lichfield, 5, 25, 31, 124, 125, 126, 127, 131, 138, 140, 141, 142, 145, 148, 151, 158, 159, 160, 166, 179, 180, 191, 203, 212, 222.
Lichfield, Will., Bishop of, 148, 153, 183.
——— Will., kt., 126.
——— Hosp. of St. John, 124.
——— John, dean of, 159, 160, 222.
——— John, Bishop of, 135.
——— Rob. ——— ——— 82.
——— Rog. ——— ——— 86, 89, 95, 99.
——— Walt. ——— ——— 90.
——— Hugh ——— ——— 113.
Lincoln, co., 111, 113, 114, 116.
Lindsell, Edw., 16.
Littleton, Edw., kt., 5, 30, 69.
——— ——— Margt., w. of, 30.
——— Edw., the younger, kt., 30, 44, 48, 57.
——— ——— Mary, w. of, 57.
——— Walt., 35.
——— ——— Alice, w. of, 35.
——— ——— Alice, d. of, 35.
——— Thom., 177, 181, 200, 202, 216, 218, 220, 222.
——— Joan, w. of, 177, 181, 216, 222.
——— John, 204.
——— ——— Joan, w. of, 204.
Littley, 52.
Lokon, Thom., of Hunttelcy, 168.
——— Rich. ——— ——— 168.
——— ——— Chris., f. w. of, 168.
Lokwode, John, 146.
——— Thom., 164, 180, 209.
Loncton, 50.
Londesdale, Will., of Throwley, 183, 185, 193, 194, 197, 199.
London, 126, 144, 146, 155, 156, 179, 182, 185, 198, 204, 223.
——— John, of Lichfield, 126.
Lone, Rich., 125, 127, 157, 166.
——— Will., 157.
——— John, 148, 157, 167, 203, 211.
Longdon, 21, 27, 41, 48, 54, 57, 62, 63, 64, 65, 66, 69, 160, 172.
Longdowne, 37.
Longfeld, 147.
Longford, Hen., arm., 130.
Longmer, John, 25.
Longnor, 11, 160, 183.
Longsdon, 34.
Longton, 65, 104.
Looker, John, 29.
Lorde, Hen., of Caldon, 136.
Lotford, 67.
Loueton, 35.
Lout, Rich., 187, 197.
Lovell, Will., 131, 137, 138, 142, 162.
——— ——— Eliz., w. of, 162.
——— John, 131, 142.
——— ——— John, s. of, 131, 142.
——— ——— ——— John, s. of, 131.
Lovet, John, 136.

Lovet, Rich., 151.
——— Rich., of Clayton, 215.
Lovot, Will., of Clayton, 215.
——— Will., of Calowhill, 216.
Lowe, 42.
——— Horton, 34.
——— Will., 34
——— Will., of Enfeld, arm., 206.
——— Humph., 163.
——— Arth., 48.
——— ——— Susan, w. of, 48.
——— Ant., 48.
——— John of the, of Heleston, 134.
——— ——— Joan, w. of, 134.
——— Nich. atte, 156.
——— ——— Joan, w. of, 156.
——— Rob., of Bromshulf, 179.
Lownes, Will., 48.
Lowton, Will., 45.
——— Thom , 45.
Loxley, 7, 20, 64, 179, 216.
Loynton, 6.
Lucas, Thom., of Gnosale, 148.
Luccocke, Rich., 22.
——— ——— Margy., w. of, 22.
Ludyngton, Will., King's Attorney, 2.9.
Lutterworth, 206.
Luttley, 70.
——— John, 123.
Luyt, Thom., 197.
Lyes, 148, 155.
Lymsey, Rich. de, 88.
——— Pet. de, kt., 93, 94.
Lynby, Hen., 217.
Lynde, Thom., 198.
Lyney, Rog., of Newport (Salop), 131.
Lynhill, 151.
——— Will., 36.
Lynley, Rob., of Newcastle, 163.
Lyote, Thom., yeo., 135.
Lytelle, Alex., of Whittington, 134.

M.

Maccleston, 46.
Maclesfeilde, Will., arm., 18.
——— ——— Ursula, w. of, 18.
——— Pet , 18, 46.
——— ——— Joan, w. of, 18.
——— Ralph, 180.
Madeley, 7, 9, 19, 31.
——— John, 36.
——— John, of Newcastle, 215.
——— Holme, 51.
——— ende, 60.
——— Ralph, of Denstone, 187, 193, 197.
——— Thom. ——— ——— 191.
Madoc ap Griffith, 181.
Madoc, Rys ap, 181.
Makeworth, co. Derby, 140, 141.
——— Thom., 140, 141.
Malbanc, Will., 74.
Malefeld, 179 184.
Malley, Agnes, lady of Westbromwych, 221.
Malpas, John, of Mavesyn Ridware, 194.
Maltby, Hospitallers of, 114.
Manchester, John, 186.
Mane, Thom., 208 209.
Manley, Thom., of Wylnale, 154, 163, 167.
Manwaringe, Edw., arm., 34, 47.
Mapulton, co. Derby, 208, 209.
Marchall, manor of, 139, 142.
——— John, 166.
——— Rob., of Aston, 210.
Marchington, 7, 12, 39, 54, 58, 59, 70, 216.
——— Woodlands, 59, 70.
Mareschal, Rob. le, 106.
Margaret, Queen of England, 184.
Marion, Rog , 97.
Marmyon, Will., 207.
Marshall, Rog., of Walsall, 130.
——— Will., 132.
——— Hen., 132.
——— John, 135.
Marske, John, 56, 65.
Martyn, Rich., 154, 213.
——— John, 186.
Maryes, John, 172.
Maryot, John, of Bydulf, 179.
Mason, Thom., 57.
Massy, John, of Walton, near Stone, 172.
——— Will., of Stanton Harcourt, 197, 198, 199, 208.
Mastergent, Edw., 7.
Mastury, John, 165.
Mathefeld, 187, 193.
——— John, 197.
Mathewe, John, of London, 185.
Mauveysin, Joan, of Mauvesyn Ridware, 133.
——— Rob., kt., 150, 152, 201.
Mawe, Chris., 40.
Maweley, Thom., of Denstone, 180.
Maxfeld, co. Chester, 225.
Mayforth, 33.
Mayne, Joseph, 61.
Maynelle, Reg., 159.
Maynil Langley, co. Derby, 194.
Maynwaryng, Ralph, arm., 154.
——— Warine de, 190.
——— ——— Isab., d. of, 190.
Mayot, John, of Lichfield, tailor, 126.
——— ——— Margy., w. of, 126.

Meare, 18, 21, 46, 58, 65, 135, 177, 184, 203.
——— lane-end, 58, 65.
Meese, 6.
Meignill, *see* Maynelle.
Melburne, Pet., 151, 152.
——— Simon, rector of Grendon, 176.
Meller, Tim , 60.
——— James, of Hope, 187, 194, 197.
Melton, 166.
Mempas, Thom., 51.
Merb, Hen., of Shelton, 166.
Mercer, Rog., 150, 160.
Mere, Will. de, 86, 92, 106.
——— Sir Rob. de, 103, 104, 105.
——— ——— Margt., w. of, 104, 105.
——— ——— Rob., s. of, 104.
Merewelane, 34.
Merihurst, John, of Dudley, 137.
Merryman, Will., 24.
——— ——— Joan, w. of, 24.
Merssh, Will., 154.
Merston, co. Warwick, 124.
Merton, 184.
Merydon, 181.
Meschin, Earl Raoul de, 102.
Metcalfe, Geo., 16.
Meuland, Rog. de, 86.
Meverell, Rob., arm., 8, 21, 52.
——— ——— Eliz., w. of, 8, 21, 52.
——— John, of Frodeswall, 138, 146.
——— Samson ——— ——— 138, 194.
——— Samson, of Tiddeswell, 182, 195
——— Sampson, kt., 167, 179, 182, 184, 185, 191, 199, 209, 210, 222.
——— ——— Isab., w. of, 182, 185, 199.
——— Rich., of Blore, 179.
——— Thom., of Throwley, 182, 185, 193, 194, 209, 210, 225.
Meylewyche, 151.
Meyreway, 46.
Michall, 68.
Michell, And., 21.
Midlemore, Geo., 31.
——— Jane, 31.
Middleton, Franc., 23.
——— Margt., widow, 24, 27.
——— John, 24, 27.
——— greene, 67.
——— Rich., arm., 181.
Miller, Geo., 25.
Milles, Rog., of Haywode, 168.
Milleward, John, of Westbromwich, 140.
——— Rob., of Ayton, 145.
Millington, John, 37.
Milne, 6.
Milnehowses, 14, 52.
Milnemeese, 68, 213.
Miloure, James, of Hope, 193.
Milton, co. Derby, 194.
Milward, Will., arm., 50.
Milwich, 41, 54, 161, 180, *and see* Meylewyche *and* Mulwyche.
Mintridge, Rich., 19.
——— ——— Anne, w. of, 19.
Mitchale, Thom., 147.
Mitton, 147, 167.
——— Will., arm., 140, 183.
Mixton Hay, 38.
Moccleston, 88, 147.
Mogynton, 149.
Moleford, Eliz., widow, 67.
Moleton, 171, 174.
Molle, Hugh, of Codsal, 199.
Mollesley, Thom., 183.
——— John, of Billestone, arm., 221.
Molyley, Hen., 183.
——— ——— Agnes, w. of, 183.
Molyneux, Rob., arm., 158, 165 178.
——— ——— Eliz., w. of, 165, 278.
Monckes. Lawr., 21.
Monke, John, 208.
Monmore, 67, 68.
Montfort, Simon de, Rebellion of, 79.
Montgomery, Anne de, 89.
——— Nich., of Cubley, 182, 185.
More, John, 125, 186.
——— Hugh, 195.
Moreage, 48, 53, 54.
Morfall, 27, 57.
Morffe, 28.
Morgan, Will., 147.
Mortimer, Hen. de, 123.
Morton, 12, 51, 163, 164, 191.
——— Thom., 12, 38.
——— Rob., 39.
——— James, 217.
——— ——— Thom., s. of, 217.
Morwhale, 148.
Moseley, 183, 185.
——— Nich., 54.
——— Mich., 70.
——— Rich., of Newcastle, 168.
Mosse, Will., parson of Langport, 210.
Mothershall, 33.
Moton, Alan, of Stapilton, co. Leic., arm., 168.
——— Rob., kt., 222.
——— ——— Eliz., w. of, 222.
Motteram, Franc., 69.
——— ——— Margy., w. of, 69.
Mouner, Thom., of Asshbourne, 187.
Mountford, John, 4.
——— ——— Eliz., w. of, 4.
——— ——— Thom., s. and h. of, 4.

Mountford, Rich., 8.
——— ——— Agnes, w. of, 8.
——— Ralph, 42, 47.
——— Bald., kt., 212.
——— ——— Joan, w. of, 212.
Mountfort, Will., chiv., 124, 188, 191, 212.
——— ——— Joan, f. w. of, 212.
Mowsley, Eras., 48.
Moy, John, 221.
Muchehale, 216.
——— John, 216.
Muleward, Thom., 226.
Mulso, Edm., kt., 222.
——— John, 222.
——— John, the younger, 222.
Mulwyche, 134, 151, 180.
Muriel, John, 85, 98, 99.
——— Will., 98.
Murrhall, John, 62.
Murywall, John, abbot of, 124.
Musden, 146, 179, 195.
Muston, Thom., 154.
——— ——— Margt., w. of, 154.
Mutton, 177.
——— Sir Phil. de, 78.
Myghe, John, of Aston, 140.
Mylls, Thom., 32.
Mylton, 21, 67.
Mynors, Walt., arm., 51.
——— ——— Mary, w. of, 51.
——— John, 124, 176, 221.
——— James, arm., 150.
——— Rich., 162.
——— ——— Margt., f. w. of, 162.
Mynshull, Edw., 15.
Mytton, John, arm., 53.
——— Thom., of Little Wyrley, 164.

N.

Nabbes, Thom., 8.
——— ——— Jane, w. of, 8.
Napton, 176.
——— Adam de, kt., 176, 177.
——— ——— Adam, s. of, 176, 177.
——— ——— ——— Adam, s. of, 177.
——— ——— ——— ——— Joan, d. of, 177.
——— ——— ——— ——— Thoma., d of, 177.
——— Rob., 176.
Narrowdall, 42.
Nassche, Thom., of Stafford, 132.
——— Thom., of Arley, 147.
Nechilles, 23, 63, 64, 163.
——— Margt., widow, 23.
——— Thom., 23.
Nechilles, Thom., Mary, w. of, 23.
——— Will., 163.
Needham, Godf., 64.
——— John, 174.
——— Rich., 181.
Needwood forest, 5, 57, 59.
Nefeve, Thom., of Rugeley, 124.
Netherpenne, 17, 32, 35, 39, 45, 58 68, 157, 169, 216.
Nether Seal, 194.
Netherteyne, 14, 16, 32, 40.
Nethertown, 25, 61, 221.
Neuplace, 134.
Neuport, 131, 132, 145.
——— Will., 124, 125, 131, 157.
——— Greg., parson of Hanbury, 221.
Neville, Edw., lord of Bergevenney, 151.
Nevodee, Will., of Colton, 140.
Nevowe, Thom., of Pipe Ridware, 163.
Newbolt, 61.
Newborow, 37, 42, 57.
Newcastle-under-Lyme, 19, 24, 27, 50, 67, 155, 160, 163, 168, 173, 180, 215, 218.
Newehall, 225.
Newland, 30.
Newman, Edw., 35.
——— ——— Joan, w. of, 35.
Newnham, 162.
Newton, 41, 140.
——— Rich., 69.
——— Rog., 150.
Nichollys, Will., 154.
Nicken, John, 36.
Noble, John, 10.
——— Edw., 10.
Nobold, 67.
Noell, Edm., 61.
——— Phil., 61, *and see* Nowell.
Norbury, 127, 132, 167.
Norman, John, 165.
——— Nich., of le Boldem, 139, 148, 218.
——— Nich., 155.
——— ——— Joan, w. of, 155.
——— Will., 7.
——— Will., of Rugeley, arm., 139.
——— Will., of Westwode, 216.
Normancote, 102.
Normicote, 58.
——— Graunge, 184.
Norris, Thom., 23.
——— ——— Jane, w. of, 23.
North, John, of Roucestre, 140.
Northale, John, 160.
Northampton, 222.
Northleye, co. Oxon., 198.
Northwood, 28.

Nortle, John de, 88.
Norton, 58, 88, 171, 173.
——— in le Moores, 4, 62.
——— under Cannock, 26, 38, 43, 48.
——— Kaynes, 37.
——— Eliz., 36.
——— Thom., 185.
Notbourne, Sentelcr, 162.
Noteworthy, 189.
Nothale, Thom., 187.
Nottingham, 172.
Notts, co., 133, 145, 156.
Nowell, James, 43.
——— ——— Mary, w. of, 43.
——— Edw., 43.
——— ——— Eliz., w. of, 43.
——— Hen., 43.
——— John, of Lichfield, 124.
——— John, of Gnosall, 163.
——— Charles, 218.
——— Thom., 222.
Nowers, John, of Takley, 198.
Nutshawe, Thom., 62.

O.

Ockley, 60, 163.
Ockoulde, Rich., 55.
Octhorp, 160.
Offley, High, 8, 39.
——— Bishop's, 59.
——— John, of Newport (Salop), 132.
——— Rich. ——— ——— ———, 132.
——— Rich., 212.
——— Rog., 212.
Okeover, 196, 197.
——— Thom., of Nottingham, 172.
——— Phil., arm., 196, 197, 208, 209.
Oklee, 60, 163.
Olcott, 19.
Old Crusader, effigy, 117.
Olde, James, 145.
Oldyngton, 133, 135.
Olerka, Thom., of Boterton, 168.
Oles, Rich., of Chorleton, 200.
Oliver, Will., 7, 68.
——— John, 68.
——— ——— Ellen, w. of, 68.
Olton, 33.
Oncote, 167, 179, 195, *and see* Ancott.
Onn, 125, 131, 147, 161.
Ony, Nich., 218.
——— ——— Anne, w. of, 218.
Orchard, John, 6.
——— Ralph, of Mulwyche, 134, 180.
——— ——— Alice, w. of, 134.
——— Hugh, of Hanford, 215.
Orgill, Rob., 29.
Orgill, Rob., Anne, w. of, 29.
Orgrave, Thom., of Abbot's Bromley, 140, 165.
Orme, Will., 3, 4, 5, 20, 64, 145.
——— Rob., 49.
——— ——— Alice, w. of, 49.
Orpley, 27.
Orslow, 164.
Orton (Overton), 8, 17, 38, 45, 51, 58, 124.
Oudeby, John, 159.
Over Penne, 32, 39, 40, 45, 46, 58, 68, 157.
Over Teane, 10, 13, 14, 16, 32, 41.
Overheytley, 62.
Overton, *see* Orton.
——— Rob., of Overton, 124.
——— Hen., 172.
Overy, 80.
Owre (Ore), 60.

P.

Packer, Lewis, 33, 49.
——— ——— Anne, w. of, 49.
Packington, 13, 17.
Padwick, 42.
Pagan, Rob. fitz, 74.
Page, Rog., of Womburne, 140.
——— John, of Aston, 203.
Paget, Will., Lord, 29, 69.
——— ——— Letic., w. of, 29.
Pakeman, Will., of Teyne, 202.
Pakyngton, 139.
Palmer, John, 147.
——— Hugh, 148.
Panton, Ivo, Baron of Wem, 74.
——— ——— Will., s. of, 74.
——— ——— Norman, s. of, 74.
——— ——— Alice, w. of, 74.
Pantulf, Sir Will., 103, 104.
——— Ivo, Baron of Wem, 104.
Parke, Hayes, 27.
——— endo, 60.
Parker, John, 18, 55.
——— Mary, widow, 18.
——— Rich., of Coven, 137.
——— Rich., of Wythynton, 169.
——— John, of Denstone, 140.
Parkes, Rich., 43, 48.
——— Samp., 52.
Parkhall, 52, 56, 58, 61.
Paston, Nich., 63.
——— ——— Joyce, w. of, 63.
Patteshulle, 133, 135, 147, 224, 228.
Paynton, Mary, 46.
Peche, John, 91.
Pedmore, 200.
Peck, Hen. del, 94.
——— Will., 94.

Pelsall, 3, 43, 68.
Pemberton, Thom., 56.
Pembrigge, Walt., parson of, 210.
Pembroke, Will., Earl of, 16.
——— ——— Mary, w. of, 16.
Pembrugge, Fulk, kt., 161, 188, 189, 190, 191, 192, 210.
——— ——— Margt., w. of, 161, 188, 189, 190.
——— ——— Juliana, sist. of, 161, 191.
——— ——— ——— Rich., s. of, 191.
——— ——— ——— ——— Rich., s. of, 191.
Pencrich, 36, 43, 44, 50, 135, 151, 159, 179, 183, 210.
Penford, 145.
Penkylle, 166.
Penne, 150.
——— Edw., 61.
Pensnet, 154.
Penynton, John, of Milton, 167.
Penystone, Thom., of Ketlestone, 223.
Peplow, 83.
Pepys, John, 46.
Percok, Thom., prior of Hosp. of St. John, Lichfield, 124.
Perkeshous, John, of Seggesley, 157.
Perkyn, John, 36.
——— Rob., of Flosbroke, 126.
——— Thom., parson of Blythefeld, 155.
Perpount, Hen., chiv., 130.
——— Rog., of Holme, 145.
Perry, Will., 21.
——— Thom., 39.
——— John, 63.
——— Hen., 135, *and see* Pyry *and* Pyrry.
Persehowse, John, 3, 40, 69, 70.
——— ——— Mary, w. of, 70.
Pershall, Rob., 59.
——— Thom. de, 81.
——— ——— Dorea., d. of, 81, *and see* Peshall.
Perton, Will., parson of Blymhill, 123.
Peshall, 77.
——— John, arm., 14, 28.
——— John, of Onn, 125, 131.
——— Rich. de, 76, 78, 107, 129, 147, 171, 173, 174, 175, 177.
——— Steph. de, 77, 100.
——— ——— Rob., s. of, 77.
——— ——— Elean., d. and h. of, 100.
——— Adam de, 97, 129.
——— Thom. de, 77, 79, 131, 147, 161.
——— ——— Isab., w. of, 161.
Peshall, Thom. de, Dorea., sist. of, 77.
——— ——— Thom., s. of, 77.
——— Nich., 131.
——— Will. de, 82.
——— Will., of Penkylle, 166.
Petitt, Walt., 38.
——— ——— Dory., w. of, 38.
Petur, John, of Norbury, 167.
Peutrere, Rob., 186.
Phaseley, 19.
Phelyp, Rich., 157.
Philips, Ant., 13.
——— ——— Alice, w. of, 13.
——— Rich., 16.
——— James, 40.
——— ——— Anne, w. of, 40.
——— Edw., 55.
——— Thom., 165.
Philyp, Ralph, of Mapulton, 208, *and see* Felip of Teyne.
Phippon, Thom., of Brokhous, 178.
Pickin, Rob., 20.
Pierson, Will., 25, 131.
——— ——— Margt., w. of, 131.
Piggott, Gerv., 44.
——— ——— Jane, w. of, 44.
Pillesburye, Will., 39.
Pilletonhall, 30, 155.
Piott (Greene), Will., 14.
Pipe, *see* Pype.
Piry, 158, 178.
——— Will., 154.
——— Thom., 187.
Planché, Mr., Somerset Herald, 118.
Plummer, Rog., 185.
Podmore, 60, 150, 166.
Pole, Pet. de la, of Rodburne, 126, 149.
——— ——— Eliz., w. of, 149.
——— Will. de la, Earl of Suffolk, 168.
——— Ralph, 149, 156.
——— Hen., 134.
——— John, of Shene, 191, *and see* Poole.
Pollard, Eliz., 27, 40.
Pollesworth, 156.
——— abbess of, 162.
Poole, German, kt., 58.
——— Hayles, 63.
——— Ralph, 188, 191.
Poolehayes, 19.
Pope Blount, Thom., kt., 7, 30.
——— Will., arm., 128.
Poteshulle, 224.
Pott., Franc., 22, 56.
——— ——— Anne, w. of, 56.
——— Rich., 49.
——— Rog., 56.
——— Thom., 56.
Pottocke, 27.

Povy, Walt., 40.
Powuder, Leon., 57.
Poynton, Rob., of Sheprigge, 215.
Poyser, Edw., 47.
——— Thom., 70.
——— ——— Kath., w. of, 70.
Pratt, Steph., 24.
——— Thom., 39.
Presse, Simon, clerk, 61.
Preston, co. Salop, 149.
Prestwood, 19, 28, 68.
Prynce, John, of Warwyk, 153.
Pudsey, Geo., 37.
Pulesdon, Rog. de, 106.
——— ——— Joan, w. of, 106.
——— John, 165, 216.
——— Will., 202.
——— Thom., of Salt, 216.
Pulton, Pacquet, 20.
——— Samp., 20.
——— ——— Eliz., w. of, 20.
Punt, Hen., of Rodburne, 194.
Purcell, John, 226.
Purfrey, Will., arm., 176.
Pursgloves, Will., vicar of Tyddeswell, 167, 179.
Pycken, Thom., 54.
Pye, Will., 52.
——— Humph., 52.
Pykkyn, Thom., of Mere, 203, 212.
——— ——— Margy., w. of, 212.
Pynson, Hen., 14.
——— ——— Alice, w. of, 14.
Pyott, Will., 14, 61, 65.
——— Hen., 65.
——— Thom., of Chedull Grange, 208.
Pype, 26, 65, 66, 151, 222.
——— Sam., 50.
Pyrry, Thom., 39.
——— John, 62, 64.
——— John, of Willenhall, 137.
——— Rog. ——— ——— 137, *and see* Perry.
Pyry, 158, 178.
——— Thom., 187.
——— Will., 154.
Pyvelesdon, Rog. de, 106.
——— ——— Joan, w. of, 106.

Q.

Quicksill, 28.
Qwytgreve, *see* Whitgreve.

R.

Radclyff, John, kt., 138, 142.
——— ——— Katr., w. of 138.
——— Geof., kt., 138.
Radclyff, James, 138.
——— John, of Kyngesnorton, 165.
——— Ralph, of Ekylston, 198.
——— Ralph, of Elvaston, 224.
——— Will. ——— ——— 224.
——— Edm. ——— ——— 224.
Radwood, 21, 46.
Ramsore, 28, 187, *and see* Romsoure.
Rancorne, Thom., 163.
Rane, Thom., 7.
Rastell, Walt., 14.
——— Rich., 14.
Rasyn, Rob., 156.
Rauceby, co. Linc., 111, 113, 114, 116.
Ravensclougle, 9.
Ravenscrofte, Thom., arm., 34.
Rawlyn, John, 59.
——— Rich., of Teyne, 203.
Redecastelle, 145.
Rees ap Thomas, 153.
Repton, co. Derby, 133.
Repyndon, 151, 166, 171, 174.
Repyngton, John, prior of, 163.
——— Will., 168.
Ricarscote, 33, 64, 153.
Richardes, John, 4.
——— Walt., 25.
Rickmansworth, co. Herts., 17.
Ridgley, *see* Rugeley.
——— John, 61.
Ridware, 61.
——— Little (Pipe), 14, 16, 133, 163, 221.
——— Hampstall, 25, 52, 55, 61, 221.
——— Hill, 30.
——— Mavesyn, 30, 38, 60, 61, 133, 150, 194, 201, 206,
——— Park, 52, 55.
——— John, of Lichfield, 125.
——— ——— ——— ——— the younger, 141.
——— John, barker, 126.
——— Hen., of Lecke, 134.
——— ——— Margt., w. of, 134.
Rigges, John, the younger, 27.
Robaston, 36.
Robotham, Thom., 39.
Robyns, Rich., 123.
——— ——— John, s. of, 123.
——— Pet., 148.
——— Thom., 224.
Rocester, 63, 67, 140.
Rocke, Franc., 6.
——— ——— Ellen, w. of, 6.
Rodbaston, 179.
Rodburne, co. Derby, 126, 149, 194.
——— John, parson of, 149.
Roddesley, Thom., of Coven, 137, 147, 153, 161.
Rode, Thom., 142.
——— John, of Tamworth, 142.

Rodesford, Thom., of Lichfield, 126.
Roe, Nich., 184.
Roger, John, of Brianeston, 214.
——— ——— Anne, f. w. of, 214.
Rokeby, Will., 204.
——— Rich., of Creek, 222.
——— Thom. ——— ——— 222.
Rokke, Will., 163.
Rolston, 17, 134.
——— Will., 134.
——— John, 208.
Romsoure, 28, 187.
——— John, 186, 187.
——— James, 187.
Ronton, 15, 59, 67, 213.
——— Chapel of, 15.
——— Hall, 15.
——— John, prior of, 140.
Rooper, John, kt., 27.
Roos, Thom., 9.
——— Pet., 9, 18.
——— Hen., of Clyfton Camvyle, 175.
Rope, Laur., 21.
Roper, Rob., 67.
Rose, Will., of Alrewas, 221.
Rossington, 167.
——— Clem., 25.
Rothwell, John, 8, 34.
Rotten, Amb., 7.
Roncester, 63, 67, 140.
——— Hen., the abbot of, 140, *and see* Rocester.
Roughey, 56.
Roulesham manor, 219.
Rous, John, 186, 197.
——— Rich., of Breredon, 220, 222.
Rowelowe, 148.
Rowley, 3, 4, 5, 20, 22, 44, 52, 55, 63, 130, 141, 177.
——— Regis, 40.
——— Somerey, 3.
——— Park, 52, 55.
——— Walt., 4, 62.
——— Will., 66.
——— ——— Alice, w. of, 66.
——— John de, 140.
——— John de, of Wolstanton, 212.
Rowton, 21.
Royle, Will., 58, 61.
——— ——— Margt., w. of, 58.
——— Walt., clerk, 61.
——— ——— Susan, w. of, 61.
Royley, Rog., 156.
——— Rich., of Ferneford, 156.
——— James, 156.
——— Godfrey, 156.
Rudge, 56.
Rudierd, Thom., arm., 15, 52.
Rudyngefeldesmore, 228.
Rudyngfeld, 228, 229.
Rufford, Will., of Grendon, 182, 185.
Rugeley, 36, 38, 60, 66, 124, 139, 141, 148, 151, 160, 218, 220.
——— John, abbot of Murywall, 124.
——— Nich., of Dunston, 134, 160, 163.
——— Nich., of Haukesert, 168.
——— Edith, 168.
——— Will., 204.
——— ——— Alice, w. of, 204.
——— Alice, 220.
——— Rob., of Shenstone, 220.
Rugge, 177, 203.
——— Will., 203.
——— Rog., 203.
——— Hen., 203.
Rugges, 169.
Rushall, 15, 43, 46, 47, 53, 54, 130, 135, 166, 215, 216, 218.
Rushton, 27.
——— Spencer, 9, 171, 174, 177.
——— James, 151.
Russell, John, 3.
——— John, of Tamworth, 151.
——— Thom., 40.
——— Rob., of Cornbrigge.
Rydge, 60.
Rydyngfeld, 228, 229.
Ryley, Rog., 29.
——— Rob., 29.
——— Will., of Shelton Wodhouse, 163.
Ryngeley, Gerard, 182.
Rypon, Rob., of Lichfield, 141, 142.
Rys ap Madoc, 181.
Ryssheton, Steph., of Eccleshale, 131.
——— Rich., 147.
——— Rob., 147.

S.

St. Barbe, Thom., arm., 198.
St. Clair, Phil., kt., 162.
——— ——— ——— Margt., w. of, 162.
Saint John, Jno., of Lichfield, 124.
——— ——— Will. ——— ——— 160.
St. Thom. Martyr, near Stafford, 100, 212, 220.
Sale, Hen., 157.
Salesbury, John, kt., 226, 227.
——— ——— Joan, w. of, 226.
——— Rich. de, clerk, 226, 227.
Salewey, Thom., of Cannock, 124, 148.
——— John ——— ——— 124.
——— Humph., arm., 141, 183.
Salford, Will., of Wolverhampton, 138, 141.
——— John ——— ——— 199.
——— Rich. ——— ——— 199.

Sallam, John, 46.
—— Ant., 46.
—— —— Joan, w. of, 46.
Salogham, And., of Lichfield, 138.
Salop, co , 125, 131, 132, 149, 167, 183, 203.
Salt, 157, 200, 216.
—— Thom., 18.
—— Thom., of Ricardescote, 153.
—— Hen., of Stafford, 87.
—— Ralph, of Wotton, 136.
Sandbach, Ralph, of Abbot's Bromley, 163.
—— Will., 182.
Sandon, 41, 54, 66.
—— Great, 124.
Sarden, Great, 50, 67, 68, 145, 228.
—— Little, 50, 67, 68, 136, 161, 221, 224, 228.
Saresden, co. Oxon., 198.
Sarrels, Rob., 49.
Saunders, Callingewood, 33.
—— Thom., 44.
Sautcheverell, John, 75.
Savage, Edw., arm., 27.
—— Thom., 224.
—— Thom., parson of Chekley, 143.
—— John, kt., 171, 173, 174, 175, 177.
—— —— Matil., f. w. of, 171, 173, 174, 175,
—— —— John, s. of, 171, 173, 174, 175, 177.
—— Rich., 171, 173, 174, 175.
—— John, of Dubrigge, 222, 224.
—— John, of Clyfton, the elder, arm., 225.
—— —— —— Maxfeld, the younger, —— 225.
Sawyer, David, 25.
Say, Rob., parson of Eton, 210.
Scheles, 153.
Scott, Will., 35, 38, 46.
—— John, 38, 46.
Scropton, co. Derby, 224.
Seabridge, 88, *and see* Sheprigge.
Seabrooke, Will , 37.
—— —— Emma, w. of, 37.
Seawall, 67, 98.
Seekerson, Anne, Mary, and Margery, 222.
Sedgford, *see* Seighford.
Sedgley, 21, 24, 33, 41, 56, 65, 68, 69, 138, 154, 157, 164.
—— Park, 167.
Segrave, Sir Nich. de, 88.
Seighford, 6, 12, 15, 24, 32, 46, 49, 67, *and see* Sesteford.
Seisdon, 17, 203.
Selman, Hen., of Bruggenorth, 132.
Selman, Hen., of Moreton, 164.
—— Rich. —— —— 164.
—— Will. —— —— 164, 191.
—— John —— —— 164.
Selvester, Thom., 19.
—— Will., 19.
Sesteford, 213.
Sewall, Hen., 38.
—— —— Mary, w. of, 38.
Seye, 215.
Seymour, Toteneys, 171.
Shadwell, Edw., 28.
—— John, 28.
Shalcrosse, John, 59.
Shaldeford, 180.
Shalford, 10, 47.
Shareshill, 50, 67, 68, 161, 228.
—— Will. de, chiv., 219, 228.
—— —— Dion, w. of, 219.
—— —— Will., s. of, 219, 228.
—— —— —— Joan, w. of, 219, 228.
—— —— —— Eliz., d. of, 219.
—— —— —— Agnes, d. of, 219.
—— —— —— Joan, d. of, 228.
—— Margt. and Katr., 228.
—— Isab. and Joyce, 228.
—— Will. de, kt., 228.
—— —— Margt., w. of, 228.
Sharpcliffe, 27.
Sharpe, Rob., 50.
—— Will., 186, 197.
Shawe, 52.
—— Ralph del, of Knotton, 94.
—— Hen., 159.
—— Rob., of Colond, 194.
Shawebury, Hen., 154.
Sheamondes, Will., 11.
Sheffield, Lord, 17.
Shelberie, John, 15.
Sheldon, Thom., 4.
—— Leon., 20.
—— Hugh, 55.
—— John, 138.
Shelfeilde, 15, 53, 65, 133.
Shelfeld, Thom., of Walsall, 215.
Shelley, Will., the elder, 39.
—— —— the younger, 39.
Shelton, 6, 35, 50, 104, 163, 166, 215.
—— Wodhouse, 163.
—— John, of Blore, 209.
Shendon, 215.
Shene, 191.
Shenston, 18, 19, 65, 220.
Shepherd, Rob., of Lichfield, 145.
Sheppard, Will., 12, 40.
—— —— Joan, w. of, 12, 40.
Sheprigge, 215.
Sherard, Hugh, of Shendon, 215.

Sherevelhales, 190, 204.
Sherman, Will., hosier, 125.
Sherratt, Will., 23, 59.
Sherwood, Edw., the elder, 69.
——— Edw., the younger, 69.
Shipton, Rich., of Yoxall, 163.
Shirard, John, of Wetton, 193, 197.
Shirley, Will., 172.
——— ——— Joan, w. of, 172.
——— Ralph, 12.
Shore, Thom., of Burton, 191.
Shorte, Thom., 9.
——— Edw., 34.
Shotesbrok, 161, 162, 167.
Shredicott, 69.
Shrewsbury, Gilbt., Earl of, 16.
——— ——— Mary, w. of, 16.
——— John, Earl of, 217.
Shugborowe, 29.
Shukburgh, Thom., 176, 177.
Shyngilhurst, John, 155.
Siddowne, Will., 3.
——— ——— Alice, w. of, 3.
Sidway, 46.
Skrimshawe, James, arm., 37, 39.
——— ——— Elean., w. of, 37.
Slayne, Steph., kt., 8.
——— ——— Margt., w. of, 8.
Slyndon, 82.
——— John, of Stanton Harecourt, 198.
——— Will. de, 226.
——— Steph. de, 79, 82, 84.
Slyngesby, John, of Milton, 194.
Slynt, Will., 212.
Smalbroke, Thom., 7.
Smethecote, 149.
Smethwick, 39, 41, 50.
Smyth, Ralph, 136.
——— ——— Joan, w. of, 136.
——— Chris., 11.
——— Simon, 15.
——— Thom., of Caldon, 187, 197.
——— Thom., 17, 41, 42, 57, 58, 60.
——— ——— Will., s. of, 42.
——— Will., 29, 32.
——— ——— Joan, w. of, 29.
——— Will., of Pencrich, 135.
——— Will., of Mere, 184.
——— Rich., 23.
——— Matt., 29.
——— Hen., of Coven, 153.
——— Nich., of Waterfall, 146.
——— John, 26, 67.
——— ——— Anne, w. of, 26.
——— John, of Calton, 187, 197.
——— John, of Mathefeld, 193.
——— John, of Careswall, 126.
——— John, 136.
Snede, Will. de, 92.
——— Nich., of Bradwall, 180.
Snelston, 167.
Sneyde, 21, 67.
——— Will., arm., 8, 19.
——— Agnes, 24, *and see* Snede.
Sogenhall, 91.
Somerfield, 20.
Somerford, 36, 49, 220.
——— John, 220.
Somerton, 8.
Somervyle, Rob., 153.
——— ——— Isab., w. of, 153.
——— Rog., and heirs, 153.
Sond, Will., parson of Blore, 195.
Southampton, co., 185.
Southleye, 136, 137.
Southwark, 142.
Southwell, Will., 25.
——— ——— Joan, w. of, 52.
——— Hen., 158, 159.
——— ——— Joan, w. of, 158, 159.
Southworth, John, vicar of Ilum, 182, 194, 208, 209.
Sparry, Will., 33.
Spencer, Leon., 16.
——— Thom., arm., 22, 28.
Spittell Brooke, 28.
Sporiour, Bernard, sporiour, 125.
——— Rog., of Walsall, 130.
——— John, 130, 154.
Spotts, 33.
Sprott, Thos., 8, 26, 37, 57, 59, 65.
——— ——— Mary, w. of, 26, 37.
——— Thom., the younger, 26.
——— Thom., 131, 133, 147.
——— ——— Alian., w. of, 131.
——— Edw., 26.
——— Rog., 8, 26, 37.
——— ——— Margt., w. of, 26.
——— Rog., of Asshemerbroke, 172.
Spycer, John, 157.
Squyer, Thom., 14.
——— Will., 14.
——— Rich., 39.
——— Hen., 39, 44.
——— John, 41, 45.
Stafford, 6, 13, 22, 33, 44, 47, 51, 56, 68, 87, 132, 140, 141, 148, 176, 177, 220.
——— Foryate, 47, 51.
——— Earl of, 228, 229.
——— Edw., Lord, 32.
——— James de, 86.
——— Will., 92.
——— Will., of Grafton, 199.
——— Nich. de Aspley, prior of St. Thomas, near, 100.
——— Rich., prior of St. Thomas Martyr, near, 212, 220.
——— Helyas, Archdeacon of, 111.
——— Nich. de, 114, 116, 227.

Stafford, Rob. de, 112, 114, 116.
—— ——Milisent, sist. of, 116.
—— Thom., 164, 212.
—— Thom., of Alveton, 133, 139.
—— Thom., of Grafton, arm., 199.
—— Humph., of Grafton, arm., 212.
—— Humph., Earl of, 125, 139.
—— Humph., arm., 198, 199, 201, 208, 212.
—— Humph., kt., 186, 197, 198, 201, 207, 208, 212, 224.
—— —— Alian., w. of, 212.
—— —— Humph., s. of, 208.
—— —— Rich., s. of, 224.
—— Rich., arm., 186, 197, 198.
Staley, John, of Throwley, 194.
Stallington, 44.
—— Hen., 155.
Standiche, John, of Brewode, 184.
Standon, 9, 56, 78.
—— Vivian de, 78.
—— Rob. de, 86.
Stanford, Edw., arm., 18, 44, 66, 67.
—— —— Mary, w. of, 18, 44.
—— Rob., kt., 18.
—— John, of Stafford, 220.
Stanhope, 197.
Stanley, Rog., 27, 41.
—— Thom. Chas., s. of, 27.
—— Thom., 124, 125, 134, 140, 146, 157, 160, 191, 198, 213, 221.
—— Edw., kt., 31.
—— Gerard, 38, 60.
—— —— Eliz., w. of, 60.
—— Walt., arm., 48.
—— Will., arm., 67.
—— Ralph, 157.
—— John, arm., 175, 176, 222.
Stansop, 136, 179.
Stanton, 28.
—— More, 22, 28.
—— Harcourt, *see* Harcourt Stanton.
Stanyngton, 153.
Stapenhyll, Will., 105.
Stapilton, co. Leic., 168.
Stapulton, Leon., arm., 186.
—— —— Joyce, f. w. of, 186.
Starkey, John, 58.
—— Rob., of Fossebroke, 194.
Stathom, John, of Throwley, 183, 185.
Staundon, 80, 184.
Staunton, Thom. de, 149, 159.
Stawne, 47.
Staynstone, 171, 174.
Stele, Rich., 7.
—— Thom., 157, 200.
Stephenson, Hen., clerk, 19.
—— —— Eliz., w. of, 18.
Stikebuk, Thom., 179.
—— Will., of Colton, 157.
Stockley, John, 40.
—— —— Agnes, w., of, 40.
—— Rog., 214.
Stoddart, Franc., 63.
—— —— Alice, w. of, 63.
Stodderd, Will., 35, 50.
Stoke, 66, 67, 115, 166, 215.
—— Priors, 212.
—— Will., of Romsoure, 187.
—— Thom., 30.
—— Rich. de, 115.
Stokes, Rob., of Thorpe, 134.
Stokker, John, of Wolverhampton, 133.
Stokton, co. Salop, 167.
Stone, 6, 13, 22, 28, 39, 44, 47, 58, 59, 66, 115, 172, 184, 210, 211.
—— Hen., 42, 47, 63.
—— Thom., prior of, 204.
Stoneor, Geo., 42.
Stotfold, 22.
Stounford, Rob., 31.
—— —— Magd , w. of, 31.
Stowe, 26, 37, 62.
Stramshall, *see* Stromshall *and* Strongeshulle.
Strange, Fulk de, 92.
Strangelford, John, mercer, 125.
—— Rob., 224.
—— —— Alice, d. of, 224.
Straungways, Thom , 124.
Strawford, Rich., of Patteshulle, 133.
Streethay, 27, 57, 148, 187, 212, 215.
—— John, Sub-Sheriff, 211, 212, 215.
Strelley, co. Notts., 133.
—— Rob., 133.
Strettey, Rob., 173.
Stretton, 12, 167.
—— en la Feld, 160.
—— Rich., 45.
—— John, 160.
—— —— Margy., d. of, 160.
Stromshall, 7, 59.
Strongarme, Thom., 10.
Strongeshulle, 180, 216.
Strynger, alias James, Will., 6.
—— Thom., 6.
Stubbs, John, 21, 145.
—— —— Pris., w. of, 21.
—— Samson, 61.
Stubbylane, 185.
Stychesbroke, 131.
Sudbury, 51.
Suffolk, Will., Earl of, 168.
Suggenille, John de, 75, 78.
—— —— Petron., w. of, 75.
Sugnal, 99.

Sugnal, Great, 76, 79, 80, 82, 85, 87, 88, 94, 98, 101.
—— Little, 76, 78, 79, 80, 81, 118.
—— Rob. de, 74, 75, 76, 79.
—— John de, 74, 75, 76, 78.
—— —— Alditha, w. of, 78.
—— Hen. de, 95.
—— Will. de, 80.
—— Little, John de, 73, 76, 77, 79, 80, 81.
—— —— —— Cecilia, mother of, 79.
—— —— Rob. de, 80, 100.
—— —— —— John, s. of, 80.
—— Great, Rob. de, 73, 79, 98, 99, 100.
—— —— —— Petron., w. of, 75, 98, 99, 100.
—— —— Rob. de (III), 98, 100, 101.
—— —— Rob. de (IV), 98, 99.
Sulney, Margt., 189.
Sutton, 136, 137, 150.
—— Great, 147.
—— Edm., 9, 22.
—— —— Alice, w. of, 22.
—— Edw., 9.
—— —— Anne, w. of, 9.
—— Steph., 22.
—— John of Dudley, 143, 144, 153, 154, 158, 163, 167.
—— —— Isab., w. of, 143.
—— —— John, s. and h. of, 143.
—— —— —— John, s. of, 143.
—— —— —— —— John, s. of, 143.
—— —— —— —— —— Const., w. of, 143.
—— John, kt., 146.
—— John, 151.
—— Constance, 146.
Swan, Walt., parson of Pembrigge, 210.
Swancote, John, 36.
Swayne, John, 18, 31.
—— —— Eliz., w. of, 31.
Swetnam, Rich., of Wolstanton, 215.
Swinfen, 17, 160.
—— Will., 132.
—— —— Alian., w. of, 132.
—— Thom., 160.
Swinnerton, 6, 18, 19, 73, 79, 83, 85, 93, 106, 113, 114, 179, 204, 225.
—— Church, effigy, in, 117.
—— Alen, the Domesday tenant of, 111.
—— —— Rob., s. of, 111, 112, 113.
Swinnerton, Sir Rob. de, 76, 79, 80, 83, 99, 100, 104, 105, 107, 113, 114, 115, 116, 118, 119.
—— —— Margy., w. of, 105.
—— —— Rob., s. of, 105, 113.
—— —— —— Mabel, w. of, 105.
—— —— John, s. of, 80.
—— John de, 73, 74, 76, 77, 78, 80, 82, 83, 84, 86, 87, 88, 89, 90, 91, 92, 94, 95, 99, 100, 104, 105, 107, 119.
—— —— Rob., s. of, 79, 84.
—— —— Steph., s. of, 82.
—— —— John, s. of, 74, 78, 84, 92, 94.
—— —— —— Margy., w. of, 74, 76.
—— Margy. de, 76, 81, 98, 99, 100, 105.
—— Margt., heiress of, 118.
—— John, 14, 166.
—— John de, of Isewall, 85, 89, 90, 91, 92, 93, 95, 107.
—— —— John, s. of, 92, 95.
—— John de, kt., of Hilton, 87, 89, 90, 93.
—— John de, of Sugnall, 118.
—— John de, of Eccleshall, 88, 91.
—— Rog. de, 76, 85, 86, 87, 88, 90, 91, 93, 94, 95, 97, 104, 105, 107.
—— —— Rog., s. of, 94, 95.
—— Steph. de, 79, 80, 81, 82, 83, 84, 85, 87, 105, 106, 107.
—— —— John, s. of, 80, 85, 98.
—— —— Joan, w. of, 82.
—— —— Rog., s. of, 85, 98, 106
—— Hugh, 14.
—— Alex., 107.
—— Thom., 14, 107, 124.
—— Thom., arm., 133.
—— Thom., of Elmesthorpe, 212.
—— Giles, 166.
—— Humph. de, of, Isewall, 82.
—— Humph., 179, 192, 204, 225.
—— Hen. de, 83.
—— Rich. de, 87, 94, 107.
—— Rich. de, the Palmer, 84.
—— Gilbt. de, 85, 196.
—— Nich. de, parson of Moccleston, 87, 107.
—— Will., parson of, 204.
Swinnertons of Eccleshall, descent of, 96.
Swynford, King's, 182.
Swynshed, Rog., 203.
—— —— Margt., f. w. of, 203.
—— Thom., 203.
Swynysco, 140.
Swytheland, 166.

Sydenhale, Will., of Compton, 159.
Sye, Will., of Grafton, 186, 201.

T.

Taillour, Rob., taillour, 125.
——— Rich., 140.
——— Rich., of Bosworth, 186.
——— John, 194, 202, 225.
——— ——— Agnes, f. w. of, 194, 202.
——— Hugh, 199.
——— Will., of Wolverhampton, 200.
Takley, co. Oxon., 198.
Talbot, John, kt., 186.
Talke, 34.
——— on the Hill, 60.
Tamhorne, 13, 31, 40, 55, 57, 222.
Tamworth, 14, 42, 43, 45, 48, 53, 127, 131, 142, 151, 195, 201.
Tatenell, 5, 199.
——— Compton in, 199.
Tavener, John, viteller, 125.
——— Walt., of Whittington, 139.
——— Aylmer, 160.
——— ——— Margy., w. of, 160.
Tayler, Humph., 40.
Taylor, Zach., 65.
Teane, 10, 146, 175, 177, 203, *and see* Netherteyne Overteyne *and* Theyne.
Teaneleas, 40.
Teddeswalle, Rich., of Mathefeld, 193.
Tempulle, Rich., of Blakenhale, 182.
Tetlowe, John, 52.
Tew, Humph., 27.
——— Will., 27.
——— Rich., 57.
Thacker, Chris., 10.
Thedyngworth, 218.
Theffesoke, near Hillewode, 178.
——— ——— Bassets Crosse, 178.
Theyne, 212.
Thickbrome, 61, 141, 180, 191.
——— Humph., 61.
——— ——— Barb., w. of, 61.
——— Rich., 141, 180.
——— John, 191.
Thicknes, Thom., 13, 15, 40, 55, 57.
——— ——— Mary w. of, 15, 55.
——— John, 59.
——— Edw., 59.
——— Nich. de, 92.
——— ——— Will., s. of,
Thikene, John, 129.
Thomas, Rees ap, 153.
Thorley, Will., 19.
——— ——— Anne, w. of, 19.
——— Thom., 51.
——— ——— Anne, w. of, 51.
Thorley, Thom., Geo., s. and h. of, 51.
Thornall, 9.
Thornbury, Will., of Blore, 179.
——— Thom., 14, 30.
——— Hall, 52.
Thornes, John, 224.
Thornton, Rog., 153.
Thorp, 134, 209.
Throwley, 21, 146, 158, 167, 179, 182, 183, 184, 185, 193, 194, 197, 199, 209, 225.
——— Thom., 199.
Thursfield, 102.
Thurstanton, 147.
Thurstone, John, Mast. of Coll. of Chap. of Corpus Christi, 176.
Tibington, 23, 137, 182.
Tichemersshe, 142.
Tiddeswelle, co. Derby, 182, 195.
——— Rich., of Mathefeld, 187, 197.
——— Will., vicar of, 167, 179.
Tillesley, John, 147.
Tillie, Thom., of London, 155.
Tillington, 33, 60.
Timmore, 13, 31, 57.
Tippyng, Rich., of Greetyate, 179.
Tiptoft, John de, kt., 144.
Tipton, 23, 137, 182, 221.
Tittensor, 115.
——— Thom. de, 78.
——— Ivo de, 78.
——— Nich. de, 115.
Tittringeton, Hen., 42.
——— ——— Dory., w. of, 42.
Tixall, 33, 34.
——— Thom., 7.
Tomkes, Thom., 47.
Tomkynson, Will., 26.
——— ——— Agnes, w. of, 26.
——— Humph., 26.
——— Rob., of Calton, 140.
Tomkys, Thom., 5.
——— Will., 12.
——— Hugh, 57.
——— ——— Mary, w. of, 57.
Tomson, Will., of Hemley, 138.
——— Will., of Netherpenne, 157.
Tonge, 184, 189, 190, 191.
——— John, 35.
Tonkes, Franc., 13.
Toone, Rob., 33.
Torald, John, of Ilum, 208.
Torkynton, John, of Teyne, 203.
Torpyng, Rich., of Greteyate, 194, 195.
Toteneys, Seymour, 171.
Towers, Rob., 19.
——— ——— Kath., w. of, 19.
Towneshend, Hen., kt., 50.
——— ——— Dory., w. of, 50.
Tranwell, 153.

Tregornowe, Isab., of London, 214, 215.
Trent, water of, 30, 38, 44.
Trentham, 37, 89, 180.
——— Franc., arm., 7, 60, 69.
——— ——— Kath., w. of, 7.
——— Rog., prior of, 100.
Trescote, 123.
Tresell, 17, 39, 203.
Tresham, Will., arm., 173.
Trevilian, John, arm., 214.
Trewbody, Will., of Rugeley, 139, 151.
Trigg, Dav., of Blore, 208, 209.
Trubshawe, John, of Strongshulf, 216.
——— Rog., 180.
Trumwyne, Will. de, 83.
Trussell, Will., kt., 88, 92, 161, 162, 167, 168, 188, 189, 190, 191, 192, 200, 207, 208, 210, 215.
——— ——— Will., s. of, 188, 189, 190, 204.
——— ——— ——— Katr., d. of, 188.
——— ——— ——— John, s. of, 188, 189.
——— John, 162.
——— John, of Byllisley, 208.
——— Will., of Castlebromwyche, 165, 190.
——— ——— Isab., w. of, 190.
——— Warine, 162, 190.
——— ——— Laur., 189.
——— ——— Will., s. of, 189.
——— ——— Marg., w. of, 189, 190.
——— Eliz., 188.
——— Theob., kt., 218.
——— ——— Katr., w. of, 218.
——— ——— John, s. and h. of, 218.
——— ——— Phil., d. of, 218.
——— ——— ——— Eliz., d. of, 218.
Trysull, *see* Tresel.
Tudman, Humph., 3, 69.
——— ——— Elean., w. of, 3.
——— Rowl., 69.
——— ——— Alice, w. of, 69.
Tummon, John of Woldebury, 183.
Tunstall, 5, 19, 39, 59, 60, 62, 68, 102, 145, 183.
Tunsteed, Ant., 66.
——— John, 209.
Tunstidd, 29.
Turner, James, 4.
——— Rich., 5.
——— Will., 140.
——— Will., the younger, 66.
——— Simon, of Gnosall, 163.
Turnocke, Rich., 32.
——— ——— Alice, w. of, 39.
Turton, John, 53.
Turvey, Nich., 131.
Tutbury, 58, 59, 150, 178, 179.
——— honor of, 169.
——— Thom., prior of, 179, 184.
Twyford, 171, 174.
——— John de, 88, 93.
——— Rob. de, 149.
Tykenhale, 166, 171, 174.
Tykkylle, Will., of Aston, 225.
Tyldesley, Thom., arm., 28.
Tymyns, John, 33.
——— ——— Beat., w. of, 33.
Tyrley, 60.
Tytley, John, 206.
——— ——— Beat., f. w. of, 206.

U.

Underhill, Edw., 65.
——— ——— Mary, w. of, 65.
Unet, John, of Holdyche, 180, 216.
Urset ——— ——— ——— 180.
Uselwall, *see* Isewall.
——— Steph. de, 82, 106.
Uttoxeter, 7, 20, 30, 41, 47, 63, 64, 67, 69, 176, 218, 225.
——— Woodland, 41.
Uveley, 67.

V.

Vall, Thom., 64.
——— ——— Anne, w. of, 64.
——— Rob., 64.
Vampage, John, King's Attorney, 144, 170.
——— Will., arm., 173.
Vaughton, Edw., 14.
——— Humph., 56.
——— Thom., 43.
Vawle, Humph., 59.
Venables, Will., arm., 126.
——— Will., the younger, of Edlaston, 126.
——— Will., 162.
——— ——— Petron., f. w. of, 162.
——— Will. de, of Careswall, 162.
Verney, John, Dean of Lichfield, 159, 160, 222.
——— Rob., of Marchington, 216.
Vernon, Norman de, 74, 104.
——— ——— Alice, d. of, 74, 104.
——— Geo., arm., 52.
——— Rich., kt., 141, 155, 161, 167, 168, 185, 188, 189, 190, 191, 192, 200, 204, 207, 208.
——— ——— Will., s. and h. of, 207.
——— Will., arm., 166.

Vernon, Will., of Nether Seal, 194.
——— Will., of Haddon, 198.
——— Fulk, arm., 162.
——— Thurs., of Haddon, 192, 195.
——— Edm., 201, 206.
——— ——— Joan, w. of, 201, 206.
——— John, of Haddon, 224.
Vicars, Ralph, of Caverswall, 126.
——— Will., 146.
Vigorys, Will., of Musden, 195.
Vyse, And., 4, 18.
——— ——— Eliz., w. of, 4.

W.

Wadesbury, 224.
Wakering, Sir Gilbt., of Rickmansworth, 17, 63.
Waldron, Edw., 54.
Waleys, John, 138, 141.
Walford, 6, 89.
Walhowse, Will., 11, 23, 26.
——— ——— Eliz., w. of, 23.
——— Walt., 36.
Walker, Rich., 13, 156.
——— ——— Joan, w. of, 13.
——— Rob., 47, 136.
——— Humph., 136, 199, 207, 217.
——— Humph., of Casterne, 194.
——— Thom., of Barre, 147.
——— Will., of Rugeley, 218.
——— Will., of Lichfield, 222.
Wall, 147, 166, 172.
——— John, 3.
——— ——— Bridg., w. of, 3.
——— Hen., 3, 22.
——— ——— Jane, w. of, 3, 22.
——— Hen. atte, 147.
——— Will., 170.
——— Thom., of Chedull, 212.
Wallegrange, 150.
Walsall, 3, 12, 15, 23, 35, 40, 43, 47, 50, 53, 63, 65, 70, 130, 133, 151, 179, 183, 212, 215.
——— Rob., of Frodeswall, 138.
Walsh, John, 138.
Walsted, Thom., 18.
Walter, Will., 135.
Waltham, Laur., 162.
Walton, 32, 39, 66, 67, 111, 130, 132.
——— near Chebsey, 226.
——— near Stone, 172.
——— John, 26, 54.
——— Mary, 54.
——— Ivo de, 74.
——— Euisan de, 111.
——— ——— Eylina, d. of, 111.
——— Hen., 146.
Walwene, of Denstone, John, 179.
Warde, Ralph de la, of Uttoxeter, 176.
Waring, Charles, 23.
——— Edm., 37.
——— Rog., of Trescote, 123.
——— Nich., of Wolverhampton, 153, 154.
——— Nich., 212, 223.
Warner, James, 39.
——— ——— Mary, w. of, 39.
——— Geo., 39.
——— Humph., 56.
Warton, 176.
Warveley, John, of Warveley, 125.
Warwick, 125, 134, 153, 156, 160, 168, 175, 186, 208, 221.
——— Thom. de, 94.
Warylowe, Will., of Normecote Graunge, 184.
Wast, 28.
Watereyton, 11, 36.
Waterfall, 15, 20, 52, 145.
——— John, 149.
——— ——— Will., s. of, 149.
Waters, Nich., of Walnesfeld, 136.
——— Juliana, widow, 136.
——— Will., 148.
Watson, Thom., of Salt, 157.
Waure, Rog. de, 79, 82, 98, 101, 104.
——— ——— Joan, d. and h. of, 79, 82.
——— Ralph de, 103.
Webbe, Edw., 36.
——— Thom., of Drayton Bassett, 134.
——— Rob., of Edynghale, 160.
——— John, of Hommerwych, 160.
——— Rich., of Wodehous, 222.
——— Rich., vicar of Albryghton, 219.
Webster, Rich., 60.
——— Will., of Ilum, 208.
Wedgwood, Ralph, 27.
——— John, arm., 27.
——— ——— Margt., w. of, 27.
Wednesbury, 11, 25, 35, 161, 172, 212, 218, *and see* Wadesbury.
Wednesfield, 19, 23, 63, 64, 68, 136, 137, 148, *and see* Wodnesfeld.
Welle, Will. atte, of Bromley, arm., 124.
Welles, Humph., arm., 26.
Welton, John, of Caldon, 136.
Wem, Ivo, Baron of, 74, 104.
Wendesley, Thom. de, kt., 149.
Wereley, Corn. de, 180.
Werestone, 180.
Weryngton, 138.
Wesebam, Rog. de, Bish. of Coventry and Lichfield, 89, 99.
Westbromwich, 3, 4, 6, 11, 35, 41, 48, 49, 53, 140, 154, 158, 200, 221.
Weston, 9, 48, 163.

Weston under Lesyord, 125, 160.
——— Coyney, 12, 146, 177, 182, 184.
——— on Trent, 33, 49.
——— John, 15, 19, 25, 34, 52, 124.
——— ——— Alice, w. of, 25.
——— Rich., 36, 51.
——— Rich., of Rugeley, 141, 215.
——— ——— Agnes, f. w. of, 215, 220.
——— Thom., 163.
Westwood, 216.
——— Sam., 63.
Wetley Moore, 48.
Wetmore, near Brewode, 217.
Wetton, 167, 179, 193, 197.
——— John, of Caldon, 136.
——— ——— Agnes, w. of, 136.
Whatcroft, John, 154, 158.
Whethales, Rich. de, 88, 107.
——— John de, 88, 107.
——— Adam de, 91, 97.
——— ——— Adam, s. of, 97.
Wheton Aston, 135.
Whichenore, 150, 181, 185.
Whiston, 12, 37.
——— Eaves, 24, 29.
——— Lees, 24.
——— Thom., 55, 61.
——— ——— Kath., w. of, 55.
——— Thom., of Peneriche, 151.
Whitby, Will., 218.
White, John, of Hixton, 166.
——— Franc., 51.
——— Rich., 56.
——— ——— Joan, w. of, 56.
——— Thom., 4, 13, 51, 59.
——— ——— Margt., w. of, 4.
——— ——— Eliz., w. of, 13, 59.
——— Anne, widow, 13, 59.
——— Humph., 34.
Whitegreve, Will., of Stafford, 141.
——— John, 159.
——— ——— John, s. and h. of, 159.
——— Rob., 66.
——— Rob., of Stafford, 176, 178, 191.
——— Thom., preb. of Colwich, 221.
——— Eliz., 231.
——— Humph., 66.
Whitehall, Geo., 66.
——— ——— Mary, w. of, 9.
——— James, 22.
——— John, 28.
——— Lawr., 37, 48.
——— ——— Jane, w. of, 37.
——— Rob., 49.
Whitehead, Rob., 29.
——— ——— Kath., w. of, 29.
Whitehurst, 44.
——— John, 22, 39.
Whitgreve, 33.
Whitmore, 19, 34, 78, 84, 88, 93, 103, 169, 177, 184, 213.
——— Humph., 53.
——— ——— Sarah, w. of, 53.
——— Will., 147.
——— ——— Will., s. of, 147.
——— Rog., 222.
——— ——— Margt., w. of, 222.
——— John, of Mere, 184.
——— John de, 84, 85, 103, 106.
——— ——— Agnes, w. of, 84.
——— ——— Ralph, s. of, 103.
Whittell, Edm., 14, 32.
——— ——— Eliz., w. of, 32.
Whittington, 13, 15, 24, 25, 27, 31, 48, 49, 50, 55, 57, 61, 134, 139, 145, 161, 213.
Whitwaltham, 162.
Whorwood, Will., 19.
——— Gerard, 19.
——— Franc., 70.
——— ——— Jane, w. of, 70.
Whytefeld, Rich. de, of Ecclesball, 79.
Whyternelhurst, 206.
Widdowes, John, 31.
Wigginton, 11, 14, 15, 42, 43, 45, 151.
Wightwick, 172.
——— Will., 7, 159, 172.
——— Matt., 7.
——— Franc., 46.
——— Humph., 46.
Wilbram, Rich., kt., 3, 34.
——— ——— Grace, w. of, 3.
——— Rog., kt., 14, 16.
——— ——— Mary, w. of, 14, 16.
Wilbrighton, 217.
Wilcotes, Sir John, 128, 129, 133, 136, 137, 150, 164.
——— ——— Eliz., f. w. of, 129.
——— Will., 129.
——— ——— Eliz., f. w. of, 129.
Wildey, Humph, 45.
Wililey, Rog., 228.
——— ——— Katr., w. of, 228.
Wilkeson, Agnes, of Tene, 146.
Willaston, Will., arm, 67.
Willenhall, 19, 63, 67, 68, 137, 154, 163, 167, 218.
——— Rog., 126, 127.
Willeslock, 69.
Willughbridge, 60.
Willymott, Rob., 70.
Wilson, John, 68.
——— John, the younger, 68.
——— Joan, 68.
Wimer, 74.
——— Reginald, s. of, 74.
Winckley, Will, 9.
Winnington, 46, 60.
——— Rich. de, 139, 142.

Winnington, Rich. de, Agnes, w. of, 142.
Wiston, 174.
Witefield, Walt. de, 75.
Wither, Thom , kt., 93.
——— John, 183.
Witherence (Witheringes), Thom., 10, 16.
Withington, 23, 67, 169.
Witindon, Osbert de, 75.
Witton Wyngates, 153.
Wobaston (Wybaston), 67, 68.
Wodecok, Will., of Chedylton, 146.
Wodeneford, Will., of Walsall, 130.
Wodeward, Ralph, of Calton, 146.
Wodnesfeld, 179.
Wodnot, John, 177.
Woldebury, 183.
Wolferston, Rob., arm., 22.
——— Edm., 22.
——— Hen., arm., 22.
Wollaston, John, 3.
——— John, vicar of Abbot's Bromley, 163.
——— Will., 13, 38.
——— ——— Margt., w. of, 13.
Wolrich, Thom., 6, 12, 24, 32, 46, 49.
——— ——— Franc., w. of, 12.
——— Phil., 10, 66.
——— ——— Anne, w. of, 10, 66.
——— Will., of Werestone, 180, 184.
Wolseley, 21, 36, 197.
——— Thom., arm., 20, 24, 62, 64, 66.
——— ——— Ellen, w. of, 64, 66.
——— Thom., 134, 160, 168, 197.
——— Ralph, 134, 160, 168, 223.
Wolsey, Thom., 164.
Wolstanton, 140, 212, 215.
Wolverhampton, 4, 5, 8, 25, 43, 46, 50, 53, 54, 55, 57, 63, 64, 68, 133, 134, 138, 141, 148, 149, 153, 154, 157, 164, 183, 195, 199, 200, 203, 212.
——— John, Dean of King's Chapel of, 200.
Womborne, 8, 17, 38, 63, 140, 147.
Wood, Hen., 49.
——— ——— Anne, w. of, 49.
——— Rob., 10.
——— John, 18, 58.
——— Will., 39, 42.
Woodford, 7.
Woodhead, 52.
Woodhowses, 4, 33, 58, 222.
——— Will., 17.
——— Anne, 22.
——— Mary, 22.
——— Margy., 22.
——— ——— Franc., 32.
Woods, John, 12, 13.
——— ——— Mary, w. of, 12, 13.
——— ——— Walt., s. and h. of, 13.
Woody, Franc., 13.
Woolstington, 34.
Wootton, 54, 67, 136, 197, 222.
——— under Weever, 28.
——— Thom., 54.
Wordesley, Thom , 48.
——— ——— Margt., w. of, 48.
Wotton, John, 222.
Wright, Rich., 26, 37.
——— Thom., 59, 65, 146, 167.
——— ——— Kath., w. of, 65.
——— John, of Fulfen, 148.
——— John, of Tamworth, 155.
——— John, of Barre, 203.
Wrottesley, Hugh., arm., 8, 17, 45, 63, 217, 221.
——— Walt., Esq., 17.
Wyatt, Rob., 10.
——— ——— Anne, w. of, 10.
Wyehenore, 132.
Wyford, 61.
Wygorn, 135.
Wylde, Thom., 181.
——— Will., the younger, 212.
Wyldeblode, Hugh, 160, 163.
Wylderley, John, of Lichfield, 148.
Wylloughby, Hugh, kt., 153.
——— Rich., 155.
Wyllys, Hen., 27.
——— ——— Edw., s. of, 27.
——— John, of Walsall, 183.
Wylne, John, prior of Repyngton, 163.
Wyndesor, Edm., 8.
——— Edw., arm., 28.
Wynneshurst, Will., 187.
——— ——— Isab., w. of, 187.
——— Rich., 212.
Wyrley, Little, 3, 38, 43, 58, 164.
——— Great, 38.
——— Humph., arm., 25, 27.
——— ——— Knightley, w. of, 25, 27.
——— John, of Werneley, 135.
——— John, of Honnesworth, 141.
——— Cornelius, 142.
Wyse, Will., of Staundon, 184.
Wystanton, co. Chester, 126.

Y.

Yardeley ende, 60.
Yate, Will., of Blythebury, 151.
——— Rich , of Scropton, 224.
Yates, Will., 11.
——— ——— Dory., w. of, 11.
——— ——— Nich., s. and h. of, 11.
Yedyhale, 222.
Yelverton, Will., sergeant-at-law, 160.

Yeo, Nich., 159.
Yermonger, Rog., 124.
Yernefield, 6.
Yewdale, Will., 206.
Yokkynson, Thom., of Knutton, 95.
Yonge, Mr. Vernon, 84.
York, John, Card., Archb., of, 173.
——— Thom., Archb., of, 226.
Yoxall, 18, 26, 35, 40, 163.
Yward, Nich., 158.
——— ——— Eliz., w. of, 158.

Z.

Zouch, Will. kt. 171.

3

HARRISON AND SONS, PRINTERS IN ORDINARY TO HER MAJESTY, ST. MARTIN'S LANE.

CPSIA information can be obtained
at www.ICGtesting.com
Printed in the USA
BVHW081155210321
603030BV00007B/1625

9 789354 412264